The Prado

The Pennsylvania State University Press

University Park, Pennsylvania

EUGENIA AFINOGUÉNOVA

The Prado

SPANISH CULTURE AND LEISURE, 1819-1939

Library of Congress Cataloging-in-Publication Data

Names: Afinoguénova, Eugenia, author.
Title: The Prado : Spanish culture and leisure, 1819–
    1939 / Eugenia Afinoguénova.
Description: University Park, Pennsylvania : The
    Pennsylvania State University Press, [2018] |
    Includes bibliographical references and index.
Identifiers: LCCN 2017019869 | ISBN 9780271078571
    (cloth : alk. paper)
Summary: "Explores the history of Spain's most iconic
    art museum. Highlights the political history of the
    museum's relation to the monarchy, the church,
    and the liberal nation state, as well as its role as
    an extension of Madrid's social center, the Prado
    Promenade"—Provided by publisher.
Subjects: LCSH: Museo del Prado—History.
Classification: LCC N3450 .A96 2018 | DDC
    708.00946/41—dc23
LC record available at https://lccn.loc.gov/2017019869
lable at https://lccn.loc.gov/2017019869

The Pennsylvania State University Press is a member of
the Association of American University Presses.

Additional credit: pages ii–iii,
detail of Carlos de Vargas,
View of the Real Museo,
1824, lithograph by Vicente
Camarón y Torra, 1826 (fig. 3).

Typeset by
Regina Starace

Printed and bound by
Sheridan Books

Composed in
Adobe Jenson and Gill Sans

Printed on
Natures Natural

Bound in
Arrestox

For Alla Libina (Shapiro),

who loved leisure and the Prado,

in memoriam

Contents

Illustrations

MAPS

TABLE

Acknowledgments

If taking on the history of one's favorite museum could be described as a daunting and humbling experience, "leisuring" it would require audacity bordering on hubris, had it not been preceded by over a decade of painstaking research. It was the support of many institutions, groups, and people that turned this work into a pleasure and a privilege. My countless months of archival research in Madrid have been made possible thanks to funding from the Fundación Carolina, Spain's Ministry of Foreign Affairs and Cooperation, the Program for Cultural Cooperation between Spain's Ministry of Culture and United States' Universities, Marquette University Summer Faculty Fellowships and Regular Research Grants, and the Robert and Mary Gettel Fund. I was successful with some of these grant applications thanks to the training that I received from the Marquette University Office of Research and Sponsored Programs and assistance from Kevin Abing. Marquette University's Klingler College of Arts and Sciences full-year sabbatical fellowship, followed by the fellowship that I received from the American Council for Learned Societies, have enabled me to take enough time off to complete the writing.

Several vibrant intellectual communities have furthered my understanding of museum history and Spain's visual culture: the hispanistasxix network, the Making National Museums program (NaMU) and its European National Museums (Eunamus) project, the American Society of Hispanic Art Historical Studies (ASHAHS), the Association for Spanish and Portuguese Historical Studies (ASPHS), the Comité Español de Historia del Arte (CEHA), and the International Society for Cultural History (ISCH). At the Prado, I am grateful for the kind attention that I received from Javier Portús. For almost fifteen years, at the archive and the library of the Prado, Yolanda Cardito Rollán, Paloma de Luelmo, Emir Moreno, Teresa Nistal, and the documentalist Rocío Arnáez have answered my questions, filled my petitions, and never failed to make me feel among friends. Curated by the Fundación Amigos Museo del Prado, the museum's on-line encyclopedia has given me access to a trove of relevant information. The Hemeroteca Digital project of the National Library of Spain has worked wonders in response to keyword queries, producing more sources than would fit even in a multivolume publication.

At the Fundación Lázaro Galdiano in Madrid, Juan Antonio Yepes, chair of the Archive and Library Department, provided me with copies of Luis Eusebi's works long before texts such as these became available digitally. At the Museum of the History of Madrid, Isabel Tuda Rodríguez and Ana Costa Novillo helped me locate several images used in this book and many more, which I used in my research. Archivists of the Royal Palace Archive and the Archivo General de la Administración (AGA) have guided me on numerous occasions. Librarians and the Interlibrary Loan Department at Marquette University Raynor Memorial Libraries have patiently handled my requests. Several chairs of Marquette University's Department of Foreign Languages and Literatures—Belén Castañeda, John Pustejovsky, and Anne Pasero—provided me with their support and encouragement, as did the deans of Arts and Sciences—Michael McKinney, Jeanne Hossenlopp, and Rick Holz.

Several sections of this book appeared previously as "Liberty at the Merry-Go-Round: Leisure, Politics, and Municipal Authority on the Paseo del Prado in Madrid, 1760–1939," *Journal of Urban Cultural Studies* 1, no. 1 (2014): 85–106, Bristol: Intellect; "The Nation Disrobed: Nudity, Leisure, and Class at the Prado," in *National Museums: New Studies from Around the World*, ed. Peter Aronsson, Arne Bugge Amundsen, and Simon J. Knell (London: Routledge, 2010), 207–24, "Leisure and Agrarian Reform: Liberal Governance at the Traveling Museums of Spanish Misiones Pedagógicas (1931–1933)," *Hispanic Review* 79, no. 2 (2011): 261–90, and "'Painted in Spanish': The Prado Museum and the Naturalization of the 'Spanish School' in the Nineteenth Century," *Journal of Spanish Cultural Studies* 10, no. 3 (2009): 319–40. I am grateful to the editors and anonymous reviewers of these publications for allowing me to rehearse my arguments and for providing meaningful feedback.

"A history of a museum—what is it the history of, really?" Over the years I was fortunate to communicate with colleagues in several countries who asked me guiding questions like this and helped me tackle the answers. As I was seeking funding to complete the research, Alda Blanco, Jo Labanyi, Susan Larson, and Alan Smith (who asked the above question) wrote numerous letters of recommendation on my behalf. Katarzyna Beilin, María Bolaños, Elizabeth (Betsy) Boone, Lou Charnon-Deutsch, Pierre Géal, Andrew Ginger, Paola Hernández, Ángel Llorente Hernández, Marga Lobo, Jorge Marí, Antonia del Rey, Rafael Rodríguez Tranche, Íñigo Sánchez-Llama, Vicky Unruh, Óscar Vázquez, and Elvira Vilches all allowed me to discuss with them some aspects of this book and gave invaluable advice. Sarah Davies Cordova guided my many decisions and read several chapters in draft. Silvina Schammah-Gesser and Alejandro Yarza (Mentor Vitalicio) helped me to revise the epilogue. John Tallmadge, whom I am privileged to call my writing coach, taught me to go straight to the point as he revised the early versions of the manuscript. Sally Anna Boyle painstakingly edited my subsequent writing, in the process becoming a necessary interlocutor and a dear friend, and not just an editor. I learned a lot from her. At Penn State University Press, I won the lottery when Ellie Goodman noticed my query e-mail and decided to give this project a try. Penn State editorial assistant Hannah Hebert, manuscript editor

John Morris, production coordinator Patricia A. Mitchell, and managing editor Laura Reed-Morrisson made sure my text and images were in order and on schedule.

And the rest is history, one would say. This history, however, would be meaningless had it not been for the support group that allowed me to indulge in all that research and writing without the pressure of having to beat the clock. Esther Hidalgo and Ángel Llorente Hernández, María Dolores Delso, Lucía Samarina, Rafael Vallejo Bretaño, and May González López all opened the doors of their apartments to me when I needed a place to stay, provided me with books and documents when asked, and kept me company. Lucía Samarina's help with wire transfers for copyright permissions was priceless. Michael Libin, my brother, made sure I never lost any data. My son Grisha was great to talk to about cultural history. My father, Victor Libin, and Irina Yelnick provided unlimited good cheer. Yance Marti, my beloved husband, accompanied me in all the travails of this journey. My most heartfelt thanks goes to them.

xv

I was fourteen years old when my history teacher, and then my parents (an engineer and a microbiologist), insisted that I join the Young Art Historians' Club at the Pushkin Museum of Fine Arts in Moscow—an institution whose origin at the turn of the twentieth century was akin to that of many educational museums described in this book. Though the Moscow of the late 1970s and early 1980s was, of course, nothing like nineteenth- and early twentieth-century Madrid, I am convinced that the experiences, ideas, and people that I encountered at the Pushkin are what brought me here, wondering about the meanings that unprepared visitors give to art. This biography of the Prado as a place where culture met leisure is also, to a certain extent, an autobiography and a tribute to museum education.

Introduction

BETWEEN THE PRADO AND THE PRADERA

THE FRENCH MUST HAVE been early risers. A. Pouyanne, a wealthy Parisian, showed up first at the museum that morning, but he could not enjoy the paintings all by himself because the Reverend Tournier, a traveling priest from Nantes, followed him into the galleries shortly after. Then came a trader from Barcelona whose name was Juan Bouquet. Later on, some people who appeared to be more working class signed the guest book: Juan García Zoralbes, a serviceman from Alicante, and an ironsmith named José Perezo, who lived in the same town. Then came a German visitor and two couples from Scotland: Mr. and Mrs. John Orr and Mr. and Mrs. John H. N. Graham. It did not take much longer for an American, S. Remington, to appear, and Francisco García, a mason from Alicante, came right after. The last to show up were Pablo Cunchillos and Mariano Herrero, a tailor and an ironsmith from Zaragoza, and a rugmaker from Cordoba, Mariano Estévez. These people, all so different from one another, had one thing in common—on Friday, May 15, 1868, along with a handful of others, they came to visit the Prado Museum and signed the guest book (fig. 1).[1]

It was the holiday of San Isidro, the patron saint of Madrid, and the year when, for the first time in Spain's history, the railway companies announced special discounted fares, making it more feasible than ever before for those wishing to see the festival to get to the capital. There was no one *from* the capital in the museum—perhaps they had all just crossed the Manzanares River to picnic on the Pradera de San Isidro, just as the characters did in Goya's sketch for a tapestry cartoon, *The Meadow of San Isidro*, painted eighty years earlier. Still, when the sun went down, those who had spent the day looking at paintings and sculptures and those who instead had spent the time browsing through the vending stalls at the Pradera, with their colored etchings and clay figures of saints and politicians, would all come together on the Prado—the promenade that was yet to give the museum its official name.

2

FIG. I A page from the guest book, May 15, 1868. Museum visitors had to sign in on the days when the collection was closed to the general public, stating their name, nationality, profession, and address. *Libro-registro de los nombres de las personas que visitan las salas del Real Museo de Pintura y Escultura de S.M., 1864-1870*. Archivo del Museo Nacional del Prado.

Long before the expanding paths of urban traffic reduced the Paseo del Prado to a rather dull setting for the Museo del Prado, Spaniards from all walks of life and foreigners had been coming, simply, to *the Prado*. In the nineteenth and early twentieth centuries, it was the place of round-the-clock gatherings and a frequent location for urban fairs: a cultural borderline in a growing city where rural and urban pastimes coexisted, clashed, and eventually merged to produce modern leisure. Overlooking the area, the Royal Museum, founded in 1819 and nationalized in 1868–70, claimed to enhance the nation's glory. In reality, however, it offered a range of sensations that its diverse public compared to those proffered on the Pradera de San Isidro and other sites of celebration, entertainment, and consumption. Rather than assume that visitors ever agreed about the terms they should use to interpret the museum, this book approaches its history as a debate about culture and leisure. Just like the people crossing the museum's threshold, who did not always trace a firm line between what they could see or do inside the museum and outside, on the Paseo del Prado and in its environs, the participants in this debate—journalists, politicians, museum directors, art critics—considered museum-going a pastime related to other public activities and therefore a part of a broader discussion concerning citizenship and voting rights, the rise of Madrid to the status of modern capital, and the growing gap between the town and the country.

On the surface, the swirling amalgam of experiences that combined the paintings and sculptures in the museum and the theatrical, sometimes grotesque, items and encounters that were initially confined to the Pradera but moved on to the Prado Promenade as the century progressed was simply a matter of evolution, of modern culture overtaking the time and space of traditional celebrations. But it was actually not that simple. The museum directors and the connoisseurs, of course, always considered it unfortunate that unregulated pastimes continued happening right next to the temple of art. In time, however, the competition with these noisy surroundings became a partnership that transformed the museum into a powerful mediator between the elites and the populace, the center and the periphery, and the citizens and the government. In the late nineteenth and early twentieth centuries, the museum—by that time officially called the Prado—would even step outside of its walls, playfully reenacted in urban parades and put on stage to entertain the visitors of the modernized San Isidro Fair. Following the winding course of Spain's modernization—the unsettling of the urban and rural worlds, secularization, and the emergence of commercial culture—the Prado Museum and Promenade coevolved in ways that made leisure just as relevant as other processes better studied by museum historians: the changing displays and collections, the refurbishing of the building, the cleavage between the old and the new regimes, the evolution of the liberal state, and the shifting definitions of Spain's nationhood, all of which are also inseparable from the history of the Prado.

A MUSEUM IN A MEADOW

There was hardly any other art institution so clearly situated between the urban and the rural worlds. What is now known as the Prado used to be precisely what the word means: a meadow; the name was sometimes not even capitalized. Before the court moved to Madrid in 1563, "the meadow" was a pilgrimage route to places of popular devotion; after that, it became the "object of constant desire for remodeling."[2] Redesigned in the seventeenth century as a thoroughfare to connect the court to the countryside, it provided a stage for royal processions, courtly festivals, and other ceremonial appearances that the Spanish Habsburgs considered indispensable for maintaining power.[3] With the change of dynasty in 1700, this area became the place for the Bourbons to make visible the lifestyles that they considered the foundation of their enlightened rule. In the 1760s, Carlos III donated some of these lands to the City

4

MAP I   The Prado and surround-
ings, 1785. *Plano geométrico de
Madrid dedicado y presentado al
rey nuestro señor Don Carlos III
por mano del Excelentísimo señor
Conde de Floridablanca; su autor
Don Tomás López geógrafo de su
S.M.,* detail.

1. Puerta de Atocha and the Alcachofa
Fountain; 2. Fuente de Cibeles and
Calle Alcalá; 3. Apollo Fountain and
Salón del Prado; 4. Four Fountains; 5.
Retiro Gardens; 6. Botanical Garden; 7.
Square off the northern entrance to the
Botanical Garden; 8. Projected Museum
of Natural Sciences, the future Museo
Real; 9. San Blas hermitage, site of the
future Royal Astronomical Observatory.
10. San Jerónimo el Real monastery.

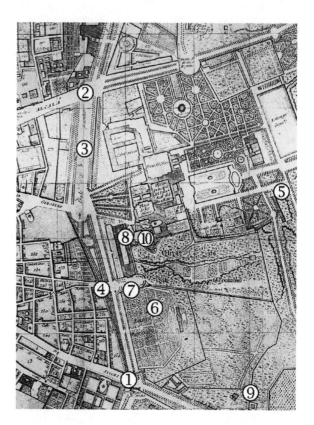

of Madrid for the purpose of an urban renovation. The result of his efforts, the Paseo del Prado, stretching from the Puerta de Atocha and the Alcachofa Fountain next to it (map 1:11) to the current Plaza Cibeles (map 1:2), was to add a final touch to the capital's rationalistic replanning. Its most attractive section, around the new Fountain of Apollo (map 1:3), then also called the Four Seasons, became known as the Salón del Prado.[4] Eventually, the name "the Prado" began to be used interchangeably to refer to the Salón, to the areas adjacent to the Salón, or to the whole Promenade between the Fountain of Cibeles (map 1:2), the Four Fountains (map 1:4), and the Alcachofa Fountain farther south (map 1:5).

Thus, in the nineteenth century, the term "the Prado" could indicate anywhere between the end of the Calle Alcalá (map 1:2) and the Puerta de Atocha. Complete with fountains and monumental benches, the Promenade seemed to facilitate the transition from old-regime courtly and religious ceremonies to the modern "public sphere."[5] In the 1770s, Carlos III opened to all visitors the palace gardens of the Retiro (map 1:5). The Botanical Garden, formerly situated on the city's outskirts, was also moved to this new location (map 1:6). The garden's northern entrance was laid out as a semicircular square (map 1:7) leading to a new structure, designed by the architect Juan Villanueva,

FIG. 2   The retaining wall separating the museum building from the San Jerónimo Monastery. The model of Madrid in 1830 by León Gil de Palacio, detail. Museo de Historia de Madrid.

which was originally intended to house a museum of natural sciences but would instead, in 1819, become the home of the Museo Real (map 1:8). The construction, funded by money confiscated from the banned Jesuit order, began in 1785. The work went so slowly that in 1790, in an effort to generate more interest, Villanueva suggested expanding the project in order to incorporate a royal library.[6] Had he succeeded with this expansion, the area would have become the site of a full-fledged academy of sciences, with botanical and zoological gardens; the Astronomical Observatory, erected after 1790 in the Retiro (map 1:9); and the grand museum, housing a library and a cabinet of natural history. Villanueva's project, seeking to reincarnate the Mouseion of Alexandria, provided space for science laboratories and a large meeting room for public debates.[7]

From the east, the site assigned to house Villanueva's would-be academy was limited by a retaining wall that prevented landslides from the hill on which the monastery of San Jerónimo was situated (map 1:10 and fig. 2). There were no streets farther east of the museum. Stretching uphill along the Promenade (fig. 3), the building was designed to make use of the height difference to mark the separation of the two themes. The Cabinet of Natural History on the upper ("main") floor could be accessed through the high northern door. The Academy of Sciences, located on the lower level, with its halls dedicated to teaching botany and chemistry, conducting experiments, and hosting meetings, had its own door in the lower southern façade facing the Botanical Garden (fig. 4). A stairway connecting the two floors was hidden inside the structure. This is why, in the words of Fernando Chueca Goitia, Villanueva's museum had "two main floors."[8]

6

FIG. 3   The northern entrance. Carlos de Vargas, *View of the Real Museo*. 1824, lithograph by Vicente Camarón y Torra, 1826. Biblioteca Nacional de España.

FIG. 4   José María Avrial y Flores, *View of the South Façade of the Museo del Prado from Inside the Botanical Garden*, c. 1835. Oil on canvas, 42 × 56 cm. Museo Nacional del Prado.

FIG. 5   Viscount Louis de Dax,
Museo Real, Main Façade, c. 1854.
Patrimonio Nacional.

This academic environment was initially supposed to include a peripatetic space off the Paseo del Prado: a long portico with a Doric colonnade and a vast semicircular square in the middle. The project that was eventually approved for construction, albeit less ambitious, also had a colonnade and a flower garden for taking a walk. Matching the style of the Botanical Garden, it was to be separated from the Promenade by an iron railing with stone posts and a gate. But the flower garden was not completed, and neither were the fence and the magnificent entryway. In 1821, when the building had already been repurposed as the Royal Museum, architect Antonio López Aguado decided against the initial plan of surrounding it with a railing or a fence: in 1821, he recycled the posts meant to be used in Villanueva's railing and made them into stone benches (fig. 5).[9] Thus, instead of being solemnly set apart from the place of public promenade, the new museum remained connected to it by a line of wide, inviting surfaces where people could rest. Though in the following decades, at one time or another, the authorities managed to put fences and gates by the museum's other façades, all attempts to enclose this western access failed. The museum would forever be linked to the Paseo del Prado.

In the nineteenth century, the Paseos del Prado and del Botánico to the north and south of the museum provided common settings for travelers' stories and Spanish sketches of the daily life of Madrid, called *cuadros de costumbres*. Still lacking a proper name, the section facing the museum was ambiguously assigned to either boulevard and suffered from an identity crisis of sorts. Although the *Vistas* commissioned by the royal administration from the Italian artist Fernando Brambilla in the 1820s suggest the court's interest in securing the connection between the museum and the Promenade (fig. 6), in his 1831 *Manual de Madrid* Ramón Mesonero Romanos, the city's best-known chronicler, still gave no name to this area, which he saw simply as a stretch somewhere between three fountains: the Alcachofa Fountain, the Four Fountains, and the Fountain of Neptune.[10] In 1848, the complete street guide by

8

Vista del R.¹ Museo de Pintura de Madrid.

FIG. 6. Fernando Brambilla, *View of the Real Museo de Pintura de Madrid*, c. 1827. Watercolor. Patrimonio Nacional.

Pascual Madoz mentioned the length and the width of this segment but neglected to give it a name. Apparently, the boulevard facing the museum was twice as wide as the Salón del Prado yet a tenth as long as both the Salón and the Paseo del Botánico.[11] Logically, then, the public imagination absorbed this section into either the former or the latter, turning the museum into the neighbor of the entire Prado Promenade. According to the architectural historian Carlos Sambricio, Villanueva's ensemble was meant to be viewed in movement, from a changing perspective as one walked down the Paseo del Prado "and not facing its main façade."[12] Similarly, the history of the museum is best understood from the perspective of people occupying and moving through this key location of Madrid's public life.

In 1808–12, when Napoleon's brother Joseph Bonaparte was installed on the Spanish throne, Madrileños saw the Promenade transformed into a center of modern consumption, a fairground, and a site of Carnival celebrations.[13] Updating commercial fairs was one of Napoleon's *idées-fixes*. In 1806, he decreed that the Paris Fair would move to a new location on the Esplanade des Invalides, an ample and accessible site with good visibility.[14] In Spain's recently conquered capital, the well-lit surface of the Prado promised a similar setting, clean and linear, so under "King José" Madrid's annual Fall Fair was held in this new place, giving the passersby on the Prado a chance to experience a temporary surge of retail and consumption. In 1812, however, when

FIG. 7   Fernando Brambilla, *View of the Real Museo from the Botanical Garden*, c. 1827, lithograph by Léon Auguste Asselineau, 1833. Museo de Historia de Madrid.

the French fled, the action returned to the Plaza de la Cebada and, eventually, was moved to the fast-developing northern extension of the Paseo del Prado, the Paseo de Recoletos.

With modern market stalls thus displaced from the Paseo near the museum, those coming to enjoy each other's company in the vicinity of the newly founded Museo Real had only itinerant vendors from whom to buy. These vendors were a colorful and noisy crowd that invariably left a strong impression on foreign writers, especially the ones eager to see Spain as an oriental destination. The areas closer to the Botanical Garden seemed particularly rural. When the French were occupying the city, farm girls brought their cows to the square between the museum and the Botanical Garden to provide the Madrileños and French soldiers with fresh milk. When the Royal Museum was founded, a vista by Brambilla depicted the square separating it from the Botanical Garden like a disproportionally large field partially overgrown with grass, with small animals that look like sheep rambling around, a woman seated on a pile of ashlar stones still remaining from the museum's construction and holding a baby (fig. 7).[15] The 1827 painting by Italian artist Giuseppe Canella reproduced on the cover of this book adds a few telling strokes to the idyllic panorama. A washer-woman balancing a bundle of clothes on her head is about to trip over the cane of an old woman resting on a bench, who looks as if she has carried her basket from afar. A beggar attempts to make conversation with passersby in the hope of obtaining small change. A mule driver enjoys the peaceful view while his animals drink from one of the Four Fountains. The area's connection to the rural world would become even stronger with time, when the Atocha train station opened in 1858 farther south of the Botanical Garden, making the Promenade the point of entry for Madrid newcomers.

If the Promenade had been designed to help urbanize Madrid, this objective had definitely not been fully achieved in the museum's surroundings. And if the museum was likewise meant to pay tribute to all things beautiful, rationally organized, and clean, it only took a step through the back door to see the rubble that essentially transformed the square between the museum and the Botanical Garden into a public toilet. By the 1840s, these stones (and the filth behind them) became as much a part of the landscape as the museum itself: they were even cast as characters—"silent yet smelly"— in a play about the museum and recognized as a location where one could also see some "pictures."[16] (Unlike the pictures displayed inside, the ones shown by the Botanical Garden were deemed "indescribable.")

Starting in 1816 and throughout the late 1820s, municipal authorities felt it necessary to forbid bringing cattle and mules to drink at the fountains on the Prado or allowing "lambs and other animals to graze."[17] The same laws prohibited people from bathing themselves and washing "dogs and other animals" in the fountains, climbing the trees, or cutting the branches. These behaviors lacking in urbanity were tolerated for much longer than we might imagine, and as late as 1904, concomitant with the announcement of the future erection of the luxurious Hotel Ritz, municipal authorities were still receiving proposals about how to keep people from using the four little fountains just south of the museum for bathing and other personal hygiene needs.

There were, however, reasons why rustic people remained on the Paseo and why the authorities accepted their presence and only focused on trying to prevent excesses. Paradoxically, it had to do precisely with the government's goal of civilizing Madrid. Since the time of Carlos III, the Paseo had served as an alternative spot for the semipagan, semi-Christian celebrations of San Juan and San Pedro called *verbenas*. Traditionally, these festivities took place on the outskirts of the city. The nineteenth-century historian Basilio Sebastián Castellanos wrote that Carlos III himself ordered the transfer of the *verbenas* to the Prado. One narrative suggests that the move might have been an effort to tame the violence and rapes that ruled in the previous location of the festivities on the outskirts of Madrid.[18] According to this version of the story, the king chose the Prado in an attempt to encourage more moral behavior. However, in Castellanos's account, people liked the location for the completely opposite reason: the trees provided shade, privacy, and anonymity.[19] In the early nineteenth century, annual royal edicts (*bandos*) still prohibited gatherings, dances, and stick fights outside city limits, singling out the migrants from the Asturias region as

FIG. 8   Fernando Brambilla, *View of the Real Museo de Pintura de Madrid from the San Jerónimo,* c. 1827, lithograph by Léon Auguste Asselineau, 1833. Author's collection.

their leaders. The fact that on the Prado it was deemed acceptable to gather in groups, make bonfires, and spend the night under the stars made the *verbenas* particularly attractive to urban newcomers because San Juan was also the day for hiring and firing servants.[20] Those losing or seeking employment were simply camping on the Prado in the hope of finding real living quarters before too long. Until the twentieth century, there were no bans on nightly gatherings on the Promenade, even when there was no patron-saint festival. On the contrary, upper classes also chose the Promenade spot for their own, quasi-rural celebrations—the Carnival and open-air *bailes campestres* (a Spanish version of *fêtes champêtres*: literally, village dances).

If the area of the Paseo del Prado near the museum and the Botanical Garden was marked as somewhat rural, a completely different view was emerging from the northern end. This is clearly visible in another vista by Brambilla, showing the museum's northern entrance (the one that was—and still is— most consistently used) as an orderly space inhabited by well-dressed people engaging in polite conversation (fig. 8). At that time the Salón del Prado, the area farther north of the museum, was Madrid's preferred place of socialization while also serving as a reminder of the 1808 anti-French rebellion, the meaning of which Fernando VII was trying to change at the time when he founded the Royal Museum—from being a rebellion against the French occupation to being in defense of his monarchy. During the war, etchings portraying the bloodshed by the feet of the Fountain of Neptune and all the way to the Fountain of Cibeles immortalized the Salón as a place of patriotic martyrdom. After the battle of May 2, 1808, the remains of the "victims of the Prado" were buried on one side of the Paseo, the place later designated as the Campo de la Lealtad (Loyalty Field) and featuring an obelisk designed in 1821 and inaugurated in 1840. In the nineteenth century, the Salón remained the place to see and be seen—an area where everyone would come, on foot or by carriage, to show off their dresses, horses, and lovers—while the Campo de la Lealtad became the center of patriotic gatherings. Still, even that square had space for a merry-go-round, a circus, and later a pavilion for exhibiting a panoramic painting of the battle of Tetuán.

If the Salón del Prado, with its spirit of civic interaction, had initially emerged as a cultural antipode to the realm of almost rustic privacy near the Botanical Garden, this contrast began to blur by the late 1870s, when the Promenade connecting them, right where the Royal Museum stood, became the location of an urban fair. The idea of moving Madrid's Fall Fairs, traditionally held on the Plaza de la Cebada, to the Prado had been circulating since 1808. Although, just like all other urban reforms introduced by the French, this one was undone under Fernando VII, after Fernando's death in 1833 the fairgrounds were transferred to the Calle Alcalá and to the Paseo de Recoletos, north of the Salón del Prado. Since the Fair, which already overlapped in time with the annual Fall Exhibition at the San Fernando Royal Academy of Fine Arts (an early prototype of the national salons), was now also held close to the Academia's building on the Calle Alcalá, the relocation spurred debates about whether the objects exhibited for enjoyment and education at the Academia were being contaminated by the objects for sale and on display at the fairs. Mesonero Romanos left a famous description of the 1838 fall exhibition, which was visited by a legion of "friends of fine arts" coming from the outskirts to "take a look at the Academia while their comrades [were] arranging vending stalls at the Fair to sell their works of kitchen sculpture."[21] Thus began the long period during which art, leisure, and commerce, whose separation from one another is usually associated with the collapse of the traditional "festival culture,"[22] competed for places and times of their own in the city and on its inhabitants' calendars. The Paseo del Prado facing the museum was where they were eventually to meet, inhabiting the same space at the same time.

After several unsuccessful attempts to disassociate the Fair and the exhibitions at the Academia, starting in 1855 the latter were rescheduled for the spring. This meant, however, that the exhibitions would coincide with the spring San Isidro Fair. Although that festival was drawing large numbers of visitors, for a while its activities were mostly held on the Pradera by the Manzanares River and thus did not interfere with the exhibitions at the Academia. For the administration of the Museo Real, however, the festive crowds coming to the Paseo del Prado during this and all other festivals—San Juan, San Pedro and Pablo, San Lorenzo, and many others—for after-hours drinks, sweets, and dances were already causing concern. José de Madrazo, who directed the museum between 1838 and 1856, described in no uncertain terms the "mob that . . . occupied the area until unruly hours or remained inside all night long during all festivities, transforming the museum's hall into a bordello."[23] Still, in contrast to the separation achieved between the Fall Fair and the exhibitions by rescheduling the exhibitions, the San Isidro celebrations were not being disassociated from the Museo Real but, rather, kept moving closer. In 1878, the city council and the Vendors' Association, determined to transform the patron-saint festival into a model for civilized recreation, moved its commercial extension to the Prado Promenade, facing the museum. The measure set in motion an unannounced contest for modernization that the traditional fairgrounds on the shores of the Manzanares would eventually lose to the better-endowed commercial fair in the center of Madrid.

On the surface of things, the Paseo del Prado and the Pradera de San Isidro were now united. Soon rechristened the "Madrid Fairs," this modern version of the San Isidro Festival added more locations in Madrid and expanded to become a fortnight of exhibitions, bullfights, theater performances, horse and bicycle races, and, after 1886, the celebration of King Alfonso XIII's birthday. Later in the century, one writer nostalgically remembered the times when the fairs "occupied the whole of Madrid, turning the town into a gigantic extension of the Rastro [street market]."[24] These were the crowded and much-debated surroundings in, against, and with which the museum developed. Merging with the summer *verbenas*, the extended San Isidro Fair transformed the Prado Promenade into an ongoing spring and summer fairground: a place where old-school popular worship intersected with fashionable vending establishments and elegant "pleasure gardens." Starting in the 1910s, municipal authorities tried to make the vending stalls look more aesthetic and even requested that the vendors have the appearance of their kiosks approved prior to the fair, "so that these *verbenas* could offer a more pleasant sight than they currently offer[ed]."[25] While the fairgrounds were thus modernizing and becoming more civilized due to their proximity to the art exhibits, the museum was, conversely, opening up to visual experiences not associated with high culture. For example, between 1894 and 1922, its rotundas were used as mortuary chambers to exhibit the bodies of museum directors and Spain's national heroes to the crowds.

In reality, as Pierre Geál demonstrates, the distinction between a museum exhibit and an outdoor artifact has always been uncertain around the Prado.[26] Sculptural compositions were often placed interchangeably on display in the museum (thereby becoming statues) or in the Retiro Park (thus assuming decorative functions); they were also placed in city squares, allowing them to be interpreted as civic monuments. Just as they often wondered if an exhibit was a monument or a sculpture, Spaniards of different social and geographic origins found it hard to tell a painting from an advertisement, an object of worship, or a freak show. This, I claim, was due to their contact with the visual culture of the Prado Promenade. If in nineteenth- and early twentieth-century Madrid even educated visitors had no basis of knowledge from which to interpret the things that the museum had to offer, they could follow the example of their laboring fellow citizens and resort to the attitudes and behaviors rehearsed on the Promenade.

Contrary to what one might think, tangling together the artistic and all other experiences did not go against the museum ideal, which, as Jacques Rancière argues, came with the recognition that "there was no longer any boundary separating what belongs to the realm of art from what belongs to the realm of everyday life."[27] Rather, taking museum-going as a pastime, Spain's emerging bourgeoisie creatively engaged with the promise of bringing aesthetic contemplation closer to other activities classified as work—or, rather, the immaterial type of work called "leisure" and previously reserved for the upper classes—that was at the heart of all modern institutions of public art and the notion of *Bildung* (self-cultivation) associated with them.[28] My looking at the Prado Museum as a leisure site will not, of course, abolish the top-down system of discourses, classificatory tools, and display strategies known as "museum culture" in order to give agency back to the masses.[29] From a leisure studies perspective, as the ensuing section explains, nineteenth-century leisure itself has little to do with liberation from constraints or any similar theory claiming that oppression is endemic to society and that freedom has to come in the form of "play," Carnival, or some other controlled, time- and place-specific "excess."[30] Instead, I follow a historicist stance on leisure, viewed as a system of activities and norms that became a decisive agent in the making of consumer society because it allowed cult, culture, and commerce—the three c's intertwined in the traditional festivals—to continue affecting each other after modernization set them apart as autonomous "fields."[31]

Bringing together museum and leisure studies, this book posits that the cultural meanings assigned to the Prado Museum can only be understood if we reconsider its interaction with the popular pastimes outside. My approach owes to recent scholarship two underlying suppositions: (1) that nineteenth- and early twentieth-century redrawing of the urban and the rural is relevant for understanding art museums, and (2) that art museums facilitated the communication between leisure, religion, culture, and commerce at a time when the boundaries between them were still in flux. Such a view of museum-going as part of a continuum where the four spheres converged to produce the embodied modern gaze gives twenty-first-century readers a glimpse of a world where visiting art museums was not necessarily about art.[32]

MUSEUM STUDIES AND LEISURE HISTORY

These days, art museums have officially become fun.[33] Their websites mix leisure and culture labels to lure visitors who, in turn, admit to seeking entertainment as well as education.[34] The growing acceptance of museum-going as a pastime is usually attributed to the rise of tourist economies that have transformed art exhibits into attractions competing for attention and government resources.[35] According to this model, visiting museums provides an "interactive experience" for those seeking authenticity and a sense of well-being.[36] "Museums are halfway between Disneyland and a church," states Mikhail Piotrovsky, the director of Saint Petersburg's Hermitage Museum.[37] Yet long before the foundation of Disneyland, art museums already provoked religious fervor and impious joy, sent mixed messages, and experimented with "schizophrenic" display principles in order to reach and satisfy the cognoscenti as well as the masses.[38] "Like modernity itself, the museum," in the words of Nick Prior, "is Janus-faced, double-coded, ambivalent. Historically, it has oscillated between contrasting sets of values and exhibited apparently self-contradictory behavior—inward-looking elitism and populist democratic pedagogy, religiosity and secularism, traditionalism and modernity."[39] Anyone wishing to understand the appeal of art exhibits before the age of mass tourism will, therefore, find it useful to pay attention to the historical unfolding of museum-going as a popular pastime and to its modern roots.

Why have the spaces of cult and leisure been able to compete with museums—the institutions of the modern "public sphere" that were specifically designed to incorporate, civilize, and supplant religious and leisure activities? The developing scholarship on the urban culture of the industrial revolution gives us an indication. The "museum age," as Germain Bazin has called the "long" nineteenth century (1789–1914), was a time of unprecedented city growth in Europe. Between 1800 and 1900, the "level of urbanization" (measured as the proportion of urban to rural population) doubled in most European countries, with the growth in urban population consistently staying above this ratio.[40] Madrid was the city that spearheaded urbanization in post-1830s Spain, when lands formerly belonging to the church and the Crown began to change hands. Providing an early example of a construction bubble, by the twentieth century the former courtly and bureaucratic center reemerged as a city of land speculators and financial and industrial capitalists.[41]

In nineteenth and early twentieth centuries, urbanization meant the creation not of new cities, but rather of new megalopoles: existing cities all across Europe began to grow taller and wider as they absorbed increasing numbers of rural newcomers.[42] Such rapid growth meant that nineteenth-century urbanity became more—not less—dependent on rural lifestyles, and "the Baudelairean experience" of the flâneur, as culture historian Hannu Salmi notes, "remained rather remote to the majority of Europeans."[43] As the workers became politicized and began demonstrating in the streets, peasant and artisan transplants—initially viewed as merely picturesque additions to the cityscape—began to be portrayed with fear and respect and became subjects of policy-makers' attention. In densely populated cities such as London, Manchester, and Liverpool, social reformers concerned with the fate of the urban poor had high hopes for public art museums. It was thought that, brought together as a group in the presence of valuable objects, the working classes would learn respect, self-control, and other habits expected in self-improving citizens.[44] Yet the new standards of urbanity could not be forged uniquely on paved streets and in public buildings. Arguing that the pastimes of modernizing cities did not occupy some yawning gap, but rather merged with those practiced in the countryside, historians of the industrial age have proposed that we look more closely at the cultural practices of urban fairs and patron-saint pilgrimage sites.[45] In places such as these, to use Lynn Abrams's apt wording, one can find a "missing link between pre-industrial amusements of the lower classes beloved by historians of popular culture and the commercial culture."[46]

In his 1938 *The Culture of Cities*, Lewis Mumford compared the metropoles of his time to "a World's Fair in continuous operation" offering "traditional pleasures of the fair—jugglers, acrobats, gamblers, sideshows, sexual license of all sorts" but expanding them in time and space to maximize revenue for the urban rich.[47] Mumford's opinion of museums was consistent with his unmasking of this urban economy of pleasure. Museums, he wrote, embodied the claims to culture made by the "metropolitan oligarchy of financiers and officeholders," who lured the public into "vast department stores of the arts and sciences, where everything is ticketed and labeled, where bargain attractions are offered, where the turnover of goods is more important than the ultimate satisfaction of the purchaser."[48] To Mumford, the connection between museums and commerce was not merely metaphorical. Still, until the 1990s, art museums were primarily addressed as a subject of aesthetics and a tool of nation-building which had little to do with fairgrounds.

In this approach, the museums' social functions were predicated on the artificiality of their space and time. In an effort to purge from the exhibits anything remotely resembling the rural world and its rude pastimes, the urban middle classes imagined the institutions of public art as separate from their surroundings: "The museum comprised a 'pure' space, symbolically opposed to the vulgarities of the carnival, where the values of civilized bourgeois culture were coded and decoded by this class itself," Prior remarks.[49] The museum's space was therefore sealed off from the outer world, while the time that it represented was rearranged to offer an illusion of "indefinite accumulation."[50] Hans-Georg Gadamer pointed out that such a setting made possible "aesthetic differentiation": a process by which "the work loses its place and the world to which it belongs insofar as it belongs instead to aesthetic consciousness."[51]

As they communicated aesthetic values, museums also developed classificatory tools allowing them to mimic (or at times anticipate) the political maps of the world.[52] Uncovering the tensions obliterated in museums' representations of history as if it were an actual signified, rather than the effect of discourse and narrativity, has become a particularly productive direction of inquiry.[53] Seeking to imitate the bordered and centralized national territories of the nineteenth century, art exhibits thus became essential for the consolidation of the liberal state. Their artful spaces, in Tony Bennett's argument, were built to create disciplined citizens and facilitate public displays of secularism, rationality, and national allegiance, which Carol Duncan has termed "civilizing rituals."[54] Importantly, as she adds, museums also ensured the gendering of the public space by making nude female bodies look natural when framed and put on display.[55]

Although art museums—especially the public and the national ones—owed much of their social impact to their founders' choices of location,[56] scholarly inquiry into the spatial history of museum-building has long been hampered by this ideal of a hermetic aesthetic display. Yet even educators and social reformers who had founded their highest hopes on the civilizing influence of the exhibits doubted whether it was realistic to expect that visitors would change their usual habits once they crossed the threshold. In the United Kingdom, a nation boasting the first state-sponsored art museum in Europe, government authorities were intrigued by the public's real reactions and even dispatched special observers to see if those gathering in the National Gallery in London were indeed paying attention to the paintings. The answers were mixed. Sir Michael Faraday, for example, reported that he had seen "women suckling their infants, and others sitting about upon the floors, and others not looking at the pictures," but that he "could not say that they had not been looking at the pictures." The Parliament's Select Committee then began to wonder whether the gallery owed its common visitors' propensity to "lounge" to its location on the city's major thoroughfare, but could not arrive at any conclusion.[57]

In every country where "museum fever"[58] had spread, writers, pundits, and social reformers who had joined forces to determine what was proper and improper in the presence of art insisted that the museums' cultural mission depended on their administrators' ability to eliminate contamination from the outer world. That was a utopian idea, as even bourgeois male spectators, thought to be the backbone of the museum public, were flocking in armed with theater binoculars to enjoy the spectacle of the opposite sex alongside, and sometimes instead of, the works of art. By the 1950s, the museum ivory tower had been shattered under the weight of unflattering comparisons with mausoleums and hospitals.[59] Yet so ingrained was the social-reformist concept of museum autonomy that the scholarly community continued focusing on the things that separated museums from their surroundings long after the illusory nature of this separation became apparent.

The balance began to shift noticeably with the publication, in the 1990s, of several works focusing on the relations between aesthetic experience, urban planning, and modern consumption. Arguing that by the second half of the nineteenth century art galleries had absorbed the display strategies of world's fairs and modern shops, scholars began to see the mid-nineteenth century as a period when association with commerce became acceptable at the museum.[60] Crucially, these studies represented the connection between the museums and the outer world as going both ways: not only were the masses drawn into museums to become better citizens, but museums

FIG. 9 Cecilio Pizarro y Librado, *Galería comercial* (Shopping arcade), 1840–73. Drawing, 165 mm × 144 mm. Museo Nacional del Prado.

themselves had to come closer to the masses in order to, as Seth Koven has it, "reshape the interior and exterior landscapes of the urban poor."[61] Similarly, in Duncan's argument concerning art and commerce, some male and most female patrons—those with limited purchasing power—experienced window-shopping no differently than admiring priceless masterpieces (fig. 9). Once the social reformers and entrepreneurs understood that exhibiting not-for-sale objects could be useful for industry and trade, newly founded department stores began to be described as "women's museums." It was at that very time that art museums took on a new function: schooling the population in the habits of civilized visual consumption.

It would be impossible to realize that art museums do not come with their own gaze, but rather offer the opportunities and positive conditions that allow such a gaze to develop and influence other experiences, without a working model of the evolution of leisure. It was sociologists and leisure historians, rather than experts in urban studies, who uncovered the continuities between premodern lifestyles, fairgrounds, and urban culture—the idea that had fueled Mumford's early thinking about city life. Mumford's own negative take on fairgrounds was shaped by debates among German politicians and social reformers concerning rural pastimes and whether or not they belonged in the industrial society. (Their answer was a resounding "no.")[62] An alternative, more favorable, reading of urban fairs emerged in the 1960s in France when Henri Lefebvre and the Situationists famously recast the Paris Commune of 1871 as a spontaneous urban festival.[63] In the wake of May 1968, the urban fairground metaphor for a revolution has resurfaced every time a group demonstrates peacefully on city streets and squares.

Counter to these persistently optimistic descriptions of urban festivals and fairs, leisure historians argue that the modern system of pastimes, with its parks, stadiums, museums, regulated gambling, and controlled drinking, itself arose as a form of oppression designed to counter the social consequences of the industrial revolution. According to nineteenth-century religious leaders, industrialization, like another fall from Eden, had isolated people from the marvels of nature and lumped them together in the cities, where the air was polluted and the hygiene poor; men, no longer spending time with their families, were succumbing to violence, drunkenness, and gambling.[64] The system of "rational recreation" designed in Victorian Britain by those concerned with morals, health, and order—and later adopted by social reformers of many other countries—gave the world some of its most lasting and popular pastimes: team sports, leisurely strolls, Sunday museum outings, family music, and board games. This is why John Clarke and Charles Critcher maintain that the masses derive no real benefits from urban leisure, at least of the organized kind, since leisure itself was designed as a set of rule-governed activities that would keep the working classes "off the street" and "under supervision."[65]

Attentive to the role that the state has historically played in encouraging behaviors consistent with its own needs, historians of leisure rely on Norbert Elias's sociological inquiry into what he called the "sportization of pastimes."[66] In Max Weber's classical argument, the modern state reserves for itself a monopoly on violence. The "civilizing process" of improving manners therefore becomes an inherent part of modernization as it channels humans' violent impulses into rule-governed activities such as hunting or horseracing and, later on, football and boxing.[67] Hence, even before Michel Foucault's lectures on governmentality were published and provided a framework for interpreting culture, leisure studies experts claimed that social resistance often takes on the guise of soccer hooliganism and other violent spin-offs of organized sporting events.[68] Conversely, nineteenth-century urban festivals, which were adding growing numbers of "sportized" activities to their programs, were fully complicit with the state's civilizing efforts and merely offered the chance for people to participate in limited and controlled excess. Rather than eradicate oppression, fairgrounds made oppression less obvious, turning attention from the distinctions of class to those of gender, color, shape, and aptitude, as in the fairground freak shows, promoting what Rosalind Garland-Thomson describes as the degrading fairground "staring."[69]

Further keys to understanding why fairgrounds remained so essential to the growing urban world are to be found in the current views on modernization as a social process that produces a split in the initial syncretic unity of religion, culture, and commerce. According to this influential narrative, before the notion of leisure was even invented, worship, merrymaking, and trade traveled together from one fairground to another. Those days of "festival culture," as Peter Burke calls it, began to fade with the development of modern cities, which brought to life the notion of "leisure" in its diverse meanings. Initially a category used by aristocrats who felt the need to protect their free time from the growing responsibilities of courtly life,[70] in the early nineteenth century "leisure" was appropriated by the working classes to denote freedom from obligation, only to be taken away by midcentury social reformers who converted leisure into a system of institutions and cultural policies aimed at controlling the population. To be sure, these ideologues did not demand a complete separation from religion, culture, and commerce but rather insisted that leisure should have its own time and space. Epitomizing this idea, gated pleasure grounds that charged admission began to emerge as sites where the urban middle classes could distinguish themselves from rural immigrants. In some cases they even took over patron-saint sanctuaries and seasonal fairgrounds. To what extent urban leisure should merge with commerce remained, for a long time, a matter of debate.

Nowhere, then, were the continuities and ruptures between the old and new forms of worship, trading, leisure, and culture more visible than on the urban fairgrounds, caught between the syncretic festival and the modern autonomous realms. No longer anchored in specific locations or locked into the rural cycle of seasonal and religious holidays, nineteenth-century fairs took on many forms and shapes. Patron-saint celebrations, of course, went on. And although journalists repudiated them as a wasteful, shameful, and backward custom, the festivals persisted, expanded, and became more commercial. In 1887, for example, the San Isidro fairgrounds on the Pradera had a *salón de descanso*—a resting spot with a view and a restaurant reserving some places for people bringing their own food—but also, on a less "civilized" side, forty-seven small and big kiosks selling wine, two liquor kiosks, only five water kiosks, seventy-nine small and large vending stalls with doughnuts, seven vending stalls with whistles (a San Isidro tradition), eight vendors selling clay figures, and fourteen toy sellers. The "sports," however, were limited to the traditional options of a shooting range and a form of entertainment that consisted of stoning running rabbits—a tradition that continued despite an official complaint to the mayor from the Animal and Plant Protection Society, an association that hosted its own, modern fair events such as dog and flower exhibitions in the current Retiro Park in the center of Madrid.[71]

Commercial fairs and patron-saint celebrations were merging and changing locations. A festival could be held without a saint to remember, and, both inside and outside traditional fairgrounds, developers started to build bourgeois pleasure grounds. These were gated areas that charged admission, and they often took pride in offering the latest technologies for their patrons' increased comfort. In Madrid, the Jardín de las Delicias advertised public bathrooms, while the Jardines de Buen Retiro featured the first electric lighting in town.[72] These venues offered amusements across the high- and low-culture divide, from acrobatic performances to dances to concerts.

Adding cross-gender mingling to the fairground "staring," pleasure grounds were crucial for modernizing the public sphere.

Peter Bailey terms these areas of middle-class amusement in Britain "leisure zones." In his argument, in places such as these, commercial stakeholders took advantage of the system of modern pastimes, marketing themselves as respectful of bourgeois moral norms yet accommodating "constraints to a more democratized consumerist freedom of behavior."[73] Tempting and testing the bourgeoisie by offering opportunities to consume and to mingle in ways that the realms of cult or culture could not offer, modern leisure spots also gave commerce a role in educating "the public."[74] In the debate about whether urban leisure could help build good citizens or whether, conversely, it prevented the public from developing civic virtue, the state would, of course, eventually take the upper hand, turning all fairgrounds into gated amusement parks. Yet as long as cities relied on the influx of rural workers, the gated and ungated pleasure areas had to coexist on the urban fairgrounds.

Several scholars have productively followed Bailey's lead by arguing that museums found a place in the bourgeois "leisure zone" alongside "the modernized pub, the music hall, the seaside pier and dance hall, the hotel and cafe-restaurant, the municipal park and the department store."[75] Approaching museums as counterparts to these gated pleasure areas effectively accounts for their cross-class appeal in the nineteenth century. Of all the visitors, it was the middle classes who found in the museum a particularly comfortable stage; seeking opportunities to consume and flirt, they also passed these habits on to the working masses. This useful model, however, has one limitation: the exclusive focus on urban middle-class lifestyles does not explain why museums were popular in countries such as Spain, where bourgeois leisure continued to compete for popularity and social recognition with popular religious, or quasi-religious, celebrations through the 1930s.

Approaching bourgeois leisure in a way similar to how labor historians interpret nineteenth- and early twentieth-century working-class pastimes, namely, as a hybrid set of spaces and activities heavily influenced by urban newcomers, offers one explanation. In recent years, historians have suggested that we reconsider the very nature of the bourgeoisie—defining membership in this class not according to income level or stakes in the means of production, but rather by the choices of values and lifestyles that certain representatives of the urban "middling classes" were making in order to distinguish themselves from their neighbors lower on the social ladder. "People were bourgeois—such is the near-tautological conclusion of extensive research and discussion—if they *considered* themselves bourgeois and gave this belief practical expression in the way they led their life," Jürgen Osterhammel writes.[76] In the regions of "peripheral modernity" to which Spain belonged at this period, the bourgeoisie wished to imitate their cosmopolitan counterparts even though their own surroundings or values were not modernizing as quickly as in the countries of the first wave of industrial development. In Beatriz Sarlo's argument, in countries of "peripheral modernity," uneven industrialization translates into a peculiar stylistic mix: the cult of the present is counterbalanced by an attachment to the past, the exaltation of urban locations coexists with nostalgia for rural lifestyles, and the values of industrial society are overshadowed by patriarchic norms.[77]

Modern cultural markers and traditional pastimes were similarly intertwined in these peripheral realms. Mark Sandberg, for example, traces the success in Scandinavia of wax and folk exhibits—the type of museums that the bourgeoisie there praised during the late nineteenth and early twentieth centuries for their educational value and aesthetic appeal—to the fairground attractions that maintained a high profile well into the 1900s.[78] Bringing this analytical framework to Spain, Jo Labanyi argues that the abundance of large canvases featuring bloody scenes of madness and assassination at the National Fine Art Exhibitions reflected the viewing habits of visitors whose gaze had been trained through habitual exposure to bullfights and freak shows.[79] The relevance of this meeting between high art and the working-class ways of looking becomes clear once we follow the scholar of early cinema Miriam Hansen in acknowledging that it was the film industry that, "submerg[ing] all class distinctions in an ostensibly homogenous culture of consumption," placed the spectators' social bonds at the foundation of the new visual mythology uniting capitalism and democracy.[80]

This book uncovers the give-and-take between several radically different approaches to public art that turned the Prado Museum itself into a cultural product, a "contact zone" between town and country (to use Mary Louise Pratt's coinage),[81] and a key player in the development of modern leisure. Michel Foucault classified museums and fairgrounds as two interrelated yet mutually opposing "heterotopias"— spaces where the linear flow of modern time is suspended and replaced by the artificial chronology of infinite "accumulation" or by the "fleeting, transitory, precarious" festival cycle.[82] The Prado Museum has always been both—a place of pure aesthetic trance *and* a festival.

A VISITORS' MUSEUM

In 1994, when the Prado was celebrating its 175th anniversary, Javier Portús, the best-known historian of the museum, lamented the institutional bias of scholarship that "has neglected foreign and domestic visitors who saw the museum as an authentic reference point where they found their true identity markers and the tools for reflecting on their own history."[83] The task seemed clear: it was time to add to the historiography of the Prado a dimension that could explain how it touched the lives of individuals and communities and what it offered in response to their needs. Although Portús's complete annotated bibliography provided ample tools to those wishing to write such a "biography," so far only the museum's building has received a more personal treatment.[84] There are, however, numerous works on Spain's visual culture, leisure, and the Prado in particular from which I draw. Contemporary studies of the Prado are steeped in a long tradition of pioneering publications since the 1930s: the books by Pedro Beroqui, Mariano de Madrazo, Juan Antonio Gaya Nuño, Alfonso Pérez Sánchez, Santiago Alcolea Blanch, Francisco Calvo Serraller, and Javier Portús.[85] Still, just as with other European museums, most recent historians of the Spanish art world are far less interested in the exhibiting institutions themselves than in the notions of power, knowledge, heritage, and taste that they projected.[86] These approaches underpin the recent histories of Spanish museums that have guided me in my work: the books by María Bolaños, Pierre Géal, and Selma Holo, as well as José María Lanzarote Guiral's overview of Spain's national museums.[87] Alisa Luxenberg's analysis of the nineteenth-century debates about Spanish heritage and its plunder has clarified the questions of transnational power and heritage even further.[88] Yet the Prado was not only a nation's treasure chest but also a museum of private collections. With its holdings coming from crowned and common donors, it relied on the shifting tastes and collecting habits of Spanish society that Oscar Vazquez has analyzed.[89]

Since the beginning of the current century, the Prado Museum has hosted exhibitions shedding light on its own past. In 2001, the Prado displayed a photographic panorama of the central gallery made in 1880 by J. Laurent y Cía,[90] and in 2003 it exhibited archival materials about the museum's rescue during the Civil War of 1936–39.[91] In 2004, it dedicated an exhibit to the first National Museum (aka Museo de la Trinidad), whose collection was merged with the Prado in 1870.[92] Furthermore, exhibits such as *The Reserved Room in the Prado* (2002) and *The Palace of King Planet* (2005) have allowed visitors to understand the changing meanings that paintings acquired when they were transferred from royal palaces to the museum.[93] In 2007, a large-scale exhibition of nineteenth-century holdings marked the inauguration of a new building designed by Rafael Moneo. The exhibition made it clear how much Spanish art owed to a museum where artists could come to copy old masters and where the government could store paintings purchased from national exhibitions.[94] In the same year, the Prado also launched a publication of unprecedented value for those wishing to understand its origins and development: *Enciclopedia del Museo del Prado*. The six-volume compendium features entries on every aspect of the museum's history, building, and collection that are made even more useful thanks to the book's online module.[95]

The museum's destiny has always hinged on politics even more than aesthetics, and never was this dependence as pronounced as during the Civil War. The controversies that triggered the evacuation of the Prado to Valencia in 1936 became the subject of José Álvarez Lopera's and Arturo Colorado Castellary's inquiries.[96] In response to this research, in 2010 Spain's Socialist government paid due tribute to those who prevented a catastrophe by protecting the collection during Franco's air attacks in

1936–1939.[97] One could see exhibits commemorating this operation on the Paseo del Prado in front of the museum and in the cities that preserved the evacuated paintings: Valencia, Barcelona, and Geneva.[98] Taken together, these events and publications have mapped the way for a new history of the Prado as a place that has defined art, taste, power, and identity in Spain for almost two hundred years.

My own perspective on these issues relies on the rich tradition of interdisciplinary research on nineteenth- and early twentieth-century Spain. I learned from the work of Ed Baker, Jesús Cruz, Daniel Frost, Jorge Uría, and Noel Valis to pay attention to the *real* class dimension of the cultural forms that are usually considered refined or middle-class.[99] Likewise, I am much indebted to the studies that approach Spain's visual culture as an intersection of race and gender: works by Alda Blanco, Lou Charnon Deutsch, Susan Martín Márquez, Leigh Mercer, and Maite Zubiaurre.[100] Modernity, leisure, and taste in Madrid in particular have become a topic of interest for a range of academic disciplines, including literature studies, history, cultural studies, sociology, and art history. This interdisciplinary work includes monographs by Andrew Ginger, Susan Larson, and Deborah Parsons, as well as the multiauthored volumes coordinated by Susan Larson and Eva Woods, Carlos Serrano and George Salaün, Marie-Linda Ortega, and many others.[101] The expanding work on urban leisure has now also retrieved a wealth of information on the ephemeral pleasure gardens, parks, and festival areas of nineteenth- and early twentieth-century Madrid: these works include publications by José María Ferrer, Concepción Lopezosa Aparicio, Rosario Mariblanca Caneyro, and Carmen Simón Palmer.[102] My understanding of the Prado's role as a cultural mediator draws from the reseach on the fragmentation of religious experience triggered by modernization, especially prominent in the work of Alfonso Botti, Derek Flitter, Íñigo Sánchez-Llama, and Begoña Uringüen González.[103]

The principles, ideas, and ideals associated with museum displays could never be confined to a nation's territory. Responding to a recent call to "transnationalize" museum studies in order to bring our analytical tools closer to the museum world itself,[104] my own approach is to reconcile the burgeoning literature concerning Spain with new studies on modern urbanization and with available scholarship on European and transatlantic networks of politicians, experts, artists, and travelers who were setting the museum standards. The book is divided into five chapters corresponding to major periods in Spain's history: (1) Fernando VII's absolutism in crisis (1819–33); (2) the constitutional monarchy of Isabel II (1833–68); (3) the "six revolutionary years" (1868–74); (4) the restoration of the Bourbons and regency (1874–1902); and (5) the rise and fall of a liberal state, corresponding to the rule of Alfonso XIII, the dictatorship of Primo de Rivera, and the Second Republic (1902–36). Each chapter is subdivided into distinct sections that look at the Prado Museum from specific angles: (1) the developments in the museum world outside Spain, (2) the ways in which the period's main political events resonated at the museum, (3) the visual culture on

FIG. 10   Luis Álvarez Catalá, *The Carnival* (aka *The Carnival on the Prado in 1800*), 1886, detail. Oil on linen, 52.7 × 102.6 cm. Brooklyn Museum, Gift of Mrs. William E. S. Griswold in memory of her father, John Sloane.

the Prado Promenade, (4) the museum's institutional changes, and (5) the learned and lay views of the museum. The book's epilogue explains the museum's evacuation from Madrid during the Civil War of 1936–39. This final section ends with General Francisco Franco's coming to power: the point at which the culture of the Prado was decisively separated from fairground merrymaking.

"Culture depends for its very existence on leisure, and leisure, in its turn, is not possible unless it has a durable and consequently living link with the *cultus*, with divine worship," Josef Pieper stated in 1952, writing against the spirit of his culture-cherishing times. In the nineteenth and early twentieth centuries, however, the three components of Pieper's equation—culture, leisure, and cult (and also and especially commerce, which is absent from his discussion)—were still on the move, just like the Madrid populace, who did not always know where the meadow ended and the city began or where fun and worship became culture. The mix of high and low cultures and everything in between on the Prado was likewise a source of inspiration for Spanish writers and artists, who even created a new type of genre scene that satisfied the bourgeois. In 1886, one such painting—*Carnival on the Prado in 1800* by Luis Álvarez Catalá—was sold in Rome for a record price of 114,000 francs (fig. 10). Though the painting, even at its creation, was staged in the past, the scene explored with gusto the modern contrast between immobile, black-clad Spanish women of old and the joyful yet fearful crowd in disguise moving under the attentive eye of the guards. A few years later, Álvarez Catalá would become the deputy director and eventually the director of the Prado Museum. Not only would he witness many modern celebrations on the Prado, he would also advance them to a new level by using technology to merge the museum and the Promenade. In 1899, on the day of Velázquez's tercentennial, he arranged for the museum's façade to be transformed into a gigantic screen on which to project images of the artist's paintings. One observer deemed the event a complete failure because its audience consisted of "a couple hundred louts, regulars of those spots near the museum," who whistled and told "all sorts of [lewd] jokes."[105] Imagining this scene now, without elitist dismissiveness and fear of the masses, one can only appreciate how well the curiosity of the "louts"—as well as their supposedly questionable humor—summed up the decades of the museum blending with its surroundings: the back-and-forth between indoors and outdoors, the easy passage from canvas to screen, the amalgam of aesthetic awe and silly gag. Indeed, the museum's diverse visitors have always approached the Prado this way.

CHAPTER ONE

A Royal Public Institution, 1819–1833

ONE CAN ONLY GUESS what potential domestic visitors thought when the Royal Museum (Museo Real) first opened. In November 1819, its founder, King Fernando VII, formerly known as "the Desired," was consumed by one desire—to retain the scepter—while his liberal challengers discussed freedom and constitution and would hardly support any project, cultural or otherwise, coming from the king. The unveiling of the museum was scheduled to welcome to Madrid Queen María Josefa Amalia of Saxony, whom Fernando had just married.[1] On November 13, the marquis de Santa Cruz, the king's sommelier du corps and the museum's first director, wrote a notice announcing the inauguration.[2] However, the majority of newspapers had been banned since 1815, and the two that remained had to have their content approved by a censor before going to press. The censoring process took so long that the announcement was not run in time, and the opening had to be delayed until Friday, November 19, the day when the museum's anniversary is still celebrated. Back in 1819, though, when the day finally came, it was raining in Madrid.[3] And while in retrospect that may have seemed like a good omen, at the time rain only meant mud, which posed a danger to the floors and thus further delayed the museum's inauguration. Two more days would pass before the building on the Paseo del Prado really opened its doors.

Asking the royal administration to extend the period of open admission that had been planned to introduce the new institution to society, Santa Cruz stated that "the public manifested grand pleasure seeing so many precious objects brought together, which honor the nation so much."[4] Yet no reaction appeared in the press. It took two more months, a coup d'état, and a temporary return to constitutionalism before the first review of the museum was published—and it was not all positive. In January of 1820, just weeks after the unveiling of the collection, General Rafael del Riego staged a successful coup, forcing Fernando to follow the 1812 constitution.[5] The hiatus known as the "three liberal years" (*trienio liberal*) did not last long: in 1823, backed by the Holy Alliance, the supporters of absolute monarchy in Spain and France organized a countercoup, dispatching to Madrid a regiment that became known as the Hundred Thousand Sons of Saint Louis to return power to Fernando. Prosper Mérimée, the French writer and inspector-general of historical monuments, would later comment sarcastically on the progress of the Museo Real after Fernando's return to full power. The museum, he wrote, offered its visitors the most comfortable red velvet couches to sit and rest on. These seats had been initially made for the parliament (the Cortes) that Fernando VII had disbanded, and, as Mérimée concluded, it did not "seem very likely that they would return to their original destination any time soon."[6] To many, the Museo Real looked like a mausoleum of Spain's failed liberalism and a storage space for the nation's past hopes. Indeed, while its founding father was alive, the museum conceived as the king's personal project did not support any other political cause.

Why did Fernando VII decide to create an art museum? People who lived during his reign and later generations have all looked at the Museo Real in awe trying to answer this question. It might be easy to attribute the king's decision to some personal circumstance or consideration. I take the view here that the reason is, instead, typological: the king was following other European rulers who were creating semi-open extensions into the "public sphere." In the aftermath of the Napoleonic wars, royal public museums were an attempt to reiterate and make visible the nations' shattered links to their monarchies. In Spain, however, the educated, well-traveled public able to appreciate the collection would have no better words for Fernando's Museo Real than it could find for the absolute monarchy that the museum was meant to exalt. It was in spite of and perhaps even against the founder's plans—and, in many ways, against the idea of art itself—that the Royal Museum eventually found a niche in the national imagination.

A POST-NAPOLEONIC ART MUSEUM

The relationship between power, museum ownership, and exhibiting principles in other countries was no secret to the Spanish elites. The monarchist *El Restaurador*, for example, in 1823 welcomed Fernando VII back as an absolute king by exalting the donations that Pope Pius VII had made to the Museo Pio-Clementino in the wake of his return to the Papal Palace.[7] Conversely, the constitutionalist *Mercurio de España* provided positive coverage of the royal Bavarian Museums, thinly disguising criticism of the Spanish Museo Real by positively describing the Bavarian Museums' chronological display as "the wise method of admission and classification that favors the instruction of artists and aficionados and protects a royal museum from resembling a storage of paintings and statues."[8]

There were four key players in nineteenth-century museums in Europe: the court, the state, the academies, and the church. Though each of these entities claimed to act on behalf of "nations" and the "public," at the time both concepts were undergoing continuous change. The term "nation" was becoming a designation for a territory and the institutions governing its inhabitants, while the "public" opened its ranks to include the middle classes, who engaged in activities such as talking in coffee shops or taking a formal stroll along the promenade. Still, as James J. Sheehan reminds us, "the public" remained a notion highly influenced by the court for much longer than the historians are sometimes willing to accept: "individuals frequently lived in both realms or moved from one to the other."[9] On the threshold between the old and the new regimes, the "public sphere" could be easily confused with ceremonial courtly "publicity." Royal public museums, neatly fitting into this transitional agenda, could give the monarchies a desired facelift while also enabling the middle classes to join the aristocrats in their dialogue with royal authority.[10] These new courtly spaces did not glorify the kings and queens for amassing artistic treasures, but rather for sharing those treasures and using them for the education and moral progress of the people.

While this would make the Museo Real a rather typical post-Napoleonic undertaking, in Spain, the decision to open royal art collections owed so much to the debates over absolutism that Fernando's museum came to life bearing many similarities with royal public galleries of the previous century: the Luxembourg Museum in Paris, the Fridericianum in Kassel, and the papal Museo Pio-Clementino. The Museo Real is therefore better understood when one compares it to the hybrid model of the nineteenth-century public museums of the German courts: the galleries of Munich and Berlin. These institutions succeeded in carving out a solid place for the social groups supporting the old regime while also successfully weathering the scrutiny of the democratically minded factions.

In the aftermath of the Napoleonic wars of 1803–15, those in Europe involved in conservation and exhibition of art could follow several models. First, there were the old-regime royal public museums, normally attached to a palace or having some section reserved for entertaining the guests of the court. Their main audience was thought of as the king's immediate circle, although the museum would also occasionally issue permissions or invitations to other visitors. For example, the Hermitage Museum in Saint Petersburg's Winter Palace, officially boasting 1764 as its foundation date, in reality did not have a separate entrance until 1852, almost a century later. In the nineteenth century, old royal palaces and new royal museums still often overlapped. The former occasionally opened as museums to the "public," while the latter could sometimes be taken over by the court for royal visits and celebrations. Such was the case with the Glyptothek in Munich, belonging to Crown Prince Ludwig of Bavaria (the future King Ludwig I), conceived in 1815 and inaugurated in 1830.[11]

Since the middle ages, the church had also exhibited works of art to the faithful. In the nineteenth century, their ranks would be joined by rapidly increasing numbers of people who only worshipped art. Historians argue that, while the post-Napoleonic political regimes were marked by continuous and occasionally successful attempts at monarchical restoration, one thing would never be the same: the cultural importance of the church.[12] Following their disentailment by Napoleon, religious communities would lose to the academies and the state their roles as patrons of the arts.

Before and after the Napoleonic wars, royal academies channeled the communication between the courts and civil society in all matters of art. Their target audience, however, was not merely aristocratic, and thus, in Holger Hoock's example, the British Royal Academy became the first of the courtly institutions to pose, and be seen, as "national."[13] In the aftermath of the plundering carried out by Napoleon's armies in all occupied lands, the academies stretched their influence far beyond the fading courts as they took on the custody of their countries' collections and spearheaded the first known movements for heritage protection. Although after the Congress of Vienna Spain's religious communities and kings would eventually recoup some of their former possessions, in other Catholic countries works of art were brought back not to palaces and churches, but to academies.[14] In the nineteenth century, the academies' trademark outreach activities consisted of making statues (or their copies) and pictorial masterpieces available to artists-in-training and organizing periodical exhibitions of works by their professors and disciples.

The youngest player, the state, entered the museum world in the eighteenth century.[15] In the nineteenth century, following the Napoleonic conquests and subsequent restitutions, the governments of some European countries began to pose as cultural authorities alongside the monarchs. The most famous of state-run museums, the National Gallery in London, was founded in 1824 without any monarchical support. Initially created by Parliament, it was later taken over by the trustees. It construed its audiences as a nation made up of voters, taxpayers, and patriots, but also catered to artists-in-training and promoted general civility by issuing requirements for proper attire. Yet, as Jonathan Conlin asserts, even the museums known as "royal" now engaged with the state institutions and thus "benefited greatly from their liminal position . . . , which guaranteed the generous support both of new Ministers of Education and monarchs."[16] The majority of post-Napoleonic museums were a hybrid type involving the royal and state administrations and the academies to varying degrees. Thus, the Berlin Museum, initially planned as an extension of the academy and financed by Friedrich Wilhelm IV of Prussia, was soon delegated to the state, with the king's role reduced to that of approving and vetoing ministerial decisions.[17]

Napoleon's conquests, the policies practiced by the occupational administrations, and postwar restitutions forever changed the repertoire of models available to anyone planning an art display. Still, the variety of nineteenth-century floor plans can be typified as a combination of three models: aesthetic, taxonomic, and rational. To a contemporary visitor, the first model, originating in Renaissance collectors' cabinets, would seem like an agglomeration of heterogeneous objects. When museums dedicated to painting and sculpture emerged, this approach, aimed at making power visible by showcasing the richness and variety of seigniorial possessions, usually took the guise of a display called "aesthetic": works combined by genre or some perceived commonality, but with complete disregard for their time and place of origin, would occupy the entire surface of a wall. These aesthetic displays were aimed at facilitating comparisons among works of art, which at that time was thought to be conducive to refining one's taste.

There was also the tradition called "taxonomic," rooted in the classification of paintings by "elements" and originating in eighteenth-century royal public museums.[18] Such floor plans assisted the dilettanti in comparing and contrasting paintings according to four fundamental traits: composition, drawing, color, and expression. Historians usually point at the gallery of Vienna's Belvedere Palace, a public museum opened by the queen of Hannover Marie-Therese in 1781, as the first example of a taxonomy adapting the "aesthetic" display model of the previous century to representing national traditions and a time line.[19] Seeking to visualize an art typology resembling Carl Linnaeus's classification of plants and other popular scientific taxonomies of the time, the planner and director of the Belvedere, Christian Mechel, organized the paintings by "schools," roughly corresponding to the political map of eighteenth-century Europe, and provided a time line that divided the artists into "old" and "new" masters. Still, although the Belvedere Gallery did not eschew the notion of a chronological development, its underlying concept was far from the nineteenth-century idea of progress: it represented the neoclassical doctrine of the "ages of man," which unfolded cyclically and did not always epitomize improvement. Since the comparison between the old and the new masters in Belvedere was not evidencing the progress of art, but rather its decadence, it was believed that a taxonomic arrangement would help stop the decline and initiate a new cycle of regeneration: by visiting the museum, the public could become aware of the crisis in contemporary art, and artists receiving access to old masters would begin imitating them. Through displays such as these, royal public museums took the lead in crafting nations' genealogies in ways that made their owners—the royalty—essential for the future of art.

Nineteenth-century museums followed this taxonomical model yet introduced important modifications. An artistic "school" was now the sum total of artworks produced in the territory of a nation, not only after the creation of nation-states but also prior to any nationhood. Such, for example, was the case with the "German school" of art, which predated the consolidation of Germany.[20] The borders were also reimagined as points of discontinuity where national cultures ended. As Christopher Whitehead argues, nineteenth-century art museums thus produced "cartographic" knowledge that inscribed time into an enclosed space laid out as a map. Museums were critical in assisting the nations' memories as well as facilitating their forgetfulness: the recent past of intranational discord was easily wiped out or resignified, while the more faraway past was reorganized according to the officially recognized time line.[21]

In the early nineteenth century, however, the definitions of time were changing as quickly as those of space, and thus an important thread of modern scholarship points to the connection between museums and the institutionalization of history as a discipline.[22] In nineteenth-century European historiography, different time lines were affecting and competing to affect the ways in which museums exhibited art. The French Revolution ushered in a new era of linear time, and in 1793 a prototype of a linear museum display was born. Planning the first national collection in France, the revolutionary Louvre, the Museum Commission and the Conservatoire determined that a new exhibit could no longer showcase masterpieces that would merely expose "men in the street" to the influence of aristocratic taste. Instead, its paintings were to be placed chronologically, documenting the origin and progress of each national "school."[23] Since then, a linearly progressing time was associated with the rationalism of the state and gained increasing popularity in nineteenth-century museums seeking to deliver a scientific picture of the world.

Still, there was considerable melancholy in the post-Napoleonic art galleries over the fact that, unlike their sister museums of natural history or applied arts, they could never fully implement an optimistic narrative of progress, as "the new way of thinking held that past artistic achievements could not be recreated."[24] In these exhibits, the present state of art continued to look like a void, irrelevant or overdetermined, implicit in—or absorbed by—previous developments. Since art history itself depended on the way in which museums exhibited their collections, achieving a consistently historical and cartographic floor plan posed a challenge that was both theoretical and practical. It was not always clear how to distribute into "schools" the collections of art that had hitherto been defined according to the artists' place of dwelling or apprenticeship, regardless of national borders. Nor did museum directors know how to represent "schools" on a time line.

Uncertainties about the intended audience of the exhibits and even about the exhibits' function played a role as well. Authorities and public opinion across Europe contended that an art-historical display was best suited for learning, scholarship, and the preparation of artists, while an aesthetic arrangement was more appealing to dilettanti. But the authorities in many post-Napoleonic museums were not sure whether they should please the aficionados or promote artists' education. This is why nineteenth-century museum planners, although well aware of the desirability of a historical display, would still resort to the old and tested "aesthetic" taxonomic arrangements, which enjoyed both a tradition and theoretical support.[25] The museum displays of the first half of the nineteenth century are thus better understood not as manifestations of consolidated knowledge, but rather as a chain of shots in the dark.

LIBERALISM AND ABSOLUTISM

Like any other post-Napoleonic museum, the Museo Real owed just as much to the French occupation of 1808–14 and Napoleon's ideas of public art as it did to the Spanish patriots' fights against the French and the ideas of the state and the nation that they spurred. The foundational moment for Spain's liberal nationhood took place at a time when there was no Spanish king on the throne, following a general convention in 1810 of the representatives of Spanish and American territories, called together by the Junta Central Gubernativa—an early precedent of a self-governing state institution ruling in the name of Fernando VII, created in the southern port of Cádiz after a chain of abdications gave the crown to Napoleon's brother Joseph. At that historic gathering, called the Cortes (a medieval prototype of a parliament) of Cádiz, "the Spanish nation" was defined as a "free and independent" sovereign, governed according to a system of laws (called the Constitution of Cadiz) that stipulated freedom of the press and promoted the separation of powers. Spain was declared a constitutional monarchy, with the Cortes elected by a simple majority of male property owners. The Cortes ended their work in 1812, and by the end of 1813 the united Spanish and British armies had chased Joseph Bonaparte from Madrid, returning the crown to the Spanish Bourbons. In February 1814, Fernando VII took an oath to uphold the Constitution of Cadiz and initiated what was meant to be a triumphant return to Madrid. Spain was awakening to independence as a parliamentary monarchy.

Before the king reached the capital on May 13, 1814, he had signed a decree restoring absolutism and denouncing the constitution. It deemed the activity of the Cortes of Cádiz revolutionary and therefore devoid of power. Then, according to the decree of May 20, 1814, all disentailed properties of the church were returned to their original owners. A month later, Fernando reinstated the Inquisition, and by May 1815 even the slightest appearance of freedom of the press was gone with the prohibition of all newspapers except two: the *Gaceta* and the *Diario de Madrid*. The governments of the former colonies reconsidered their attitudes and, with the exception of Cuba and the Philippines, preferred to fight for self-determination over depending on an anachronistic regime.

Where did the foundation of the museum fit into this picture? On May 22, 1814, Fernando VII adopted a decree reestablishing the institution of the *mayordomía mayor* (royal administration), with the purpose of "separating entirely the government and the interests of . . . the royal house from those of the state."[26] The split put the royal house on a state budget, even though the king could temporarily control its allocations. It was this dual structure of the court vs. the state that allowed the king to create the Royal Museum while also arranging for all competing projects to fail. The story of how it happened gives us an image of a king who aptly manipulated emerging artistic patriotism in order to win the right to pose as a cultural authority.

Everywhere in post-Napoleonic Europe, the royal fine arts academies were leading the museum movement. Yet although the same transformation was underway in Spain, the Academia San Fernando had to face unexpected competition from the king, who now decided to fashion himself as the absolute ruler, not only of his nation's territory, but also of its artistic heritage. Initially all seemed peaceful. Upon his arrival in Madrid, Fernando VII received a proposal from the academicians to create a public museum, approved it, and even encouraged the corporation to move to a larger building—the Buenavista Palace (confiscated property of ex-minister Manuel Godoy; it is currently the site of the Ministry of Armed Forces).[27] There was a caveat, however: the royal administration provided no funding to repair the building. This deficiency seemed to be palliated in September 1815, when the royal administration authorized financing from the proceeds from Godoy's impounded possessions.

It was then the turn of the state—in particular, the institution advisory to the king, called the Council of Castilla—to oppose the plan, suggesting that, instead of the Buenavista Palace, the king consider giving the Academia a half-destroyed building on the Paseo del Prado, designed by Villanueva in the 1770s for the Museum of Natural History. A patriotic, anti-French narrative that emerged later, when the building was already destined to be the Museo Real, asserted that in 1808, once the adjacent royal palace of Buen Retiro had become the headquarters of the invading army, the new inhabitants stripped the expensive lead roofing off Villanueva's beautiful structure, thus leaving the interior exposed to the elements, and repurposed what remained of the building as a stable.[28] In 1830, Mérimée asserted that he could still see on the walls the graffiti and inscriptions left by French and British soldiers. Restoring for a noble cause a building known to have suffered at the hands of the French made the Museo Real a nationalist enterprise before a single painting was even brought there.

The academicians still thought the museum would be theirs. Yet they also knew that once the king and the religious communities retrieved the paintings the Academia had preserved during the French occupation, its own holdings would be insufficient for a museum.[29] They therefore expressed a wish that the king set an example by not reclaiming his belongings or at least leaving a portion of them for a museum.[30] In June 1816, Fernando responded positively by sending to the Academia works of art from his palace that were needed "to complete a collection of the originals of all most famous Spanish and foreign schools and masters."[31] In the meantime, religious communities, brought back to life by the absolutist revival, now wanted their artwork back. The Academia's position was therefore weak: it depended on the royal will without the counterbalance of the state, which felt shaky and underfunded and had no interest in running a museum.[32] Fernando's administration did not fail to use this weakness to the king's advantage. Initially acting on the Academia's behalf, it then sided with the state, embodied by the Council of Castilla, played it against the Academia, and became the sole creator of the Museo Real, soon declaring Fernando the winner. "Thus cheaply did he earn the title of an Augustus," was the summary of the outcome by the British writer Richard Ford, the nineteenth century's best-known expert in all things Spanish.[33]

Indeed, early historians of the Prado experienced some unease with the fact that they owed the museum to one of their least favorite kings. Even Pedro de Madrazo, a faithful royalist and the son of Fernando's protégé, would admit in his 1843 catalogue that it would have been more logical for the museum to have been founded under Carlos III. Yet the Enlightenment was the age of science, and the "reformer king" Carlos III, although he had indeed planned a museum, envisioned it as a cabinet of natural history. In reality, the idea that a collection of paintings alone could be a relevant public exhibit was slow in establishing itself in Spain. In 1814, when Fernando VII decided to display art in Villanueva's building, not even the architect López Aguado, who was in charge of the restoration, understood that art exhibits would not share the space with natural specimens.[34] For decades after its inauguration, the officials of the royal administration, unsure about the character of the institution, still called it "the gallery of paintings at the museum on the Prado": they thought that the rest of the building would be reserved for natural history exhibits. The connection between exhibiting art and science was not severed until much later. In 1826, the administration agreed to "temporarily" deposit some objects from the Cabinet of Natural History at the museum, and in 1839 the Museo Real incorporated a part of the former cabinet, a collection of precious objects (known as the *Tesoro del Delfín*) that Felipe V, the first Spanish Bourbon, had inherited in 1712 from his father, the heir to the French throne.[35] A century later, the director, Francisco Javier Sánchez Cantón, would find another, much less glamorous legacy of the cabinet left at the museum: an "enormous oval box filled with dried birds," by that time reduced to dust.[36]

Spanish historians have made a special effort to trace the early projects to make royal paintings available to "the educated and the intelligent." These projects had existed since the times of Felipe IV (Velázquez's patron) and, closer to the nineteenth century, Fernando VII's father, Carlos IV.[37] Yet the first official plan for a public museum in Spain was formalized by Joseph Bonaparte, assisted by his Spanish supporters, such as Luis Mariano de Urquijo, who prior to the invasion had planned a museum for Carlos IV. Caring as much for education as for palliating the bad press caused by unofficial looting and official export of Spanish paintings to France, in December of 1809 Joseph Bonaparte decreed the establishment of the first museum of different "Spanish schools" in Madrid with a collection originating from the royal palaces as well as the convents whose property was being confiscated. Still, some works, of course, had to be sent to Paris for the Musée Napoléon.[38]

On the side of the Spanish patriots, alternative projects emerged that represented museums as places where the "national patrimony" could be protected from plundering, "placed under custody" in the absence of their legitimate owners. The owners were the Spanish royal family, the church, and private collectors like Godoy; the custodian was the Academia San Fernando, acting on the behalf of the "nation."[39] After the Congress of Vienna, the passion for recuperating and exhibiting works of art spread around Europe, and the fascination with Spanish paintings, shared by all foreign participants in the Peninsular War, made Fernando VII aware of the value of these works and inspired him to favor the idea of exhibiting his collection.[40] It was clear that considerable benefits could be reaped, both internationally and at home, by opening a museum of Spanish art.

Yet, although the Museo Real became an early post-Napoleonic museum, it was conceived as a royal institution and a semiprivate extension of the king's own property. Having alienated the Academia from the museum initiative, Fernando VII put an end to the projects that conceived of artistic heritage as national without needing the institution of the Crown. Simply put, the task of the Museo Real was to make the monarchy essential again. One way of achieving that was to portray the king as a true patriot and the guarantor of the nation's future. Hence, the inauguration announcement for the museum, penned by the marquis de Santa Cruz, attributed to the king a number of patriotic feelings, ranging from his care for the "common good" and a "burning desire to bring happiness to his vassals and propagate good taste" to his striving to "beautify the kingdom's capital and contribute to the nation's shining and splendor."[41] In its ongoing confrontation with the liberals wishing to transform Spain into a constitutional monarchy, the court was attributing to the king functions that would otherwise remain neglected.

The royal administration was well aware that some image-making had to be done to humanize absolutism, and this is perhaps why so much effort went into crafting a narrative about the king's wife, Isabel de Braganza, as the founding mother. Fernando VII married this Portuguese princess in 1816 when he was still deciding whether to open a museum himself or entrust the enterprise to the Academia San Fernando. As a newcomer to the court—and a young and beautiful one at that—Isabel was a perfect figure to be put in front of a project aimed at showing the monarchy's amiable face. Indeed, Isabel was reported to have financed the restoration of Villanueva's building with her share of income from the royal post. (Contemporary sources, however, suggest that at the time of the construction this income was growing scarce.)[42] In a posthumous portrait, Bernardo López Piquer immortalized the queen pointing at the museum building through the palace window while reaching with her other hand for a pile of floor plans.[43] In the meantime, oral and written tradition seemed to accept that the person who influenced the king most was one Isidoro Montenegro, a courtier in charge of overseeing royal costume, entertainment, and the furnishing of the palaces. According to his contemporaries, Montenegro, "undisturbed by the scandalous contrast between his own opulence and the public misery," was always on the lookout for new projects with high potential for personal enrichment.[44]

According to Pedro Beroqui, who in the 1920s and '30s scrutinized the archives of the royal palace, Montenegro's influence on Fernando VII was crucial when the disputes with the Council of Castilla made it clear that if the king wanted a museum he would have to finance it by himself, exhibit paintings from his own collection, and install it in Villanueva's building. This insider version, mixed with the official legend, is present in Ford's 1845 account, although the British author seems to confuse Montenegro with the marquis of Montealegre, who had been the mayordomo of Fernando's father, Carlos IV. In Ford's story, when "one Monte Allegre" persuaded the king "to refurnish much of the palace with French papers, chandeliers, and ormolu clocks—his particular fancy," only the influence that the marquis de Santa Cruz had on the queen saved the paintings from imminent destruction by removing "them to the unused building on the Prado."[45] Whether or not it is accurate, the marquis de Santa Cruz was indeed put in charge of the museum in February of 1818 and energetically began retrieving paintings from royal palaces. At that time, the king assigned to the project monthly expenses from his own discretionary fund; upon completion, the total cost of repairs to the building was assessed at seven million reales, all of them coming from the king. In September of the same year, the marquis, already called "director," reported that two of three projected galleries were restored and ready for hanging the paintings. In the meantime, Queen Isabel de Braganza had died in childbirth. (This is why the museum's inauguration was timed to celebrate Fernando's second wife.) Nevertheless, Isabel's memory had become so essential for the museum's founding legend that in 1822 we still find the mayordomo mayor looking for the right type of marble for sculpting her bust to adorn the building alongside the bust of her widower.[46]

37

GAZING AND ENTERTAINMENT ON THE PASEO DEL PRADO

The Madrid of Fernando's times was not yet the fast-growing capital that it would later become. The major demographic accomplishment of the late 1810s and 1820s consisted in merely bringing the size of its population back to what it was before Napoleon. Until the disastrous cholera epidemic of 1833–34, the numbers of Madrileños grew steadily yet slowly and did not reflect a strong influx from the rural areas. By 1833, the censuses registered, with adjustments that historians now consider necessary, from 120 to 140 thousand inhabitants, of which approximately ten thousand comprised military garrisons and thirty thousand more were foreigners and "floating population."[47] The scarcity of incomers kept the cycle of Madrid's celebrations intact. The May pilgrimages to nearby sanctuaries on the Manzanares River, the near-pagan spring rites immortalized in Goya's tapestry cartoons, the Fall Fair, and the local Our Lady de la Paloma festival, also held in the fall, continued without change. The Paseo del Prado still housed the nightly *verbenas* in June and July.[48]

The municipal authorities of Fernando's time seemed little concerned with working-class pastimes, dances, or even bonfires, because it was not the masses, but rather the educated citizens, who were challenging the regime in 1814–33. Unlike the common people, Spanish antiabsolutists favored the forms of consumption and celebration modernized by the French: modern cafés, open-air elegant gatherings, and Carnival, which Joseph Bonaparte revived after decades of prohibition.[49] Since these innovations had clustered around the Paseo del Prado (because it used to be the buffer zone between the invading army headquarters and Madrid), the bulk of Fernando's regulatory measures after the French retreat also targeted this area. Between Fernando's return in 1814 and his temporary ousting in 1820, all commercial establishments disappeared and all Carnival celebrations were banned on the Prado; during the ensuing three constitutionalist years, masked balls were once again allowed in Madrid theaters and cafés, but not outdoors, while cafés and theaters made a timid return, only to disappear again after 1823.

Under the guise of debating consumption and celebration, old and new politics clashed, transforming the Prado into the place where the Spanish "public" was being created and new social behaviors were being rehearsed. It is hardly surprising, then, that close to the end of Fernando's rule in 1832, seeking to answer the title question of his famous essay "Who Is the Public and Where Is It Found?," writer Mariano José de Larra would point directly to the Salón del Prado.[50] For Larra, individuals became part of the "public" merely by stepping outside their homes, and the Prado, "the great resort whither all the world throngs to see and to be seen," epitomized this new reality.[51] Yet while the Salón was also bringing strolling people to adjacent promenades, it is important to remember that the land donations described in the introduction turned the stretch facing the museum into a space between the fringes of royal and municipal domains, which were the subject of an ongoing dispute between the City and the Crown. As the liberal elites were learning to relate the pastimes that the French had allowed to flourish on the Prado to progressive politics, the question remains whether or not they were also visiting the museum, and if so, whether they experienced museum-going as one of these modern activities.

On the surface, it appears that visitors to the Prado Promenade during that time cared little about the museum but interpreted their walks as a visual experience comparable to admiring paintings. "And now for our glasses to examine the ladies," wrote an anonymous contributor to a London magazine in 1820.[52] "We derive no less entertainment from a review of the riding passengers, who may be very plainly examined by the curious eye, on account of the open glass windows or panels," another writer acknowledged, suggesting that the sight of people riding in their carriages along the Prado could sometimes take the shape of framed portraits.[53] Taking into account "the benches near the botanical gardens, the chairs in the principal alleys and the turf seats . . . full of spectators," many foreign authors claimed that for Spaniards their

FIG. 11   Anon., *The Paseo del Prado in the times of Fernando VII*, c. 1850, etching on the cover of
Ramón Gómez de la Serna, *El Paseo del Prado* (Madrid: G. Hernández y Galo Sáez, 1919).

daily walks on the Prado were a "public amusement" alongside theater and bullfights.[54]
Indeed, the thrill of people-watching penetrated the depictions of the Prado, domestic
and foreign, and left its trace in caricatures and illustrations. These illustrations, featuring men and women, standing or sitting, gazing at each other, suggested that the
daily promenade was a compelling visual experience that could just as easily continue
inside the museum (fig. 11).

Foreign authors have also noted the working classes on the Prado: the later the
night, the more picturesque the crowd. After the evening Angelus prayer, well-dressed
visitors cleared the space, and people whom the foreign travelers considered to be
homeless would move in: "it is at this time that poor creatures who have obtained a few
octavos by begging during the day, and laborers whose hard destiny allows them no
better shelter than the open sky, succeed to the gay world of fashion: . . . they lie down
to sleep upon the benches and seats which have been just occupied by the most bloom-
ing beauties and most elegant beaux of Madrid."[55] This anonymous writer remarked
that the déclassé night shift also danced on the Prado to the sounds of guitars and
castanets, making modern-day readers suspect that they are reading a mere fantasy.
Another author, Christian Augustus Fischer, likewise remembered "the aromatic and
vivifying exhalations of the fanning evening gales, the magic lunar beams playing in
the shades, and the romantic sounds of the melting guitar!"[56] Fueling the passion for

treating the lower classes as "picturesque," the nightly camping on the Prado thus did not shock foreign visitors but only added much-needed bohemian zest to their time in a city that they otherwise considered too modern.

The sections of the Promenade closest to the Botanical Garden, where the museum was located, in particular retained much of this rustic appeal. Alexander Slidell Mackenzie described this area as especially attractive for those looking for bucolic privacy: it gave young couples a chance to forget that "they are not alone in the world" even in broad daylight.[57] Mesonero Romanos stated that people of "provincial or foreign" origins, lured by the garden, most commonly came to the stretches of the Prado Promenade south of the museum.[58] Unlike the lower-class people gathering at night, these strangers had access to the Museo Real not only during the times it was open to the public (then Wednesday and Saturday mornings) but anytime they wanted, since the museum admitted on any day "traveling *señores*" who could show a passport or a temporary address in Madrid.[59]

For the duration of Fernando's rule we only have the testimony of upper- and middle-class locals and foreigners from which to trace the Spanish public's perception of the museum at that time. Not knowing much about art, these visitors often gave themselves humble pen names that suggested that they did not identify themselves with the museum. Ostensibly, then, these reviews can give us a glimpse of attitudes beyond the narrow circle of the dilettanti. Although the Spanish reviewers were less likely than their foreign counterparts to comment on the people occupying the Prado Promenade at different times of day, they did describe their visits to the Prado Museum not as aesthetic practice, but rather as an exercise in people-watching. One author, who introduced himself as "Not knowledgeable" (*El que no sabe*), portrayed another visitor and his strange behavior: "he would walk ahead and then suddenly back; bend to the left, then to the right; other times he would nod his head to the side; since it was a silent action I had to ask him if he was not feeling well."[60] The strange man turned out to be a connoisseur seeking the best light in the badly lit rooms by which to admire the Spanish paintings on exhibit. Apparently, while some contemplated art, others enjoyed the embodiment of what they deemed to be a pantomime, one of the popular genres of both legitimate and street theater.

At that time, the Prado had not yet become a place to see theater and marionette shows, which were concentrated closer to the Puerta del Sol and Calle Caballero de Gracia. Still, even if theatrical entertainment did not come close to the museum, early nineteenth-century visual culture provided experiences and sensations not too far removed from the contemplation of art. Take, for example, vision machines, popular spin-offs of neoclassical perspective painting. In the nineteenth century, entrepreneurial performers used these apparatuses to offer miniature "picturesque mechanical" theaters, automaton shows, cosmoramas, and phantasmagorias.[61] Featuring a combination of painted scenes, optical illusions, light projections, and "recreational physics," these shows offered moving pictures of spaces and people—real or imagined—that responded to the new passion for watching other humans and the Romantic obsession with nature and the irrational.[62] At different times these shows also included cosmoramas of the Paseo del Prado itself and a perspective of its fountains.[63] The visual culture of the Prado Promenade thus became itself a subject of artistic illusion and an object of street entertainment.

John E. Varey's summary of the street theaters of Madrid makes it clear that these optical attractions appealed to the middle and upper classes. Some shows advertised themselves as having been enjoyed and officially approved by the monarchs, but not all of them were highbrow. For example, one exhibitor showed a monstrous bull with two heads, three eyes, and a small baby bull connected by an umbilical cord on its forehead, claiming to have presented this freak of nature to the king and the royal family.[64] Others directly addressed upper- or middle-class audiences. Such was the enterprise conceived by the "famous professor of physics" Étienne Gaspard Robertson, who even asked "art-lovers and decent people" in the audience to intervene when other spectators became too excited and needed to be pacified.[65]

Quite a few of these attractions involved paintings. On his tour to Madrid in January and February of 1821, Robertson added to his program a phantasmagoria featuring a "historical gallery" of portraits of famous Spaniards: Pelayo, Hernán Cortés, and Cervantes.[66] Although their subject matter was akin to the canvases exhibited in the Museo Real—such as the formal *Portrait of Hernán Cortés* by Alonso Sánchez Coello—these mechanical figures were much more entertaining. In 1826, to celebrate Fernando VII's marriage to his last wife, María Cristina de Borbón y de las dos Sicilias, Robertson's competitor Juan González Mantilla arranged an ambitious show: an enormous cloud would appear on stage and be "gradually dissolved by a large sun, . . . turning into a portrait of our beloved sovereign, and then into that of his precious spouse."[67] In the eyes of anyone not versed in the rules of aesthetic appreciation, this type of visual pleasure offered strong and sometimes insurmountable competition to poorly lit, silent, and immobile images on display inside the museum.

While these visual attractions could easily beat a museum visit, the museum's immediate vicinity itself had little to offer in the way of entertainment beyond a mere view of people passing by, a rustic sight captured in the 1827 *Vista* by the Italian artist Giuseppe Canella, reproduced on the cover of this book. The only exceptions occurred at the Tívoli Park and Pavilion (currently the site of the Ritz Hotel), just across the street from the museum, but only when Fernando VII was not in power. The French had used the Tívoli to establish the first modern café in Madrid. With Fernando's return, the café was abandoned, but it came alive again after the 1820 coup. Mesonero Romanos would later describe the Café del Tívoli as one of the most "useful, comfortable, and entertaining public establishments." It was a high point of nineteenth-century civic and industrial development.[68] For years to come, the liberals would nostalgically remember it as a "public garden, an inn, and a café in which . . . splendid concerts were given."[69]

Modeled on the Ranelagh and Vauxhall Gardens near London and funded by Antoine Perret, a French developer, the Café del Tívoli became Spain's first pleasure garden. Still, although looking at paintings fit well into the model of leisure that such gardens promoted in other countries, the Tívoli did not exist long enough to generate a habit of visits to the Museo Real by the gallant sort of people who frequented its grounds.[70] In 1823, when Fernando returned and reclaimed his ownership of the spot, the new city government refused to give the owner permission to operate during the winter season—that was a privilege of "legitimate" theaters only. The former café had to host less-refined entertainment such as the acrobatic performances and pantomimes of "Madama Marcial," and the owners were forced to charge an entrance fee, turning the Tívoli into Madrid's first gated leisure area.[71] Still, the business continued going downhill and had to close in 1829. A year later, Fernando VII, who had always considered this site a royal possession, leased it "for perpetual use" to the Real Establecimiento Litográfico, run by his acolyte José de Madrazo, the future director of the Royal Museum.[72] That institution, operating under the king's exclusive license, used the location to make copies of vistas of royal sites and paintings from the collection of the Museo Real. For over twenty years, all pleasant diversion at the Tívoli would cease, and this gated park next to the Museo Real would remain excluded from the new pastimes emerging elsewhere on the Prado Promenade.

In the years after Fernando's death, modern leisure would return to the vicinity of the Museo Real each time Spain's political regime took a course of rapprochement with liberalism. In the meantime, under Fernando's rule, only one public activity succeeded in securing a real spot on the Prado: the commemorations of the the 1808 anti-French rebellion, aimed at bringing the area back into the courtly orbit by promoting a patriotic celebration where old-regime royal rituals and modern publicity converged. It was in the king's best interest to insist that the patriots had died defending Spain's monarchy, the one that he was now poised to carry on. This opening of the areas next to the Prado Promenade to civic commemorations was in stark contrast to the closure of the same areas to middle-class leisure venues, emphasizing the role of the Museo Real in legitimizing Fernando's rule. The museum display of the time included patriotic compositions to underscore this fact, including *The Defense of Zaragoza* by José Álvarez Cubero (1825; it now welcomes visitors to the museum's new wing) and *Daoíz and Velarde* (the heroes of the 1808 rebellion in Madrid) by Antonio Solá (1830). In the following decades, these sculptures would periodically leave the museum to become civic monuments adorning the places relevant for commemorating the war, the exact interpretation of which had become a point of contention among the Crown, the church, and the liberals.

For the time being, however, the museum remained the fortress of absolutism, at whose gates the battle between the liberals and the court about the civic profile of the Prado Promenade had to stop. Cafés and other spaces of modern consumption were ousted from the museum's environs, leaving the area to ambulant vendors. Inside the museum, the first thing that visitors would encounter was a room dedicated to Spain's contemporary art, featuring numerous still lifes with fruits, flowers, and jugs of water that these vendors also sold. The display included genre scenes of the old Feria de Madrid on the Plaza de la Cebada by Manuel de la Cruz Vázquez and several tapestry cartoons by Francisco and Ramón Bayeu depicting picnics and dancing by the Manzanares River.[73] Although one cartoon by Francisco Bayeu captured people promenading on Madrid's Paseo de las Delicias, and works by, or attributed to, Velázquez hanging in the same gallery referenced hunting, this exhibit traced a nostalgic bridge to the pre-Napoleonic past and did not suggest a connection between the Museo Real and the debates concerning the public uses of the outdoors.[74] The relationship between the museum, modern leisure, and the Promenade hinged on anti-French memories, just as the Crown wanted.

EXHIBITING THE KING'S NATION

Like the commemorations of the 1808 uprising, the Museo Real was seeking to connect the royal and the public through a patriotic idea: collecting in one place and making available the works by Spanish masters that were already beginning to be smuggled all across Europe. Fernando Brambilla's *Vista of the Rotunda of the Royal Museum*—an early view of the museum's interior—had the words *Escuela Española* (Spanish school) written in large letters across the entrance arch into the central gallery (fig. 12); the title of the museum's first catalogue ran, *Catalogue of the Paintings of the Spanish School That Exist in the Royal Museum on the Prado.*[75] Yet in reality, in the 1820s and all the way through the 1830s, the best of the Spanish school was displayed in the rooms to the left and right of the central gallery, and the only Spanish paintings one saw by walking under the archway were those belonging to modern artists "provisionally" located "at the entrance." If the inscription in Brambilla's painting indeed existed in the museum, it worked as a patriotic dedication and a declaration of intent. Indeed, the display that opened in 1819 contained works by Spanish artists only. In 1821, an Italian collection was added. In 1826, the restored central gallery and an octagonal room farther south created the possibility for exhibiting more Italian art, as well as paintings representing "schools" that the catalogue called "German and French."[76] Following the 1826–30 expansion, two more rooms, facing the Botanical Garden, were completed to house Flemish and Dutch art, while on the lower level a sculpture gallery was created.

FIG. 12   Fernando Brambilla, *View of the Rotunda of the Real Museo*, c. 1830. Watercolor. Patrimonio Nacional.

The early layout of paintings indicates that the founders followed the international exhibiting criterion of presenting art divided into national traditions. In fact, in 1826, when the central gallery was fully restored and prepared to accept paintings, the marquis de Ariza y Estepa (the museum's director from 1823 to 1826) wrote a memorandum that made it clear how much the administration cared about complying with these standards. He cited the "order and practice that other museums observe: that of maintaining the schools separate."[77] As he wished to adhere to these principles, he thus described his dilemma—how to distribute the national "schools" in a space designed for a different purpose. Villanueva's structure dictated that the "Spanish school," which was the museum's *raison d'être*, be located in the grand central gallery, while other "schools" could be placed in smaller adjacent rooms. However, since Spain's royal collection contained far more Italian than Spanish paintings, the national display was not large enough to fill the space. "If the rooms where the Spanish school is [now] located are emptied for the Italian one, many [Italian] paintings will remain unexhibited and will have to go to the general deposit, leaving [the Italian] school devoid of its importance and grandeur, while there will be not enough Spanish paintings to complete the Grand Salon. This will lead to a confusion of schools, lack of beauty in the new floor plan, and new expenses for moving the paintings."[78]

No matter how straightforward and clear one might have thought it would be, for the classification by "school" prevailing in the early years to appear fully justified, two crucial issues needed to be resolved. First, the directors had to fit the artistic traditions of Spain's weakly related historical kingdoms into a single definition of a unified "Spanish school."[79] Second, they had to choose a chronological model to underpin the exhibit. The explanations contained in the early catalogues written by Luis Eusebi testify that both issues were initially resolved by following the models inherited from the previous century. In his 1824 and 1828 catalogues of the Museo Real, Eusebi referred to all artistic traditions of Spain as a "Spanish school," and in just the same way he called all Italian traditions "Italian." However, when describing old Spanish masters (those who worked prior to the eighteenth century), he also recognized the local "schools" of Seville and Valencia. As far as time was concerned, Eusebi's 1828 catalogue explained clearly that the exhibit was arranged according to the old-modern divide in the style of Mechel's Belvedere: the two rooms accessible through the rotunda were dedicated to the "old Spanish school," while the entrance to the central gallery "provisionally" housed "paintings from the Spanish school by artists who are still living or have recently passed away."[80] Other national traditions had no separation by epoch; the Italian "school" was interchangeably called either "different schools of Italy" or the "Italian school."[81]

The debates about how to define and display the "Spanish school" would develop in the press in the following decades. In the 1820s and early 1830s, both the museum administrators and its visitors were easily satisfied when they saw all paintings originating from Spain collected together, and did not question the basis of their juxtaposition. Yet in José de Madrazo's Lithographic Establishment (at the time still located in the same building), the question about the feasibility of a unified "Spanish school" loomed large. In the foreword to his 1826–32 collection of lithographed copies of paintings from the Museo Real, the first artist of the court and director of the Establishment only included a description of national artistic schools, starting, logically, with the Spanish one.[82] The theoretical introductions were initially commissioned to Juan Agustín Ceán Bermúdez, Spain's biggest authority on art history. An Enlightenment thinker, Ceán distinguished three schools in the history of Spanish art: the school of Castile and León, the school of Navarra, Aragón, and Murcia, and the Andalusian school.[83] When Ceán died in 1829, Madrazo's friend José Musso y Valiente was asked to take over the work. In an 1832 letter to Madrazo, Musso y Valiente defended Ceán's threefold classification: "Why can't we signify in some way that we had artists in different provinces who worked without communicating with each other, learning from what they had at hand? What I want to say with this is that the distribution into three groups is not entirely unfounded and in some ways it contributes to national glory."[84] Apparently, despite his agreement with Ceán about the matter, and somewhat against his will, Musso y Valiente was specifically charged with creating a narrative of a unified "Spanish" tradition.

However, it was not the unity of Spanish art, but rather its progress, that caused the most debate. While the exhibit of Spanish artwork was still underway, Eusebi also attempted to account for the "Spanish school" and arrive at a certain notion of its history.[85] His writings, published and unpublished, show his ongoing efforts aimed at understanding and summarizing current ideas about art, schools, and epochs, and his work on adapting them to explain and justify the collection of the Royal Museum. In 1822, under the protection of the British chargé d'affaires Lionel Hervey, he published a book called *An Essay About Different Schools of Painting*, which was on sale at the museum. In 1826, as work was beginning on the last rooms of the first floor, Eusebi anticipated the need for scientifically arranging their future displays by drafting a thick, three-volume compendium about how to classify Flemish, Dutch, and German art. The manuscript, currently conserved in the Museo Lázaro Galdiano in Madrid and marked "for personal use," bears witness to the author's inability to distinguish a classification by theme or genre, steeped in the tradition of aesthetic comparison, from the more recent chronological arrangements.[86] Thus, the very possibility of gathering and exhibiting paintings next to each other in the museum was intertwined with the theoretical thinking about classifying and interpreting them.

In the history of Spanish aesthetics, the museum's display at its inauguration seemed to fall right through the conceptual gaps between eighteenth-century taxonomies and the interest in postulating a linear history of art, which was still in its infancy. In Eusebi's chronology, the Spanish "school" emerged during the general demise of art, which it could never fully overcome. This is why in his *Essay About Different Schools of Painting* Eusebi attributes to the Spanish school a number of virtues as well as defects.[87] In his time, there was only one comparable effort to write a time line for Spanish art: Ceán Bermúdez's unpublished eleven-volume magnum opus "The History of the Art of Painting."[88] But Ceán, who viewed the unfolding of Spanish art after the sixteenth century as one uninterrupted decline, argued that only the work of royal academies could redeem Spanish art from its imminent demise. To a nineteenth-century museum, that kind of view was truly polemical. Suffice it to say that Ceán considered Velázquez and other masters of the time of Felipe IV, the gems of the exhibit, merely "good naturalist artists . . . enchanted by the brilliance of coloring and the seductive imprecision of tones."[89] As mentioned above, Ceán also distinguished multiple Spanish schools. In his rendering, by the eighteenth century the school that he called Andalusian had disintegrated, while those of Castile and Aragon still possessed their own unique traits.[90] Such an approach completely undermined the plans to use the exhibit for cultural nation-building. Since Ceán was Spain's only living authority on art, some theorizing clearly had to be done in order to justify the museum's floor plan, and Eusebi jumped on the task.

Eusebi's chronology of Spanish pictorial tradition prolonged the flourishing of the Spanish school until the end of the seventeenth century in order to include

Velázquez and other masters showcased at the Museo Real. Although he agreed with the eighteenth-century cyclical time line, Eusebi was eager to stretch the cycles just enough to postpone the decadence to "the latest times," when Spanish art "could not avoid falling into mannerism as all others did." This, of course, made the museum more relevant than ever because it could provide artists with good examples from old masters. If Ceán entrusted the revival of Spanish art to the academies, Eusebi's writings left the reader with the impression that Spanish art could be saved by the Museo Real and Eusebi's own explanations of its collection.[91]

Taking a look at the arrangement of paintings in the early decades of the Museo Real, one can therefore detect an intellectual development similar to the one offered in Vienna's Belvedere. The works appeared to be divided into large national traditions. Although the catalogues mentioned the local schools to which each painting belonged, they were united under a common denomination. Meanwhile, Eusebi's book, on sale right at the museum entrance, could assist visitors in understanding how to define this tradition. Time was also present at the Museo Real, but only to a limited extent: works of art were divided into two epochs, old and new. "Old" Spanish paintings were distributed in the two salons on both sides of the central gallery. "New" works occupied a special place. While the artwork in the room that Eusebi initially called simply the "Third Salon" was, in fact, at the end of the time line, the room itself was actually positioned at the beginning of the tour: at the entrance to the central gallery, right after the entrance rotunda. Such a nonlinear time line corresponded to the old-regime model of royal public museums. In the nineteenth century, however, this presented a major challenge for any historically minded visitor seeking to learn about the progressive evolution of art: the comparison between old and new Spanish masters offered a sight of "not merely decadence, but of ruin, death, and complete oblivion of art and its traditions," in the words of the French writer Louis Viardot, who saw the collection in 1823.[92] Later in his life, as the French government's museum inspector, Viardot would return to the Museo Real and often speak warmly of it, but this early verdict proved hard to erase.

The progress of art was indeed a problem difficult to resolve. Although Eusebi clearly agreed that progress was a concept that could not be demonstrated in a display of the Spanish school, his comments contain no irreverent words about the museum's contemporary collection. Rather than dwell upon these holdings' artistic merits or lack thereof, all catalogues after 1824 emphasized their symbolic and historic subject matter. In this way, modern paintings were resignified to suit the museum's ceremonial function. Excluded from the narrative of the development of Spanish art, they now served as props for the display of royal power and as testimonies to the monarchy's historical mission. Instead of telling a story about Spanish art, they spoke of a nation in harmony with its rulers.

This was to be expected from an institution run as an "extension of the palace."[93] In Fernando's lifetime, the Museo Real showed up on the state budget only in 1821 and

1822, when the constitutionalist liberals revoked the privileges conceded to the royal house. Still, even at that time, the king's support continued in the previous amount, requiring the state to supplement only when there were additional costs.[94] On the days when the public was admitted, royal guards occupied their posts in front of the museum. The staff who did not have apartments received the right to live in the museum or in the small house next to its eastern wall. Just like anyone in the palace, they were assigned the privileges of "uniform, doctor, surgeon, and pharmacy."[95]

The first museum directors were selected from prominent courtiers who also had ties to the Academia San Fernando. The marquis de Santa Cruz (the director until the liberal coup of 1820) had been the royal mayordomo mayor and Fernando's tutor under his father. In the 1780s, the marquis's father was the one who convinced Carlos IV not to follow through with Carlos III's orders to destroy the collection of nude paintings amassed by the Spanish Hapsburgs, but rather to deposit them in the Academia.[96] The next two directors, the prince de Anglona (1820–23) and the marquis de Ariza y Estepa (1823–26), did not belong to the palace hierarchy but were instead honorary members of the Academia. The former, whom the king was forced to appoint after the 1820 constitutionalist revolution, had been a colonel in the Royal Guard and was named a grandee of Spain only after his appointment as the museum director.[97] The latter, put in charge of the museum after the 1823 countercoup (when his predecessor exiled himself to Italy), did not even reside at the court.[98] So the royal administration came up with a new model. Vicente López Portaña, the first artist of the court, was put in charge of the collection, while the newly appointed director was responsible only for the museum's administrative and economic aspects.[99]

Thanks to such a separation of powers, the next director, the duke de Híjar (1826–38), was not affiliated with the Academia at all. Acting on behalf of the royal administration, he could therefore turn against the Academia's interests, retrieving for the Museo Real some of the paintings that the king had dispatched in 1816 for the potential Academia museum and was now claiming back. The duke de Híjar proceeded to reclaim the collection of Habsburg nudes to install in the Sala Reservada (Reserved Room) on the museum's lower level and, later on, took possession of several sculptures, including the bronze nude figure of Carlos V by Leoni. In the letters requesting the canvases from the Academia, the duke de Híjar insisted that the museum, the "exclusive property of H.M. the king,"[100] was a better place for the works of art.

The Academia, however, did not give up its museum plans so easily. It retained the vast collection confiscated from Manuel Godoy (which, among other masterpieces, included both of Goya's *Majas*) and some paintings not reclaimed by churches or private owners. These works, together with the Academia's own collection and the vast number of original sculptures and copies that it owned, were the basis for the public exhibition of paintings and sculpture in the building on the Calle Alcalá. The first catalogue was published in 1821, right after the constitutionalist coup. The title, in calling the Academia "National," suggested that having just regained political power, Spanish liberals were investing high hopes in this institution. Fernando's return would halt the Academia's plans. Yet the antimonarchical appeal still made this corporation seem liberal and allowed it to compete successfully with the Royal Museum. During the Fall Fair, the Academia hosted annual exhibitions of the work of its pupils and member artists; on those days, everyone was also admitted into the galleries of painting and sculpture.[101] While Fernando was stripping the Academia of its holdings, new ones were coming in as donations from antimonarchical collectors. It would take the museum a whole century to win from the Academia the right to be considered the main custodian and exhibitor of art in Spain.

All across Europe, state authorities were joining forces with the academies in founding museums—but not in Spain. In September of 1818, the marquis de Santa Cruz doubted whether, upon inauguration, the court should transfer the museum to the state. Having considered the possibility of government funding, he came to the conclusion that "in practice it is ridden by no small complications and its results will not be entirely advantageous and happy" and drafted a proposal to maintain the museum and its staff at the exclusive cost of the royal administration.[102] The king approved of the plan, and, except for the three "liberal years," the royal house was the only entity involved in all processes and works.

Competition with the church was a different matter. The Peninsular War had generated a market for Spanish artwork, and the religious communities were happy to traffic in it, especially because they felt the continuing threat of another round of disentailments. Indeed, during the *trienio liberal*, more were announced. In between these campaigns, however, monasteries and convents were recovering their properties and works of art and would occasionally contact the museum authorities. Their correspondence indicates that they understood very well the separation between religious and museum uses of art but were reluctant to stop collecting. For example, when Fernando donated sacred paintings from the monastery of El Escorial to be hung in the future museum, the abbot of the monastery protested and issued a claim. The paintings, of course, were needed for worship, but the prior sounded as much like a collector as the museum's director, declaring that he would gladly stop trying to reclaim from the museum the two works by Andrea del Sarto if he could trade them for something by Murillo, since his monastery "had nothing by this master."[103] More often, however, the religious communities used the Museo Real as a reserve for pious images. Such petitions for art were usually accompanied by clear statements that the community was not looking for valuable works, but rather for images satisfying the needs of worship. This is why in 1830 the director sent several copies and second-rate paintings to the restored San Jerónimo Monastery.[104] The tendency of the church to consider the museum as both a storage place for religious art and a competitor in collecting would continue throughout the century, while the museum also kept its reserves open to churches and monasteries' petitions for the loan of artworks.

The debates over the custody, ownership, and administration of art spurred by the foundation of the Museo Real channeled the Crown's claims to cultural hegemony, which dominated Fernando VII's rule. Inside the museum, the court signaled its intention to participate in artistic life with the reserved space in the building's south wing for the king and his family.[105] Though having an art museum double as a royal residence was not unique for its time, the surprising part of this story is how rarely, in fact, Fernando visited his creation. Protocol required the king to be the first to see all new exhibits, so the directors repeatedly invited His Majesty to examine the sculptures arriving from Rome: José Álvarez Cubero's figures of Fernando's parents and his *Defense of Zaragoza* and Antonio Solá's *Daoíz y Velarde*.[106] Fernando's reluctance to stop by sometimes delayed public exhibitions by months. While the connection to the museum was meant to improve the king's image, and the monarchical propagandists did all they could to remind Spaniards about it, on only one occasion, in 1828, did the newspapers recount a royal visit.

The royal administration preferred to declare the Crown's ownership symbolically, multiplying the representations of monarchical authority in direct proportion to the challenges that Fernando had to withstand as a ruler. According to the 1819 catalogue, a canvas by Luis Paret, *The Oath of Fernando VII as Prince of Asturias* (1791), greeted the museum's early visitors from the walls of the first room.[107] After the 1820 coup, however, the directors found more forthright ways to assert royal patronage. In 1822, as the king was retreating to Seville, a yard-wide sign stating, "Royal Museum. Property of the King" was hung by each of the entrances, while the prince de Anglona was asking the royal administration to commission the busts of Fernando and the deceased Queen Isabel de Braganza for the two sides of the museum's only open (northern) entrance.[108] When the "Hundred Thousand Sons of Saint Louis" finally cleared the way for Fernando's return, a royal portrait was placed by the main entrance.[109]

Contrary to the tendency of the royal museums all across Europe to let the signs of monarchical presence elapse with time, the renovations and major reorganizations of the Museo Real in 1826–30 made this presence more noticeable. In 1826, Álvarez's statues of Fernando's parents, Carlos IV and Maria Luisa, were added to the collection. (Their painted portraits by Goya had been on exhibit since 1819.) Then, in 1827, the portraits of Fernando's grandparents, Carlos III and his wife, both by Mengs, were dispatched from the royal palace and hung in the museum. To complete the genealogy, in 1828, a statue of Fernando himself was delivered from Aranjuez. During that same year, the display of "contemporary" artists that visitors could see on their way to the central gallery added its most solemn royal portrait: *Fernando VII on Horseback* by José de Madrazo.[110]

The guidebooks published after Fernando's 1823 absolutist comeback carried this symbolic reframing of royal power even further as Eusebi's brief notes developed into full-fledged reference books. A painting by José Aparicio, which the 1824 catalogue described as *Spanish Provinces Rising Against the 1808 Invasion*, received the following annotation in 1828: "Spanish character has always distinguished itself by its thorough love of Religion, King, and Motherland, and one may find among the largest proofs that it has given of this noble virtue the indescribable passion and enthusiasm with which it repulsed from its bosom the host of the most treacherous of tyrants in the short space of time between 1808 and 1813."[111] Even after Fernando's death, the tendency to pin Spain's nationhood to the display of monarchical loyalty continued, and thus another of Aparicio's canvases, which in 1824 was titled *The Scene of Famine in Madrid in the Years [18]11 and 12*, in Pedro de Madrazo's 1843 catalogue was introduced as an "allegorical composition representing Spanish endurance and the character of the people refusing nourishment from oppressors and preferring death to a life under the rule of anyone other than the legitimate king."[112] Thus, even when Spanish aesthetic thought, grounded in the neoclassical tradition, would normally have classified the recent art as decadent, the paintings at the entrance to the central gallery were nevertheless to be admired, albeit for reasons other than their beauty.

Since the paintings' subject matter, rather than their quality, was employed to make the museum look patriotic, the exhibit gave very little agency to visitors wishing to experience Spanish nationhood through a display of its art. The nation's essence was cast here as merely a bundle of Catholic faith and loyalty to the "legitimate king." The important nation-building role given to the contemporary exhibit also explains why, although Eusebi's catalogues stated that this room was merely provisional, it proved to be the museum's longest-lasting section. For most of the nineteenth century, visitors to the Royal Museum had only one way to come inside: through the Ionic colonnade of the northern door (currently the Goya entrance). If Villanueva had initially conceived of it as the royal entrance, in the Museo Real this door was rededicated to the public, who therefore, upon entering through it, found patriotic paintings front and center as they first took in the grandeur of the rotunda. Since the inauguration of the central gallery in 1826, virtually no visitor could miss this display, and even in the 1990s, long after all the paintings had changed places, some of these spectacular compositions were still greeting guests in the rotunda. Instead of illustrating the decline of taste, they sang the praises of the Spanish monarchy and the nation that it sought to represent.

A PATRIOTIC MUSEUM

By the time the Museo Real came into existence, the liberal-leaning press, including *Mercurio de España* and *Crónica Científica y Literaria*, had covered enough European galleries, old and new, to create well-informed public opinion about museum funding, floor plans, and collections development.[113] At the end of 1818, an anonymous review of the Luxembourg Museum in Paris introduced Spanish readers to the idea that the best way to exhibit art was to create a representative government institution (in this case France's Chamber of Peers) and adorn its walls with paintings. Camouflaged to maintain the illusion that the author was merely overviewing a new Parisian display, the commentary seemed to declare that the art museum and good governance belonged together: "these masterpieces' relevance for public prosperity had never been declared so solemnly and with such authority; and never had art received a nobler and a better-conceived impulse."[114] From the liberals' standpoint, the display of domestic art appeared a national necessity inseparable from fair political representation.

Expectations such as these made it hard for the liberals to accept the Royal Museum, even though their interest was clearly sparked. The first review of the museum, published in March 1820, as soon as censorship was lifted, already criticized the display, deeming it similar to "a private cabinet of curiosities or an antiquarian's storage," not following any order, but providing instead "eurhythmy and symmetry to please the ignorant, leaving the intelligent in a need of making guesses about different artistic epochs in our Spain."[115] Another reviewer, calling himself "Your fellow citizen" (*Su paisano*) and a stranger to the court, took issue with Aparicio's *The Famine in Madrid*, wondering why someone would still display monarchical propaganda disguised as art. "The spectacle of a poor family that, facing a difficult choice—to die or to accept nourishment from those who unjustly occupy their land—preferred the first option to the second, is lacking in both verisimilitude and dignity" was the author's verdict.[116] It was not clear, however, that he even knew that the painting occupied a privileged spot in the museum; he was simply criticizing an etched copy that some bookstore owner had hung on the store's exterior wall.

Like that reviewer, those who voiced an opinion against the museum during the "three liberal years" focused on its location, its external appearance, and the works popularized by printed media but did not seem to have any firsthand knowledge of the collection. In 1821, a contributor calling himself "An eyewitness" (*El testigo de vista*) proposed adding stairs to the building's northern façade but seemed unaware that the museum *occupying* the building displayed works of art and not natural specimens. Another, more subtle way for reviewers and critics to protest against the Royal Museum was to rechristen it as "National," thereby casting doubt over the royal ownership of its holdings. So while the official *El Diario de Madrid* continued labeling the establishment the "Real Museo of Paintings at the Prado," *El Nuevo Diario de Madrid*, a liberal competitor, ran the same announcements calling the museum "National" for the duration of the constitutionalist years.[117]

When French troops restored Fernando to the throne, debates about the course of his rule occasionally took the guise of discussions of his museum. Fernando's supporters welcomed the ahistorical arrangement of the items on display. *El Restaurador*, an ultra-Catholic paper published with Fernando's undercover funding, exalted the collection of masterpieces, "where grace invigorates the human heart," arguing that the view of paintings removed from their original surroundings and brought next to each other offered a quasi-religious experience that awakened feelings of "gratitude" to the creators of art analogous to a higher gratitude to the Creator himself.[118] While the promonarchical elite thus found the museum's aesthetic display spiritually elevating, the critics in the opposite camp did not demand to see a historical evolution of national schools either, as one would expect in a post-Napoleonic world.

During Fernando's lifetime, the liberal dream of a "progressive" floor plan simply amounted to an inoffensive patriotic claim that the best rooms should be reserved for displaying Spanish art. Conversely, the museum's purpose of projecting a royalist attitude meant that the order of the display could be neglected as long as it conveyed its underlying virtue. This became particularly noticeable after the crucial 1826–28 reinauguration, when new rooms were dedicated to the French and German schools while the old Spanish and Italian exhibits stayed the same. When the Museo Real reopened in March of 1828, a writer calling himself "Unknowledgeable" remarked that he could not understand why Italian paintings were housed in a better-lit and more imposing central gallery while Spanish masters had to suffer, lumped together in small rooms on either side.[119] Meanwhile, the official press insisted that the museum was invaluable for the nation because it was turning young artists into "men worthy of general appreciation."[120] These early reactions suggest that the public had a whole array of ideas about what an art museum was, and that these ideas all differed from what the Museo Real actually offered.

Reflecting upon the mission that the Museo Real was called on to fulfill in its early years, Géal has traced it back to the neoclassical triad of "learning, leisure, and international prestige."[121] In his announcement of the museum's inauguration, the marquis de Santa Cruz mentioned all three: the museum made the nation shine while also "providing the aficionados with an occasion for the most honest pleasure" and giving "to the students of the art of drawing most efficient means of making fast progress."[122] Yet, during the early decades, the three priorities were not evenly distributed. As they planned and updated the exhibits, the museum's authorities emphasized the patriotic mission, to which the royal administration responded favorably. In 1826, Vicente López, the museum's artistic director at the time, retroactively approved the funding for Eusebi's publication of the museum's catalogue in French, for which he had received no authorization, on the sole ground that foreign generals who had come to Madrid in 1823 to restore Fernando as the absolute king "desired to explore and examine the paintings."[123] In the decades and centuries to come, the visits of foreign dignitaries would invariably include a tour of the museum—the longest-standing relic of courtly ceremony that has survived to the present day.

Although the museum authorities took great care to ensure that foreigners left with the best impression possible, the display itself was making their task difficult.

In the absence of a chronological display of art, the directors were well aware that museums of their time most clearly served their nations by displaying their domestic art in its full glory. Still, there were three main obstacles to creating that sort of display. The first obstacle was that, historically, the Spanish monarchs had less interest in collecting Spanish pieces than in collecting the more prestigious Italian art, and so the museum's holdings simply did not have that many national works to show off. The second obstacle was the museum's building, which was designed for a different purpose and offered insufficient light. The interiors could, of course, be rebuilt, but the court's budget for the museum was the third challenge that made all such innovations unlikely. Foreigners and Spaniards alike criticized the lack of proper light needed to see the Spanish art. More expert visitors such as Louis Viardot, who was among the French soldiers and officials coming to see the exhibit in 1823, did not appreciate the mixing of art and propaganda on the museum's walls. This did not, however, entirely prevent Viardot or anyone else from admiring artists such as Velázquez and, especially, Murillo. Viardot, who returned to Madrid in 1833, signaled in a strange way the paradoxical success of the museum's patriotic mission among the foreigners. Looking at the rich display of the Spanish school, completely unknown to the French, he proposed to turn Madrid into a new mecca for "independent" artists seeking inspiration beyond that to be found in Rome. Viardot also lamented that the "Sons of Saint Louis" had not asked Fernando VII to pay them back in paintings and proposed dispatching to Spain an expedition that would purchase art from religious communities and impoverished aristocratic families.[124] If the museum was really contributing to the fame of domestic art, it also seemed to be endangering its endurance on Spanish soil.

Though it seemed by the early 1830s that the ideal of international prestige had been accomplished, it was not in ways that could satisfy those who cared about the exhibition and protection of Spanish art. The museum's other mission—the education of artists—figured less prominently in early accounts about the Museo Real. Before the nineteenth century, the need to improve the national production of art was cited as the main reason for creating royal public museums, but at the Prado that priority had not yet been given full attention. Concern for the accommodation of young artists, which would eventually become the main focus of the museum's admission policy, was nowhere to be found in the first instructions for concierges and staff.[125] Mérimée and Viardot alike praised the empty rooms, where "a few rare pupils come to establish their nomadic easels and paint in haste their poor copies."[126] The few artists working at the museum most likely did not even come from the Academia San Fernando, which had its own proper collection and a canon, steeped in the neoclassical tradition, that was quite different from what was exhibited in the Museo Real.[127] There were, however, French copyists whom José de Madrazo invited to produce the sketches and drawings for his lithographs. More time would have to pass before the museum was recognized as important enough to be used to train artists.

The last of the museum's missions, to please the dilettanti, seems the most interesting, because it closely connected the Museo Real with the evolution of modern leisure. Originating in the Enlightenment ideal of self-cultivation (*Bildung*), museum "pleasure," as the marquis de Santa Cruz conceived of it, was an edifying activity conducive to refining good taste and producing the rational subjects whose civic involvement ensured a nation's progress.[128] According to this mindset, nations whose citizens had access to art museums had a better outlook for the future. It is hard to determine, however, whether or not the Museo Real worked that way. Both Mérimée and Viardot suggest that, in actuality, the museum's visitors were scarce. For Viardot, there were even fewer "curious people, . . . promenading their domestic carelessness or foreign admiration," than there were artists-in-training.[129] Mérimée explained the silence reigning in the museum as a result of its admission hours, which were much more conducive, in his opinion, to attracting people who had come "to see things instead of just walking to and fro."[130] At that time, the museum was open on Wednesdays and Saturdays only, and, as Mérimée correctly deduced, the few laboring folks who had sacrificed a day of work in order to see the paintings acted responsibly. "How many artists have come from the artisan's class!" he concluded, suggesting that these select dedicated citizens could be the nation's future geniuses.

Imagining Spain as a country of art-loving masses led the French writer to assume that unlike the museums of London, where only well-dressed visitors were admitted, the one in Madrid did not have a dress code. That was not true: the museum regulated its visitors' appearance, refusing admission to individuals "badly dressed or not wearing any shoes." Patrons also had to leave their canes and walking sticks by the door, except for those whose social status entitled them to carry one.[131] In contrast to what happened in the ensuing decades, there is no glimpse on record of any real pauper coming into the museum during these early years. The admission hours praised by Mérimée had an important consequence for the future of Spanish museum leisure: this royal establishment kept itself completely separate from the celebrations, be they religious or civic, taking place around it. While festivals were clearly noticeable on the Promenade outside the museum's windows, nothing but the summer heat or winter rain would change the museum's admission hours. Unlike the Academia San Fernando, which modified its schedules to accommodate more patrons during the Fall Fair, the Museo Real did not pay attention to the festive crowds.

The correspondence of the museum directors frequently mentioned the "curious" public. The word, however, did not necessarily carry positive connotations. The museum authorities seemed to have a lurking dread that they would eventually have to allow the public to "finally satisfy its curiosity."[132] A similar attitude is apparent in the royal order mandating that the administration close the Reserved Room, where nude paintings were exhibited, to visitors.[133] The same correspondence sheds some light on which exhibits really caused the most interest—or were thought to cause the most interest in the eyes of the directors. In July of 1827, the duke de Híjar reported that an "infinite number of distinguished personalities stopped by" the museum wishing to "see and examine the perfections" of José Álvarez Cubero's sculpture *The Defense of Zaragoza*—a patriotic composition that had just arrived from Rome.[134] In August of 1831, he mentioned the public's interest in seeing another sculpted reminder of the war against the French: the group of *Daoíz y Velarde* by Antonio Solá, also brought from Rome and kept in a box until the royal family found time to see it.[135] In both cases, the interest, either real or assumed, had more to do with the disputed legacy of the War of Independence and Spaniards' patriotic feelings than with art or taste.

There is one text, however, that testifies indirectly to the idea that the elites still considered the eighteenth century-style aesthetic floor plan an unrivaled arrangement. The first Spanish translation of Mérimée's "Les grands maîtres du musée de Madrid," which appeared in the weekly *Cartas Españolas*, came with footnotes by an anonymous patriot ready to defend from criticism every inch of Villanueva's building and the collection that it housed. Commenting on Mérimée's lack of appreciation for Spanish artists beyond Velázquez and Murillo, the commentator proposed a retrospective intellectual experiment: forget for a time the real display and put next to Spanish artists the best representatives of the French school (Nicolas Poussin, for example). "Then any mutual understanding between Mr. Mérimée and us would cease and a huge fight among great colorists would begin."[136] The annotation suggested that some art-loving Spaniards might have had a patriotic appreciation for a comparative "aesthetic" display that would far surpass the appeal of a rational exhibit by "schools."

Against this background, it becomes clear just how difficult it was to explain a museum that neither followed the neoclassical example of juxtaposing masterpieces from different traditions nor pretended to be scientific and illustrate the progress of national art. Old-school connoisseurs would love the former; new-century liberals could understand the latter. Still, there was no theory yet to support the layout of the Museo Real. The possibility of seeing works of art together in one place had set in motion a debate about paintings and the best ways to display them, but the general public visiting the museum was then indifferent to the results of that debate. In the absence of a recognizable narrative or time line, visitors noticed the lights, the paintings' subject matter, or each other. Spaniards were only beginning to understand the museum and the roles that it could take on, and time was needed before they could infer what its exhibits were trying to teach them. In the meantime, the moving and talking pictures that magicians and illusionists offered outside might indeed have seemed much more fascinating.

CHAPTER TWO

Inscribing Monarchy into the New Regime, 1833–1868

AFTER FERNANDO'S DEATH, the same passion for imitating his predecessors that had brought the museum to life almost caused its destruction. Seeking to revive another of the Bourbons' traditions—merging the royal persona and the institution of the monarchy—the king did not separate the possessions that his family could inherit from the property of the Spanish Crown. Everything except the palaces and the crown jewels was to be divided among Fernando's widow and their two daughters, Isabel and Luisa Fernanda.¹ The canvases were to be handed down as family heirlooms, and the lack of an undisputed—male—heir to the throne was not helping the museum's cause. Fortunately, with very few exceptions, the court understood the museum's importance better than the family of the king who had created it. Still, the fights to preserve the Museo Real would take a high intellectual toll. As foreign art lovers, dealers, and smugglers were raising the stakes of the Spanish school abroad, the directors would have to convince the regent María Cristina and her daughter Isabel II that the museum was more valuable than a dismantled collection of paintings.

Although the connection to a dispirited monarchy was not making the post-Fernando Museo Real an easy object of love and admiration, civic attitudes toward its exhibits also continued to evolve. Affiliated with the new Moderate Party, which was steering the transition to the new regime, the museum directors—the duke de Híjar (1826–38), José de Madrazo (1838–56), and his son Federico de Madrazo (1860–68)—eventually turned its displays around to match their beliefs in court-led representative rule. The Moderates' liberal opponents, who supported Isabel II in the hope that her monarchy would be parliamentary, were no fans of her father's heritage at the museum, which they wished to see replaced by an exhibit reflecting a fairer balance between the Crown and the people. Those who envisioned Spain as a republic, on the other hand, enlisted the Museo Real in their own cause by rechristening it as simply the Museum of Paintings (Museo de Pinturas). The three groups, however, now followed with equal dismay the sight of common Spaniards on the Prado Promenade and lamented their behavior during popular celebrations, considering it a sign of their poor preparedness to become citizens.

Although the state began to gain force on the arts scene, the general scarcity of funding made royal patronage seem unavoidable even in the eyes of those who wished for it to remain unacknowledged. "There is no rich and robust old aristocracy that could invest copious amounts in acquiring paintings and statues and in constructing palaces," wrote the journalist who signed his reviews "Edgardo." "Our modern Stock Exchange aristocrats . . . hardly spare any remaining income for art objects; the only pictures they can boast of having in their dwellings are those painted on the wallpaper."[2] Without the rich religious communities to commission artwork for cloisters and altars, artists could only rely on "the throne and the people," both of which looked "weak and poor," the writer continued. Against this background, the political position of the Museo Real and the allegiances that its directors were choosing in the competition to represent the nation became a matter of importance beyond the sphere of art.

ART AND NATIONHOOD IN MIDCENTURY EUROPE

The bleak political and financial beginnings of Spain's new regime hindered the adaptation of the Museo Real to what had been regarded as indispensable in a national or public museum since the foundation of the revolutionary Louvre: a chronological encyclopedic display by "schools" and epochs. Such an inability to achieve a "universal survey" ideal, however, was not unusual, as all across Europe royal and post-Napoleonic museums were facing a new set of challenges that resisted clear-cut distinctions between aristocratic (aesthetic), transitional (taxonomic), and democratic (rational) arrangements.[3] At the time of the July monarchy, Second Republic, and Second Empire in France, the rise of Victorianism in Britain, the Risorgimento in Italy, and the centralization of the German principalities, who it was that museums represented or served could be anyone's guess. As the old-regime society of orders and privileges was slowly ceding place to a class-based hierarchy under a limited royal power, the imagery of people united around their "national" monarchs, which had seemed so powerful in the aftermath of Napoleonic invasions, fell out of fashion.[4] State-based nationalisms called for exhibits that spoke directly to patriotic feelings while also harnessing popular movements. Meanwhile, the fight to lower the suffrage census (the income level required to become a voter) fueled a need for public art for voters and taxpayers to identify with and judge.

The revolutionary recipes for a museum without a king that rearranged old-regime collections rationally no longer seemed to work for this new audience. Moreover, the idea that visitors were best served by permanent exhibits, whose directors still had to maneuver between the governments and the monarchs, lost strength when the governments began to assert their cultural monopoly by commissioning artwork for public buildings. Having to withstand new and varied competition from venues with more clear-cut appeal, ranging from government institutions to commercial art exhibitions and world's fairs, public museums outside of Spain saw their prerogatives reduced. Contemporary art, not old masters, was gaining popularity, and museum directors found artists' education to be their last remaining niche—and proceeded to adjust their politics and discourses to fit this new calling.

Museums, which had so recently represented the nations' most powerful, were downgraded to the bottom of the "exhibiting complex"—a growing group of institutions offering displays aligned with the needs of the liberal state.[5] High in this emerging hierarchy, history painting was quickly expanding its uses, bringing to life a new type of exhibit that depicted key moments in world and national histories. In the 1830s to 1850s, several nations followed the French example of visually empowering the representative institution—the Chamber of Peers—by turning it into an exhibition hall.[6] Still, monarchies survived all across Europe, and, in an effort to reinvent themselves, kings also commissioned art for new throne chambers telling the stories about what their rule meant to the people. This was, for example, the idea behind Peter Cornelius's and Wilhelm von Kaulbach's frescoes in the palaces in Munich and Dresden.

Pierre Nora and his team classified the diverse array of midcentury public art offerings as inculcated memories: "memory-royalty, memory-state, memory-nation, and memory-citizen."[7] In Nora's account, the royal memory predated the times of the museums, yet its sacral mode of approaching time, "obsessed with its origins" and concerned with "presenting itself as a timeless ritual," prepared the ground for all ensuing developments. In this typology, toward the 1850s Versailles and the Louvre no longer encapsulated a royal genealogy, but rather the "memory-state," whose "affirmative and unifying" force left the visitors with a certain liberty of interpretation.[8] Such a competition for configuring the nations' memories, and thereby influencing their present, explains why the Crown and the state still considered museums relevant for settling their respective claims to power—something resembling the *juste milieu* of the July Monarchy in France. After the 1830s, the number of European "temples of art" continued to increase, and all but the National Gallery in London had a royal past to celebrate or work around. What the administrators of these museums did was to use the eclectic style fashionable at the time to produce hybrid floor plans that added new values to the royal "sacred" genealogies.

Although these displays were spurring fewer discussions in the press than temporary exhibitions and the decorations of public buildings, they effectively addressed the need to reinscribe the past and present monarchies into the new configurations of nationhood. The historical galleries of the Versailles Museum were opened by Louis-Philippe in 1835; unlike the paintings in the Louvre, these compositions occupied the entire walls, thereby taking modern academic painting away from the museum tradition and bringing it closer to the old frescoes. Versailles became a popular object of imitation. A Belgian Historical Gallery was planned in 1850; the National Portrait Gallery in London, initially called the British Historical Gallery, was inaugurated in 1857. In the German-speaking lands, no special historical gallery was created, but Eduard Bendemann's and Karlebach's historical compositions for the New Museum in Berlin (inaugurated in 1855) conveyed nationalistic meaning allegorically by depicting six "turning points" in history that also illustrated the "gradual selection of 'superior races.'"[9]

Joining forces with the new discipline of art history, museums became the place to delineate national cultural territories. The debates concerning the National Gallery in London reaffirmed the ideal of a state-funded institution that had originated in the 1790s Louvre: "illustrate styles or schools, not men," as one British reviewer stated in 1848.[10] This brought to life displays that focused on mapping national space while avoiding the difficulties of representing a progressive time line, which some historians still found debatable.[11] Without a clear consensus about the chronology, the creators of the National Gallery proposed a floor plan based on the history of art yet also relying heavily on aesthetic comparison.[12] By 1851, the static forms of display found their way back even to the "rational" Louvre: its refurbished Salon Carré contained highlights from the collection that represented different schools. Hence, though floor plans featuring "a progressive chronology combined with the idea of a 'school'" were still considered the preferred strategy for a rational arrangement of paintings, museum directors continued to encourage aesthetic or taxonomic juxtapositions—of individual pieces or national styles—with the idea that these arrangements most easily allowed art to "speak" in order to make it speak to both connoisseurs and laymen.[13]

The princely power that the royal museums had traditionally visualized was also recast to speak across the social divide. The continuous public scrutiny of a museum's collection and a shared desire to expand it generated lively discussions in which the number and quality of paintings and sculptures figured as a measure of the nation's wealth and economic promise. The rising popularity of realism facilitated this interpretation, as faithfulness to an original and attention to detail now became the ideal for artisans and craftsmen seeking to promote national industries. Visitors' judgments about the representational credibility of paintings that had sounded naïve toward the beginning of the century were now considered patriotic and received respect. At a time when economic competitiveness was becoming more valuable than military might, educators in Britain, France, the German principalities, and the United States argued that the future depended on cultured artisans, the ones who would ultimately ensure the flourishing of their nations.

As the triumph of verisimilitude in art also revived the debates about "ideal beauty," the press started a discussion about the function and the place of nudes. Now that the museums spoke for the state alongside the monarchs and no longer counted on the upper class for their audience, the consumption of nude art, which had not attracted attention in the past, became a mark of bourgeois "distinction." Adapting the cultural institutions inherited from the old regime to their own quest for identity, the bourgeois used the concept of the nude to chastise their two antagonists on the grounds that they did not understand this safe, "disinterested," and socially acceptable form of nakedness. According to bourgeois morality, the aristocrats were all hypocritical libertines who erred on the side of public discretion by pushing nakedness into the privacy of their sumptuously decorated alcoves, while the working classes made the opposite mistake of accepting in public lewd images and behaviors that had not been properly aestheticized.[14] Needless to say, while such an approach to the female body secured art museums as gendered male territories,[15] it also revealed a moral double standard: bourgeois males enjoyed the very same display of nakedness that they were trying to idealize as art—they were, of course, not any more "disinterested" in nudity than men from any other class.[16] And of course, as Charnon-Deutsch demonstrates, the debates concerning nudes had their counterpart in another, equally hot topic: the status-defining nature of women's dress.[17]

When it came to art, however, the bourgeois freedom to judge was best exercised when looking at contemporary artistic creations and not at established masterpieces, bringing to prominence three alternatives to museums: the exhibitions held by the artists' associations, the Paris salons alongside their national varieties all across Europe, and, finally, their transnational version at world's fairs, the first of which took place in London in 1851. Crucially, it was no longer the exhibits' perfection, but rather their defects—a notion impossible in the old-regime exhibiting institutions—that made art attractive, generating heated debates among visitors and in the press. Art criticism became a new profession and a good occasion for any writer to launch a career. Yet although writers destined to be classics in the future, like Heinrich Heine, Théophile Gautier, Charles Baudelaire, and Stendhal, to name only a few, critiqued the salons, their most popular reviews approached public art as a pretext to discuss the "public" more than the "art."[18]

The numbers of those wishing to act and speak as the "public" far surpassed those who understood painting and sculpture, and hence the conversation was dominated by concerns such as admission policies, museum location, and picture hanging. In these debates, the leading arguments and positions mimicked the fights for political participation waged in other arenas. In the age of rising socialist movements—and the dawn of communism—every cultural undertaking had to become a double-edged sword just as useful for entertaining the bourgeoisie as it was for appeasing the working classes. And so, with the press connecting the artistic realm to the muddled world of politics, museumgoers' views of their fellow visitors also acquired political overtones. Their aspiration to good manners supplied the bourgeois with plenty of occasions to set themselves apart by discussing decency and good taste. Religious leaders and social reformers used the same arguments to encourage the working classes to attend art exhibits as well. Unsurprisingly, though, the ideologues of monitored "recreation" in the interests of bettering society, before they came up with the idea of arranging special exhibitions for the poor, deemed temporary exhibitions such as the Paris salons hectic, questionable, and less likely than traditional museums to educate the masses.[19]

Traditional museums, however, were also influenced by the aesthetics of temporary exhibitions. The public so clearly preferred ephemeral displays to permanent collections that directors wishing to retain relevance came up with their own innovative formulas for how to mix old masters and contemporary art. In an effort to withstand the competition from expanding private patronage, starting in the 1860s states and kings all across Europe began to found museums of contemporary art following the model of Louis Philippe's Museum of Living Artists.[20] Art dealers and artists' associations responded by organizing temporary exhibitions of old masters. Selective displays offered clearer and more coherent national narratives than traditional museums, whose directors were still concerned with representing a universal history of art. This is why "historical exhibitions," as they were sometimes called, became especially popular in the unifying Italian and German principalities.[21]

In the middle of the century, the growing cross-national demand for temporary exhibitions moved to a whole new level of transnational mega-displays—the world's fairs, arranged by the governments and funded as joint private-public ventures. The 1851 Great Exhibition in London, which was followed by the exhibitions in New York (1853) and Paris (1855) before returning to London (1862) and Paris (1867), enlightened the Western public about the benefits of transforming old-school fairground fun into educational yet spectacular bourgeois leisure. The 1851 London fair was held in the Crystal Palace, a technological marvel whose glass walls supplied natural light and heat while also eliminating nuisances such as wind and rain. Inside, "the mixture of palms, flowers, trees, statues, fountains, the organ (with 200 instruments and 600 voices, which sounded like nothing)," as Queen Victoria described it in her diary, offered a new world of nature, art, and artifice combined, without seasons or climate zones.[22] The unique technology and ambition behind the Crystal Palace did not stop architects from every nation claiming to be industrialized from trying to imitate its design inside and outside the world's fair circuit, creating the "arcade" spaces of total visibility that the philosopher Walter Benjamin considered the most emblematic bourgeois settings. One such structure, built in the 1880s, is now an exhibition space in Madrid's Retiro Park.

The entrance fee and the sheer cost of the trip to the world's metropoles would banish the working classes from these fairs. Yet though upscale in their appearance, these events had to admit the masses—at least the ones that were employed and could consume goods in addition to producing them—whose lifestyles they promised to improve. The French government paid for groups of workmen to visit the 1851 exhibit and report on their impressions. In 1862, it was decided that each ensuing exhibition should have a theme. "The History of Labor" was chosen for the 1867 fair in Paris. Starting in 1851, assembly rooms were provided at the fairs in an effort to foster international exchange of opinions on matters of import for workers. The working people, however, did not respond to these gestures of patronage as the bourgeoisie hoped. The facilities at the 1862 fair in London were used for a meeting between the French and British labor leaders which became a stepping-stone for creating the International Working Men's Association, better known as the First International (1864). In 1867, the British government even refused to fund craftsmen's reciprocal visits to the Paris exhibition, arguing that the workers had abused its trust.[23]

Even the contradictory names given to these events reflected the confusion about their class agenda. Were these gatherings indeed the dignified "international exhibitions" that the organizers imagined, or were they, rather, "world's fairs"—"museum, factory, market, and festival in one," as the French poet Guillaume Apollinaire would later describe them[24]—providing fun for all? Utilitarianism and aesthetic "disinterestedness" were also conflated in the selecting and exhibiting criteria. Every object was vetted by national boards and considered for a prize by an international jury as a potential masterpiece. Yet at the 1851 and the 1853 fairs, the only "fine art" accepted was sculpture, on the grounds that it was an industrial art since its execution required mechanical tools. This brought to general attention the fact that there was no longer an agreement about what "art" really was. In 1845, the academy in Munich had already caused a stir when it exhibited works such as architectural designs and lithographs that other national academies were still rejecting as "industrial" arts.[25] Now that the dispute about the importance of such arts seemed settled, in 1852 the continuity between these and "fine" arts became the foundational principle for the South Kensington Museum (now the Victoria and Albert Museum). This new institution would inspire all major innovations in the exhibiting world through the end of the century, making it difficult for the directors of traditional museums to display art without feeling the pressure to combine arts and crafts.

A different approach, meanwhile, was emerging from France, where the quest for a balance between monarchy and democracy had spurred debates about artistic education. It was Victor Cousin's political philosophy that best captured the role that painting and sculpture would play in the slowly democratizing nations when he linked "ideal beauty" to truth and civic virtue. Wishing to secure a niche in the increasingly mechanized world for this kind of beauty, the designers of the 1855 Paris fair dedicated an enormous exhibit just to the paintings and sculptures from all the participating nations. The intention was to make France look competitive by magnifying culture so that the spaces needed to exhibit it matched the exhibiting facilities needed for industry, in which Great Britain appeared unrivalled. Still, the Paris world's fair overtly declared the autonomy of art and famously maintained the relevance of "fine art." It thus happened that, in the second half of the century, the display of a nation's artistic might was the promise that invigorated traditional museums and revived their appeal.

The competition and communication between the permanent and temporary exhibits, between museums and public buildings, between old masters and young artists, between arts and crafts, that caused such deep changes in Europe's major museums could not help but influence the Museo Real. As its directors exhibited their works at the world's fairs and Paris salons, received commissions for historical galleries outside of Spain, or facilitated the export of works by Spanish old masters, democratically minded art critics were striking a deep nationalist chord in their discussions about permanent museums. Reviewing the 1849 annual exhibition at the Academia San Fernando for *El Popular*, the critic who signed his name "S. Rejano" stated that Spain really needed a permanent museum that would be like "an Iliad painted with brushes, where the Spanish people could worship their God, their religion, and their heroes."[26] For the time being, however, Spain had for its major permanent exhibit the Royal Museum, which thus had to become many things to many people.

A "MODERATE" MUSEUM FOR A TRANSITIONAL REGIME

In 1835, the writer Mariano José de Larra saw the unfinished building of the Royal Museum as an accurate reflection of the state of affairs in a "*quasi*-nation" of "*quasi*-men" united in a "*quasi*-certain hope to become someday *quasi*-free."[27] As Spaniards proceeded to dismantle absolute monarchy, could an institution depending on the royal administration for funding afford to finish the construction? And if so, could it offer to its visitors anything other than a glut of royal imagery?

To be sure, art was becoming a commodity in Spain just as much as it was all around it, although art's commercial promise remained more visible in the international arena, where old Spanish masters were rising to posthumous stardom thanks to exhibits such as Louis Philippe's Spanish Gallery at the Louvre, inaugurated in 1838, and its later addition of Frank Hall Standish's collection.[28] Spanish artistic elites with foreign connections were also trying their hands at this new business, with consequences that promised a bleak future for the arts domestically. Meanwhile, inside the country, José Madrazo, who had added the aristocratic "de" to his family name in exchange for his support of Fernando VII and who ran the Museo Real between 1838 and 1856, and his son Federico, who became the museum's director in 1860, knew better than anyone the value of Spanish art. José de Madrazo evaluated the acquisitions for the Spanish Gallery at the Louvre, while Federico, from Paris, was sending him reports about the press that these exhibits received.[29] This did not prevent the

Madrazos from leading the heritage-preservation debates at home and from undertaking at the Museo Real a series of expansions that glorified the Spanish Crown.

Two approaches to art—the sacral and the commercial—clashed at the Museo Real as Spain entered a period of battles for the "golden mean" of political power. In 1830, when the aging Fernando VII announced that his wife's future child, no matter if it was a boy or a girl, would inherit the throne,[30] the absolutists were already preparing their own candidate—the king's brother Carlos María Isidro—while the liberals were hoping for a successful revolution. When the queen gave birth to a girl, both the liberal and conservative factions redoubled their efforts. As the king was going back and forth on his decision and Carlos's anti-queen faction continued to threaten a civil war (and almost started one), the reformists at Fernando's court recognized the need to negotiate with the liberals. What the transitional reformists had in mind was a partial resurrection of the parliament (the Cortes) as an advisory body to the Crown. This would make Spain similar to parliamentary Britain or, at least, to the restoration France of Louis Philippe's Charter.

Thus a prototype was set for a new-regime state working together with the Crown. From his office in the Tívoli, José de Madrazo had his son Federico, then a promising eighteen-year-old artist, paint an unusual composition encapsulating the consensus reached in Spain as it was losing its king, Fernando. Conceived as a large-sized historical scene, yet depicting a recent episode, *The Grave Illness of Our Lord the King* portrayed the future governing queen María Cristina supporting her husband prostrate on his bed, surrounded by a team of physicians. It was clear to anyone looking at the painting that, in that difficult time, the king's faithful wife constituted a real support for the throne and would carry on the royal will in harmony with the court, suggesting, of course, that it would be thus in reality. It did not turn out that way. After Fernando's death, not only did court politics and the will of the royal personae rarely coincide, but, as they were fighting or negotiating with the liberals their right to lead the transition, the courtiers who supported the Moderate Party eagerly manipulated the reputations of the malleable females to whose service they were appointed.[31]

Both José and Federico de Madrazo fit the behavior pattern of those reformist leaders. First artists of the court, they created numerous flattering portraits—verbal and painted—of both queens, whom they nevertheless did not hesitate to call "useless" in their private correspondence.[32] This leads one to take a nuanced approach to understanding the Museo Real during this period—not as a mere projection of monarchical aspiration, but rather as an institution offering the vision of monarchy that the elites wanted.[33] Although the radical changes in the museum displays undertaken at that time reflected the moderates' course and never came close to supporting the liberals' vaguest hopes, under the pretext of crafting an image for the monarchy without absolutist power, the museum provided a crucial setting for a debate over the relative weight of the forces that claimed participation in nation-building: the state, the church, and the select group that did not believe in self-governance.

The museum's future depended on the outcome of the legal dispute over Fernando's succession. Fortunately, the two executors of the will were also two former museum directors, the marquis de Santa Cruz and the duke de Híjar. Their correspondence with José de Madrazo makes it clear that all three were mortified at seeing the paintings being inventoried and assessed. In 1834, the judicial branch of the royal administration decreed that execution of the will be suspended until Queen Isabel's coming of age. Over the course of the decades-long struggle between Fernando's widow and the court, it was determined several times that the king's inheritance belonged to the ruling descendant only, not to the surviving family members. In 1836, when the governing queen's Carlist contenders started a war and the court's finances became unsustainable, the Crown's financial responsibilities were centralized in an entity called the Intendencia General de la Real Casa y Patrimonio. The Intendencia put in charge of the museum a new governing body called the Junta Directiva, presided over by the museum director, the duke de Híjar, but also incorporating the royal accountants and aided by the first and second artists of the court.[34] Putting the museums under collective leadership might well have been a good idea, but in 1838 the governing queen dismantled that junta and appointed José de Madrazo the director. For many decades to come, the museum was entrusted to court artists.[35]

The Crown's continuing claims to power over the collection made it hard for the directors of the Museo Real to downplay the monarchical cause or even embrace the aesthetics of a balance between monarchy and the nation such as Louis Philippe was then proposing as a path to a liberal restoration in neighboring France. Considering the establishment her property, María Cristina, the governing queen, did continue supplying artwork from the palaces for the museum. Yet, since she was an amateur artist, the copying of pieces from the collection of the Museo Real never stopped in the palace, adding to the list of the directors' responsibilities the difficult task of tracking down and retrieving the works dispatched to the royal family's residences for copying. In 1845, when María Cristina decided to copy Rafael's *La Perla*, a reporter for *Clamor Público* noticed the bare spot on the wall and suspected that José de Madrazo was conspiring with British agents to sell the museum's treasures.[36] The royal "rest chamber" was still at the museum and even received more adornments, while ceremonial coverage of the governing queen's, and later the queen's own, visits to the museum also continued as it had with Fernando.

The connection to the royal palaces and the lip service continually paid to the monarchy helped the directors protect the niche occupied by the Museo Real from the state when it decided to establish its own Museo Nacional de Pintura y Escultura with works confiscated from Spain's religious communities. The state's National Museum was initially located in the former Trinity Convent, which gave the establishment its best-known name, the Museo de la Trinidad. However, the state's constant and enduring financial hardship meant that the museum, designed to counter the church's patronage of the arts, had to move to the building occupied by the Ministry of Development (Fomento, currently the location of the Ministry of Agriculture). The paintings were hung in the hallways and the ministerial offices, making it impossible to offer a coherent display. Still, this competitor of the Museo Real was becoming an important referent for those dreaming about "putting a nation" (in Carol Duncan's wording) unrelated to its Crown in a Spanish art museum.[37] In a provisional catalogue published in 1865, the director of the National Museum made a bold attempt to trace a state-centered genealogy of Spanish art, paying attention to the regional traditions and referencing the collections of the recently founded provincial art galleries.[38]

Just as was happening in other countries, both the court and the state chose the academy, in this case the Academia San Fernando, when they wished to demonstrate their partnership in nation-building. The Museo Real could not compete in popularity with the Academia's annual fine arts exhibitions, where young artists displayed their work next to canvases by their professors and to paintings signed by the governing queen and Isabel II.[39] (Federico de Madrazo, however, privately revealed that all works that María Cristina exhibited as her own were painted by him, his father, and his brother Luis.)[40] Held at the time of the Fall Fair, the exhibitions at the Academia drew diverse and picturesque crowds.[41] While both Madrazos were among the exhibitors and on the jury of these exhibitions, they wished to minimize the importance of these events for a state-based idea of nationhood, causing extremely heated debates in the press. A fervent opponent of the state's claims to nationhood and cultural leadership, José de Madrazo wrote to Federico in March 1839, while the liberals joined the masses on the streets of Madrid, "What does this nation do for the arts . . . ? Hardly anything at all, and one would be foolish to expect such a thing. . . . Nations are only good at destroying and selling what honors them most."[42] Starting in the mid-1840s and throughout the 1850s and 1860s, many demanded that the Academia exhibitions be held in the central gallery of the Museo Real, just as the Paris salons were then held in the Salon Carré of the Louvre, but the Madrazos were vehemently opposed to this idea.[43] Unlike their French counterparts, the directors continued to defend the borders of the royal institution and did not open it up to exhibits that could potentially reflect a type of nationalism that they disapproved of. At a time when public debate revolved around the issue of participation, this reluctance to engage with groups beyond the throne hindered the political relevance of the Museo Real.

Another debate, however, was already emerging that would make the museum important, albeit in different ways than the supporters of political nationhood were expecting. In the 1840s, the Catholic Church was actively mobilizing the elites close to the court, paving the way for a movement in support of a theocratic notion of the state that would become known as Neo-Catholicism.[44] In 1845, a new constitution,

more conservative than its 1837 predecessor, replaced the principle of national sovereignty, so dear to the 1812 liberals, with the idea of "shared sovereignty" of the Crown
and the people and proclaimed Spain an officially Catholic nation. This new "period
in civil-ecclesiastical relations" was ratified in the 1851 Concordat with Pope Pius IX:
the Spanish state conceded to Rome its agency in determining changes in the Spanish
Church and defining Spanish Catholicism.[45] The directors of the Museo Real fully
aligned themselves with this new cause, allowing it to determine their approach to the
royal imagery during the so-called Moderate Decade of Isabel II's early rule (1844–
54), when the Crown would become the laughingstock of Spain.

Proclaimed an adult at thirteen, Isabel at sixteen had to accept a marriage to her
cousin Francisco de Asís, who was chosen by her mother over two other candidates.
Either of the two would have been better: the rejection of Carlos Luis (the son of
Don Carlos María Isidro, the Carlist candidate) triggered the Second Carlist War
(1846–49), and the duke of Montpensier's failed ambitions (he was offered the hand
of Isabel's sister instead) prompted him to seek the throne through a conspiracy that
would dethrone Isabel in 1868. The young queen's marriage to a man whose homo-
sexuality was widely known perpetuated the image of an adulterous and hypocritical
royal family whose members could not even call themselves to order, much less rule
the nation. The liberals' take on the unusual union between a libertine court and its
ultrareligious *camarilla* was captured with a particularly titillating twist in an anonymous series of pornographic drawings of Isabel II, her husband, and their spiritual
advisers, called "Naked Bourbons" (*Los Borbones en Pelota*) and attributed to the artist
Valeriano Domínguez Bécquer.[46] Meanwhile, while the court guaranteed a steady
supply of juicy gossip, a small portion of Spain's Moderate Progressives joined forces
with conservative intellectuals to try to protect the monarchy from the damage it had
suffered in the hands of Spain's actual monarchs.

This marked the birth of Neo-Catholicism in Spain. Unlike Germany, where
the term denoted Catholics who supported a church depending on the state but not
the pope, or France, where Neo-Catholicism acquired socialist overtones, in Spain
it was initially a derogatory epithet coined by the liberals to denounce their diverse
political enemies. Only some of the people who were called "Neo-Catholics" wished
to bring the institution of the church back into the new regime—for purposes ranging
from the suppression of revolutionary movements to the opening up of the debate
about historical heritage. Others were reacting to secularization by seeking new
ways of preserving the idea of the sacred: these Neo-Catholics proposed to modernize Catholicism by disassociating religious experiences from places of worship and
bringing them into state institutions, public art, and the press. This was the outlook
that the Madrazos shared. Although the two oldest "Madrazo boys" (as the novelist
Benito Pérez Galdós called them) were initially known in Madrid for their moderate
Romantic liberalism, in the 1840s Federico, the artist, and Pedro, who at the time

was writing a new catalogue of the Royal Museum, founded a Catholic newspaper.[47] In 1846, Federico dedicated his acceptance speech to the Academia San Fernando to examining that institution's collection of religious art.[48] Pedro's publications of the same period invoked Christ as the "social link" that would deliver Spain from class struggle and suggested an interest in a "providentialist" interpretation of history as a revelation of God's will for individuals and nations.[49]

The reality of Madrid's streets, however, defied Neo-Catholic imagery of social peace. Though Spain did not experience anything on the scale of the 1848 revolutions in Europe, in 1854 it became apparent that urbanites all around the nation were willing to bring their wives and children, build barricades, and assault rich men's homes. In Madrid, during what would have been the festival of San Pedro, the government moved troops in and lined them up, occupying the entire length of the Prado Promenade. Although the queen mandated the banning of the San Pedro *verbena*, there was no shortage of other bonfires. The people, initially quietly watching the army occupy the Prado, armed themselves, freed political prisoners, and set fire to several private residences, including the palaces of María Cristina and the statesman and financial speculator the marquis de Salamanca. The price of peace was the royal family's public *mea culpa* and the announcement of a new Constituent Cortes that brought the liberals back into power for two years.

This first episode of street politics around the museum since the 1808 rebellion against Napoleon stirred up issues of authority that had seemed long forgotten. Only two weeks had passed since Isabel's pacifying manifesto, and the Madrid newspaper *La Iberia* was already charging the museum directors with getting too close to those who used to hold power.[50] Part of the settlement of the rebellions of 1854 was the Crown's promise to sell its properties and pay its debts, and it was the turn of the state to look into the royal administration's handling of the museum. The commission appointed by the Cortes decided that the division of royal property had nothing to do with "national pride, artistic spirit, [and] the patriotism seeking the country's glory" and hence did not recommend, once again, that the Museo Real be sold.[51] Nor, however, did it define it as national property, thus leaving its identity in limbo.

Unlike the earlier waves of disentailment, the liberal policies of the 1850s involved a redistribution of land between the state and the court. In Madrid that meant that the dispute over the area surrounding the museum had to be resolved. And since the Crown, of course, could not simply cede its possessions, the 1865 Law of Royal Heritage separated the personal property of the royal family from the possessions of the persona occupying the throne. Sensing that the era of monarchy acting as a nationalistic synecdoche was coming to an end, Pedro de Madrazo wrote an ode glorifying the queen for donating a "large part of her patrimony to the nation," where the "nation" already referred to the state and not to the Crown.[52] Though limited in its reach, the ruling was a huge step forward for the Royal Museum, which could now distance itself from the monarchs and join the nation-building project in terms that presented less compromised views of the monarchy. On the surface, however, and for a long time, the change was only manifest in the museum's northern entrance. In 1865, the gate that separated the building from the road to San Jerónimo (no longer royal property) was opened, allowing people on their way to the Retiro Park to pass right next to the museum's door.

The consequences of this apparently innocuous act would soon be revealed. In September 1868, a group of armed civilians came down from the Prado, disarmed the guards, and continued along to the Retiro barracks. The museum became an unwilling participant in the revolution that dethroned Isabel II, bringing to power a state council that declared that the nation was ready to pick her own kings. The era of the Royal Museum personally belonging to the monarchs seemed to have ended.

THE NEW MADRID

While political fights were taking the shape of disputes over the area around the Royal Museum, the uses of the Promenade near the museum's façade—the area that the Crown had donated to Madrid in the eighteenth century—were also becoming sources of tension between two groups rising to visibility in mid-century Madrid: rural immigrants and the bourgeoisie. Their growing claims on the Paseo del Prado changed the debate around the Museo Real and the roles reserved to art outside of the "exhibitionary complex."

In the early nineteenth century, the church still owned properties on 44 percent of the streets, and hence the selling of these possessions during the 1836 and 1855–56 disentailment campaigns led to "a landslide-earthquake-like torrent of purchases, demolitions, and construction sites" that began to transform Madrid—a city of clergy, courtiers, bureaucrats, and artisans—into a capital of land speculators, statesmen, and financial oligarchs.[53] Seeking ways to replenish state coffers while also asserting state power, the liberal governments that carried out these campaigns sold the majority of the confiscated lands to the highest bidder, refurbished a few of the larger monasteries as public institutions, and left almost no area in which to build public spaces.[54] Importantly, these plots were confined to the perimeter of old ("Habsburg") Madrid, which could no longer fit the expanding population. In the half century between 1804 and 1857, Madrid added over 100,000 people, reaching 281,170; by 1860 this number was recorded as 298,426.[55] This was the result of ongoing immigration alone, because in a town suffering from continual epidemics (most notably the cholera outbreaks of 1834 and 1854, and an 1865 repeat in the vicinity of Madrid) and deficient food and water supply, the internal population growth was negative.

The immigrants' living conditions could be inferred from the City's ban on def-
ecating in the streets during the 1854 epidemic and its subsequent mandate that all
rental rooms for workers meet the minimum size of three square meters (32.3 square
feet). To stop rental speculation and bring Madrid's available housing up to speed with
its population growth, in 1857 the City approved the plan known as Plan Castro (after
the name of the engineer Carlos María de Castro), which stipulated the expansion of
the city's territory in all directions except toward the Manzanares River. Still, renting
rooms without facilities and ventilation to immigrant workers remained such a lucrative business that some political reformers demanded control over urban planning:
"here we decree replastering the façades, yet no one wants to stick their noses into the
dirty and unventilated courtyards and stairs," Ángel Fernández de la Ríos would later
comment.[56]

Although the effects of Plan Castro and other modernizing developments did not
appear on the map of Madrid until the end of the century, the changes in lifestyles and
values that came with urban expansion made Spain's alignment with other European
nations inevitable.[57] The former peripheral meadow and the Enlightenment Paseo del
Prado that Madrid had received from the Crown and reserved for the urbanites' leisure
was becoming an entryway to new districts built according to the new living standards
and marked in Castro's description as "aristocratic," "middle-class," and "working or
trade class" neighborhoods (map 2).[58] Though Castro's plan reserved for recreation the
area east of the Retiro Park (map 2:3), multiple gated pleasure gardens also emerged
on the Paseo de Recoletos north of the old Prado (map 2:4) and on its extension, the
Paseo de la Castellana (map 2:5). Complete with cafés, stages, and dance floors, they
also became the testing ground for urban innovation, offering everything from public
bathrooms to gas (and later electric) lights for their visitors' comfort.[59] The clear-cut
distinction between the public and the private, the cult of the body, the attention to
health, the love of order and comfort, and consumerism were the norms that ruled in
this new Madrid and spilled over into its older sections.

So, if under Fernando VII the Prado Promenade had looked either rustic or civic,
a plethora of new values battling for dominance was planting the seeds of discord
in the museum's vicinity. Representing the new "public"—the one that aligned itself
with the bourgeois norms—state authorities and private investors now shared an
interest in imposing order on the city lands that were coming too close to the modern
Madrid. Meanwhile, social reformers wishing for a truly representative state began to
reconsider the uncontrolled leisure customs that potential voters were practicing in the
Prado and demanded that the city do a better job of promoting public virtue in the
areas that it controlled but could not properly civilize. Clashing with the state, which
sided with the Crown and investors, the municipality, as owner of the promenades,
now paradoxically found itself united with the "liberal populace" on the old-regime
side of the debate over the use of urban space: the city favored open leisure spots at

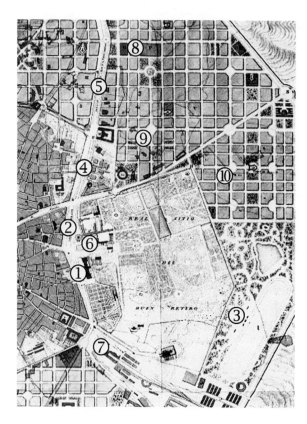

MAP 2 The expansion of Madrid (Plan Castro): a preliminary draft, 1861. *Ensanche de Madrid. Anteproyecto. Plano General de la zona de ensanche y distribución del nuevo caserío. Ejecutado por Real Orden de 8 de Abril de 1857*, detail.

1. Museo Real; 2. Salón del Prado; 3. Planned recreation area; 4. Paseo de Recoletos; 5. Paseo de la Castellana; 6. Tivoli and Plaza de la Lealtad; 7. Atocha train station; 8. Planned upper-class neighborhood on both sides of La Castellana; 9. Planned middle-class neighborhood, Barrio Salamanca; 10. Planned working-class neighborhood (current neighborhoods of Retiro and Pacífico).

a time when everyone else wanted more fences and gates. Even the liberal Larra, who chronicled this evolution in the 1830s, firmly identified as "public" the pleasure grounds that were privately owned and gated—and not the Paseos or the Botanical Garden, which belonged to the City and accepted everyone without charge.

The paradoxes of transitional urbanism did not end here: it was the modernization of the areas that the City did *not* own that was instigating the calls to order over the open areas that *were* municipal property. The masses causing dismay on the public lands were composed of rural immigrants hired to build the new Madrid that they were not invited to inhabit. Bahamonde and Toro state that the numbers of temporary workers, most of them from the provinces and rural areas, hired in Madrid in 1854 grew almost twofold by 1869, from eighty-five hundred to sixteen thousand.[60] Until later in the century, these workers and their families were excluded from the system of professional training—an omission that spurred the growth of so-called people of bad behavior who dedicated themselves to beggary and prostitution. Their presence became prominent on the Paseo del Prado, where some of the immigrant workers were also seeking shelter.[61] An anonymous "Resident Officer" from Britain described people sleeping by the Botanical Garden: "rolled up in their cloaks, their persons carefully

FIG. 13 Anon., "La Linda del Prado" (Pretty woman on the Prado), c. 1851. Etching. Museo de Historia de Madrid, fondo Casariego.

bestowed in the corners between the pillars and the railing, secure from the wheels of carriages and hoofs of horses."[62]

At that time in Britain evangelical leaders were already claiming that the only way to restore health, morals, and social order was to expose the urban poor to man-made nature, in the form of public parks, and organized distraction, in the form of "rational recreation."[63] Under Queen Victoria, monitored leisure evolved into popular culture—that is, culture designed for people to partake in with the goal of social engineering. In Catholic countries, the term "recreation" prompted enough associations with the pastimes laid out by the social reformers of the Enlightenment that it received a warm welcome there as well. In Madrid, for a while the only novelty was the contexts in which the term appeared: commercial advertisement and public health. In April of 1834, we already see the motto "Recreation is good for the conservation of life" used to advertise El Jardín de las Delicias.[64] During the 1834 cholera epidemic, the Madrid health department was known to instruct inhabitants that taking a walk was one of the "innocent distractions" helpful against "strong passions."[65] Meanwhile, from London, the exiled Spanish liberals introduced their readers to the public promenades in different European cities.[66] Madrid and other Spanish capitals, they thought, fared quite well against nations such as Britain or France that had no spaces of comparable size and beauty.

Still, if one compares the design of the bourgeois recreational spaces, supporting the mingling of men and women of different ages and classes, with the domestic descriptions of the Prado, the differences become apparent. Spanish authors were now seeing uncharted yet perceptible borderlines everywhere along this ungated promenade. Everyone ought to know when exactly the *crème de la crème* took a walk, and where rich women would sit, and where to go to find "pretty women" (a male euphemism denoting anyone from the eligible daughters of middle-class families to prostitutes) (fig. 13). Time on the Promenade became just as ritualized as its space. "Two o'clock is when the elegant begin to flow to the Prado, and the Promenade achieves its greatest splendor, its apogee, at three."[67] According to the same journal, Sunday mornings were the best time to take a walk. The reason? "At that time, the smoke rising from the chimneys of all kitchens guarantees you that by their side there is a fantastic number of *povere cenerentole* [poor Cinderellas] busy with their domestic chores, producing the aristocratic majority on the Prado."[68] The variety of classes was not new on the Prado, but the bourgeois were now doing everything they could to avoid getting confused with members of the, "so to speak, more democratic crowd."[69] While the authors of these accounts saw the Paseo del Prado as a place to figure out political representation, however, they seemed ill at ease in the presence of middle- and working-class people, especially women.[70] Unlike the British public parks, the Prado therefore remained a gendered and class-segregated place.

The long-established tradition of people-watching on the Prado now mostly meant that women and the working classes were becoming a spectacle to the male literate "public" to contemplate and enjoy describing in detail. These experiences, usually referred to as *cuadros* ("pictures" or "scenes"), became the most important part of the period's "culture of display," which, in Leigh Mercer's analysis, constituted the essence of modern middle-class urbanity.[71] The regent queen, and later Isabel II herself, set the stage. Using the area to modernize court ceremony, both would appear on the Promenade to communicate with their subjects, especially in times of crisis. Further down the social ladder were the "elegant" women, who sometimes came alone. *Correo de las Damas*, a women's magazine, described the hats and mantillas seen on the Prado in much the same way present-day celebrity journals describe the fashions worn by movie stars. The emerging genre of *costumbista* sketches ushered in equally detailed "pictures," written and drawn, of lower-class women by middle-class men.[72] Some writers were now commenting on the parallelisms between the rituals of people-watching and looking at exhibits; their metaphors, however, did not come from art exhibitions but rather from the fairgrounds. In 1847, Antonio López de Guzmán, writing for the liberal *Eco del Comercio*, called the Prado Promenade "a perennial exhibition, where just as at the animal fair one picks animals to take to the slaughterhouse, or to employ for hard and brutal work, or to make it serve for entertainment and recreation."[73]

Not only were working-class folks visible on the Prado, but the discussions about their appearance and manners were directly tied to the issue of political rights, triggering the earliest opposition to the popular festivals in Madrid. For example, among the newest sights on the Prado inspiring the writers to dip their pens in ink were pauper boys. In 1834, a whole campaign broke out against ragged children offering a light to smokers for a tip. The monarchical *La Revista Española* denounced the "youths covered with disgusting rags, . . . whose actions, gestures, and conversations breathe the deepest ignorance, the utterly corrupted customs, the highly obscene expressions, and the most complete abandonment."[74] The street boys that one could see in many European cities had not yet received the name of *gavroches*, after a character in Victor Hugo's *Les misérables* (1862). Still, the social fear that they inspired was clear. When the municipal authorities reacted and decided to bring to the Prado uniformed boys from a local orphanage who would be an example to their uninstitutionalized fellows while also undercutting their jobs, even the liberal *Eco del Comercio* welcomed the idea.[75]

The writers and intellectuals now considered the days and, especially, the nights of the patron-saint festivals particularly useful for studying the "common people." For liberals demanding wider suffrage, the nightly *verbenas* became a testing ground to probe the maturity of the lower classes. Their conclusions were far from optimistic, as carelessness and drunkenness—the markers of popular pastimes—did not produce rational voters. "This entertainment (and no one will dispute that it is entertaining to walk all night long without sleeping); this, I repeat, popular entertainment has its own high style, its own aristocratic air," wrote a contributor to the satirical newspaper *El Jorobado*, before remarking on the suspicious presence of "young women and not so young, seamstresses . . . or something" in the open-air cafés.[76] In 1839, Modesto Lafuente (who between 1850 and 1867 would author a thirty-volume *History of Spain*) sarcastically described the actions of semi-drunk crowds during the *verbenas* as a "people's parliament" with its "grand assembly" divided into "numerous circles or groups or, as one could say, dancing electoral colleges."[77] Using these hapless individuals as examples made it clear that the festive crowds were not ready to be voting members of a democracy.

Still, the midsummer festivals were on their way to being recast as one of Madrid's traditions, especially after 1841, when the erudite Basilio Sebastián Castellanos wrote the first history of the *verbenas*. In the following years, newspapers would regularly reprint his text in anticipation of the spring and summer cycles of celebrations. The City of Madrid was actually interested in expanding these activities and issued generous licenses to street vendors. Thus, on the nights of San Juan, San Pedro, and San Pablo, the stretch between the Plaza de la Lealtad next to the Salón del Prado and the museum would become a fair, hosting music and dances and selling pastries and alcohol.[78] The merger of the *verbenas* (rural noncommercial festivities) with vending activity on the Prado Promenade would eventually become the norm. Yet at the time this was still a novelty, and it did not fail to awaken writers' moralizing zeal. On many occasions they used irony and sarcasm to repudiate the crowd without succumbing to class animosity: "Many were the good-humored folks that danced and sang under the accompaniment of guitars, tambourines, timbrels, and other musical instruments, and not a few decided to spend their night dedicating themselves to doughnuts, cakes, and alcohol," one reporter remarked in 1851.[79] Another made it a point to describe in detail the "unholy" nature of the festival's after-hours on the Prado: vending stalls covering the full length of the Promenade, "improvised doughnut factories" by the Tívoli, and a late-night shift of "hot-blooded" music-lovers "occupying a preferred spot in front of the Museum of Paintings."[80]

The emerging debate concerning the pastimes available on the Prado allowed the directors of the Museo Real to demand that their vicinity, too, should become less open and more bourgeois. The Promenade at that time was the only area adjacent to the museum building that did not belong to the Crown, and this is why the museum directors could recast their political sympathies as the court's debates with the city government over its handling of popular gatherings. The municipal authorities, however, did not limit consumption or regulate morals, but simply dispatched more guards on festival days. Since 1837, the annual reminders about the norms of behavior during the *verbenas* had become minimal, and the only things banned were lewd gestures, personal offences, and the sales of tree branches (for hitting each other—a pagan tradition associated with San Juan) after curfew.[81] Entrepreneurial minds would soon learn how to turn the lack of regulation into a source of income, setting the foundations for commercial gaming and competitions in Madrid. In 1838, a "juego de sortija" (ring jousting) attraction that required an admission fee was already installed in front of the museum during the Fall Fairs, with monetary prizes given to the riders who could pierce a ring while racing.[82] Even though these competitions, which dated back to the eighteenth century, approached the rule-governed bourgeois idea of leisure, they also made the museum administration that was now leading the crusade to civilize the Paseo unhappy. In 1843, just as the Cortes were gathering in Madrid to end the regency and proclaim Isabel II an adult, Madrazo voiced his protest against the city's continuing tolerance of the midsummer *verbenas* and, especially, the horseracing that it now included, which, in the director's words, brought in the "mob."[83]

This was just the beginning of a fight to keep leisure activities off the Prado, one that used the preservation of the museum and its reputation as its main argument. A decade later, in an article titled "Hygiene," the monarchical *La España* complained about youngsters playing a ballgame against the museum façade, when they "could perfectly well be working on the construction of the [new water] canal."[84] Making fun of the city authorities' ingratiating approach, the author did not conceal his scorn, proposing that a "municipal guard be kind enough to inform the precious young men, very tactfully of course, that amusing things bring more pleasure when enjoyed sparingly, and that exercise in excess can harm one's health and can even be a cause of death."[85] A note no less sardonic about "lazy slackers enjoying themselves in pleasant company" while throwing balls against the museum façade appeared also in the liberal *El Clamor Público*.[86] Interestingly, however, while the contributors ridiculed the ideologies of public recreation, at no time were the "slackers" invited to leave their ball under a tree and check out the museum.

These articles appeared during Madrazo's campaign to restore the civil guard post, which had been eliminated by an order from the local military commanders.[87] In his correspondence with court authorities, Madrazo also complained about "abuses that are committed at the external façades of this Royal Museum, where they play ball, break windows, and steal lead separators from the stained glass."[88] When these requests proved ineffective, he created a position at the museum for uniformed guards, charged with reporting any activity in the museum's vicinity that posed a potential threat. An 1856 royal order featured requirements for these guards that give us an idea of the objectionable actions that might be observed, and policed, from inside the museum: "[Do] not allow anyone [to] lean against the walls of the Establishment, . . . see that no announcements are glued to the fences and columns and no one touches or dirties the sculptures on the façade, . . . prevent any harm to its walls, doors, glasses, etc., . . . [do] not allow playing ball against its walls, or throwing stones in the museum's vicinity, and also prohibit playing cards and engaging in any other similar activities."[89] The discussion seemed to be moving in a direction that had nothing to do with the Victorian definitions of culture and recreation.

The conflict between the museum and the working-class (especially young) people relaxing around the museum engaging in activities previously unheard of is easily explained by the changing composition of Madrid's fast-growing population. Playing ballgames against a wall, a typical pastime in the rural areas of Spain, was now brought to the section of the city which was traditionally associated with nature: the Botanical Garden. Similarly, one can recognize another pastime, this time from the south, happening on the Prado during the *verbenas*: singing and dancing in large circles, to the accompaniment of guitars and castanets. In 1858, when the first public railroad line to the capital (Madrid–Alicante) was completed, Spaniards from the rural areas and the provinces became even more numerous on the Prado because the nearby Atocha station became the point of entry to the city (map 2:7).[90] The "country hicks" (*paletos*), as they became known in Madrid, included temporary visitors from Spain's provinces as well as workers coming in search of a job.[91] The latter often made the Promenade their home until they found a place to stay, causing journalists to complaint that the lack of proper lighting and the failure to respond to the Promenade's new role as a "transit point" was giving rise to "scandals and scenes incompatible with good morals."[92]

As for the temporary guests, Madrid's journalists, deeming them unrefined and materialistic, made fun of their interest in the Royal Museum. In May of 1868, as the railroads began to offer discounted packages to the San Isidro Fair, the fairground-goers became a subject of ridicule alongside the *paletos* when they considered it their duty to take a walk through the museum as well: "Saw it on Sunday. Ugh, was it hot! There are a lot of paintings and rooms are very big. What can I say: been there, done that." This imaginary diary entry belonged to one such visitor: a "conservative old Castilian" created by Eusebio Blasco, the editor of Madrid's satirical liberal newspaper *Gil Blas*. It came with the editor's own comment: "You would have had a better time visiting a cold-drinks pavilion [*horchatería*]."[93]

Consumer alternatives to museum-going were indeed moving closer to the museum, thanks to the city's liberal licensing policies. In 1835, a new, gated pleasure

FIG. 14   Charles Clifford, *A View of the Jerónimos from the Calle Alcalá*, The building, the garden, and the railing of the Tívoli are visible in the background toward the center, with the museum to its left, next to the San Jerónimo Monastery. Biblioteca Nacional de España.

area was inaugurated on the Promenade, facing the current Spanish Treasury (Banco de España): Las cuanto estaciones. It welcomed both sexes and, during the festivals, offered reduced fees to young women wishing to attend the open-air dances, which charged admission. Writers did not fail to insinuate that the mix of sexes was not quite innocent; in 1835, *Correo de las Damas* recommended that the "elegant" female readers stay on guard "since after eight o'clock in the evening the menu there is just for show."[94] The writers' glee at seeing women alone in public spaces suggests that as long as gendering remained the norm, the admission fee was no guarantee of the decency that the bourgeois were seeking. For the time being, both the common and privatized areas of the Promenade shared its reputation for being the center for sexual encounters of all kinds.

The ownership of the Tívoli estate, facing the museum's northern entrance and housing the Madrazos, was a subject of dispute between the City and the Crown. But the Tívoli was still leased out to José de Madrazo's Lithographic Establishment, where the artist had also moved his residence and his personal art collection. Federico de Madrazo's star was rising, too, and in 1842 he added his studio to the Tívoli, where the cream of Madrid society would come to have their portraits made. The fact that the two inhabitants of the Tívoli also ran the Museo Real made the ideological subtext of the clashes over leisure particularly clear: despite their moderate monarchism, the museum directors supported commerce and regulated leisure instead of the old-regime leniency toward the masses in the open and the businesses catering to them.

The Madrazos were, indeed, an entrepreneurial family. In 1854, when the legal framework of leasing royal possession became blurry, Madrazo Sr. rented the Tívoli to a family of French investors, the Méric brothers, who used the site to launch a factory, Compañía Colonial, producing French-style chocolates. A view of the area made in 1853 by the British photographer Charles Clifford shows how close it was to the museum (fig. 14).[95] Compañía Colonial used steam engines, which in 1856 and 1859 caught fire, but advertised itself as a "model factory." In 1867, it moved its production to a new facility. As long as it remained in the Tívoli, the owners were supportive of Madrid's charitable organizations and often lent out their garden for fundraisers: yearly concerts, dances, and fireworks to collect money for the education of poor children. The Madrazos apparently did not consider the fires or the fireworks on their fenced-in property to be as dangerous to the museum as the popular gatherings on the neighboring Prado.

Subletting the estate, of course, was not the same as expropriating the land, but when José de Madrazo died in 1859, the family considered itself the owner. So when the factory moved out, Madrazo's numerous children decided to tear down the buildings and divide the land into several lots for auctioning. In February 1867, the former casino—which had also been the site of Madrid's first French-style café—and the surrounding pavilions went down, as did the trees of the Tívoli's garden and the tents of the Tívoli Dance Society. The area became a vacant lot, and remained so for many years, as the transaction was not finalized until 1874. This created, right next to the museum, an empty spot where people were robbed and corpses were disposed of.[96] The blight was especially striking because by that time the inhabitants of Madrid had already begun to value the trees and preserve public gardens.[97] In 1868, the daily *La Época* deplored the "ruins, ditches, desert dust, and horrendous erosion" that made the area a "truly pitiful sight."[98] One is left to wonder what Federico de Madrazo, the museum's director at the time, thought when he passed by on his way to work.

In comparison, there were few disputes—but plenty of protests—concerning the museum's southern entrance. Until 1871, this nameless area was most often referred to as "the small square between the museum and the Botanical Garden." The city's lands used to end right behind it, so its eastern side was fenced, blocking the passage to the orchard of the San Jerónimo monastery.[99] But that was no longer the case after Fernando VII opened the Retiro Park to the public. Newspapers periodically demanded the opening up of the square so that one could pass through it to the Retiro—or announced that it would be opening up—but this did not actually happen until the 1880s.[100]

Given the square's privileged position, there was no shortage of other projects proposed for the space. In 1846, Mesonero Romanos suggested putting an arch or a gate in the fence to open it and erecting a statue of Carlos III in the middle of the square.[101] In 1847, the liberal daily *El Clamor Público* reported a plan to install a circus there, "pending only Her Majesty's approval."[102] In 1860, there were talks about transforming the square into a "beautiful French garden."[103] In 1864, the daily *La Época* proposed moving the obelisk commemorating the heroes of the 1808 uprising against Napoleon to the square.[104] Anything, some concluded, would be better than the sight of underskirts and sheets (presumably belonging to museum guards and their families or the people camping by the Botanical Garden) hung out to dry that the square most often offered.[105] Despite all the interesting proposals, neither the City of Madrid nor the museum could develop the area because the land belonged to the Crown. In the meantime, upper-class visitors used the cul-de-sac to park their carriages, and in 1839–40 the Royal Intendancy approved the construction of a formal carriage access.[106] The south entrance itself was not always in use. It was only opened in 1864 after the museum's major reorganization and was usually closed except on days of public admission.[107]

While the uses of the museum's immediate surroundings were still just being discussed, the area behind the museum promised an actual change (fig. 2). At the time, this section was still visible in full only from a narrow courtyard accessible through a gate next to the museum's northern entrance; there was just enough space in the corner between the apse and the retaining wall for a building big enough to house some of the employees. This was the façade that the museum directors now wanted to improve by finishing the construction of the apse that Villanueva had laid out following the outline of a large conference hall. Since this hill was also part of the San Jerónimo monastery, discussions about this and ensuing improvements set in motion a long chain of territorial disputes.

If relations between the museum and the changing owners of that land had never been cordial, they had been particularly tense ever since the 1836–37 disentailment campaign, when the former church became an artillery depot, the convent cells were transformed into barracks, and the former monastery garden was ceded to the Royal Residence for Invalids.[108] Imagining an explosion of the powder stored in the artillery depot and leaks from the garden being watered, the museum directors began to protest, but the garrison commander insisted that there was no other place to move the ammunition.[109] As for the garden, in 1847 Madrazo was still complaining about "a pile of composted manure" being burned next to the museum's entrance.[110]

In July of 1848, poking fun at such an unusual cohabitation, the Madrid comical newspaper *El Papamoscas y su tío*, in the spirit of revolutionary optimism that was coming from France, published a "Tragedy" representing a conversation between two characters—called "The Museum" and "The Former Convent"—"accompanied by trees, a pile of ashlar stones, and the silent but stinky filth that twenty classes of people left behind." In the play, San Jerónimo complained about the new inhabitants and the decay of morals in its bosom that they brought with them. The museum sat quietly listening and tried to console its neighbor, only to perish in an explosion when an artilleryman dropped a burning cigarette on a box of ammunition.[111] Although the play portrayed the museum and the convent as friends, in reality the administration of the Museo Real was very interested in the monastery lands and buildings and would consequently fight any institution located there.[112] The ownership over the site was the subject of a long trial between the court and the City of Madrid, with as many resolutions as appeals.[113]

The depot finally left the museum's vicinity in 1851, and, taking his fight to the next level, Madrazo tried to annex the building. However, in that same year, Spain's government signed an agreement with the Vatican that reversed the church disentailments. The expansion that the modified land codes had seemed to promise to the museum thus ended in nothing, as the City of Madrid could not come to an agreement with the two institutions with which the museum sympathized—the Crown and the church. All that José de Madrazo could obtain were funds to add the final touch to Villanueva's building by completing the apse.

By 1853, the museum could boast a new eastern façade. Yet as the San Jerónimo was fighting back and as the bourgeois's love for segregation was becoming the norm, the museum directors' policies did not differ from what the sympathizers of every political cause wanted at the time: more fences. Since the apse was protected from the east by the retaining wall, the directors, unwelcoming as they were of the City's policies, concentrated their efforts on setting a barrier between the museum and the Promenade, establishing a gated garden. This was Federico de Madrazo's project, for which he commissioned two sequoias to be brought to Madrid—the first tree of this type in Spain. The garden was finished in 1862, but its only fence was a series of low posts with a rope, making the separation only symbolic.

NEW ARRANGEMENTS AND OLD GENEALOGIES

In 1851, someone apparently enthralled by the Crystal Palace in London proposed to turn the entire Promenade in front of the museum into Madrid's first glass pavilion, defying the separation between indoors and outdoors.[114] Inside the museum, however, things were changing faster than around it, even though the directors' complex relationship with the Crown did not translate into an easy partnership with the state in configuring Spain's national art. Instead, the directors of the Museo Real, coming from the Madrazo family, sided with the other contender for influence over Spanish nationhood—the church. With this choice, they had both a justification and a foundational philosophy for rearranging the museum in a way that denied the secularization of the state and the Crown. As a way to achieve this goal, the Madrazos rearranged the exhibits in a retrospective order that could suggest that Spanish art unfolded according to a sacred time line. A floor plan resulting from this idea distinguished the Museo Real from its European counterparts even as, in transition to the new regime, it employed the strategies rehearsed in other countries. Although the directors also commissioned historical galleries, rearranged "old masters" on a chronological time line, and gathered the gems of the collection in one special room, at the Museo Real, while other European museums were focusing on national space, time became a contentious matter.

Representing national history as a spiral movement toward a predetermined divine mission, the chronology underlying the reorganizations of the Museo Real as Spain was transitioning toward the new regime viewed time itself as a mere element in an ontology where the results of human activity were always preset.[115] Historian Derek Flitter finds such a retrospective "providentialist" time line—linear yet also, paradoxically, cyclical and static—pervading all nineteenth-century Spanish historiography, both liberal and conservative. In his view, even progressive and secularized representations attributed to both the state and the nation a quasi-religious destiny and quasi-royal genealogy. This was also the chronology that prevailed in the Museo Real once it became clear that the danger of its being dismantled had passed.

Unlike her father, Isabel II could not pose as the creator of the museum, even though she compensated her sister for her share of the collection, thereby "buying" it for the Royal Museum. After the 1865 separation of the royal and national properties, her role was further reduced to acting as a custodian of the treasures belonging to the Crown as an institution. This is why the museum propaganda did not focus on the persona of Isabel II, but rather on her rule as a part of the history of Spain and its artistic collection. When José de Madrazo became the director in 1838, he effectively used its liminal status, caught between being personal and national property, to enrich the museum's holdings, collecting exhibits from palaces and the monastery of El Escorial, property of the Crown. He also opened to the public and incorporated into the exhibit the Sala Reservada, where paintings deemed immoral had been kept away from the uninitiated. In his private correspondence, the director explained that putting royal treasures on display was the right way to glorify the nation and to make Spaniards understand how much they owed to their monarchs culturally.[116]

The question was, of course, whether such cunning royalism could allow the museum to offer a portrait of the nation convincing to anyone besides the monarchs themselves. Soon after his appointment, Madrazo requested permission to visit all the royal possessions and retrieve the portraits for a new project that would become known as the historical (or sometimes chronological) gallery of kings and queens of Spain. By that time, Louis Philippe of France had already inaugurated the historical galleries in the Palace of Versailles. Madrazo had firsthand knowledge of this project, since his son Federico had received the commission for one of the panels for Versailles. Madrazo's historical gallery, although never fully accomplished, constituted a similar attempt to merge the royal and the national genealogies. What we know about it suggests that it took very limited steps to unearth from the Spanish past a notion of authority other than the kings and queens. Thus, the text of the decree establishing the gallery signed by Isabel II in 1847 called for the inclusion of not only the sovereigns of all the historical kingdoms of Spain, but also "the counts and judges of Castile."[117] The decree specified that they had to be exhibited "separately," together with the "portraits" of the medieval rulers of Aragón and Navarra and the counts of Barcelona. These works, however, were the last to be commissioned and apparently were never created.

There were other attempts to represent the civil authorities. By the end of 1847, when Isabel II made the above decree, Madrazo, under the pretext of planning a "collection of portraits of celebrated men,"[118] had started transferring to the museum paintings from the Royal Topography Cabinet. Whether or not he actually intended to follow through with such an endeavor, this collection can be considered an early prototype of an iconographic gallery that supported a definition of nationhood without monarchy. According to another memorandum, in 1847 Madrazo also planned to dedicate one room of the museum to the paintings of battles.[119] Although incomplete, these projects planned for the 1830s and '40s followed the late absolutist cultural standards heralded in France: that the monarchies and the nations would justify each other on the grounds of each other's successes, yet the kings would enjoy a surplus power to own, commission, and exhibit national imagery to the people comprising the nation.

The idea was inspiring enough to elicit an attempt from the Academia San Fernando to take over the commissions, which Madrazo was dispensing at will, by creating an alternative display of national history. In 1848, just months after the decree creating the historical gallery, several artists and sculptors requested a personal audience with Isabel II, where they handed the queen a proposal for a national historical museum made up of works by contemporary artists.[120] The proposal had no effect. For the Crown, the historical gallery already planned was enough to fill the need for nationalistic imagery, and the Museo Real had the prerogative to carry the plan out. Yet the sacred royal genealogy figured prominently in the Royal Museum's version of Spain's nationhood, leaving little space for the linear progressive time line most commonly associated with nation-building under the new regime.

Madrazo's proposed series was conceived in retrospective genealogical time, "starting with the Bourbons, continuing with Austrian until the Catholic kings as the head of the Austrian dynasty, continuing then with the kings of Castile, Leon, Oviedo, and Asturias."[121] Furthermore, while the last two dynasties and, for some reason, the kings of Aragon were exhibited chronologically, the display of other medieval rulers took place in a kind of timeless past, and the commissioned "portraits" were hung in the order in which the different artists were finishing them, with complete disregard for chronology.[122] Additionally, a special effort was made to represent the role of the queens in Spanish history by commissioning the images of the medieval rulers Berenguela and Urraca. Isabel's own presence was to be signified by an equestrian portrait by Bernardo López Piquer.[123]

According to Federico de Madrazo, Isabel II visited the Museo Real only twice in her lifetime, and the head of the palace administration visited only once.[124] Their only visit together in June 1848 was prompted by the planning of the Historical Gallery. According to some newspaper reports, for that occasion the inscription

"Museo Histórico" (History Museum) was placed by the main entrance to the muse-um's central gallery, suggesting that the director was planning a prompt, high-profile inauguration. Yet in reality, the collection was relegated to the attic, and in 1850 the liberal press was still asking why it was not yet open to the public.[125] By 1856, the year when the National Portrait Gallery opened in London, four rooms in the museum were reportedly refurbished for historical galleries.[126] Contemporary guidebooks also referenced the exhibit, but there were no reviews of it in the press, suggesting that, until the 1868 revolution, the series did not yet take full shape, even though the idea itself proved popular.

Had it been accomplished, Madrazo's chronological series would have provided the first public representation of Spain's national history—albeit one that served the monarchy well. Never before had royal portraits played a role other than demon-strating to the kings their origins. In the Museo Real, the complete genealogy of the sovereigns of all Spanish territories was planned so they would be manifest to everyone. And even though the collection was hardly, if ever, seen by the public, it reframed the debates about the role of royal images for the nation. Even the royal chambers in the museum, still reserved for the monarchs and their families, acquired new meanings, as they were now described as a part of the same historical collection housing the portraits of the Spanish Bourbons.

Crucial for raising awareness about the national iconography, Madrazo's initiative prepared the ground for a wide range of historical configurations of nationhood, from the publication of etchings from Valentín Carderera's *Spanish Iconography* (1860) to the foundation of the National Archaeological Museum (1867). In 1864, an author signing himself "M.L." claimed that the scarcity of historical compositions in the Museum of Paintings was making it necessary that there be representations of his-torical subjects in the National Theater. "M.L." was, most likely, none other than the historian Modesto Lafuente, mentioned earlier.[127] His interest signaled that, through the conduits of theater and history, the museum was becoming relevant not only for monarchists but also for liberals. Furthermore, the debates opened the eyes of the Spanish public to the need to expand the nation's civic iconography. In 1853, *Clamor Público* campaigned to collect the portraits of Spain's most famous men and, on a more playful note, create a portrait gallery of the globe's most beautiful women.[128]

For the time being, however, the museum's service to women was limited to its glorification of the queen. In that same year, 1853, her name was immortalized in a new exhibit space called the Sala de la Reina Isabel, made possible thanks to the completion of the museum's eastern façade with the apse that had remained unfinished since the eighteenth century.[129] Back then, the two themes of Villanueva's museum—the exhi-bitionary (cabinet of natural history) and the knowledge-producing (chemistry and botany laboratories)—were supposed to merge on the two communicating levels of the grand Conference Hall located in that apse. The two-story Sala de la Reina Isabel

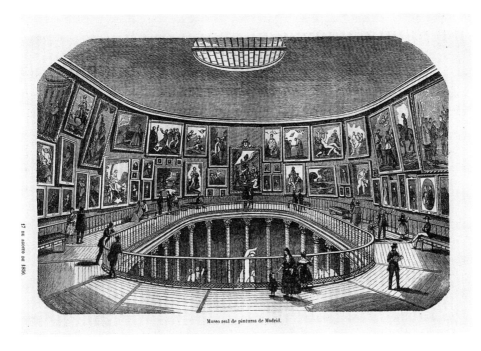

Museo real de pinturas de Madrid.

FIG. 15   Interior of the Sala de la Reina Isabel. *Semanario Pintoresco Español* 33 (August 17, 1856): 257.

that opened in its place in 1853 continued this unifying idea by opening to the visitor's eye all the museum's treasures at once: its most cherished pictorial masterpieces on the top-floor balustrade and its most outstanding sculptures visible underneath. Not only did the new exhibit room connect the two levels; it also occupied the altar-like symbolic center where the museum's northern and southern wings met (fig. 15). Supported by columns positioned too close to each other, this two-level structure, however, spurred comparisons to "vulgar" places of entertainment, whose spectators were also encouraged to look down from the balustrades: the circus (Teatro Circo Price) and bull- and cockfighting arenas.[130] Art critic Federico Balart would later note that the only proper view of the paintings on the balustrade could be obtained from the chandelier hanging in the middle. Contemporary images, however, suggest that there was no such chandelier but rather an early version of a skylight.

The gallery continued the tradition of nineteenth-century aesthetic displays. It did not feature contemporary or exclusively Spanish art and thus did not identify the queen with her nation's artistic production. And since the room had no chronological order, it did not propose any version of Spain's history. Rather, the gallery delivered the monarchy's image as the guarantor of cultural abundance, the recipient or collector of artistic masterpieces, and the center of gravity for artists from different parts of the world. The idea that the monarchs were custodians of paintings and their courts melting pots for talents had never before been applied to Spanish art. It first appeared in the catalogue published in 1843, the year of Isabel's coming of age. In the catalogue, Pedro de Madrazo told readers a new story about the twofold role of the Spanish royalty. Of course, they were still glorified as collectors. But Madrazo also exalted the Spanish kings since the Habsburgs as international cultural intermediaries "guided by the generous idea that the cult of beauty is not subject to the miserable limitations of lands and climates, nor of an exclusive nationalism, contrary to the propagation of enlightenment." In such a rendering, the Spanish monarchs, "protecting with dignity artists from all nations" and employing "their gold" in order to "purchase" for Spain "an artistic civilization and the elements from which the Spanish school was created," laid the foundation of the national art.[131] Although it sounded lofty, Madrazo's account no longer had any ritual to offer: the kings simply used their (or the nation's) treasury to employ artists who would make Spanish artistic production possible.

Among the meanings hovering in and around Madrazo's explanation, several ideas were taking shape: the centralism of the Castilian court, the monarchs' merit as patrons, and the emergence of the national artistic school from international influences. And these were, precisely, the underlying principles of the Sala de la Reina Isabel, which exhibited masterpieces of all "schools" of all times, from Raphael to Velázquez. Symbolically, its exhibit glorified the queen as the heiress and the culminating figure of the two dynasties that commissioned and collected the paintings. The gallery's name, in not specifying which of the three queens it commemorated, transformed Isabel II into a spiritual daughter of her namesakes: Isabel the Catholic queen, who was officially considered the founder of Spain's first dynasty, and Isabel of Braganza, who was considered the founder of the Royal Museum. After the nationalization of the museum in the 1870s, it was decided that the gallery was, after all, dedicated to Isabel of Braganza, the founding mother, whose name was then written above the entrance. Yet in 1858, a statue of Isabel II was installed in the middle of the sculpture gallery, visible from the balustrade. Thus, in the museum's most innovative endeavor there lay a new definition of monarchy as an entity that invested its resources wisely enough to foster competitive domestic production.

With the Crown becoming a force behind Spain's artistic development, the Museo Real ought to account for the school of art that supposedly resulted from this benefaction. Yet two issues still had to be resolved to tell such a story: time and space. The battle over the representation of the Spanish school as unified and centralized had been unfolding since the early 1830s in José de Madrazo's Royal Lithographic Establishment. The catalogue of José de Madrazo's own private art gallery, however, classified schools by localities, according to what he called the "most general opinion."[132] When in 1833 Spain was divided into provinces modeled on the French *departements*, it would have seemed natural to allow the Museo Real to represent the local artistic traditions as manifestations of provincial idiosyncrasies, as the catalogue of the Museo

Nacional did. In fact, this is how Spanish art was also classified in the Spanish Gallery inaugurated in 1838 in the Louvre. Yet although they were personal friends with the author of that gallery's catalogue, Baron Taylor, the Madrazos considered it a mistake or even a "stupidity" (as Federico de Madrazo stated in a letter to his father) to use these classifications.[133] For thinkers like José de Madrazo, rooted in Enlightenment ideas, which did not account for progress in art, the historic evolution of the national school over time was a problem more complicated than its stylistic unity across Spain's territory. This is why, as director, Madrazo left virtually intact his predecessors' taxonomic principle of dividing the collection by national "schools" without a time line.[134]

If both generations of the Madrazo family agreed that it was unpatriotic to distinguish multiple artistic traditions in Spain, they also found it convenient to centralize the "Spanish school" by uniting it around the royal court of the country's capital, Madrid. Hence the national cultural map constructed under their leadership was not a federated space or even a territory divided into provinces, but rather a token of royal sovereignty oblivious to the peripheries. In the early 1860s, Federico de Madrazo explained the new display that he implemented once he became director in this way: the "endless and pointless dividing and subdividing" only reflected "how costly the formation of the political unity of the Spanish nation must have been, considering the deplorable tendency, so common among us, to divide ourselves into small fractions instead of grouping in order to form one unified totality."[135] Such an interpretation of Spanish art went explicitly against the cultural policy of the state, which was interested in redistributing artistic traditions among its new administrative entities, especially when Federico de Madrazo affirmed that "the motherland of Velázquez and Murillo, Ribera, Zurbarán, Juanes, and Alonso Cano does not need to subdivide its school into provinces."[136] In the meantime, from the liberal camp, there was a movement to configure a "Madrid school" as merely another provincial tradition rather than the center of the national art.

Creating a plausible exhibit of diverse artistic threads interwoven into one became a task that Federico de Madrazo took on during his directorship in 1860–68. We know about his reorganization, as well as his motives, from his brother's 1872 catalogue, published after the museum was nationalized but featuring quotes from Federico de Madrazo's 1864 memorandum. Apparently, the reform implemented the project that Madrazo's predecessors had rejected in 1826: exhibiting Spanish art in the central gallery. With the museum's main entrance, facing the Prado Promenade, never open, visitors would step inside through the northern doors (currently the Goya entrance). Then, the grand enfilade would open before their eyes, leading from the northern rotunda and then through the "contemporary" gallery, all the way to the exhibit dedicated to old Spanish masters. Having reached the middle of that gallery, visitors would see to their left a door with curtains into the sacrosanct Sala de la Reina Isabel. If they continued straight, however, patrons could find works by old Italian masters who influenced the Spanish artists whose paintings they had just seen. In other words, Federico de Madrazo's new floor plan unfolded in a genealogical timeframe, from the "contemporaries" to the "old masters" to their Italian teachers.

Thus, if the original Royal Museum was mostly taxonomic and devoid of any history besides the division of Spanish art into old and new, the expansions undertaken by José and Federico de Madrazo starting in the late 1830s, from the historical galleries to the reorganized exhibit of the Spanish school, had consistent historical claims. The chronology that the museum conveyed was immersed in the genealogical time of sacral royalty and in the timeless cult of individual geniuses like Velázquez and Murillo, whom one Catholic newspaper even called "the chiefs [*jefes*] of our pictorial school."[137] Nonetheless, the Museo Real was not immune to the idea that an intimate connection existed between arts and crafts and the nations' industrial development. Following his father's lead, Federico de Madrazo added to the display of Spanish art objects made of semiprecious stones from the royal collections. In 1865, the director of London's South Kensington Museum, on a visit to Madrid, appreciated his efforts and was reported to have "especially loved the crystal chalices" whose display was about to be unveiled.[138]

MUSEUM AND SPECTACLE

Despite the directors' intentions otherwise, this modest yet undoubtedly modern admission of crafts connected the museum to the displays emerging all around the Prado. As Oscar E. Vázquez convincingly argues, there were no private art dealers in Spain until the later part of the century.[139] Public exhibitors—the Museo Real; the Academia San Fernando, hosting the annual exhibitions that in 1856 morphed into national art salons; and the state, organizing its own Museo Nacional—thus did not have to compete with modernized commercial venues.[140] Rather, the main competitors for displaying public art to the Spanish domestic population were flea markets, churches, and fairs. Since the 1830s, this list also included new visual shows clustered on the Prado Promenade. Take, for example, the diorama installed in the summer of 1838 in front of Martínez's Silver Factory (Platería)—one of the few places in Madrid where young men from working- and middle-class families could receive lessons in drawing and life modeling.

The location in front of the Museo Real, as Lee Fontanella states, was more than appropriate for such an innovative illusion: this was a triumph of art as artifice.[141] The drawings of the monastery of El Escorial by Jean Blanchard, a French engraver who also made copies of paintings for José de Madrazo's Lithographic Establishment, were combined to create a realistic illusion complete with light and sound effects: the smoke of incense, "the light evanescing and coming back again, . . . solemn religious chants accompanied by an organ instilling them with respect and veneration," and "a choir and a community of Capuchin friars looking as if they were real."[142] Three additional "vistas"—by that time a common genre—accompanied the show.[143] Enclosed, perfectly accessible, and transparent, this miniature world satisfied the bourgeois obsession with visibility while also creatively playing out the voyeuristic interest in grasping the inside and the outside at a glance. Crucially, though, the modern technology employed in this diorama created an effect of complete immersion that, in Luxenberg's incisive reading, "produced a visual characteristic that was closely associated with the Spanish school of painting: unmediated realism."[144] Concomitant with the opening of the Spanish Gallery in the Louvre and drawn by French artists, this attraction thus directly connected the Museo Real with both the foreign art markets and the emerging bourgeois culture in Spain—something that no conventional art exhibit could offer at the time. No wonder that even the governing queen took her daughter, Queen Isabel, to see the diorama.

That installation was popular enough to last until 1846,[145] but two decades would pass before, in 1867, another optical spectacle came to the Prado: a telescope. For a fee of one real, one could use the telescope to see the moon and the stars. Journalists and poets seemed uneasy with the presence of both sexes at the apparatus (fig. 16). Poet Antonio de San Martín even pushed the rules of the Spanish language to account for gender diversity in the audience:

> melancholy planet
> so close to Earth
> is contemplated with great attention
> by all men and all women [todos y todas].[146]

The power to capture unobstructed space with the help of drawing, perspective, and light that the diorama and the telescope conferred was one pillar of midcentury visual culture. The other was the ability to capture human nature by means of technology-enhanced eyesight. Scholars have argued that the fascination with eyesight itself, with the process of looking as a way of deciphering an illusion, was partially responsible for the success of photography.[147] In the middle of the century, this new medium stole the crowd's attention away from the visual attractions of late eighteenth- and early nineteenth-century "popular physics."[148] In 1837, Mesonero Romanos introduced his audience to the predecessors of Daguerre's method: the pantograph, the diagraph, and the torno de retrato, an invention useful for making copies of bas-reliefs.[149] The photographic experiments of Daguerre and others, well known in Spain, highly interested the Madrazos. Federico authored early descriptions of the camera obscura built by the artist José Ramos Zapetti, with whom he studied in Rome.[150] José de Madrazo personally met Daguerre and was the one who introduced his method in

EL TELESCOPIO DEL PRADO

—Yo voy á ver el planeta Vénus; ¡y ustedes, señoritas?
—Nosotras quisiéramos ver si por allá arriba queda todavía algun primo.

FIG. 16 "The Prado telescope." "—I am going to see the planet Venus; and you, Señoritas?""—And we'd like to see if we still have a cousin over there." *Gil Blas*, August 14, 1867.

Spain. The Madrazos' support for modern technology that seemed to challenge the value of pictorial art shows just how closely the interests of the elites were intertwined with emerging bourgeois culture in Spain.

The rapidly accumulating technological innovations, however, were not helping to unveil the mystery of vision or abolish the power of the unseen, and so, according to Gillen D'Arcy Wood, the spectacular visual experiences produced a countermovement: the Romantic cult of the imagination, the only human capacity for grasping the invisible and the hidden.[151] Thus, although the directors of the Museo Real were interested in photography, they also had the option of staging, inside the museum, a world that appealed to the imagination and resisted the almost overpowering realm of illusion, commerce, consumption, and sports unfolding right outside the museum's walls. The museum's role in cultural modernization was enormous, but its tensions with the visual culture of the Paseo del Prado were, for the time being, making it invisible.

For example, the new schedule of admission, introduced by José de Madrazo, adapted the Royal Museum to modern regimes of time in Spain's capital, where, as evidenced in Mesonero Romanos's 1831 *Manual*, days were now being sliced by a timetable of meals, work, and recreation and where the agrarian cycle had already been split into weeks, further divided by workdays and weekends, and interrupted by holidays that no longer corresponded to festivals. Until 1838, while the museum was open to the "public" on Wednesdays and Saturdays, middle-class liberal writers denounced its servility toward the aristocracy by keeping the museum closed on the workers' only free day, Sunday. In 1836, the satirical daily *El Jorobado* published a story about a woman (supposedly a cultured bourgeois) who only succeeded in receiving a pass to visit the collection outside of the general admission hours when she convinced her cook to write a letter to the director in her name, full of vulgarities and spelling mistakes and confessing her disgust for the common people who flooded the museum on the days when it was open to the public. (The underlying critique was that for a Spanish bourgeois, the aristocrats were just as vulgar and illiterate as the masses with whom they did not want to mix.) In 1838, when José de Madrazo was appointed director of the museum, the day it was open to common visitors became Sunday.[152] The working classes would have to be content. There was, however, a particular reason for the change: considering the museum to be a place where artists could copy classical paintings, Madrazo wished to leave artists alone and undisturbed on other days of the week. He even enlisted the queen's supposed "maternal interest" in making the institution serve the needs of artists-in-training. On a day when the museum was not open to the public, one could still receive access by presenting a foreign passport or a temporary address in Madrid.

José de Madrazo's interest in improving national pictorial production through the training of artists was rooted in the Enlightenment approach. Now that the Romantic cult of artistic genius was capturing the attention of the younger generation, including Madrazo's sons Federico and Pedro, it was even easier to justify the museum's narrowing of its intended visitorship beyond the already limited definitions of the "public" that the emerging bourgeoisie was rehearsing elsewhere. Both José and Federico de Madrazo had interacted with that public at the Academy exhibitions. At the museum entrusted to them, they avoided dealing with this public's claims and did not miss an opportunity to criticize the "profanes," even when these were distinguished courtiers and politicians.[153] In the meantime, the catalogues written by Pedro de Madrazo avoided mentioning the dilettanti, and distinguished instead between "intelligent people and professors who do not need to know someone else's judgment or feeling in order to judge art," on the one hand, and the "nonintelligent" viewers who "only learn certain vague and indefinite terms which they tend to apply at whim," on the other.[154] Pedro de Madrazo was a Romantic fiction writer and essayist, and beyond the museum catalogues, his other publications tended to exalt the geniuses, "beings privileged by nature, predestined to cause admiration of those similar to them," those "who would not trade even for royal powers the sublime secrets unattainable to those who call themselves *aficionados*."[155]

Of course, the midcentury dilettanti were not the old aristocrats engaged in self-education, but rather uninitiated middle-class visitors. Consider this self-named art-lover who wrote to Federico de Madrazo:

> Sr. Madrazo: I would like to ask, as a favor, for one of your passes, the green one (that does not expire) because, fortunately or unfortunately, I have a lot of free time on my hands with which I don't know what to do. I am an aficionado of painting and, although I am not an artist, when I see a good picture I cannot get it out of my head [en viendo un cuadro bueno *no se me despinta*]. I really want to see all that because it's been *at least* fourteen years that I haven't been there.[156]

It is easy to see why laughing at such expressions of the "love of art" became a part of the denunciation of "fake culture" (*la cursilería*) that, in Noël Valis's analysis, middle-class laymen used in order to appear more distinguished.[157] For example, Antonio Flores, a writer from the circle of the young Madrazos, described as pseudo-cultured the dilettanti flocking into the museum on Sundays: "men without . . . brains, . . . spending their entire lives in finding out about the society's taste, only to believe that it is their own."[158] This is how the idle spending of free time in the museum, which had hitherto been encouraged, became an activity that was somewhere between laughable and base, while the notion of taste, so fundamental for the Enlightenment, was reserved for artists only.

Still, the directors' neat scheduling plans did little to keep different groups of visitors apart, revealing instead how much the notion of the "public" itself was changing. Romantic aesthetics dictated that one could only understand art by practicing it, and hence copying paintings gradually became a part of education. The governing queen took the lead; the paintings taken to her and her daughters' residence for copying ranged from Raphael's *The Holy Family* (*La Perla*) to Dutch genre scenes. The fashion for copying canvases also reached the middle classes. For the circles outside of the Academia San Fernando, copying was not only educational but also a commercial activity fueled by an expanding market for utilitarian paintings—at the time, mostly religious compositions and still lifes (often advertised as "dining-room paintings"), used everywhere from chapels to taverns.

Starting in 1843, all visitors coming into the museum when it was closed to the general public had to sign a guest book. Until 1856, copyists signed the books together with other visitors; afterwards, a special list was instituted for them to sign every time they entered the museum. In comparing the numbers of visitors featured in Géal's compilation, one can estimate that in 1843 there were between sixty and one hundred copyists per month working at the museum.[159] Given these numbers and the commercial side of their activity, it would be hard to imagine that these people were quietly immersed in their work. And in fact, in an 1856 letter José de Madrazo admitted that he had to move Velázquez's *The Surrender of Breda* to another room so that it could be copied without disturbance from "those who under the pretext of painting come to the museum to talk and waste the time of the artists who are productively working."[160] In the early 1860s, then, the directors felt a need to regulate the copyists' behavior.

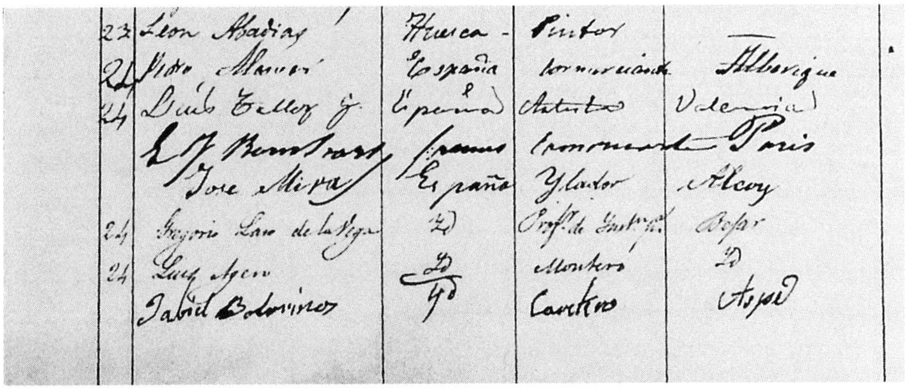

FIG. 17   Guest book of the Museo Real, September 24, 1859, signed by José Mira, a spinner (*ylador*) from Alcoy, Luis Agero, a beater (*montero*) from Béjar, and Gabriel Bolovinos(?), a cabinetmaker (*gavetero*) from Aspe. The last visitor's handwriting suggests limited proficiency. The Fall Fair of 1859 opened three days earlier. Archivo del Museo Nacional del Prado.

According to the rules adopted in 1863, museum employees had to prevent the copyists not only from coming too close to the canvases or measuring their surfaces, but also from "smoking, singing, whistling, placing announcements or drawings on the walls, speaking in loud voices, reading newspapers or other print media, walking up and down the rooms, [and] gathering in a circle with other copyists, thereby distracting others from their occupations."[161] The gathering in groups, walking, and shouting that the directors did not tolerate inside the museum were normal activities on the Prado Promenade.

Géal's calculations show that by the 1860s, even on the days when the museum was closed to the public, foreigners did not constitute the majority of the visitors. In 1860, for example, there were 1,113 visitors from Spain's provinces—excluding the copyists—and fewer than 1,000 foreigners (319 visitors from France, 213 British visitors, 70 Italians, 62 Germans, 58 Americans, etc.).[162] The French and British travelers were distributed rather evenly over the year, showing only slight increases in May. Meanwhile, the numbers of domestic visitors doubled or tripled in May and September through October, the months when Madrid celebrated festivals and fairs from the San Isidro to the Fall Fair. Many of these guests had considerable difficulty even writing their names or professions (fig. 17): "shoemaker," "employee," "salesman," "laborer," "ironsmith," "blacksmith," and "baker" were often written in shaky hands and misspelled.[163] Although these museumgoers did not leave us written accounts of their impressions, middle- and upper-class writers did not fail to notice their presence and reflect on, or imagine, their reactions. The result was a new genre of writing—narratives about lower-class visitors that supported the pundits' growing discomfort with the "contamination" of museum art with attitudes rehearsed in the street. In the middle of the century, debates about the Academia San Fernando's annual fine arts exhibitions already revealed a need to mark a clear distance between museum art and popular visual culture—to show that art was not "some sort of cosmorama or fantasmagorama to fascinate village folks and service maids," as one writer put it.[164] Others, conversely, argued that popular culture was no different than the scenes displayed in the museum. In 1849, when the city authorities banned a circus advertisement from Madrid's Puerta del Sol under the pretext that its colors were too vivid and its content too bloody, the liberal writer and publisher Wenceslao Ayguals de Izco claimed that images such as these were no different from the gems of the Museo Real.[165]

At a time when the most popular paintings that artists produced were large-sized spectacular compositions, highly influenced by these very "cosmoramas" and "fantasmagoramas," separating high art from popular visual culture was becoming a common concern. In 1834 and 1835, Pedro de Madrazo penned the earliest essays reflecting on the changing museum visitorship. Though he followed Mérimée's earlier criticism of visitors attracted to realism and disappointed with the old masters, unlike Mérimée, Pedro de Madrazo did not spare anyone who was not an artist. He made all visitors equally guilty of loving verisimilitude and of looking at the paintings' subject matter as if it were merchandise on display. Madrazo's 1835 essay equally repudiated a clerk charmed by a painting of partridges and an upper-class aficionado "who . . . neglected to study or dedicate himself to anything" on the grounds that they avoided the paintings looking "old and dark" and could not resist the attraction of a "really well *taken* . . . calf's head"—as if the still life was a vending stall.[166] In an essay published a year earlier and reportedly reflecting an equally true event, Madrazo described the same adoration of nature "well taken" by "soldiers and village folks."[167] Engaged in a discussion about "whether *The Surrender of Breda* did or did not represent Our Lord giving the keys to Saint Peter," these visitors criticized Velázquez's generals for being "hardly well taken." Madrazo described everybody's tastes as equally "profane" and portrayed their remarks as coming from idle "men for whom fine arts are solely a pastime, a distraction, a *pretty entertainment*." Meanwhile, he continued, in the Italian room, an "unexpressive twelve- or thirteen-year-old with a wicked face looking like he had escaped from a Latin class" was observing too closely Titian's *Venus and Adonis*, obviously enthralled by the composition's erotic charge.

For Madrazo and others considering themselves authorities, these clueless museumgoers erred on multiple accounts: seeking recognition for their tastes, using the museum for leisure, being unable to interpret the nude, and confusing public historical art with commodities or objects of religious worship. It was a battlefield reflective and symptomatic of the new reality of an expanding museum visitorship. "Have you been to the Museum of Paintings on the days when it was open to the public?" asked Eladio Lezama on the pages of *El Arte* before confessing that he sometimes allowed himself this "entertainment": "[The] first thing that I find in the museum is the inevitable group of people in ecstasy in front of a painting that shares with the 'house of beasts' [a small zoo in the Retiro Park] and the Chinese tam-tam its appeal to all hicks coming to the capital: the *painting of hunger* [*The Famine in Madrid*, by José Aparicio]. Rarely have I stopped next to these innocent simpletons who gather around this canvas as if they were its guard of honor, without hearing them say: 'that little bread roll looks real!'"[168] The author's aesthetic zeal notwithstanding, his repudiation of the masses' excessive love for realism and fascination with represented food was accompanied by the tacit use of the museum for people-watching and entertainment, which were, in reality, just as far (or further) removed from the aesthetic appreciation that the exhibit was intended for as what the subjects of his joke were doing. The debate between the approach to art as object—denied legitimacy—and as a part of middle-class entertainment—considered acceptable—would fully take shape in later years when the museum acquired new meaning as a national institution. But one can already see the three opposing positions.

On one side of the triangular debate were the writers, described above, who demanded greater autonomy for the arts and greater recognition for artists. On another were middle-class writers who portrayed their uneducated fellow citizens sympathetically. The writers of the liberal *El Clamor Público*, for example, displayed solidarity with those who had a realistic take on art, and even revealed a curious lack of knowledge about the architect who designed the Museo Real:

> The widows and the unemployed . . . pay frequent visits to the public exhibition that we . . . know as the *Museum of the Passive Classes*. This museum, whose treasures all our subscribers, no matter how indifferent to . . . fine arts, have admired, does not occupy a separate building, similar to the one that the famous architect Juan de Herrera [*sic!*] erected on the Prado. . . . Rather, it is spread in a series of galleries that do not connect to each other. Nor is it a museum of paintings or etchings or sculptures but rather of four-legged animals, birds, fishes, and sea creatures: its rooms are none other than the sumptuous store windows of taverns, eateries, and restaurants, where the hungry populace's eyes are exposed to the splendor of a heavy lamb shank, innocent dove, fresh monkfish, and putrid oyster. Poor passive classes pay daily *external* tribute of blind idolatry to the scandalous attraction of such masterpieces, daughters of wise nature.[169]

On the third side were writers who opposed the utilitarianism that they attributed to the working classes while also seeking other uses for art. Albeit less practical, these uses were related to the bourgeois entertainment of both the serious and the naughty kind. Paintings could, for example, provide inspiration for theatrical costumes. In 1847, one reviewer advised his readers to "pay a visit to the Museum of Paintings and consult Titian's portrait of Carlos V" to see how that character had to be represented.[170] In

1865, the reviewer of Verdi's *Hernani* at the Teatro Real in Madrid praised the clothing designed by decorator Aldighieri for being copied from Titian.[171] Less respectable uses of art for entertainment brought erotic overtones into the museum experience. "Who would not remember a woman's naked belly and the beginning of a thigh half-covered by a gracefully wrapped fabric?" fantasized a contributor to *Arte en España*, describing the restoration of the marble statues.[172] Surprisingly, these associations were still considered more acceptable than the working-class quest for realism that the bourgeois writers attributed to the influence of commerce and entertainment.

Some democratically minded commentators, however, felt a need to empower the masses and encourage their active engagement with the museum. In his highly successful 1843 serial novel *Maria, a Laborer's Daughter*, the republican writer Wenceslao Ayguals de Izco suggested that the lower classes had an innate understanding of artistic technique and composition, portraying his humble female protagonist as intuitively drawn to Velázquez (fig. 18). As for the supporters of entertainment, for a while they could not be unequivocally classified as bourgeois either: the museum imagery was most popular among the practitioners of *tableaux vivants*, a middlebrow theater genre and an upper-class pastime coming from France that involved the imitation of pictures by actual people and was only beginning to approach bourgeois standards of refinement.

In the middle of the century, the growing fascination with *tableaux vivants* created a connection to the Museo Real in the minds of the inhabitants and the visitors of Madrid, though only a few of them ever saw the actual paintings upon which the *tableaux* were based. Unlike the earlier prototypes projected on the streets and in ephemeral seasonal venues, midcentury "living pictures" initially were less a historical gallery and more an erotic display. Just as in midcentury London, relocating the images from the highly encoded museum space to outside and making them "live" spurred recurrent debates about the female body as an object of representation and the difference that it made when no longer painted on canvas. A journalist covering a French show by Mme. Tournour, on tour through Spain in 1849, even refused to discuss the live paintings' artistic merit, announcing instead that "the aficionados of good lines will not stop directing their binoculars at the company's female constituency."[173]

A year later, coinciding with the City's authorization of masquerades during Carnival, Madrid's aristocrats started staging their own shows, this time with bourgeois women taking the lead. The author covering one such event seemed pressured to assert that this was a decent entertainment, performed for a "circle of immediate friends" from "good society" and quite different from the spectacle offered by Mme. Tournour: "this . . . is nothing like imitating that [show], but rather . . . mak[ing] it greater, rehabilitat[ing] it, return[ing] to it its artistic qualities, transforming what used to be an inconvenient and almost repugnant show into a respectable and entertaining performance." The paintings represented on this occasion were religious and allegorical compositions, most of them from the collection of the Museo Real.[174]

FIG. 18   "This half-nude figure in the center represents Bacchus." Vicente Urrabieta, illustration for
Wenceslao Ayguals de Izco, *María, la hija de un jornalero* (Maria, a Laborer's Daughter), vol. 2, 31
(Madrid: Wenceslao Ayguals de Izco, 1847).

The references to *tableaux vivants* became a common cliché ensuring wide circulation of the museum metaphors beyond the context of art. Some of the printed
descriptions of "living pictures" revealed their authors' continuing ignorance about the
museum and the paintings that they evoked. *El Clamor Público* attributed Aparicio's
Glories of Spain to José de Madrazo, just as in the quote above it ascribed the museum
building to Juan de Herrera. Because until 1856 there were no plates with the authors'

names on the frames, it was hard to keep track of the collection without an in-depth study of the catalogue. However, even after the name plates were added, the liberal publications did not show any deeper knowledge of the art. In 1865, for example, the pro-republican *La Discusión* seemed to know so little about the actual paintings in the collection that it portrayed a son and a father, on a visit to the Prado for the San Isidro festival, engaged in a dialogue in front of an imaginary allegorical painting supposedly capturing the current state of political oppression in Spain.[175]

Apparently, their ignorance about the paintings did not stop writers or their read-ers from relying on these works in political debates. Selected exhibits at the museum, such as Aparicio's *The Famine in Madrid*, became especially popular material for liberal jokes, suggesting that in Spain's imagination the Museo Real continued to represent the Crown, albeit in ways that encouraged a light, easy discussion about its pressure on society. In the 1840s and '50s, those advocating a greater police presence on the Prado Promenade claimed that the museum surroundings featured "indescribable pictures" (*cuadros que no son para escritos*),[176] while journalists covering politics visualized current events as allegorical compositions similar to Aparicio's *Glories of Spain* or the infamous *Famine in Madrid*.[177] One writer joked, "[Neo-Catholic] newspapers insist that Spain's capital offers a picture of fear and consternation. With their permission, we would say that it actually offers many more than one such picture, as anyone who has seen the Museum of Paintings can testify."[178]

"Living pictures" were also bringing attention to the role that women played in the museum. Still, it is not clear whether the frequent references to women signified that their visitorship was on the rise or simply denoted the scandal that middle-class writers, not initiated into upper-class aesthetics, felt when facing the museum's queens or nudes. As described above, enough stories depicting male fascination with the painted or sculpted images of women or comparing real women to the images from the collection were published at that time to support this view, although the visitor books do not reflect any growth in female museum-going compared to the increasing number of women who copied paintings. Analyzing the guest books, I found no signature by a female visitor who was not a copyist or a wife of a foreigner signing together with her husband. This does not mean, of course, that women did not come to the museum on the days of public admission. The etching by Vicente Urrabieta for Ayguals de Izco's *Maria, the Laborer's Daughter* (fig. 18) playfully por-trays female visitors in front of Velázquez's *Bacchus*, but neither the artist nor the writer seemed to consider a woman looking at an image of a nude man a moral problem; this suggests that the museum space was so masculine that female spec-tatorship was simply not an issue. Yet while the respectability of some of the figures featured in the museum was a matter of dispute, women's journals did their best to dignify the experience of public art by referencing the religious imagery on display. Murillo's *Immaculate Conception*, in particular, became one of the most frequently cited exhibits following Pope Pius IX's dogmatic proclamation of immaculate conception in 1854.

And how did the museum now treat its foreign visitors? In its internal documents and official propaganda, foreigners still occupied a disproportionally high position. For example, when in the mid-1840s Richard Ford criticized the disorganization of the museum and the poor restoration of its paintings, Pedro de Madrazo felt so alarmed that he devoted eight (out of the total of ten) pages of the prologue of his new catalogue to refuting Ford's impressions.[179] One would imagine that close attention to international opinion corresponded to the Royal Museum's representative function. Thus, documents from the Madrazo family archive suggest that, at least until the end of Maria Cristina's regency, a circle of friends close to the ambassador of Denmark in Madrid used to patronize the museum by paying regular group visits during the late morning and afternoon. This group was like a civil society in miniature, or rather, the type of a society that was still cosmopolitan and dominated by aristocracy like the "public sphere" of the old regime. It was international, cross-generational, and did not discriminate against women: it included "ambassadors, the secretary of the French embassy, and other reputable characters, such as the minister from the United States with his daughter, famous for her beauty in Madrid society, different Spanish political figures, . . . and people whose names were linked to the palace administration."[180]

In time, domestic public opinion would become more critical of the museum's organization, while foreign visitors would continue filling the role of elitist art-lovers, providing the directors with much-needed support.[181] Starting in the 1850s, when the monarchy's financial shortages became a continuous challenge, the directors used a set of standard references to foreigners, "whose notable representatives of all classes come specifically to admire artistic treasures,"[182] in order to attract the queen's attention to the museum's needs. Foreign writings also constituted a huge proportion of literature about the Museo Real and were thus frequently used as a reliable source of information. Through the end of the century, everyone writing in Spain about the museum repeated Mérimée's description of it, popularized by Viardot in his *Les musées d'Espagne, d'Angleterre et de Belgique* (1843), as "one of the richest in Europe," while seemingly ignoring the fact that Viardot's was a very qualified message: reflecting the changing international expectations from art museums, it was undergirded by complaints about the lack of historical or any other order in the Spanish display and the comparison of it to an "amateur cabinet."[183]

The demands for a rational display representing the history of all pictorial traditions, which dominated the debates in other European museums, were only making their way to Spain. The author of the most comprehensive critical overview from this perspective was none other than Francisco Pi y Margall, prominent liberal politician and the future president of Spain's First Republic. Deploring the lack of chronological order and separation by schools, he reminded his readers that "to reason means to serialize" and that "a museum should be art history." Pi y Margall proposed two solutions: one, exchange holdings with other museums to complete the "schools"; and two, avoid altogether the question of the schools, which was "dictated more by national spirit than by the need of critique," and reclassify the paintings according to a new dichotomy loosely resembling the separation between the classics and the romantics.[184] For the time being, his remarks, in saying that the museum's galleries, in lacking classification, resembled an *espectáculo*, repeated—yet also explained—the standard comparison of art to theater.

The museum's affinity to a theater and other types of shows was the subject of a discussion that was taking shape. Since bourgeois entertainment had yet to become a legitimate model for looking at art, most commentators found equally reprehensible the religious or utilitarian approaches taken by the common visitors, whom they blamed for comparing art to merchandise and shows, and by the dilettanti, who exhibited fake knowledge. Uncertainty among Spaniards about the museum's role allowed writers such as Eugenio de Ochoa, José de Madrazo's son-in-law, to claim that the Museo Real showcased the state patronage of the arts.[185] As late as 1867, Ochoa interchangeably credited the monarchs and what he called "government" for developing a "public spirit favorable to the support of fine arts."[186] Yet Ochoa reserved no agency for the middle or working classes, arguing instead that the government's role consisted in giving examples to the upper classes in order to spur their interest in art.

Meanwhile, the preferences of the Spanish middle-class visitors were most noticeable in their repeated demands to see Goya exhibited. Many liberals asked why they could not find Goya's works depicting the scenes of the anti-French rebellion in Madrid, imagining that José de Madrazo kept them in a "dark jail."[187] When Madrazo extracted both works from the vaults and put them on display in one of the Spanish rooms, critics still continued asking why he couldn't find a better place for them. The museum's consistent disengagement from the liberal cause and its reluctance to embrace vernacular viewpoints on art spurred the comparisons between the museum and the pantheon[188] and made more democratically minded authors reject it altogether. In 1867, Gregorio Cruzada Villaamil, the director of the state-run National Museum, lamented the fate of "works of art that have lost their true and personal mode of existence" and found refuge in the museum, dusty like the "attic of an old castle abandoned by its owner."[189] A year later, the owners would have to abandon the Royal Museum, ushering in a whole new set of questions about what it exhibited, how, and why.

CHAPTER THREE

Museum and Revolution, 1868–1874

ON THE NIGHT OF September 29 1868, "several groups of armed countrymen" approached the museum, took the sentries' rifles, and went on to disarm the remaining royal guards quartered in the Retiro.[1] Thus came to the Prado the revolution soon christened "Glorious" (*La Gloriosa*), which turned Spain into an elected monarchy and then a short-lived republic. The revolution coincided with the Fall Fair, and, according to the museum guest books, the dethronement of Isabel II did not keep artists-in-training, foreign visitors, or Spanish traders, students, and agricultural workers from turning up in large numbers to visit the Museo Real.[2] Two weeks later, as a royal possession, the museum was entrusted to a new council responsible for the former properties of the Crown.

The Museo Real could not go national overnight. There was no final handshake, no decisive single stroke of a pen that made it so. In December of 1868, the council responsible for it was transformed into a department within the Ministerio de Hacienda (Ministry of Finance), thus bringing the Museo Real as it had been to an anticlimactic end. Spanish publicists were unsatisfied with the limited degree of the museum's change. Foreign travelers insisted in calling it "Royal" long after its takeover. The real question, however, was what social agenda the institution would promote now that it did not have to channel monarchical propaganda or the social will of the elites. As fights continued in the streets and in the Cortes and as the identity of Spain's new rulers remained in flux, the museum's administration listened to everyone, from the supporters of constitutional monarchy to those who wished to see Spain a republic or even a federation of independent cantons. Such a shift toward representing the community rather than the government, thereby becoming national in a deeper, truer sense, was one of the revolution's least noticed but most lasting impacts on the museum. Even though the monarchy and later the very same Bourbons would soon be back, the National Museum of Painting and Sculpture, a prototype of today's Museo Nacional del Prado, would emerge from the turmoil as an entity engaged in the most pressing issues of the time: the workings of democracy, the impact of art on individuals, the progress of trade, the development of realist aesthetics, and the spread of socialist and anarchist ideologies.

Although artists were still running the museum, they were no longer recruited from the nobility of the times of Fernando VII and Isabel II. Unlike their predecessors, Antonio Gisbert (1868–73) and Francisco Sans Cabot (1873–81) easily found common ground with the authorities of Madrid in matters concerning the pastimes on and around the Prado: both wanted more street activity, but of a better-regulated kind. This did not mean, however, that the museum entered an epoch of harmony with its surroundings: instead of approaching its desired standards of a bourgeois "leisure zone," the Prado Promenade was becoming a setting for political demonstrations and class struggle.

DISPLAYING NATIONHOOD

If the former Museo Real was becoming national, what kind of national museum would it be? In 1868, there were a great variety of approaches to making "the nation a visible reality"—the process by which, as Susan Pearce argues, a "political abstraction" receives a "symbolic form in the shape of tangible 'masterpieces.'"[3] Spain's most radical reformers had plans for a cultural overthrow reminiscent of the Great French Revolution. In October 1868 (just weeks after the dethronement of Isabel II), the publisher and future urban planner Angel Fernández de los Ríos had already cited the proclamations issued by the 1790 Convention in France as an inspiration for demolishing old buildings and streets in Madrid.[4] Yet Spain's "liberal populace," and even some intellectuals, who now considered any exhibition of paintings and sculpture to be the heritage of a corrupt regime that sacrificed the nation's scientific flourishing for a self-congratulatory display of its rulers' artistic possessions, already found the French example wanting.

By 1868, the Louvre, whose rational floor plans continued to be an ideal that no European museum could yet rival, was no longer offering a revolutionary display. Napoleon III's commitment to finishing the construction of the building and enlarging the collection, now including the Museum of Sovereigns, which had opened in 1852, supported the identification of French nationhood with strong monarchy. The French museum exhibited works owned by the state together with those purchased by the new kings and the emperors, who would take these exhibits along with them each time another revolution forced them to leave.[5] The new leaders of the former Museo

Real had no desire to awaken the ghosts of royal restitutions—a matter only recently settled in Madrid—and wished to steer the meaning of "national" away from questions about the transfer of power for as long as the future of Isabel II's crown remained unclear. The near-destruction of the Louvre during the 1871 Paris Commune and the subsequent plans for making all museums and art galleries report to a self-governing artists' federation gave further proof that museums were better served by more inclusive images of community than those defined by their princes, whether they were called kings or emperors.

Luckily, there were other options when it came to the way in which a museum could put itself forward as "national." One such option was to define a museum's "national" relevance by its ability to showcase economic might and purchasing power. Since these were related to modern markets and territories, such museums took great pains to impress the viewers by emphasizing the positive effects of centralizing art collections. The museums choosing this approach could support any form of political power whose claims over a territory they could assert. The British Museum and National Gallery in London represented the state working together with civil society, while the Museums of Art History and Natural History in Vienna exhibited the imperial collections. The Belgian museums, on the other hand, still carried on the name of "Royal," although the holdings of the Royal Museum of Fine Arts of Belgium initially belonged to the City of Brussels (they were purchased by King Leopold I and donated to the state). Reflecting the territorial conflicts that centralization was causing, the collections of this type of national museum sometimes moved around the country.[6] Their ownership, shifting from the city to the state and back again, could just as often support the central government's claim to power as it could enhance a city's cultural might as a consolation prize for its loss of political importance.

Such territory-oriented displays often included artifacts from different regions—alongside items from current or former colonies in nations with overseas possessions—as well as antiquities, which were in steady supply thanks to the expanding numbers of archeological sites. It was Giuseppe Garibaldi who gave the Western world the first example of a revolutionary nationalization of a collection that did not merely contain paintings and sculptures when he renamed the Real Museo Borbonico in Naples (a collection of artifacts discovered in Pompeii) a *National* Museum (Museo Nazionale). When the Italian republic was founded in 1860, its government also acquired a reputation for centralizing heritage institutions and nationalizing formerly private collections, teaching the world how to use the "complex inheritance already imbued with its own meanings" to tell the story of a new nation.[7]

Meanwhile, in the German lands, other new museums calling themselves "national" supported different dynasties' claims to leading the unification efforts or reflected the need to balance royal, state, and municipal powers. Such was the case with the Germanisches Nationalmuseum in Nuremberg, inaugurated in 1852 with exhibits from private collections and later state purchases; the Bayerisches Nationalmuseum, opened in 1867 with the purpose of supporting Maximilian II's aspiration to revive the Holy Roman Empire; and the Alte Nationalgalerie on Museum Island in Berlin, created as a monument to the 1871 Prussian-led unification and the leadership of Kaiser Wilhelm I.[8]

In Catholic countries, the transfer of power from individual rulers—princes, kings, and emperors—to the state ran parallel to secularization efforts that brought to national museums works confiscated from religious communities. Regardless of their definition of nationhood, these displays depicted nations shedding their cults. This was, for example, the case with the Portuguese national museums, which would emerge only in 1880s but whose holdings, confiscated from suppressed monastic orders, were on exhibit at the Royal Academy of Portugal starting in the 1830s. In Italy, where disentailments followed unification, the nationalist identification with the church remained so strong that nationalization of its possessions was considered unpatriotic, and gossip soon began to spread that Italian revolutionaries were about to sell the papal treasures abroad.[9] Each government's handling of the collections that it was taking over therefore became a measure of state's ability to represent the nation.

While these approaches to nationhood reflected conflicting political claims, a few museum founders and curators were already of the opinion that nations did not need the mediation of monarchs, religious authorities, or state institutions to be represented. Seeking to invigorate communities and define the "people," some museums added special portrait galleries displaying the images of citizens in an effort to close the class, gender, and generation gaps between museum visitors and the subjects of paintings and sculpture. Though later in the century portrait galleries dedicated to contemporary men and women would appear all across Europe, the male prototype was already set in 1826 in the Hermitage Museum's gallery of the heroes of the Russian campaign against Napoleon in 1812, and later expanded by the British National Portrait Gallery, founded in 1856, which included portraits of British women.[10] In most European countries, however, civic art still projected the images of communities onto the nostalgic visions of their foundational moments recreated by contemporary artists. Museum authorities supporting this view of the nation preferred to commission works or purchase them from national salons and stayed away from the old historical compositions that figured prominently in some princely collections, seeing those works as glorifying the authority, whatever it was, rather than the "people."

What the "people" meant and whether the nationalist projections of it could withstand the test of class warfare were questions the European museum authorities were already trying to address. Hence, while the historical compositions and civic portraiture privileged the privileged, the creators of London's South Kensington Museum took on the task of recasting artisans as the nation's backbone by putting crafts and everyday objects on display. Archaeological findings exhibited alongside material heritage and samples of contemporary craftsmanship were believed to convey the spirit of the common people underrepresented in paintings and sculptures. Reflecting a view of society as a project of the educated elites working together with a small number of producers of artifacts, yet retaining the exclusive right to collect, classify, and exhibit their work, had, of course, its own class agenda, steeped in fear of the proletarians who were already organizing themselves on the grounds of class—not national—solidarity. In 1872, from Versailles (the provisional capital after the Paris Commune), the French National Assembly went so far as to refuse its support for workers' travel to the world's fair in Vienna, claiming that the previous London exhibition of 1862 had been a pretense for creating the Communist International.[11] Meanwhile, in Britain, where late Victorian liberal reformism was gaining force, making former privileges such as the contemplation of art available to the masses was becoming a tool of social co-option. Still, the view that nations could be represented by their artisans set in motion the most innovative thought about the museums' service to their people in the second half of the nineteenth century. Transmitting culturalist values inspired by the elites, promoting the attitudes of contemplation and reflection as prime human activities, and privileging the consensual notion of citizenship against the emerging awareness of class differences, art education and exposure to exhibits combining arts and crafts seemed to offer a magical remedy that would guarantee social peace while also moving forward the nations' economies.[12]

By the mid-1870s, as the outcomes of the Crimean and Franco-Prussian Wars made it clear that armies could only implement the economic forecasts scripted in the nations' factories, education reformers began to popularize the idea that craftsmen— and not the military—held the keys to their countries' future.[13] Deemed equally useful for educating artisans and taming the proletarians, museums acquired relevance that they had never enjoyed prior to the era of class struggle. Social reformers now judged cultural institutions by their effect on the masses, thus making art museums as important as other places of public leisure. In Britain, this reassessment of museums had been happening since the 1840s, when social reformists began to encourage museum-going together with membership in working men's clubs, athletic activities, and music hall entertainment.[14] Building on Michel Foucault, Tony Bennett has argued that as soft versions of madhouses and prisons, museums proved to be even more effective in disciplining the masses by making them visible to each other in the presence of objects organized as displays.[15] Although the origins of "rational recreation" lay in private entrepreneurship, it was the state, Bennett argues, that would capitalize on the effects of this and other programs aimed at encouraging people to become self-improving citizens. The fact that monitored leisure did not pretend to forge group identities or class consciousness seemed particularly useful given the fears of revolution.

The economic competition, wars, and class struggle that had marked European political life since the 1850s reinvigorated art museums by opening new possibilities

105

for them as entities capable of representing the nations while also palliating class conflicts. There were many concepts of nationhood that Spanish government officials taking over the Museo Real could choose from. Spain's new National Museum could give more prominence to the state's efforts to make Spain an elected monarchy and a secular nation, downplay or enhance the role of Madrid, choose a social group to represent, pick a new genealogy for a post-Bourbon country, or opt for a progressive forward-looking time line; it could even forget about history altogether and put Spain forward as a country savoring its present and looking into the future. The museum could, furthermore, focus on old or new paintings, religious or secular art, scenes of war or peace, portraits or landscapes; its displays could give greater prominence to the marble statues of ancient democracies or sculptures of Spain's current rulers or add to the collection archeological findings or artisanry. Each of these options came with its own idea of how museums should use admission policies and collection development to shape their relationship with society at large. Yet although those who would debate the future of the royal art collection in Spain showed remarkable awareness of these options, and even added some more of their own, their proposals rarely left the pages of official memoranda to be presented to the general public. This was, in part, due to the complexities of postrevolutionary restitution in a country whose territorial integration was weak and whose tradition of representative government was still in its infancy.

SIX REVOLUTIONARY YEARS

What Spanish historians call the "six revolutionary" or "six democratic" years started on September 19, 1868, when Admiral Juan Bautista Topete, stationed on a warship in the Bay of Cádiz, printed proclamations of rebellion against the government of Isabel II and arranged for them to be scattered around the town. In the following days, the uprising, initiated by navy officials offshore, spread to the mainland, where it received official backing from generals and politicians who had been conspiring against Isabel II from abroad and who now returned home. Soon all the garrisons of Andalusia in southern Spain had joined the movement, demanding a new constitution, universal suffrage, guarantees of individual freedoms, and, eventually, the abolition of army conscription. The queen, who at the time was taking sea baths in the northern resort town of San Sebastián on the far side of the country, quickly reorganized her cabinet and moved the remaining loyal troops against the insurgents. Nonetheless, by the end of September the loyalist army had been defeated and Isabel had escaped to France, from which she later issued a manifesto announcing her imminent return. In the meantime, power in Madrid had passed to a revolutionary junta that declared the creation of a provisional government.

The new government's first concern was to disassemble the revolutionary juntas in the provinces and suppress those claiming that the revolution's logical outcome had to be a republic. In order to join forces against the growing republican mood, in November of 1868 the parties that had led the revolution created the so-called Great Liberal Union, whose stated objective was the establishment of a constitutional monarchy. They promised that the new regime would not be a "monarchy of divine right," but rather a "popular" one that "we will establish by our own votes."[16] The provisional government set February 1869 as the date for the election of the Constituent Cortes. On that date, for the first time in Spain's history, liberals saw in action direct "universal" suffrage without any property qualifications for voters (though they still had to be male). Yet the voting age, set for twenty-five instead of twenty as the Republicans had demanded, excluded many young men leaning toward republicanism, and, additionally, the property qualifications were kept intact for citizens of Spain's remaining colonies.

Many were not satisfied with these improvements of Spain's political culture by the provisional government and thought the reforms should be broader and more far-reaching. Already by December of 1868 the army had to be called in to suppress new uprisings around Cádiz. When the Constituent Cortes were finally elected, the Republicans found themselves in a solid minority, and although Juan Prim, one of the fathers of the Revolution, had promised that the Bourbons would "Never! Never! Never!" return to the Spanish throne, there were no Republicans on the committee in charge of drafting the new constitution. The new constitution thus defined Spain as a monarchy, naming the president of the provisional government the "regent," compensated by the title of "Highness."

A month after the election, the statue of Isabel II, the old-time symbol of the new regime that had adorned the building of the Cortes, was reclassified as a work of art and transferred to the sculpture collection of the former Museo Real. While the revolution had happened during the Fall Fair, the arrival of the new rule in Madrid coincided with the circle of spring festivals between San Isidro and San Juan and was celebrated with the customary fireworks and bullfights. But as the government was debating the options for future governance, the museum's status as royal property remained undecided. In late November of 1868, Federico de Madrazo, who had run the museum since 1860, was fired and the provisional government appointed Antonio Gisbert as his successor. Gisbert was a history artist known for his liberal political views and his personal friendship with the leaders of the revolution.

General Serrano became the regent of Spain, and the presidency passed to Prim. A committee was soon established to lead the search for a democratically elected monarch. Prim's first speech on that subject, however, made it clear that even in the eyes of the leaders it was hard to find a king for "a country where there have occurred events such as we have ourselves seen."[17] This is how it happened that in June 1870, almost two years after the revolution, there was still no indication as to who would become Spain's next king. Some negotiations, though, were continuing behind tightly closed doors. The reason for so much secrecy became clear when a new finalist, the Prussian Prince Leopold of Hohenzollern, was announced. The French government, already on the verge of war with Prussia, was not amused; they demanded that Spain withdraw the offer and pressured the Prussian ambassador to seek Leopold's refusal. Even though Leopold did eventually renounce his candidacy, France declared war on Prussia anyway. Meanwhile, Spain announced neutrality and continued the negotiations with another candidate, the prince of Aosta, second son of the king of Italy, Victor Emmanuel II, and Maria-Adelaide of Habsburg-and-the-Lorraine. In November of 1870, the prince accepted the invitation to become King Amadeo I. As for France, it eventually lost the war with Prussia.

Since Spain's government, involved in a search for a new king, had to select the properties to offer to the finalist, the former Museo Real was officially separated from the possessions essential for the royal family and became the property of the state. The formal takeover was now finalized. But the reorganized entity needed statutes and a payroll, and as the future ruler remained uncertain, the government was in no hurry to create this legal framework. It took a disaster to bring the museum's status to its attention. In January of 1870, the public official in charge of the former property of the Crown announced the disappearance of several cartoons for the Royal Tapestry Factory which had been stored in the basement of the royal palace. Among them were six works by Goya. The next month, after a public outcry, the remaining cartoons were transferred to the Museo de la Trinidad, and the Ministerio de Fomento, concerned about the fate of the artistic property of the former monarchy, demanded control over the Royal Museum.[18] Five days later, the Fomento officially reclaimed the museum from the Hacienda, and in another month, on March 22, 1870, the regent of the kingdom issued a decree putting the former Museo Real under the new entity.[19] The museum would report to this state institution until the beginning of the twentieth century, when the Dirección General de Instrucción Pública y Bellas Artes became an autonomous government ministry.

The sculptor José Gragera, who had worked at the Museo Real since the mid-nineteenth century and became deputy director after the revolution, was appointed to represent the government at the official takeover. His diligent report gives us a glimpse of what kind of institutional culture the state was inheriting together with the former Royal Museum. Some paintings and sculptures had been decommissioned; other objects had disappeared without any written order or even the smallest indication of where they had gone. Thirty-five topazes, emeralds, and rubies were missing from a mosaic table that apparently no one had checked for decades. In the 6,037 pages of "a book inappropriately called *inventory*" (emphasis in original), "everything is in conflict and in disarray and nothing is in place," Gragera reported.[20]

"Next to famous canvases which the entire world admires there is an old mask, a chair without a seat, and objects destroyed by time, humidity, and dust." It took a month to verify the inventory, and upon reading his report the government officials were quick to understand that a new and better-organized list was the first order of business. In October of 1870, the regent of the kingdom set up a special commission for writing a new inventory and finding the missing paintings and sculptures.[21] But the work of this commission was soon to be overshadowed by a radical change of plans.

Ever since the former Museo Real began to report to the Fomento, there had been questions in the air about how this new National Museum would relate to the other National Museum, the Museo de la Trinidad, under the auspices of the same ministry. Merely a month after the takeover, Gisbert sent to his new superiors an extended memorandum proposing to merge the two museums. In the director's view, eliminating their redundancy would allow the government to save money, while the nation would obtain a "center of the arts . . . promoted to occupy the first place among all museums of Europe."[22] Specifically, in Gisbert's view, the merger would result in a more complete and coherent collection, make it possible to keep the museum open every day of the week, and generate funds to support additional staff, including a gardener who had formerly been employed by the court.[23]

The proposals for the merger of the two museums had actually circulated for decades.[24] But although by September of 1870 the idea definitely had supporters even in the government, the details were not easy to negotiate. It was hard to decide what had to come first: the new and expanded physical museum or a legal entity with statutes and regulations. Or perhaps it was hard to decide whether anything at all should be done for as long as the country's political future remained unclear. Nevertheless, in November of 1870, Prim created a special commission charged with putting together a proposal for the merger.[25] The decree that created the commission also mentioned the prompt creation of a separate museum of contemporary art with paintings purchased from national and international exhibitions. If realized, the three tasks would bring Spain up to speed with the exhibiting institutions in Britain and France. On December 2, 1870, just a few days after the commission was created, Pedro de Madrazo, who was asked to catalogue the merged collection, proposed to name the new institution the "Museo del Prado" to eliminate any possible confusion with the old National Museum and, perhaps, obliterate the question of ownership altogether.[26] With time, this would become the museum's most famous name.

The merger of the two national museums was one of the regent's last decisions before the elected king Amadeo's planned arrival in Madrid. Yet a chain of unexpected events would make it harder than ever to predict the future, not only for the collection, but also for Spain's governance. On December 27 1870, General Prim, the main supporter of the elected king, was assassinated. Allegedly, it was a high-profile crime orchestrated by people as influential as the regent, Serrano, and the duke of

Montpensier, in the hope that the king-elect would be too frightened to accept the offer and Spaniards would rush to crown the duke. But by the time Prim fell victim to eight hired guns, the Italian prince was already on board a steamboat on its way to Spain. He did not hear about his supporter's ominous death until he reached the port of Cartagena, and when he did, it was too late to turn back. To his enemies' chagrin, Amadeo proceeded to Madrid, where he swore loyalty to the new constitution and was crowned soon afterwards, in January 1871.

King Amadeo laid no claims to the former Royal Museum. The most palpable consequence of this was the loss of its ceremonial function. No longer serving as a proof of the monarch's generosity and without a king to glorify, the museum started charging admission every day except Sunday. In 1869, Gisbert had been adamant about keeping the doors open every day without charge.[27] But the admission fee was already stipulated in the 1871 draft of the new regulations; it was authorized in April of 1871 by the provincial government and confirmed in a royal decree in August of 1871. The relatively high fee—2 reales, formally explained as a means of funding an orphanage that the royal family used to support—was enforced at the end of September 1871. Even after the Bourbons were restored to the Spanish throne, admission charges did not go away.

It took King Amadeo's administration one year to sort out—or, actually, to blur—the museum's position vis-à-vis the state and the elected Crown. On February 22, 1872, a royal decree again declared the collection the property of the nation, thus potentially putting the monarchy back in, as it had been determined in 1869. It seemed that the change would slow down, even stop, the merger of two national museums. But another disaster made it clear that something had to be done to the former Museo de la Trinidad. When in March 1872 a fire destroyed eight paintings from its collection still located in the building of the Ministerio de Fomento,[28] the government finally understood that it was dangerous for the works of art and burdensome for the Treasury to maintain two museums. On March 22, 1872, Amadeo issued a decree mandating an immediate transfer of the best paintings from the former Museo Nacional to the Prado. The text specifically stated that the merger would take place without a clear understanding of the entity's statutes, bylaws, payroll, or classification of its exhibits—a task deemed to "require painstaking investigations, meticulous work, and long time lines."[29] A commission was appointed to select works to be brought into the Prado. The official takeover was formalized in June of 1872, and in July of 1872 newspapers reported the transfer of several paintings, giving particular attention to how the unification of the two museums expanded the potential display of Goya's works.[30]

In the end, only about a hundred paintings found a place in the new National Museum. During the later Restoration, the bulk of the collection would be disseminated to provincial galleries, schools, universities, government offices, and other locations.[31] The draft of the new regulations stipulated that until enough room was generated for the paintings from the former Museo Nacional, its usual facilities at the Fomento would remain open to the public and operate as a branch of the new unified National Museum. However, it would soon become unnecessary. In 1886, someone noticed that the keeper of the former national collection was not showing up for work. Asked about the keeper's health, Federico de Madrazo, by then again the director of the Prado, had to acknowledge to his superiors at the Fomento that the man had not been coming to work for the last three years because there was no work for him to do. The former National Museum had no art to exhibit, and the keeper's position had only been conserved out of respect for his long years of service.[32]

Back at court, Amadeo was having to withstand challenges that would have brought down even a more experienced politician. At a time when the new Carlist War in northern Spain threatened the nation's territorial unity, and the fights for independence arising in Cuba and Puerto Rico announced the imminent end of what was left of the Spanish Empire, Spain's already ruined treasury was collapsing under the demand for military funding. The ubiquitous electoral fraud paralyzed any attempt at making parliamentary democracy work. The influential old-regime factions sabotaged things every time the new royal family tried to promote a new lifestyle and new habits. Terrorist attacks (one aimed at the king and his wife, María Victoria) made everyone question the mere survival of the monarch, let alone his monarchy, and the exiled Bourbons and their numerous domestic supporters did not fail to use the new king's bad press to their advantage. In February of 1873, Amadeo I abdicated and left the country. The parliament, now reluctant to accept any king at all, proclaimed Spain a republic. During the first eleven months of relative order, followed by another eleven months of increasingly unruly provisional governments, the First Republic had to continue both the Carlist War and the Cuban War (known as the Great War to Cubans) as well as face a new political force: a "cantonalist rebellion" in 1873 that sought to turn Spain into a Swiss-style federation. The peaceful path to a federation enjoyed the support of one of the presidents of the Republic, Francisco Pi y Margall, whose in-depth critique of the Museo Real was reviewed in the previous chapter.

When King Amadeo abdicated, the museum's national status had to be reconsidered once again vis-à-vis the possessions of the latest monarch. By a decree of July 24, 1873, the museum regained its former status as the property of the state.[33] The abdication also triggered a change in directorship. As soon as King Amadeo left the court, Gisbert, his vehement supporter, fled to France without giving notice, leaving it again to his deputy, Gragera, to go over the inventory to make sure the collection was complete.[34] The government of the Republic had to find a new director. Federico de Madrazo, considered an "honest" and "fitting" candidate,[35] was invited to return to his former duties. He was appointed in September 1873 but resigned in just a few weeks, recommending other artists to replace him. One of them, Francisco Sans Cabot, would become a director capable enough to steer the museum through the

Republic's many governments and through the early years of the ensuing Restoration. (Curiously, soon after his appointment Sans would marry the widow of the writer Wenceslao Ayguals de Izco, who, as we saw, had claimed that a lower-class woman such as his character María could intuitively understand Velázquez on her first visit to the Museo Real.)

It was precisely at that time that the question of educating the audience was raised in Spain. The new government's decree of November 14, 1873, directed the museum to initiate a "series of public conferences on the subjects of aesthetics, criticism, and history of fine arts," to be carried out by persons "of recognized artistic and literary reputation."[36] During these final months of the Republic, the museum's new director did all he could to implement a small version of this forward-looking educational program that the government had mandated. The revolutionary administration did not have enough time, however, to bring these plans to life. In hindsight, the Republic's most effective measure relating to the museum appeared in article 1 of the decree, mandating that the directors submit annual reports about the museum's collection and visitorship. Both measures were aimed at putting the National Museum at the Prado, as it was now officially called, in control of art education and of the changes in its holdings and floor plans. These measures were also aligned with the most advanced institutional agenda of the time, which was emanating from Britain: outreach and self-study. Thanks to the new legislation, statistical data about the museum have been available since 1874.

Instead of carrying out the rest of these revolutionary changes, however, the museum soon had to prepare for the return of the Bourbons. Trying to take the last opportunity to complete the collection, in June of 1874 the Fomento petitioned the Hacienda to transfer several paintings from the former royal property to the Prado, arguing that "in no other places will they find more, or more intelligent, admirers."[37] The president of the Republic authorized the transfer but ordered the museum to send back other, less valuable paintings of equal shape in order to cover the holes and the outlines on the walls. Few doubted the former owners' approaching return, and the palace had to be prepared. The nationalization of the Museo Real thus proved to be a long and change-ridden process stretching over the six years without the Bourbons, which ended as abruptly as they had begun. In late December of 1874, General Martínez Campos issued a "pronouncement" declaring his allegiance to Isabel II's son Alfonso. The government of the Republic offered no opposition, and in January of 1875 the prince arrived in Spain to be proclaimed King Alfonso XII. In the course of the "six democratic years," the state found sources for the museum's financing, accepted responsibility for its collection, and started learning the basics of planning and management. No wonder every step of the transformation was fraught with accidents and negotiations. This institutional adjustment and the emerging awareness of the museum's new responsibilities were the most important factors in the restructuring of the museum as national.

REVOLUTIONIZING THE PROMENADE

As the museum was changing hands and names, its surroundings were gradually becoming unrecognizable. In October 1868, Fernández de los Ríos published an essay with an interesting title—"Mental Walks Through Spain's Capital: As It Is and as the Revolution Should Leave It"—calling for the destruction of every reminder of the old regime in Madrid.[38] Indeed, the following years would leave a lasting impact on the museum's building and environs, which were now becoming the property of the state. The projects that would create new streets and construct blocks of flats in the former Retiro and San Jerónimo had been approved since 1865, but the new government's power to lease or sell the old royal and church possessions to developers was virtually limitless. A number of foreign firms were bidding for the right to invest in the area; some of them sensed enough potential for profit that they proposed building and beautifying the streets for free, in exchange for one lot of the former royal lands. By 1874, the burden of dealing with these new forces caused the Hacienda to create a special committee responsible for negotiating the terms of the area's redevelopment. The committee included, alongside the ministry's own officials and city negotiators, a community representative, who happened to be none other than the abovementioned Fernández de los Ríos.[39] While the authorities were making plans for the area, public opinion about their projects was increasing, becoming prominent in both the pages of newspapers and the fast-spreading gossip on the street.

When the provisional government had its hands untied to begin drafting a new Madrid in 1868, the cornerstone of this imaginary city seemed to be located right in the museum's backyard (map 3). Very soon the wall that separated San Jerónimo from the Retiro was gone, the Retiro itself was transformed into a public park (Parque de Madrid), and the former convent became, once again, a topic of debate. The commercial development behind the museum and in the former Tívoli had also started, and amidst the spreading construction the museum's territory needed legal protection. The official act of the takeover by the state in 1870 endowed the building with land occupied by its garden and the adjacent areas (marked as ovals on map 3:1). To the north, the museum's territory stretched up to the Calle Felipe IV, which had been projected in 1865 (map 3:2). To the east, the new resolution modified that 1865 plan by extending the museum's grounds beyond its northern and southern pavilions to separate it from the projected Calle Ruiz de Alarcón (map 3:3). The small square between the museum and the Botanical Garden, formerly a royal possession, now became a part of the museum grounds, and its western limits were set to match the garden's fence (map 3:4).[40] This 1870 border would remain unaltered until the museum's expansion of 2007. Were there any plans to turn it into a gated area? The 1872–74 *Plano Parcelario of Madrid* showed very detailed outlines of the garden, with a continuous line behind the benches (map 4:1). However, as contemporary images demonstrate, this line was

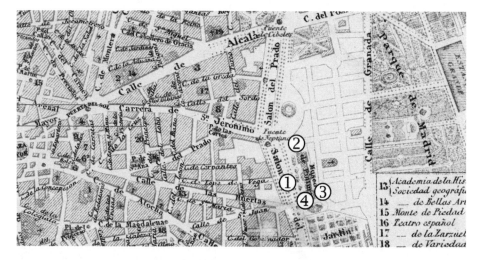

MAP 3   Decisions made after the 1868 revolution about tracing streets behind the museum. Carlos (Charles) Lasailly, *Plano de Madrid*, 1877, detail.   1. Western limits of the museum's territory; 2. Calle Felipe IV; 3. Calle Ruiz Alarcón; 4. Southern limits of the museum's territory.

not a tall railing, but rather a sequence of low, unimposing posts with banisters that would be closed with a chain to separate the museum from the Paseo at night.

It took some time for the museum authorities, the government, the City, and the public that now symbolically owned the building to understand their rights and obligations with respect to the adjacent territory. Still, only a month after the revolution, the liberal daily *Gil Blas* was criticizing the new landscaping that was planned. In the editor's view, Villanueva's northern (initially royal) elevated access was an old-regime construction hiding "under a hunchback" the building's noble façade. He asked that the slope be done away with and that new access to the museum with a stairway be installed.[41] The author clearly envisioned a stairwell and a portico as democratic architectural emblems of antiquity, contrasting with the "outdated" world associated with Victor Hugo's hunchback.[42]

Federico de Madrazo, still director of the museum, was of the same opinion: in November of 1868, he also requested that the hill be leveled in order to prevent humidity in the rooms buried underneath. The Municipal Works Commission diligently submitted and corrected plans following Madrazo's wishes. However, the work would take several more years and the intervention of another architect to be accomplished. And although the slope north of the museum would remain until 1881, its eventual annihilation would be one of the revolution's most visible results. The consensus about "excavating" the museum denoted a new social preoccupation: ensuring that its bold and unpretentious building conserved its prominent position in the middle of growing urban high-rises.[43]

In contrast, the area south of the museum, now officially under the museum's jurisdiction, did not take as long to change. Since the mid-1860s, it had been designated as the site of a monument to the artist Bartolomé Esteban Murillo, from which the square takes its current name. This ambitious civic enterprise marked the arrival of citizen-driven urban planning. It was the Madrid militia that raised the question of erecting the monument using the statue that had been donated by the sculptor Sabino Medina and initially "cornered" in the museum (in one commentator's description) as a part of its modest collection of contemporary sculpture. The money for the pedestal designed by the city architect came from the provincial deputy of Madrid, who also coordinated the works pro bono, while the command of Madrid's popular militia paid for paving the square. In the early 1870s, each step in the monument's construction and inauguration, covered closely by the press, gave the authorities another chance to pose in a favorable light.[44]

The landscaping of the museum's southern entrance became a civic cause just as street politics was transforming a semi-rural oasis next to the Botanical Garden into a site of class struggle. The first public demonstration next to the museum, organized by the Young Republican Party, took place in August of 1869 to protest capital punishment and the provisional government's reactionary policy, and was accompanied by minor acts of violence. A year later the same square, still under construction, would host a workers' demonstration.[45] Street protests were still a rarity in Madrid, and the efforts made to celebrate civic involvement and investment in the area, under the eye of benevolent authorities, seemed to signal new ownership of urban space.

Yet not only violence and class struggle, but also gendered politics, was already haunting the coverage of these meetings in press. On March 22, 1869, as the Constituent Cortes were still in session, a group of working women, mostly from the nearby tobacco factory, used the Prado as a gathering spot for a peaceful march to the building

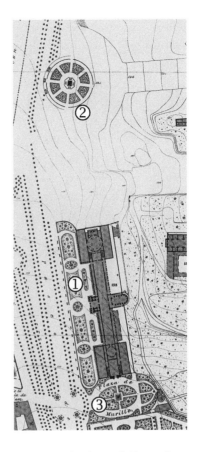

MAP 4   Carlos Ibáñez de Ibero, ed., *Plano Parcelario de Madrid*, 1872–74, detail.

1. Enclosed garden planned to limit the museum's western extension; 2. The Tívoli 3. Plaza Murillo.

where Congress met. Their official claim, which one observer qualified as "legal yet unnecessary," was to ban military conscription, which the Republican minority at the Cortes was also unsuccessfully trying to combat.[46] The women's placards, however, included demands for a federated republic. Newspapers reported that large number of "village" men and youths infiltrated the gathering. Some of them attempted to oblige nonworking women who had come to the Promenade for a leisurely stroll to join the march, and others behaved in such a way that, when the protesters reached the Congress, the delegates felt threatened and blocked the entrance.[47] Under King Amadeo, women of opposing political views also took their demands to the Prado, albeit in a different form. In March of 1871, upper-class women began to gather on the Promenade to show off their traditionalist head coverings in defense of Spanish values that they now considered endangered. These manifestations, known as the "revolution of the mantillas," were among the earliest examples of upper-class political action on the Paseo del Prado.

Reading through the accounts of the 1871 Paris Commune, Henri Lefebvre famously argued that urban festivals and class struggle merged in revolutionary France. Yet the testimonies from Madrid seemed to support the opposite conclusion: the rise of political activity on the Prado contrasted with unusually low participation in popular celebrations. Commenting on the first postrevolutionary Carnival, the journalist Nicolás Díaz Benjumea concluded, "freedom does not make people want to wear masks and hoods, which are a necessity at the times of oppression and servility."[48] His forecast was that, should Spaniards remain free, people would lose the need to cover their faces, bringing to an end the "spectacle born in the times of slavery." The reviews of that year's San Juan and ensuing festivities repeated the motif, which became characteristic of middle-class writers. In 1872, *La Ilustración Española y Americana* even published an unusually respectful sketch of the San Isidro celebrations, in which the customary imagery of the masses engaged in eating, drinking, and other excesses was replaced by the figures of peacefully conversing individuals (fig. 19).

The bourgeoisie's acute awareness of the masses and the times and places of their gatherings also brought back the liberal fantasies of a respectful, civilized Carnival on the Prado. Wearing Carnival masks in the streets—allowed during the French occupation of 1808–14 but banned by Fernando VII—had been legal since the 1850s (the only exception being that it was still illegal to dress up in the costumes of religious orders or military uniforms). During Carnival, the Prado was heavily policed; however, Valeriano Bécquer's etchings comparing Carnival on the Prado with that in a laboring-class neighborhood depicted an upper-class gathering in the museum's vicinities that had little to do with the real carnivalesque spirit of drunkenness and obscenity that ruled elsewhere (fig. 20). Channeling the bourgeois's unsatisfied desire to reserve the area for people of their liking, these images were possibly caused by fear

FIG. 19   "Madrid. —A View of the Pradera de San Isidro, May 15 of the current year in the afternoon," *La Ilustración española y americana* 20 (May 24, 1872): 312.

of the masses' unpredictable and aggressive behavior during the celebrations, which
was occasionally confirmed by actual events reported in the press.

Eagerly exploiting this emerging controversy, Gisbert, the new director of the
Prado, continued the Madrazos' efforts to chase idle people away, even though his
political views differed drastically from those of his predecessors. In 1869, he denied a
request to install a stage for a band along with chairs for its audience in the museum
garden, citing the somewhat dubious reason that this would "block the view of the
beautiful façade while also being incompatible with the building's serious nature."[49]
Still, the presence of the masses and the violence that the press now customarily associated with them was evident. During the Fall Fair of 1870, for example, the corpse of
a small girl was found behind the stones still piled up between the museum and the
Botanical Garden. And the San Juan celebrations of 1871 were marked by a fight that
left a man dead and a woman in jail. With time, common people must have declared
their presence with less restraint—or it may have simply become more acceptable to
complain about them. During the Fall Fair of 1873, under the revolutionary government, the next museum director, Francisco Sans, even felt it necessary and possible
to request protection from the mayor of Madrid. He asked that the round-the-clock
water kiosk next to the museum entrance be banned; it was owned by a woman

FIG. 20   Valeriano Domínguez Bécquer, *The Carnival in Madrid: The Prado de San Fermín and the Pradera del Canal*. Etching. *La Ilustración de Madrid* 1, no. 4 (February 27, 1870): 9.

whose apparently fierce character became a cause of "scandals sometimes reaching the extremes of shooting firearms and at other times making people hide in the bushes, evading the guards' vigilance in the darkness of the night."[50]

On a visit to Spain during King Amadeo's reign, Italian journalist Edmondo de Amicis described the Prado Promenade as an ongoing feast with "the joyous excitement, the noise, the whirlwind, the feverish gaiety of a fête."[51] In reality, class divisions were becoming more ominous in Madrid's public places, as the revolutionary events made the masses more visible and less predictable. Hence, while the working classes expanded their public presence, those who preferred nightly gatherings without the company of nonpaying fellow Madrileños would patronize with growing frequency the celebrations in gated areas such as the Campos Elíseos on the new and fashionable continuation of the Prado, the Castellana Promenade. During the revolutionary years, this and other leisure areas with paid access hosted regular nightly dances and occasional theatrical performances during the time of the festivals.

The increasing popularity of public places in postrevolutionary Madrid thus included not only the democratization of space but also class divisions, fear, and flight to gated grounds. Empowered middle-class citizens even began to design nation-building as well as entertaining alternatives to traditional gatherings, such as the transfer of the remains of select citizens of Spain to the new Pantheon in 1869.[52] Timed to coincide with the first postrevolutionary *verbena* of San Juan, it was marked by events that were just as playful as they were solemn. One newspaper even published an imaginary dialogue between resurrected architects Juan de Villanueva and Ventura Rodríguez (who were among the first to be reburied in the Pantheon), trying to figure out what was happening.[53] For the procession from the cemetery to the Pantheon, carriages were built that looked like the buildings that these architects had planned. Thus, those passing by the Prado on June 20, 1869, could see a carriage disguised as the museum following the body of its creator. From then on, the visual culture of Madrid would have a special fondness for mobile images of the museum. As for development inside the museum itself, in the years to come it would be indelibly marked by the continuous presence of these three forces: middle-class public opinion overseeing access to the space, the citizens who selected the museum as the privileged site of civil visibility, and the apolitical yet loud majority still gathering on the Promenade during the festivals.

RECLAIMING THE MUSEUM

Although it required less expertise to debate about the museum's surroundings than to form and express ideas about its collection, floor plan, and social importance, nationalizing the museum demanded that the general public and the few existing museum professionals and art critics form opinions about these matters for the new state administration to work with. For thirty years, the museum directors had catered to artists and educated foreigners while repudiating the Spanish middle classes, who knew little about the fine arts. But they now had to be welcomed in. "The fact that the public is lacking in expertise doesn't mean that it doesn't enjoy the masterpieces of our national museum," stated a contributor to *La Iberia* in early 1869.[54] In the past, lay audiences had learned in the street their ways of approaching museum art. But these approaches were becoming suspicious now that the pundits considered the *verbenas*, Carnival, and other premodern pastimes outdated. Thus, the revolution did not cause an easy reversal of public opinion about the museum, instead relegating it to a conceptual void between the criticisms and proposals of experts, on the one hand, and simple, uncultured enjoyment by the inexpert middle and working classes, on the other. What made the museum debates revolutionary, however, was how quickly and easily writers started channeling matters of art into morals, politics, and entertainment.

The word "museum" was losing its serious overtones, and nothing exemplified this better than a funny and slightly indecent cartoon published in *Gil Blas* a month after Isabel II's dethronement, titled *A Projected Painting Representing the Spanish*

120

GALERIA DE PINTURAS DE GIL BLAS.

Proyecto de un cuadro que representa la revolucion española, para el Museo del porvenir.

Revolution, for the Museum of the Future (fig. 21). Showing two plump female legs and a crown floating over the surface of what must have been the Bay of either Cádiz or San Sebastián, where the rebellious generals on the boats are ditching the dethroned queen, the cartoon promised a revolutionary liberation of aesthetics tied with a loosening of morals and interclass relations. The ensuing months would make it clear that the state and its citizens would first have to rethink their relation to art in order to begin talking freely about it.

Revolution made the bourgeois powerful, yet there was no celebration about this in the museum. The introduction of the entry fee marked a radical change in what the "public" meant and in how the relationship between the museum and its audience was described. First, two tiers of "public" were now identifiable: the paying and the nonpaying. Since the museum's inception, the "days of public admission" had traditionally been ones when the doors were open to anyone, while on other days access was regulated by the person's credentials (a passport or a special authorization note from the museum director). The new decree distinguished between two different days of "public admission": "public" were now the days when one had to pay, while Sundays were "public and free." This measure had far-reaching consequences for the new National Museum, as it expanded its intended audience while also limiting its "public" to those with the means to pay. Transforming access from a privilege into a paid practice benefited the domestic middle classes: those without special qualifications, who in the past would have had to request a pass or procure a passport, could now come in on any day provided they could afford the ticket. The meaning of free Sunday visits, which the decree explained as ensuring "artistic recreation," also changed to reflect the new class agenda. The museum was morphing from a privilege-governed institution into a modern arena for the enjoyment of paying citizens and for the "civilizing" of the nonpaying ones.

Outside the museum, lowbrow realistic exhibits called "cabinets," "exhibitions," or "galleries" of wax figures representing historical characters had appeared shortly before the revolution and were now mushrooming in popularity. In late 1870 and early 1871, two new establishments opened in Madrid featuring figures from the past and recent history, such as Garibaldi and Don Carlos, the latest Carlist contender for the throne. In 1871, one such exhibit attributed to an "artist-woodcarver" from Valencia was called the "New Museum of Sculpture," suggesting a growing rivalry between high art and the down-to-earth, realistic shows. Yet although the advertisements praised the wax figures for their artistic perfection and historical accuracy, their relation with the fairgrounds had not been severed. Postrevolutionary legislation classified the collections of wax figures in the same category as domesticated circus animals and other "objects for traveling theaters."[55]

While these lowbrow history exhibits were attracting growing attention, the status of high art had also changed. In early 1874, the satirical daily *Periódico para Todos* introduced a new type of short sketch that laughed at pretentious visitors trying to pass for experts. One author depicted a dialogue between a humble visitor and a quasi-expert claiming that "he had dedicated his best days" to Murillo's art and could recognize immediately the author of any painting. When the humble visitor asked who had painted a Crucifixion on display, the supposed connoisseur replied that "only a blind man would not see it: INRI."[56] (Apparently, the connoisseur was unaware that INRI [initials of "Jesus, King of the Jews" in Latin] represented the words attributed to Pontius Pilate and figured on most crosses.) As noted earlier, such a pattern of behavior, called *cursi* in Spanish, and the humorous interpretations of it had already evolved in Spain into a standard middle-class response to cultural change.[57] After the revolution, many people and many things became *cursi* in a museum that had hitherto treated uneducated visitors as laughingstocks.

This did not mean, however, that Spanish newspapers stopped ridiculing laymen. Instead, they repurposed the depictions of common museum-goers to convey everybody's sense of bewilderment viewing the collection, which the press now described as an experience that could challenge a visitor's moral convictions. By the time the revolutionary turmoil had subsided, Spaniards had firmly placed the National Museum as a leisure spot competing with cafés or opera or operetta houses, whose numbers were growing, and had associated it with bad morals and sexual innuendo. This interpretation was already noticeable in the 1869 naturalist novel *La condesita* by Francisco de Sales Mayo. The narrator—a young middle-class woman who would eventually become a prostitute—confessed that she used the museum to familiarize herself with nude bodies, mostly male, which she later enjoyed recreating in her fantasies.[58] She also remembered being followed around by men during her museum visits. Reflecting upon the exhibits' effect on the education of her senses, the narrator concluded that the museum fueled her sensual imagination and allowed her to see and display some flesh in ways similar to what happened at the theater and opera.

This was, as far as research can show, the first time the former Royal Museum was compared to a titillating place of entertainment. Such an ability to tickle the senses, however, corresponded to the standards of bourgeois leisure, which needed to be sorted out and weighed against the standards of high culture, of which the museum was still considered the main guardian. In response to this need, metropolitan writers conjured images of people confused by the museum exhibits: uneducated out-of-towners, village folks, and women—the social groups that did not vote and could therefore demonstrate questionably civic attitudes.

The complex tasks that these fictional characters were asked to perform firmly encoded the museum space as not only urban and bourgeois, but also male-gendered. Consider, for example, a short story published in *La Ilustración Española y Americana*, an upper-middle-class illustrated weekly, which featured the following dialogue between a bourgeois widow and a male family friend in the presence of the widow's two young daughters:

—Welcome, don Casimiro, where were you last night?
—Having some fun . . . I went to see some women . . . .
—Did you mean "some ladies"?
—Well . . . sort of . . . I went to see some ladies . . . nude.
—Sir!
—I must say, there was nothing sinful: these ladies were . . .
—. . . painted?
—Exactly.
—So, you were at the museum; but why at night?
—Oh, no, the ladies I am talking about, although there was a lot of color on them, were of bone and flesh, all of them young and some very pretty.[59]

He had, in fact, attended Offenbach's *Geneviève de Brabant* at the popular Teatro del Circo. In this comic sketch, both the opera and the museum were places to spend time surrounded by women, naked or nude, without committing a sin. However, it is clear which one seemed more respectable to the widow, a female character conjured to confirm the male gaze as standard in all entertainment venues, which now included the National Museum.

Journalists and writers began to discuss the role of women just as women themselves began to show up in greater numbers, as evidenced by the guest books for artists-in-training. Between March 1, 1864, and December 31, 1868, approximately twenty Spanish and three foreign women received permission to copy at the museum. Over the same length of time, between January 1, 1869 and October 31, 1873, approximately forty-eight permissions were issued to women, of whom thirteen had foreign names, surnames, or titles.[60] Yet while these numbers clearly mean that there were more women working at the museum, the growing presence of foreign *artistes* coming solo also suggests that the museum's most professional visitors were becoming more diverse, not only in terms of gender, but also in terms of language and social status. It should be noted that the Prado was simply becoming more popular among artists-in-training of both sexes, and after the Revolution the proportion of men to women remained as it had been, 10:1.

One of the women who applied for permission was the eighteen-year-old Emilia Pardo Bazán, who came in 1869 to copy paintings with her mother and husband while her father was busy attending the meetings of the first postrevolutionary Cortes. Pardo Bazán would later become Spain's first feminist novelist; yet the interest in visiting the museums for pleasure, self-improvement, and education had already been emerging in the writings of women publicists since the late 1860s. In 1869, María del Pilar Sinués de Marco, the author of the monumental multivolume biographic compendium called *Gallery of Famous Women* (1864–69), portrayed the lack of exposure to museums among her middle-class female compatriots as one of the many forms of their "martyrdom."[61] In the early 1870s, texts on aesthetics began to circulate in the women's press. The author of the first such publication stressed that unlike contact with natural creations, the understanding of beauty in art required an education and special preparation.[62]

Many writers continued the old ways of using paintings as religious illustrations, but now these stories were also directed at the female audience. New times demanded new moral teachings, and the lives of artists could make indoctrination seem educational. As Lou Charnon-Deutsch has pointed out, romances of love, betrayal, and triumphant virtue that ushered art into the domestic sphere also served as an appealing conduit for secularized moral preaching for women.[63] Replete with clichés, they reinforced bourgeois morality and prevailing opinions about art. For example, in 1870, *La Moda Elegante*, a women's weekly known for its illustrated advice on crocheting and hairstyling, began to teach its readers about Velázquez as well. Or did it? The Valencian writer Salvador Maria de Fábregues had published a tantalizing story in the tradition of Alexandre Dumas: the adulterous King Felipe IV, lusting after the artist's wife, blackmails her with a bracelet that she has lost at a fairground celebration, but Velázquez forgives his faithful Juana and sets off to paint *Las Meninas*, aided by Murillo (in the story, his pupil).[64] It was clearly a bad idea to participate in the festivals and nightly *verbenas*, mingling with the lower classes and losing personal property, but a wife could avoid disgrace by confessing her peccadilloes to her loving husband. Still, no matter how reductive the moral of the story, it did reference Velázquez's presumed portrait of his wife and even quoted the museum catalogue.

Such stories capitalizing on the moralistic potential of paintings showed how art could be brought to middle-class homes, but they offered no guidance to those venturing into an art museum. So humorous narratives, whose authors made fun of the popular puzzlement concerning the paintings about which even the experts could not agree, offered some help. The progressive satirical newspaper *Gil Blas* was particularly successful in voicing the unsettled debate about what was good or bad in a national art institution. When, in the weeks following the Revolution, the editor began to scrutinize the actual postrevolutionary museum, José Aparicio's 1808 painting *The Famine in Madrid* immediately caught his eye. In his opinion, a national exhibit was no place for canvases representing king-loving Spaniards who allegedly preferred to starve, eat rats, and see their children die than surrender to Napoleon's troops.

After fifty years of unending criticism from the liberals, hardly anything new could be said of *The Famine in Madrid*. Still, the Revolution gave the critics one more reason to demand the removal of this canvas: the museum was to be the mirror portraying the nation through the prism of triumphant realist aesthetics. Thus, a comical effect was achieved each time one established a connection between *The Famine in Madrid* and Spanish society without the Bourbons. In mocking tones, Eusebio Blasco (the editor of *Gil Blas*) described the composition as if it were realistic, as if the loss of the monarchs truly would cause people to starve themselves, and drew terrifying conclusions about Spain's new political regime and values. He portrayed himself as being so shocked by what he saw at the new National Museum that he decided to seek shelter in other public spaces, including the Senate, but when he noticed alarming signs of famine on the statesmen's faces, he had to run away in fear.[65] From 1869 until the proclamation of the new monarchy in 1871, *Gil Blas* kept insisting that the *Famine* be removed. In 1873, another satirical magazine, *El Mundo Cómico*, entered the fight with a vignette that featured a visitor asking a beggar where he could find "the picture of famine." "You are looking at it," the beggar replied.[66] By that time, however, the painting had already left the museum by popular demand.

Enjoying the humorous parallels between the museum and other places was one thing; having a voice in the museum was another. Pundits rarely mentioned art (about which they did not know much) when they touched upon the institution: the use and ownership of space was a far more debated concern. On April 4, 1869, the liberal newspaper *La Iberia* asked whether it was true that the new director, Gisbert, had established his personal studio in the former royal quarters.[67] In March of 1872, the Republican Federalist newspaper *El Combate* informed its readers about "more than scandalous" activities taking place in the museum to provide living quarters for top management.[68]

A second thread of opinion commented on the collection's expansion.[69] Special attention was paid to Goya, whose reputation had become associated with the liberals' fight against absolutism. All through the nineteenth century, Goya's exhibits tended to attract public attention after every political upheaval.[70] But in the late 1860s and early 1870s, Goya was not yet considered a canonical artist, and his works, dispersed among various public offices under irregular conditions, were prone to all sorts of damage. In 1868, a group of militiamen had fired into his *Portrait of the Actor Isidro Maíquez* hanging in the Ministerio de Gobernación, apparently mistaking the sitter for one of the Bourbons. And in 1871, *El Imparcial* reported that Goya's portrait of Fernando VII had been discovered among the trash at the Dirección de Comunicaciones, another government institution.[71] So it is no wonder that the public wanted to exercise some control over the Goya collection. In 1871, *La Época* reported that a special Goya room was being planned at the Prado. At that time the idea sounded like a fantasy, but it would actually be implemented at the end of the century.

Though sources point to a surge of robberies and violence in the National Museum's vicinities, they do not deliver any indication of a lower-class "occupation" of its interior. Rather, the "uncivil" behavior was coming from a group that in the past enjoyed considerable privileges: young artists allowed to copy paintings now clashed with the administration over demands that the conditions of their work be improved or at least kept as they were. Indeed, the loss of the symbolic authority of art professionals caused by the museum's transition from royal to national manifested itself in many ways. The most noticeable was the change in admission policy that no longer allowed the copyists exclusive access on weekdays. The copyists complained about this both privately and in the press but obtained only temporary amelioration. They also lost the privilege of selling their copies in the museum's portico. Their protests about that situation brought no results at all. Add to all of this the fact that, since the Revolution, the directors themselves had repeatedly complained about the negligence, misbehavior, and insubordination of the staff, and one can see that the postrevolutionary museum authorities were suffering because of the disintegration of the old system of loyalty and privilege. Gisbert was "urgently" requesting new museum regulations by April of 1871; Federico de Madrazo, the museum veteran, had to step down in 1873 after several weeks of reappointment because he could not handle the ushers' insubordination. In the following year, his successor, Francisco Sans, weathered a mini-rebellion of the copyists and again insisted that new regulations were "indispensable."[72]

Although the finalization of new rules would have to wait until 1875, the multiple drafts shed light on the changing balance of power among the directors, the staff, and the visitors. A simple comparison between the three versions (1871, 1872, and 1874) reveals the matter of most urgent concern at each time. In 1871, it was clearly most important to address the issues raised by the staff, who were no longer the servants of the court and tied by old-regime personal loyalty. This is why, unlike the 1863 rules (which were only intended for copyists), the 1871 regulations addressed "the staff, the copyists, and the people coming into [the museum's] rooms and galleries." Significantly, the requirements for the general public remained essentially the same as the rules that had been designed for the copyists. Article 54, for example, reproduced the 1863 prohibitions against smoking, singing, whistling, hanging signs or drawings on the walls, speaking in a loud voice, gathering in large groups, and "committing acts or professing expressions which would go against the decorum of this institution." Only two changes were made: the word "copyists" was replaced by "employees as well as the public," and the prohibition against "walking in the rooms from one extreme to the other" had been removed, making the Prado Museum now officially an indoor companion to the Prado Promenade.

The distinction between staff, copyists, and the public, however, was back in the next, 1874 draft. Reflecting the spirit of the Republic and much more permissive, this document provided virtually no guidelines for visitors' behavior but added new provisions for copyists that prohibited them from "mov[ing] the banisters, tak[ing] paintings off the wall without the director's special authorization," applying water, oil, varnish, and other substances to the walls or floors, and transferring to third parties the permission to copy paintings.[73] Meanwhile, the general public was only asked to follow in the museum the rule by that time standard in Madrid theaters: to leave walking sticks, umbrellas, and parasols with the concierge. Apparently, the new museum administration was mostly thinking about the paintings' safety and about the artists' protests. By the same token, the lack of any debate, either internal or public, about possible dangers coming from common visitors suggests that these were not an issue.

In the same vein, contemporary sources also do not allow us to witness any discussion about taste. This is partially due to the fact that even after the Republic's 1873 forward-looking legislation the museum did not become the center for teaching art history. While in the Academia and in universities aesthetics was still embedded in the study of philosophy, the historical approach to art was temporarily confined to the institutions of secondary and higher education. In 1868, Juan Facundo Riaño taught the first monographic courses on the history of the arts in Spain at the Diplomacy School of the Universidad Central in Madrid. Shortly after the revolution, the provisional government fired him and eliminated the position. In the same year, however, Francisco Giner de los Ríos became the first Chair of the principles and history of the arts at the private Instituto del Noviciado.[74] Although in 1873 the Republic reestablished Facundo Riaño's courses at the university, it was not until the early twentieth century that the educational provision of the 1873 decree would become reality at the Prado Museum. So if in France the revolutions were associated with wider social groups receiving and enjoying the right to judge art, in Spain the nonprofessional audience was left to its own devices. Despite the new government's legislation and educational program, postrevolutionary journalists appeared remarkably indifferent to the museum's teaching potential and simply indulged their delight at the feeling of freedom at the National Museum. This was a silent revolution whose full effects would become visible in the next decade.

LOOKING FOR A FLOOR PLAN

At a time when art was in other countries becoming a pedagogical tool for palliating class conflict and achieving industrial progress, the Spanish government's forward-looking provisions were understandable and timely. The reality was, however, that the museum was still largely irrelevant as an institution of active citizenship. In 1869, 250 students of science, medicine, and pharmaceutics from Madrid signed an open letter reminding government officials that the museum—a monument of an epoch just ended when "sciences were put behind arts"—was unfairly occupying a "palace initially built for the [sciences]."[75] The Academia San Fernando, as usual, stayed attuned to changing tastes and began to privilege archaeological exhibits over paintings whose merit was no longer obvious to educated youth. Only three months into the Revolution, it was already showing a collection of prehistoric objects.[76] Under the leadership of a prominent historian, José Amador de los Ríos, the National Archaeological Museum was also becoming a strong competitor for the public's attention.[77]

From the opposite political camp, the monarchical newspaper *La Esperanza* sarcastically warned its readers that it "would only appear logical" if the provisional government tried to use the museum as collateral when seeking credit from Parisian banks, given that "artistic treasures that the museum contains are the heritage of the times of obscurantism, the remembrance of which must be disturbing to this government."[78] After the 1871 Paris Commune in France, however, even the old-regime elites began reconsidering the state's cultural mission and decided to support the government, which they deemed a lesser evil—in the museums and elsewhere—than the educated will of the masses. Arguing that the public should have no power over the former Royal Museum even if the collection had been classified as a "public good," Pedro de Madrazo, for one, now wanted to empower the state: "the state has acquired it; the state is conserving it . . . , and the state that administers this priceless national property is entitled to regulate the limitations of its use as required for better public service."[79] Still, the new directors were not forthcoming with an explanation of their institution's place in postrevolutionary culture and could offer little in the way of revolutionary rhetoric. It was again the press, now aided by government officials, who were quickly educating themselves in the matters of art, which took on the responsibility of producing an outline of a revolutionary museum program. This time period, 1868–74, was indeed the true birth of Spanish museology, and that is largely due to the depth and reach of expert discourse about the subject, set in motion by a rising number of art critics, thinkers, and statesmen.

Museum professionals were the first to address the need for a reorganization, proposing changes so forward-looking and relevant that all of them would eventually be put in place, even though in some cases it would take half a century. During the six years after the Revolution, however, the only proposal actually implemented belonged to Vicente Poleró, a former restorer of paintings from the Royal Museum. In a pamphlet written prior to the Revolution and appearing shortly after, Poleró advocated for a merger between the Royal and the National Museums on the grounds that closing the lacunae in their holdings would elevate the prestige of Spanish artists, transforming what were little more than "rich collections of paintings . . . unworthy of their names" into a "true museum."[80] What he really envisioned was an institution that would exchange its holdings with provincial museums to achieve a display representative of the entire territory of Spain. He would repeat the same idea in 1871, producing a list of all the Spanish works in thirteen museums (some of them provincial and some former royal collections), totaling 3,970, ready for a redistribution. Although the new Museum of Art and Sculpture was ostensibly Poleró's main concern, he also proposed consolidating all objects related to the art of war in a museum that would inherit the Royal Armory's collection, sending all objects pertaining to the history of labor to the new Archeological Museum, and "uniting and classifying" all other museum centers, including the Gallery of the Academia San Fernando, the Navy Museum, and many others. Masterpieces would find their place next to exhibits hitherto considered applied or unimportant, transforming a picture of aesthetic decline into a history of the nation's creative abilities and making available "important data concerning portraits, types, and characters, as well as ammunition, furniture, fabrics, and products."[81]

Such a grand and extensive plan required a new vision of space, and so, in 1871, Poleró suggested that no movement of paintings should begin until the completion of the spacious new building on the Paseo de Recoletos that the government had been planning since the mid-1860s for the National Museum and Library. Showing a sophisticated understanding of what an art museum could do for the progressive development of Spain's economy and society, Poleró envisioned that a comprehensive mega-museum attract "erudite persons and artists," improve trade, and address the "much-neglected education of the popular classes."[82] For a government looking to make some powerful moves, this was a very attractive proposal. Logically, then, several postrevolutionary decisions would bear traces of Poleró's vision of the brave new museum world.

Another museum expert, the former director of the Museo de la Trinidad Gregorio Cruzada Villaamil, was also quick to draft a revolutionary art agenda in his 1868 article "What Revolution Has Done, and What It Yet Has to Do, to the Personnel, Administration, and Teaching of the Fine Arts."[83] If in the previous decades, Cruzada Villaamil wrote, public art conflated nation with monarchy, it was now the turn of the state to show generosity and appreciation of beauty. Hoping that the government could become a better patron of the arts than the departed Bourbons, he envisioned a museum where abundant government funding would facilitate a new floor plan similar to "several museums of Germany and Italy" and provided with a new catalogue not authored "by anyone named Madrazo."[84] When (and if) this finally happened, there would be harmonic interpenetration between the museum, its visitors, and the artists: "the public will . . . see its demands satisfied and the young artists will harvest the laurels and the public's praise."[85] Such was the liberal fantasy of a participatory museum.

Yet the Spanish writers who understood something about art by 1868 also realized that it was not merely the type of ownership that was changing. So when the government ensured its grip on former royal properties, it became imperative to redefine the relationship between the museum, its authorities, and Spanish society. New ownership required a new *raison d'être* for the art display and a new way of addressing its audience, wrote Francisco María Tubino, a liberal positivist thinker from Seville who offered the first comprehensive program of reform for both the museum and the system of art education in Spain. In so doing, Tubino launched one of the most innovative directions in Spanish thought: the quest to bind together art, personal development, and democracy.[86] Pointing to the fact that the museum's definition as "national" simply meant that "Spanish people" were now accepting a huge financial burden, this author argued that "people" could "demand" that the government make the museum into something more than a site "of mere recreation and pastime."[87]

Unlike many others, Tubino only accepted the state as a temporary and palliative structure made necessary by the fact that Spanish citizens "were not in a condition to obtain the use of their autonomy."[88] This included the sphere of the arts, in which, for Tubino, Spaniards were likewise unprepared to participate directly and would therefore have to accept some temporary mediation of the government. Contrary to the prevailing mood, which somewhat absentmindedly passed on to the postrevolutionary state the former monarchy's privilege of representing the nation, Tubino was seeking ways to bring the nation—that is, the voters—into the museum. To this effect, he drafted a plan for universal public art education that would transfer the teaching of aesthetics from universities, where it had been attached to departments of metaphysics, to museums, and would turn the former Royal Museum into "an institution with its own life, chartered and independent, enjoying in itself sufficient means to meet the needs of culture."[89] It is hard to overestimate the potential impact of this proposal on the future of art museums in Spain. Although aesthetics was not actually removed from the university curriculum, this was the path that the social reformers would take in the following years, eventually transforming the National Museum of the Prado into a place of education for people of all ages and social groups.

Tubino's specific proposals were respectful toward the museum's traditions and took into consideration the existing limitations in space and holdings that were commonly cited as an excuse for a lack of art-historical display. In his view, it was not these defects, but rather the general exhibiting principle, that hindered the museum's ability to meet the requirements of science as well as the "interest of the learned and the unschooled visitors." Tubino's critical eye focused on the museum's enshrinement of the Spanish canon, which had been erected into a norm by Federico de Madrazo's floor plan: "We constantly hear talk of, or praise for, the divine Morales, the mystical Murillo, the energetic Zurbarán, or the always under-celebrated Diego Velázquez, but very rarely if ever does one come across meditations on art as an idea, as an activity, as a series of original facts and manifestations . . . that had its beginnings, its high and low points, its falls and its triumphs, receiving influx from other social domains and exercising, in turn, undoubted and deep influence on how the masses felt and thought."[90]

Like other European progressive thinkers of his times, Tubino considered art a social activity interdependent with other aspects of a nation's life and the "history of labor," which required a positivist floor plan: a display recognizing that art was merely one of many social variables.[91] Tubino therefore envisioned a twofold system similar to what John Ruskin was advocating in Britain. The main section would exhibit the "development of domestic art" according to the established tradition "of a reasonable comparison," offering the most accomplished and representative works "with indication of their dates, name of author, the year when each was born or died, place of birth, all in a way [that was] not too hard to read," while the other would bring together paintings of the second order "by masters and nationalities."[92] Although Tubino dedicated less space to describing it, the purpose of this section apparently was to present an outline of development of art as a process without romantic "geniuses," infusing the "pure aesthetic concepts" with social relevance and a sense of national history: "some honorable aspiration of the time, some egregious memory worthy of being exalted and popularized."[93] Tubino was the first to look at the former Museo Real through the prism of a realist aesthetic, declaring as the most valuable those works that were not only "sublime" but also "inspired in universal consciousness" and satisfying for the "collective sentiment of the time."[94] Furthermore, deeply immersed in the federalist debate, he proclaimed the principle of "variety within unity," whereby Spanish art was represented as united when compared to that of other nations, while remaining internally diverse.[95] Demonstrating that the heterogeneous nature of Spanish art could be explained in terms of positive philosophy, this proposal would acquire fundamental importance over the next decades when Spain's increasingly vocal progressive critics would rethink the nature of the Spanish school and its display.

The third thread in the critical evaluation of, and proposals for, the new museum came from Ceferino Araujo Sánchez, Spain's leading expert on the provincial museums of his time. Now that the former Museo Real was reporting to the state, he argued, "we have the right to demand the reforms that we consider necessary; we have the duty of being demanding people until [the museum] is raised to the position at which it needs to be."[96] The strongest point of Araujo's proposal, however, was his remarks on the museum's weakness, which, in his view, prevented that institution from meeting the public's needs. The chronic lack of personnel was still forcing the administration to keep some rooms closed. The floor plan still offered an unconvincing distribution by "large groups of different schools" and lacked any classification—apart from simply trying to achieve the best possible exhibiting conditions for Velázquez, a "petty task if one cares for the interests of art."[97] The admission fee was prohibitive to domestic visitors and was damaging Spain's reputation among those coming from abroad, who perceived it as a form of state-supported begging.

Araujo's proposals for the museum's reorganization were less articulate than his criticisms. Although he demanded a strict taxonomy of schools, his definition of an artistic school, based on the place of the artists' birth rather than education, did not differ much from those of Pedro and Federico de Madrazo. He did, however, require a chronological display. Developing these ideas in a later book, *Los museos de España* (1875), Araujo explicitly proposed that the museum "organize works by nations, by chronological order, and keeping works by the same artist always together."[98] And, as Poleró had done, he approved confiscations and induced donations in order to complete the collection. By the time Araujo's book was published, however, the Bourbons were back, and it was not clear whether the reorganized museum would remain national. Hence, when juxtaposed with his plans for a museum intended to be national, Araujo's proposals contained goals that also began to sound dated: "the development of taste"[99] and the nurturing of the love of arts.

Although these three writers lamented the lack of museum reform, they did not do justice to the savvy of the new leaders, who were quick to connect the need for a rational display at the nationalized museum with improvements in education and industrial development. Thus, while the 1870 decree reclaiming the museum for the Ministerio de Fomento, written by an official from the Department of Public Instruction, envisioned the new expanded museum as a collection of masterpieces, the document's final version, signed by José Echegaray (the playwright who became the minister of Fomento of the provisional government and who in 1904 would be awarded the Nobel Prize in literature), made it clear that the state expected more: "Together [the two museums] will form priceless collections where all epochs of art could be represented, with different schools written on the pages of its history."[100] As the decree was being finalized, the fantasy of an old-regime patriotic display in the earlier draft—which claimed that little-known Spanish works could now finally be exhibited alongside those of internationally acclaimed artists—was replaced by a vision of having all schools complete and neatly separated. The direction of future change was now remarkably similar to that outlined by Poleró: bring together and redistribute, in the most rational way possible, the holdings of the former Royal and National Museums, the National Archaeological Museum, as well as provincial museums, churches, religious corporations, and even the Academia San Fernando. In 1871, the authorities' interest in integrating art, industry, and the history of labor became even more articulate as the Fomento drafted the topics for its nationwide essay competition. Those aspiring to receive an award in the category "Museums" had to rehearse the following argument: "Extension and limits of archaeology, art history, and industry. Can these studies be separated or do they constitute different directions of one and the same science? Groups of knowledge that they embrace. Their synthesis."[101] Clearly, as early as 1870 and 1871, Spain's provisional government seemed to be looking for a theory to undergird a museum reorganization far more ambitious than the one actually implemented, one that would pursue a new system of knowledge and a new exhibiting structure.

In the early 1870s, many still expected that different types of exhibits would soon be united under a common roof in a new National Museum and Library building on the Paseo de Recoletos. But construction was soon halted, and, in any case, there would not have been space for the former royal collection in the projected "rickety" building, which, when it was finally finished in 1892, only had room to house the Museum of Contemporary Art, the Archaeological Museum, and the National Library.[102] Still, the state would not be deterred from trying to amass national treasures. In November of 1873, as the new Republic decided to enhance art education, the Fomento requisitioned works of art from all the former royal palaces and residences without distinguishing between painting, sculpture, and applied arts such as tapestries. Even the most liberal newspapers criticized the measure, citing the lack of space at the Prado and proposing instead to refurbish the palaces as museums.[103] Still, the requisitions continued.

Comparing the range of criticisms and ideas provoked by the nationalization of the Royal Museum to the array of issues guiding the creation of the national art museums across Europe, we can see that Spanish thinkers and public officials were just as aware of the relation between art and governance as their foreign counterparts. What was different in Spain, however, was that no one assumed that the state would play the same role in the National Museum that it did in the nations that had undergone revolutions earlier. This is why so much thought went into defining the role of the museum audience and the authority that it should receive. In 1868 and 1871, Poleró could still dream of a strong government capable of designing a new network of mix-and-match museums where artisans and tradesmen could come to learn skills beneficial for art and industry. In 1872, Tubino already envisioned and tried to resolve the main problem of the audience's agency, which would haunt the educational reform programs of the next decades: how could a public accustomed to royal patronage achieve a level of understanding of, and involvement in, its institutions that was appropriate for the owners of the nation's artistic heritage? Later on, Araujo ascribed to the state the role of permanent patron and protector of the arts. Despite its pessimism, this is the approach that proved most fruitful in the decades to come. For a government whose prior museum experience had been limited to the hugely mismanaged Museo de la Trinidad and the underdeveloped network of provincial galleries, it seems that the short-lived cabinets of 1868–74 successfully climbed a very steep learning curve.

Given the clarity of this agenda, what stopped a new floor plan from being implemented, or rather, perhaps, what made the public think that nothing had changed? The new museum directors, in fact, shared many of the goals and convictions that were circulating in the public debate and even made some reformist steps. But so much was in the air in the new museum culture, and so entrenched was the narrative underlying the Royal Museum's last floor plan, that six years were not enough for the new authorities to offer and implement a convincing alternative. In the history of the Prado, this was therefore a time of experiments and battles involving every possible issue, from the nature of state patronage to the questions of copyright.

The directors had always worked to expand the museum's collection and territory. Thus, when the Revolution broke out, even Federico de Madrazo welcomed it as an opportunity. On October 16, 1868, he submitted to the Administration of Former Royal Patrimony a proposal which, in his words, would enable the museum to stand out among its counterparts in Europe, where improvements were encouraged and motivated by "competing princes and states."[104] Since the mid-1860s, Madrazo had been reminding his superiors that if they did not allow an expansion, other European museums would steal the Spanish museum's fame, and now the Revolution presented a chance to tell the government what he really wanted: an annexation of San Jerónimo and the Casón del Buen Retiro and a collection enriched by works from all the royal palaces, selected by a special commission.[105] Curiously enough, the Prado as we know it today corresponds rather neatly to Madrazo's plan, although it would take a century for it to be implemented: the Casón was added in 1971, and the cloister of San Jerónimo had to wait until 2007 to become a part of the museum.

Though Madrazo would soon have to leave, future directors and civil servants agreed with both items on his agenda.[106] Unfortunately, the former palace architect who examined the buildings stated that he would have recommended the proposed expansion had the buildings not been in need of unaffordable refurbishing.[107] So those who planned to amplify the institution in the following years understood that they could only count on Villanueva's building, at least for the moment. The official who drafted the 1870 decree for the Ministerio de Fomento about the merger of the two national museums offered an imaginative solution: since there was no space to exhibit all the works from the former Museo de la Trinidad, the most important of them could find a place at the Prado, "and in view of such a splendor funds will be assigned, resources will be dedicated, and sacrifices will be made to expand the galleries, and we will finally see most notable works from both museums shine according to their merits."[108] In other words, the government decided that enriching the collection should come first, and once the new exhibit did its work in persuading the politicians, they would understand the need for more space.

This is why, instead of a grand expansion, the merger of two national museums triggered only a modest refurbishment. In 1874, looking for ways to increase the wall surface, the architect Alejandro Sureda pioneered a system of room separators in the former Flemish Gallery on the first floor.[109] Even Pedro de Madrazo, a vehement defender of his family's principles for hanging art, could not help applauding, calculating that the separators could generate enough wall surface to accommodate fifty additional paintings that could now be "classified with method, clarity, and good sense."[110] The new gallery and three others where this system prevailed had just been finished when the Bourbons returned, and these three galleries were then named after those monarchs. In the end, at the official inauguration ceremonies, no thanks would be given to the Republic, which, even in its last days, granted the money to improve the museum.

The lack of space had made it necessary to expand; public officials had dictated that it was socially meaningful to reorganize the collection. So it now became urgent to articulate, and agree on, the underlying principles for a new classification. Of course, as discussed above, every group had its own ideas and lists of demands: the art experts insisted on a complete reorganization according to art-historical principles; the less prepared journalists were content as long as they could see more of their Goya and the monarchical propaganda was chased away; and the government officials, always following a scientific method, leaned toward a radical fusion and redistribution of all the collections. Facing these conflicting needs, Gisbert did not propose any new floor plan. Once he realized that establishing his headquarters in the galleries that used to be royal chambers was a faux pas, he had become a faithful servant of public opinion. He retrieved and hung as many works by Goya as possible, including his cartoons for the Royal Tapestry Factory, and got rid of Aparicio's *The Famine in Madrid* along with a number of other promonarchical paintings. Of course, critics such as Araujo Sánchez criticized Gisbert for maintaining the Romantic love for exhibiting geniuses, but the democratically minded journalists were pleased.[111] As far as the war against monarchist propaganda was concerned, the new director proved to be so determined in this crusade that in 1872 even the government had to beg for his mercy. In November 1872, Gisbert received an order mandating that Aparicio's work, alongside other canvases "that by their merit and the importance of their subject matter should not be stored in a roll," be unrolled and exhibited in the rooms in the Fomento that the Museo de la Trinidad used to occupy.[112]

Sans, appointed with Federico de Madrazo's recommendation under the First Republic, took a more determined approach to the display. From his correspondence with the Ministerio de Fomento it becomes clear that by at least June of 1873 he was working to expand the collection of Spanish art by exchanging holdings with provincial museums.[113] Although the state officials were of the same opinion, Sans was more realistic in his ambitions and also more systematic: he focused on the most pressing need—a satisfactory classification of Spanish art—reasoning that "it would be more difficult to achieve the same goal with the foreign ones."[114] The acquisitions and requests that Sans was making at that time confirm that he had been trying to familiarize himself with what was happening in other European museums and in the Spanish art world. At the end of 1873, he ordered for the library the catalogues and regulations of the Louvre, London's National Gallery, and the museums of Dresden, Brussels, and Berlin.[115] His financial reports show money spent purchasing and binding the catalogue of the Louvre, the magazine *El Arte de España*, Rejón de Silva's 1788 *Diccionario de nobles artes*, and a catalogue of Goya's cartoons.[116] But something must have gone wrong in Sans's plans, for in January of 1875 he wrote to his superiors asking to redirect the funding for a reorganization of the Spanish Gallery toward reorganizing the Flemish one instead.[117] Only a week earlier, Alfonso XII had made his triumphant return to Madrid, and we can reasonably assume that even if Sans indeed planned to reorganize the Spanish collection, he would have wanted to postpone it until he knew which way the wind was blowing. There is, however, no indication as to what kind of classification Sans would have implemented if given a chance, and although he remained the director until 1881, he never proposed a new floor plan.

Thus, the writers who claimed that nothing had changed since the museum became national were both right and wrong. Indeed, very few changes were visible, and the ones that had been planned took too long. However, the modifications that *were* implemented signaled an important shift in museum policy toward embracing public opinion. And the public did not demand radical change. Rather than trying to adapt the display to their taste or their notions of nationhood, Spain's middle classes used the museum inherited from the old regime as a tool to help define themselves. Meanwhile, the country's new leaders had articulate ideas but still needed a more convincing classification of Spanish art than those available at the time. This is why the directors showed more concern for producing such a classification than for an all-encompassing restructuring of the museum. Yet while they were still guarding the limits of "fine arts" at a time when the government was looking for ways to combine art and industry, the directors were gradually coming to a realization that, no matter how complete the collection, the history of Spanish painting taken in isolation from other arts could not reveal a clear progression. By the end of the revolutionary period, the museum's display by schools and chronology was back to square one. Still, taken together, the government measures and the intellectual debates of the revolutionary period suggested a wide social commitment to breaking the museum's identification with the monarchy and bringing the concept of nationhood closer to the models of territorial unity, centralism, and the accumulation of wealth that were becoming popular among Spain's neighbors. Most importantly, there emerged a new museum culture, where the directors, state officials, and the public worked together on the expansion or modification of the collection.

CHAPTER FOUR

Becoming National, 1874–1902

THE "SIX REVOLUTIONARY YEARS" of 1868–73 sped past and through the museum, leaving it transformed in every way except for the building and the floor plan. But these changes were as deep as they were swiftly made, and it would take a long process of engagement before Spaniards themselves began to recognize the museum as a national institution. The nature of its service to Spain and, consequently, the reasons for the state to maintain and develop it would generate debate even as late as 1898. That was the year of what many Spaniards called "the disaster"—the loss of the last colonies, Cuba and the Philippines, in the Spanish-American War. While the conflict was still unfolding, left-leaning writers brought up the question of whether the nation needed to sell some paintings to support the war effort.[1] The emerging consensus was a felicitous one: putting a price on the museum "would be as foolish as trying to assess the blueness of skies, or the scent of flowers, or the light of the day."[2] At the time, even Rodrigo Soriano, the author of this eloquent defense and an influential socialist thinker, would not call this an uncontested statement.[3]

When the press defended the museum, its reasons for doing so ranged from the museum's importance for the progress of representative institutions to the improvement of theater costumes. The novelists, delighted to find a new and intriguing setting for their protagonists' acquaintance and courtship, added motives less lofty but no less potent: the proximity of female nude images on the walls or the growing presence of the opposite sex among the spectators. And while the domestic audience was coming to terms with the museum's presence in the national imagination and in the state's budget, the museum itself, led by directors of quite different political and aesthetic convictions—Francisco Sans Cabot (1873–81), Federico de Madrazo (1881–94), Vicente Palmaroli (1894–96), Francisco Pradilla (1896–98), and Luis Álvarez Catalá

(1898–1901)—was undergoing enough internal transformation to face the new century with a clear, if not fully realized, agenda. These years of "becoming national" were a time of experiment and trial that would show what people could do, not only *in* the museum but *with* it.

End-of-the-century Spain was a country of maturing capitalism, and its entrepreneurial energy made possible some of the museum's most visible external transformations. While construction continued in and around Villanueva's building, the city government selected the Prado Promenade to become a modernized fair. Supporting the City's efforts to limit uncontrolled gatherings while also expanding commercial entertainment and consumption, the museum directors spearheaded the "civilizing" transformation of Madrid's leisure activities. At the end of the nineteenth century, the Prado Museum would accommodate the new conceptions of art spectatorship as a pastime that was not as much about art as it was about shared pleasures and civic values. This chapter looks at how an emerging museum culture negotiated a place for the Prado in a time of expanding citizenship, educational reform, economic development, and military crisis.

END OF THE NINETEENTH-CENTURY MUSEUM WORLD

In a Europe of dissolving empires and consolidating nation-states, public art was called on to promote national allegiances. When political borders did not correspond to the claims for self-determination, statesmen and people now called "intellectuals" appealed to ethnic, religious, cultural, and linguistic unity to justify national allegiances. With the exception of the Nordic countries, only a fraction of Europe's population was literate, and late nineteenth-century definitions of nationhood still had to be communicated visually. Stateless nations championed the images of peasant and urban populations united in a common destiny.[4] In areas where nation-states were already a reality, the political need to negotiate subnational—local or regional—self-identifications created folk-based regional styles. This was a contradictory setup. The well-oiled machinery of world's fairs, international fine arts exhibitions, national salons, and private exhibits was transforming art into a cosmopolitan commodity peddling national spirit yet supportive of regional identities. Although artists could still pose as heirs to Romantic "geniuses" and claim to channel the spirit of their people, the language of art had to be calibrated to conform to the international style labeled in different languages "art nouveau," "secession," or "modernism." By the turn of the century, as Eric Storm argues, European artistic elites came to an understanding that a cross-border regionalism was most appropriate for reflecting the national gestalt regardless of the country's political status or level of centralization.[5] Regionalist art thusly understood relied on folk crafts as well as their industrial imitations. Bolstered by the fear of the urban proletariat, with its internationalist demands, this new aesthetic quest opened traditional art museums to rural forms of artistic expression and more democratic types of gaze.

The governments did not lose their taste for supporting the arts, but state patronage came with a mandate to unite fine and "mechanical" arts. Church sponsorship seemed a thing of the past (but not in Spain, as we shall see). The academies were still the de facto authority over painting and sculpture, but civil society was demanding to take over. Using the model of artists' guilds and associations, educated aficionados created their own clubs with activities that ran the gamut from producing art to exhibiting, critiquing, and commercializing it. Private dealers, already present on the art scene since the first half of the century, became more powerful and poised as collectors and benefactors. Museums began to emerge across Europe with a nation-building mandate yet without any government support. In Switzerland, the federal government had no role in museum-building, which was considered uniquely a municipal or cantonal prerogative. In Sweden, linguist Arthur Hazelius single-handedly founded the Scandinavian Ethnographic Collection (1873), later renamed the Nordic Museum, and the Skansen, Europe's first open-air museum (1891). Donations started to pour in, and a few years later the founder declared his museums the property of "the Swedish people." In this situation, the collection belonged to the state, but an independent board of trustees ran the museum.[6] In Russia, the Alexander III Museum of Fine Arts, reporting to Moscow University (currently the Pushkin State Museum of Fine Arts), was created from private donations by the members of its founding committee (1898). In comparison with these civic endeavors, art collections that still officially belonged to kings, states, or both seemed outdated. In order to retain relevance, old art museums had to cease supporting royal personae or state institutions in their fights for representing the nation, and had instead to think of and address the middle and working classes, in addition to the aristocracy, as citizens, regardless of how they understood national art.

Museum directors could no longer avoid giving a role to civil society or offering some representation to the people. As the majority of European governments lowered property qualifications for voters—still only male—classes hitherto denied participation were drawn into politics. The socialization of the masses meant that they had to be recognized as the "public" when attending events and exhibitions. Though images associating communities with their rulers or their shared historical experiences were still in circulation, this sort of iconography was not acceptable at a time when the nation's maturity was measured by the cultural participation of its civil society. In an effort to assert the relevance of their institutions, exhibitors argued that the greater the size and quality of museum collections, the more able citizens were to undertake concerted efforts to secure the competitiveness of their countries beyond the sphere of the arts. Social reformers, in the meantime, came up with new schemes for attracting the expanding public to the museums—schemes that now included arranging special exhibitions for the poor, children, and other groups considered unable to grasp traditional art collections.

The idea that museums ought to represent the history of art was replaced by the need to illustrate the history of the nation. Yet since traditional art collections alone could not sustain the multiplying definitions of nationhood, museums were turning into agglomerated institutions, nested in the same space or adjacent to each other, displaying old and new paintings and sculptures, portraits, and archeological findings, and sometimes also incorporating national libraries and archives. The Louvre, which had been exhibiting historical crafts and antiquities since the Second Empire, added a Museum of French Furniture in 1891 and a Department of Art Objects in 1894. In the meantime, the German national museums scattered on Museum Island in Berlin offered an even fresher look, reminiscent of the world's fair pavilions. The National Gallery in Berlin (1876) and the National Gallery of British Art (the Tate) (1890) in London contained contemporary works retrieved from national exhibitions at home and abroad. By the end of the century, almost every national art museum would have some type of museum of modern art erected in its vicinity whose competition it had to withstand.

There were now more museums run by boards of trustees and similar collective bodies than those directed by artists or bureaucrats. These museums often had their own endowment that allowed them to become partially or fully independent from the government ministries to which they reported. In 1890, the Louvre acquired the status of "civil personality," with its own treasury, independent from the funds assigned to other French galleries.[7] In Britain, both the British Museum and the National Gallery had enough private funding to operate independently of Parliament, even though some of the trustees were also Members of Parliament. The Swedish museums, mentioned above, were put under the control of a similarly independent body even when the ownership of the collection was entrusted to the state.

As they were acknowledging that civil society, and not state structures, had agency in collecting, protecting, and exhibiting artifacts, museums were also expanding their target audience. Now that the masses were acquiring civil rights and museum authorities were admitting organized visits and field trips, the question of how and why people should look at art also became political.[8] In the past it had received a range of responses. Romantic aesthetics had suggested that civil harmony could result from the effect caused by monitored exposure to beauty, and this is what museum founders had counted on in their approach to mass visitors. In the 1880s, inspired by the idea, made popular by John Ruskin in Britain, of aesthetic education for all, the reformists agreed that urban industrial workers were the ones who needed art the most because they were left without access to nature, which was conceived to be the object of contemplation leading common people to virtue. Thinking that art could mitigate this deficiency, late Victorian educators insisted on exposing the masses to the fundamentals of aesthetics.

The pedagogical doctrines of object-aided learning created even stronger reasons to transform museums into educational institutions. Faced with the workers' resistance, turn-of-the-century reformists brought the "rational recreationists" experiment to schools in an effort to shape the leisure and visual experiences of working-class children.[9] Since drawing was already recognized as a crucial trade skill, educators were determined to introduce the children of the poor to the fundamentals of art interpretation. Permanent and loaned school exhibits were soon being created in the working-class neighborhoods of industrial cities such as Manchester, Sheffield, Birmingham, Aberdeen, and Glasgow and quickly gained popularity beyond Britain. Educators began transforming classrooms into galleries where reproductions of paintings and objects related to the curriculum were put on display. While some schools established their own permanent art galleries, others received actual paintings or sculptures on loan. Following the British example, in many European countries "pedagogical museums" amassed collections of books, objects, and art reproductions that could be lent out. They also helped to organize exhibits and hosted lectures, seminars, and excursions for teachers.

Such attempts to inculcate the unity of "the beautiful, the good, and the virtuous" through art, as prescribed by Victor Cousin, generated a strong backlash in the last quarter of the century. In the late 1870s and throughout the 1880s, art's emancipation from virtue became the motto of the new generation of aesthetes, who knew enough of art theory to despise moralizing lectures and all other forms of didactic mediation. Philosophers, writers, and art-lovers from Nietzsche to Huysmans to Oscar Wilde defended the idea of an antisocial, impractical, and apolitical "decadent" art, and the belief in the transformative power of museums hit a low point among the elites.[10] While on the whole the art-savvy middle and upper classes resented the moralizing uses of art, workers in Britain began to educate themselves though workers' clubs, which resisted middle- and high-class patronage.[11] Jonathan Conlin, the historian of the London National Gallery, notes that when the British Parliament debated whether art collections should be kept open on Sunday afternoons, members of workers' unions were surprised to see old-time advocates of working-class museum-going like Lord Shaftesbury be just as skeptical as they were about the helpfulness of museums in offering a good alternative to "gin-houses."[12] "Up to this point nobody had noticed that museums can be boring," Conlin states, adding that in the utopias of William Morris, Matthew Arnold, and Walter Pater there was no place reserved for an art museum.[13] In the 1880s, he continues, descriptions of "museum horror" became ubiquitous.

This swift reaction to the plan for a pedagogical takeover of museums further strengthened the position of the skeptics who were already doubtful of the usefulness of public displays for all.[14] Hence in the 1870s and '80s, despite their best intentions, the supporters of museum education did little besides creating specialized exhibits and segmenting their audiences by class and age (although not gender). In the new world of multiplying niche displays, authorities and entrepreneurs preferred to create for the uninitiated their own special galleries, and museums no longer tried to adjust their collections and floor plans to the "man in the street." When E. M. Barry's new wing of National Gallery in London was opened in 1876, the directors rejoiced in organizing new rooms following the principle of aesthetic compatibility, rather than the much-exalted linear chronology. In 1881, in London's East End, the laboring classes were invited to attend a special art exhibition, which in 1901 would give birth to the popular Whitechapel Gallery.[15] In 1890s, old art museums were still resisting didacticism, while educators were looking for ways to craft their own exhibits on demand. But at the turn of the century, when socialists entered European politics—initially on a local scale—politicians' interest in traditional art museums would be renewed and the question of catering to the masses would be back on the table.

The fact that the promoters and the detractors of museum education widely discussed their positions opened the viewing of art itself to public scrutiny. Hitherto classified as a lonely pleasure with the promise to assist individuals in self-cultivation, art spectatorship was now officially recognized as a group—and sometimes a crowd—activity. Thus, even as museum directors were moving their institutions back to aesthetic floor plans, they could no longer expect that the dilettanti would come in one by one to enjoy them. Rather, they had to find ways to accommodate a fun-seeking, sensationalist, and detail-oriented collective gaze that was identical to the one usually associated with the early films shown at fairs and in pubs.[16] In this way, art museums prepared the ground for the "relational economy of leisure, entertainment, and representation," which in the twentieth century would reap full benefits from this modern—embodied and collective—way of looking.[17] It would be a mistake, however, to attribute such dispositions to the "masses" only: by the turn of the century, as Mark Sandberg argues using Scandinavian visual culture as an example, fairgrounds were just as popular as museums with the middle-class audience. As Didier Maleuvre suggests, end-of-the-century debates simply confirmed the symmetry between the treatment given to objects of art in museums and the "aesthetization—neutralization and autonomization—of the bourgeois subject in industrial society" that had made museums essentially modern phenomena.[18] All across Europe, the investments in the "leisure zone" (Bailey's coinage) had already been consolidating for decades around the art museums and had resonated inside, where looking at other visitors instead of the masterpieces had become standard.[19] The aesthetization of crafts, initiated in the museums in the 1850s and increasingly popular, moved this capitalist gaze into every bourgeois home. Now politics was turning citizens into objects of aesthetic contemplation.

World's fairs, which Walter Benjamin called "pilgrimages to commodity fetishism," had been modeling a world where everything, from industry to private life, was displayable and classified according to current political maps. Since the late 1870s, these events had also incorporated forms of nationalist entertainment that blurred the distinction between display and performance. As Sharon L. Hirsh and Terri Switzer point out, although national pavilions and the shows that accompanied them were formally delimited, they were frequented by an audience that was cued to apply an identical gaze to the moving subjects and the static objects.[20] Logically, then, humans figured as exhibits, and those whose social standing would not allow them to pay their way to see the displays were themselves cast as displays within the native environment of their humble living quarters. Merging the fashion for exhibiting colonial tribes in the central parks of major cities (recorded since the 1850s) and the bourgeois fad for *tableaux vivants*, the organizers of national pavilions, with "autoethnographic" gusto, put their own cultures forward as a continuum of objects and performances imbued with an ethnic spirit.[21] Absorbing people and objects of display, professional performers and the spectators coming to enjoy them, these nationalistic installations also found new uses for traditional art. For example, some displays at the Swedish Ethnographic Museum were materialized replicas of earlier historical paintings, suggesting that academic art and the reality of folk life could merge long before live peasants were paid to live in the Skansen open-air museum.[22]

Since not all types of nationalism practiced the same approaches to class, it would be a mistake to think that aestheticizing the everyday only channeled the power of the bourgeois gaze down to common or colonized people. In 1890s France, for example, as Debora Silverman explains, everyone from art critics to politicians argued that modernization and national vigor were mostly visible in the homes of the national bourgeoisie.[23] After that, it did not take too long to recast the daily life of the middle classes as a museum exhibit, and so, at the 1902 world's fair in Turin, the fine arts section was arranged as a succession of bourgeois rooms decorated with paintings and artful furnishings.[24]

End-of-the-century nationalism thus conjured two types of displays giving different agency to national subjects—one focusing on the rural population and the other privileging the urban middle classes. Requiring a gaze that could glide with ease across performances, objects, and artistic representations, they were aimed at the same audience but did not exclude each other. Working-class entertainment figured prominently as the source of this gaze: in the agrarian-inspired exhibits, it was the fairground entertainment; in the urban ones, it was the local festival. By the end of the nineteenth century, both types of activities were urbanized and enjoyed popularity among all classes. Once this nationalistic gaze was recognized as standard, socially committed writers regained the territory that they were losing in the museums. Asserting that even if there was nothing inherently educational in looking at the exhibits themselves, museum-going was still a civilizing pastime capable of uniting the nation, they began to cite museums alongside fairgrounds and *fêtes galantes* (courtship parties) as examples. The oft-cited scene in Émile Zola's *L'assommoir*, depicting common people retreating to the Louvre when their wedding party got rained on and being startled by the view of nude statues, reflected, in a comical way, the consensus among French nation-makers that museums should satisfy the tastes of the working-class urban population.[25]

Considered equally valid for viewing art and merchandise across the domestic and the public spheres, this way of looking accommodated women better than the art-lovers' aesthetic gaze, which sublimated female nudes.[26] This was the time when the female gaze was recognized as different from the male one, and while, for the time being, it was confined to the commercial sphere—as in the department stores being described as "women's museums"—women's rising artistic activity could not keep questions of gendering away from traditional institutions of public art for much longer.[27] In France and Britain, women were admitted to the art academies and struggled hard to receive access to nude models. In Britain, the Society of Female Artists was founded in the 1850s and grew strong enough in the 1870s to limit its membership to professional women artists.[28] There were more women copying paintings in Europe's art museums, but the humorous coverage they received suggests that men resisted acknowledging them as equals. As Brown and Dodd point out, the growing artistic activity of women still could not protect them from the male-dominated system of exhibiting institutions.[29]

All across Europe, national art museums—the intellectual children of the nineteenth century—were turning into *enfants terribles*, casting doubt on the validity of the public art of the previous decades and the aspirations associated with it, and Spain's traveling, reading, and writing public was well aware of this. The press reviewed changes in existing galleries and covered the inaugurations of new ones, from Philadelphia to Antwerp, Berlin to Melbourne. Illustrated weeklies published etchings of their buildings, while newspapers scrutinized their budgets. And although Spaniards would customarily remind themselves that their museum was "the richest in the world," even they knew that the Prado was losing in the international competition. "The idea that Madrid's Museum of Paintings is the best in Europe is so widespread that it might seem strange if I say that it is only true if one comes to Europe from Morocco; otherwise, as a museum or gallery, it cannot compare to the French, Italian, or British ones," ran the introductory paragraph of Araujo Sánchez's 1887 series of articles about the Prado.[30] Along with other liberal critics, Araujo ascribed to the National Museum an extensive list of social responsibilities; inevitably, for these critics, the museum was woefully underperforming and inadequate. Whether the Prado was indeed falling behind its counterparts, or whether its critics simply were hard to please, politics had a lot to do with it.

THE RESTORATION

Although the Restoration monarchy was not one of divine right, and although Spain's political regime, now remarkably independent from the person occupying the throne, favored evolutionary rather than revolutionary changes, the stop-and-go course of Spain's politics made it hard to envision a museum that could rely, like its foreign counterparts, on the health of the nation's governmental institutions, the self-awareness of its civil society, the progress of education, and the robustness of its treasury. After the "six revolutionary years," the trend set by Fernando VII's and Isabel II's turbulent debuts and farewells continued. Isabel II's son was eleven years old when he had to flee to France in 1868, and was thirteen when, still in exile, he was proclaimed the heir to the throne. At seventeen he became King Alfonso XII. Ten years later, in 1885, he would die of tuberculosis, survived by two daughters and his second wife, Maria Cristina of Austria, who at the time was expecting. Until the birth of the baby and the revealing of its gender, it was undecided whether the oldest daughter would wear the crown. In the meantime, María Cristina was proclaimed regent queen. In 1886, she gave birth to a boy who became King Alfonso XIII. Until his coming of age in 1902, his mother would rule in his name.

While those who had supported the Glorious Revolution or had acquired voting rights in its aftermath saw their political influence hindered and even silenced by the returning Bourbons, journalists and politicians, some in favor of and some opposed to such silencing, began to use the museum as a political touchstone. In 1877, in his acceptance speech on his induction into the Royal Academy, the writer and politician Pedro Antonio de Alarcón—a former and now repenting republican—exalted aesthetic beauty as an idea that rendered laughable any democratic project embodied in universal suffrage.[31] In the 1890s, as voting rights were back on the table, the museum was, once again, positioned as a mirror. When a new electoral vote was being debated in Congress in 1890, the right-wing *La Monarquía* covered with pleasure the claims filed by participants in the National Art Exhibition against the decisions of the jury "elected by universal vote": "if our suffrage brings similar results in our first [direct] elections, a fine mess we'll be in!"[32] (When the law of universal suffrage was finally approved in 1890, authorities asked if the museum could host an electoral precinct. The answer was a firm no.)[33] During this time period, whenever the government limited or debated citizens' rights, young artists and democratically minded art critics would direct their voices and their questioning at something they still had a voice in— the system according to which Spanish art was selected, judged, and exhibited. In this respect, developments in the Spanish art world followed the course earlier witnessed in France, where each postrevolutionary step back meant greater participation in the debates about the location and jurying of the salons.

In contrast to what happened in France, however, none of the three monarchs of the Spanish Restoration were art enthusiasts. Instead, and fortunately for the

Prado Museum, understanding art was becoming the fashion among government officials. Antonio Cánovas de Castillo, the former leader of the conservative minority in the postrevolutionary Cortes and the designer of the Restoration regime, was a keen supporter of the arts. A connoisseur of ancient sculpture, he would eventually become a member of the Academia San Fernando (1887). In his acceptance speech, he praised the National Museum's pictorial masterpieces and denounced the "unpleasant confusion" reigning in its collection of ancient marbles.[34] One of Cánovas's most transcendent cultural experiments was the foundation, in 1877, of the Museo Nacional de Reproducciones Artísticas (National Museum of Artistic Reproductions).[35] Having planned it as the center of artistic and educational innovation, he commissioned the museum design and development of the collection to the anglophile Juan Facundo Riaño, who had created the Spanish section of the British Museum and had earlier participated in the development of the Central Archive and the British Library.

Somewhat unexpectedly for an admirer of the "marble nations" of ancient democracies,[36] Cánovas's system gave enhanced influence to the nobility, the clergy, and the army. Conversely, the workers' associations had to go underground, since freedom of assembly was no longer guaranteed. A number of professors from Universidad Central were fired because their teachings, inspired by the pantheist German philosopher Karl Christian Friedrich Krause, did not agree with Catholic dogma. By 1876 these professors would regroup and found a private Institución Libre de Enseñanza, which soon became the platform for Spain's educational reform. The college featured among its honorary members the world's most renowned scientists, including Charles Darwin, and included among its faculty Spain's most committed liberal statesmen, such as Nicolás Salmerón (ex-president of the First Republic in 1873–74) and the writer Juan Valera (the former director of public instruction). There were a number of elected officials among the college actual or honorary professors, and they would use their positions to promote social reforms, becoming part of a growing government minority unsatisfied with the status quo. Their plans for improving public education, inspired by the philosophy of the Institución, included provisions for teaching art theory in secondary and even elementary schools. Friedrich Froebel's thinking on early child development and British social reformism—the traditions underpinning the Institución's art curriculum—gave high priority to aesthetic education in general and museum-going in particular. When reformers from this circle took the lead in the Museum of Artistic Reproductions, its collection was expanded, with items ranging from plaster copies of ancient statues to all kinds of artifacts from world and Spanish history. In 1882, this group even founded its own exhibiting venue, the National Pedagogical Museum. (Its influence on the Prado will be discussed separately.)

There was thus no shortage of national museums in Restoration Spain; just like the European niche exhibits, they focused on education and seemed to leave the former National Museum, now merged with the former royal one, completely outside of their plans and endeavors.[37] Yet did they? In the last quarter of the century, the Prado had five directors, all renowned artists. We already know two of them: Francisco Sans, appointed under the First Republic, directed the museum until his death in 1881, after which Federico de Madrazo was invited back. In addition to running the Prado, presiding over the Academy, and receiving numerous commissions for portraits, Madrazo had been a senator since 1877 and still served as the director of the School of Painting, Etching, and Sculpture of the Academia San Fernando.[38]

Even though Madrazo's return to the museum and his extensive obligations would seem to have precluded any reform measures at the Prado, the museum had a new social mission to fulfill that did not allow it to turn into an ivory tower of art for art's sake. Having successfully recovered from revolutionary secularism, the church figured prominently again in Spain's nation-building project. Federico de Madrazo was one of the champions of this neo-Catholic program, giving the National Museum a role of paramount importance: mediating between the state and the church by circulating religious imagery in the public sphere. The museum's reputation as a middle ground where cult and culture met proved to be particularly important for attracting middle-class women who were chastized for stepping out into public or visitors from the provinces, where the local priests were still held as higher authorities than local political leaders. If in the eyes of the clerics the National Museum became an enshrined public place for citizens to enjoy the splendor of Spain as a Catholic empire, the supporters of secularization meanwhile found in it a comfortable alternative that could take certain social groups and their rituals away from the temples.

Unlike the church, the court would never re-emerge as a decisive political force in Spain, despite the return of Isabel II and the issuing of over three hundred new noble titles under Alfonso XII and Alfonso XIII.[39] As for the army, it seemed content with the status quo and stopped staging coups once the government ceased interfering with its internal affairs. But this also meant that Spain lost an opportunity to modernize at a time when other nations, having witnessed the triumph of Prussia over France, were reorganizing their armies. Failing to improve its organization, the military could not respond to the challenges of colonial wars, which were reflected close to the Prado only in the colonial exhibitions at the Retiro. In 1898, the loss of Spain's last colonies would precipitate the most painful national crisis in Spanish history. The population blamed the government for the failure, and the intellectuals would receive official backing for their programs of national "regeneration."

Restoration democracy took the form of an obligatory rotation (called *turno pacífico*) between two ruling parties, Cánovas's Liberal Conservative Party and the Liberal Party, led by Mateo Sagasta. Yet since at least some of the senators could be elected rather than appointed, the new president of the Senate drafted a plan that would make the institution as visible and dignified as a democratic institution could be: he decreed the transformation of its old building, a former sixteenth-century convent, into a "sort of gallery of contemporary Spanish painting, to be visited by everyone wishing to have a precise, exact, and fair idea of its importance in our times."[40] Inspired by the throne chambers of the royal palaces of Dresden and Munich, the Royal Gallery of the British Houses of Parliament, and the staircase of the Berlin Museum, the president of the Senate included an impressive list of major events in the world's and Spain's history that these paintings and sculptures would depict. Belatedly, the country was joining the fad that had taken hold all across Europe—raising the status of parliamentary monarchies by turning their parliaments into museums.

Until a smooth parliamentary process became a reality, however, museums provided a popular arena for rehearsing positions on the issues that required attention, from centralism to slavery, from urbanization to class struggle.[41] More of these controversies could be articulated in the representative institutions after Alfonso XII's death in 1885, when Cánovas opted to unite all political parties under the common cause of supporting the constitutional monarchy. This ushered in changes so forward-looking that in 1895 Emilio Castelar, former president of the First Republic, called Spain "the most democratic state possible in a monarchical form,"[42] despite its royalty and the officialdom of the church. But parliamentary democracy and the advances it brought about also gave rise to social polarization and violence. Even the 1890 universal suffrage law, ratified by the Senate, was approved only after a heated debate in Congress, whose members were not sure whether it would be a good idea to allow the masses to express their will. And although its implementation gave voting rights to peasants and landless middle-class men over twenty-one, voter abstention would remain between 33 and 40 percent. Normally the lack of stability in the understanding of citizenship translates into a culture where social groups dispute in public spaces the hegemony that is denied to them politically. This is why end-of-the-century discussions about the National Museum would channel the clashing aspirations of the nostalgic elites, the supporters of church privileges, middle-class men tired of seeing their rights continuously redrawn, women seeking public recognition, and the federalist supporters of independence in Catalonia, Basque Country, and Galicia.

At the Prado, the conflicts over citizenship rights resonated in the form of heated debates surrounding the nomination of museum directors. Madrazo died in 1894, succeeded by a former pupil, Vicente Palmaroli (1894–96), whose tenure at the museum was brief: he died two years after his appointment.[43] For many, Palmaroli's death promised a new era in the administration that would give civil society, or at least the artistic community, a role similar to the one it played in running the salons in nearby France. When the news of Palmaroli's passing away became known, artists and journalists demanded that the history painter Francisco Pradilla, at the time residing in Rome, be appointed director.[44] Never before had the public had a voice in these questions, and Pradilla, although a famous artist, was not even an academician. But, despite it being an unusual outcome, the people got their way: the Ministerio de Fomento decided to "get inspired by the wishes of public opinion" and asked the regent queen to ratify the proposed changes in the museum's statutes in order to make Pradilla eligible.

The era of universal suffrage was therefore ushering some democratizing changes into the Prado as well. A true celebration followed: journalists hailed Pradilla's appointment as no less than "a 'reconquista' of good taste and beauty" and a "national issue that should make us proud."[45] Hailed as "an extraordinary Spaniard,"[46] Pradilla assumed the position in November of 1896.[47] But he did not remain long in the post. In April of 1897, a woman copyist discovered that one of Murillo's paintings (which was actually a copy) was missing. Worst of all, it had disappeared on a Sunday, a day of free public admission. The masses of nonpaying visitors flooding the building were now under suspicion, as were the changes brought by Pradilla, who had decreed that more entrances be open on Sunday in order to make the museum more accessible. A widely publicized investigation ensued, and criticisms aimed at the director, who resigned a year later. Something was achieved, however: the next director, Luis Álvarez Catalá (1897–1901), was also a much-praised artist (mostly of historical and genre paintings) but not a member of the Academia San Fernando. Like his predecessor, he resided in Rome and was called back to Spain to be the director of the Prado. But Álvarez Catalá's years were also numbered: he died in 1901, one of the first victims of the infamous "Spanish flu."

The quasi-general election of the museum's director reflected the struggle of urban middle-class men for political participation. But workers' voices were also becoming stronger. Fearing a revolutionary outbreak, the government took measures to examine and regulate not only labor conditions but also the living conditions of Spain's workers. In 1883, a special Commission for Social Reform was created under the Ministry of the Interior. During the 1885 debates at the Cortes, José María Labra (an *Institucionista* politician) quoted the British statesman Robert Lowe: new voters were becoming "our new masters," and the government therefore had to spare neither time nor money in educating them. Nothing would have more impact on the future of the Prado Museum than this seemingly fortuitous meeting of class anxieties and political possibilities under the umbrella of end-of-the-century debates about social reform.

The government used the occasion of the remodeling in the Prado to create jobs that would palliate the so-called workers' crisis, while inside the museum the staff, which was undergoing a deep generational change, demanded participation in governance.[48] At the end of 1877, a little over half of the employees at the Prado had arrived after 1868, with mostly just lower-level workers such as ushers and doormen still belonging to the old guard who had been hired under the system of old-regime privileges.[49] These privileges had always allowed workers to pass their posts on to descendants and even to live inside the museum, so they did not welcome the prospect of becoming simply hired labor. In 1884, when a fire almost destroyed the Royal Armory—another old-regime establishment—Federico de Madrazo ordered that the remaining living quarters at the Prado, housing seven guards and two doormen, be removed from the museum and negotiated a small monthly compensation for those who now had to rent their own apartments.[50] It was then that the Prado became a site of class struggle. The ushers, none of whom were affected by the change and so received no extra compensation, considered themselves offended and began demanding raises. By 1887, they showed enough corporate awareness to cite the working conditions of the staff of foreign museums, using somewhat threatening overtones to remind their employers that "trust" was what made their work successful.[51] With time, the qualifications required to get a job at the Prado became more numerous and specific, and by the early twentieth century the museum directors would have guards and ushers doubling as in-house spies, whose undercover obligations included finding out the whereabouts and morals of the staff, their families, and their friends. The increasing number of robberies that accompanied the growth of the art market made such knowledge about their staff very important to the directors.

While civil society was slowly developing an interest in museums, the returning Bourbons did not try to reappropriate their ancestors' art collection, and it was left to the government to establish its museum policy. As a faithful representation of the parliamentary monarchy, the directors now had to recognize both the cultural role of the Crown and the administrative prerogatives of the state. Whenever museum policy came under discussion, the government found itself mediating among the public voices that were debating the state's role as the guarantor of the citizens' education and well-being. This is why in 1887 Ceferino Araujo Sánchez dedicated to the "current and future Ministers of Fomento" his newspaper columns criticizing the deficiencies of the Prado. He also demanded that more information about the directors' decisions be released in the press.[52] Federico de Madrazo, then the director, responded in print, but, after the author's persistent follow-ups, he stopped replying. In private, however, someone in the museum's administration collected and studied Araujo Sánchez's columns and other journalistic articles, clippings of which, abundantly underlined in red, are still preserved in the archive of the Prado.

THE LEISURE ZONE

The confiscations of land during the Revolution had transformed the areas east of the museum into one big construction site for the growing Barrio del Buen Retiro (map 5). The developers, promising safety and quiet to their future renters, vehemently supported the regulation of leisure in the area, regulation that both the liberal reformers and the directors of the Prado had so long and unsuccessfully demanded. Control of pastimes on the Promenade became inevitable, and while work was underway to limit the times and places of the traditional semirural activities by enforcing rules

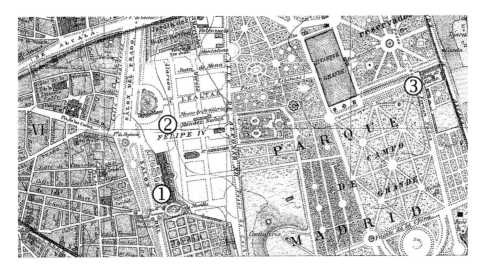

MAP 5   José Pilar Morales, Pedro Peñas, Otto Neussel, *Plano de Madrid*, 1879, detail with streets behind the museum still only traced.

1. Prado Museum (still called the Museo Real) with the outline of its garden; 2. The projected Barrio del Buen Retiro; 3. The old Royal Zoo (La Casa de Fieras).

and arranging gates, the Paseo del Prado became a model of bourgeoisie-led class consensus.

Civic festivities and patron-saint celebrations continued with ever-increasing allure. Yet unlike their revolutionary predecessors, rather than discourage the uses of the Promenade for leisure, the post-1874 government of Madrid chose to make old-school fairgrounds commercial. Aimed at promoting "civilized" consumption and replenishing the city treasury, the politics of leisure during the Restoration was marked by three processes: festivals were unchained from the cycle of religious festivals, secularized, and became increasingly nationalistic; patron-saint, "fun," and commercial fairs merged and began to offer similar attractions; gated areas for leisure and entertainment mushroomed around open-air fairs and occasionally abandoned these old locations to be closer to the areas of urban renewal. During this period, traditional and modern pastimes peacefully coexisted on and around the Prado Promenade because modern urbanized activities and spaces were adding to—not replacing—the ones with ties to the rural world. The city and church authorities worked together with private investors to conflate religious and civic holidays, patron-saint and neighborhood celebrations, and their commercial and free offerings. The growing importance of gated leisure spots is reflected on the 1883 map of Madrid by Emilio Valverde, where all such areas with limited admission—gardens charging entrance fees, theaters, commercial exhibits, and private mansions hosting balls and parties—are marked in capital letters (map 6). The fact that this is how city monuments and state-run museums, including

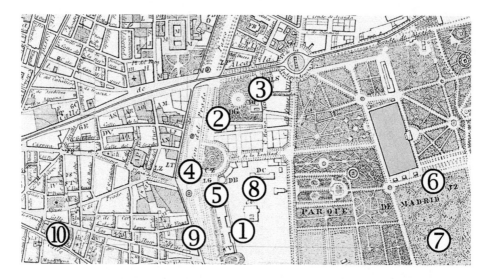

MAP 6   Emilio Valverde, *Plano de Madrid*, 1883, detail. Capital letters point to indoor and outdoor leisure areas, both state-run and private. Small letters refer to churches and convents.

1. CV: Prado Museum; 2. DG: Jardines del Buen Retiro; 3. DF: Theater of the Jardines del Buen Retiro; 4. LG: Circo Hipódromo; 5. Mr. Bidel's Exhibition of Wild Beasts; 6. Palacio de Velázquez; 7. Palacio de Cristal; 8. DB: Panorama of the battle of Tetuán; 9. Platería Martínez; 10. Museum of Anatomy and Pathology in Hospital San Juan de Dios.

the "National Museum of Paintings," are also marked suggests that they were classified as places akin to these other venues. Conversely, there are no special markers for the open gathering areas and for the promenades.

In the early years of the Restoration, the continuing festivals projected the same image of apparent social unity interrupted by hidden class differences that they had acquired under Isabel II. In 1875, a reporter covering the first San Isidro held under the Restoration still contended that personally he would not lament too much the disappearance of an event "from which public morals gained so little and which would so often give rise to abuses and bloody excesses."[53] The report made it clear, however, that, while the crowds in the traditional pilgrimage–cum–fun area by the Manzanares River were mostly working-class and the celebrations themselves seemed lacking in taste, at night the neighborhood of the museum continued to be their favored locale. The masses here were still rubbing elbows with the bourgeois on the Promenade, and even the king would occasionally pass by.

The real, gated "leisure zones" emerged on and around the Paseo, sometimes in close proximity to the ungated gathering spots. This was the case with the Jardines de Buen Retiro (Buen Retiro Gardens, which should not be confused with the current Retiro Park), located next to the Salón del Prado. (The garden, formerly a royal possession given to the City, was eventually eliminated in 1905 to build the grand Palace of Communications, which currently houses the government of Madrid.) The City turned this area, marked as "DG" on map 6, into a pleasure garden complete with cafés, elegant vending kiosks, gazebos, band kiosks, a theater (marked as "DF"), and dancing grounds (map 6:2, 3). Even though the development of the Jardines was entrusted to private investors, the City reserved the right to regulate the admission fee (one peseta) and hours of operation and to ban the use of fireworks. No one could remain in the area one and a half hours after the end of the last theater performance.[54]

153

Closer to the museum, by the Plaza de la Lealtad, an establishment called "Hippodrome Circus" (marked as "LG," map 6:4) advertised clown performances and a show of a "tiger-woman." Right next to Villanueva's building, the developments in the Tívoli further questioned the traditional definitions of art, adding more fun and variety to the mix while also capitalizing on the blurring of distinctions between a display and a performance. In November of 1877, pedestrians on the Paseo del Prado were surprised by the sight of a strangely shaped building erected on the former site of José de Madrazo's residence. It was "Monsieur Bidel's Exhibition of Wild Beasts," also known as "M. Bidel's Zoo" (map 6:5). *La Ilustración Española y Americana* jokingly warned the museum's director not to leave the facilities at the animals' feeding time, in case the cages were not quite secure.[55] In order to generate hype for his enterprise, Bidel had put together an "exhibition," as reporters called it, of images of the animals that would soon actually inhabit the space. By Christmastime, passersby could already see tigers and lions walking up and down their cages, being fed, and demonstrating their prowess.[56] Admission was twice as high as at the National Museum, but this did not seem to deter the public. Bidel's show was not the only one involving animals in Madrid: during the holiday season of 1877–78 it had to compete with two theatrical and circus enterprises.[57] Reviewing the theater season of 1877, *La Iberia* humorously listed Bidel's zoo among other "achievements of Spanish art."[58]

At the time, the conflation of subject-object and human-animal distinctions and the absorption of art into entertainment was already becoming a marker of modern visual culture all across Europe, and it was no different in Spain. In Madrid, the fascination with animal exhibits became so overwhelming that newspapers satirized it as representative of Spain's postrevolutionary public life in general. Both the conservative and liberal press shared this tongue-in-cheek approach to the fad, stating that Madrid, as it filled with animals, was getting dangerous. "The woods must be empty [by now], let's run into the woods!" the note concluded.[59] Meanwhile, those who did not run to the woods could enjoy the now-municipal Parque de Madrid (Madrid Park, currently the Retiro) east of the Paseo del Prado, where since 1881 special gated areas had been arranged in imitation of the world's fairs, and were called La Feria de Madrid (the Madrid Fair). This became the prime location of the "Madrid Fairs," in plural, the name given in 1879 to a bourgeois sequel to the San Isidro celebration that turned the month of May in Madrid into an ongoing commercial celebration competing with the old-regime Fall Fair. That same year the May Fairs included a flower exhibition at Madrid Park.[60] In 1883, the flower exhibit moved to the Jardines del Buen Retiro, and a Metallurgical and Mining Exhibition was opened instead in a special pavilion built for this purpose in Madrid Park (map 6:6). Now known as the Palacio de Velázquez, after its architect, Ricardo Velázquez Bosco, the pavilion was later followed by the Palacio de Cristal, by the same architect, a miniature copy of the Great Exhibition's Crystal Palace.

In 1887, the territory of Madrid Park adjacent to the old Casa de Fieras (Royal Zoo, map 5:3) was fenced in to become the site of the colonial Philippine Exhibition and its sequels, which displayed an Alaskan Eskimo tribe next to an exhibition of tropical animals, and then a village of "Santiago Indians" with their church.[61] This was not unusual, given how common it was to collide and combine together people and exhibits in the second half of the nineteenth century.[62] As mentioned earlier, the participants in world's fairs not only used this technique for legitimizing the continuity between art and spectacle but also sent such colonial installations on an autoethnographic spin. More disturbing was how neatly this arrangement, in Alda Blanco's incisive analysis, dovetailed with modern museum culture: the products and artifacts "appropriated" from the colony were collected in the central exhibition pavilion and arranged as an innovative museum of art and industry.[63]

In this context, it is hardly surprising—although still disturbing—that after 1895 the same gated section of Madrid Park became the pleasure ground to celebrate other fashionable events combining industrial displays, animal exhibits, "sportized" leisure, and fine arts salons that the bourgeoisie of Madrid put together in an effort to relocate the traditional San Isidro festival away from the Pradera and the excesses associated with interclass mingling there. Railroad companies offering discounted tickets, ongoing civil and international wars and recruitments, and the centralist policies of the Restoration state brought growing numbers of people from the provinces to join the crowds of celebrating Madrileños, and the city authorities and commercial associations saw new financial opportunities. The program featured events taking place in the gated sections of the Madrid Park: an exhibition of livestock later renamed the Livestock and Agricultural Machinery Exhibition, a commercial show of paintings and sculpture organized by El Círculo de Bellas Artes (a private fine arts association in Madrid), a dog exhibition, and, eventually, the *batallas de flores*—competitions of carriages or automobiles adorned with flowers—which became a participatory artistic activity for the rich to display themselves artistically adorned in the streets, on the move.

The model "leisure zone" was therefore emerging in a special area freshly built in the park, not on the promenades. Still, for the inhabitants of Madrid, many of whom were urban newcomers, these innovative facilities were a place to retrain—upon payment of an admission fee—centuries-old Carnival attitudes as a fairground "stare" modernized and disguised as a civilizing force. The caricaturists got plenty of opportunities to bring the exhibited people, animals, and fairgoers together in their cartoons that traced parallels between the races observable in the dog world and the social divisions within the human race (fig. 22). Since the "laborers of the pen"—as Margot Versteeg calls the journalists working in late nineteenth-century Madrid—often hailed from the provinces, these images put the bourgeois culture of the capital on display through the eyes of fictionalized outsiders with no less scorn than the urban dwellers themselves were directing at their rural and provincial countrymen.[64]

Amid the modern leisure areas emerging within walking distance, the Prado Promenade retained its old popular appeal, even though the city authorities, seeking ways to reimagine the area, began to dispense abundant licenses to vendors and providers of commercial amusement. During the San Isidro of 1875, the merry-go-round and the doughnut stands were located in the former Tívoli, across the street from the Prado Museum. But in May of 1878 "the provincial and city governments, associations of commerce and industry, and some private entre-

FIG. 22   Cilla, illustration for Eduardo de Palacio, "Odios de raza" (Racial hatred). *Madrid Cómico* 15, no. 640 (May 25, 1895): 189.

preneurs" came together in a joint effort to establish "magnificent recreation pavilions" and "attractive and elegant stalls selling all sorts of objects," thus de facto turning the Paseo del Prado into a new, commercial continuation of the San Isidro festivities.[65] The items offered for sale included such objects as wigs and hair extensions, and the buyers were referred to as a "public" coming to learn about the advantages of this merchandise, suggesting a strong parallelism between exhibition, entertainment, and commerce.[66]

Faced with the need to protect the importance of Villanueva's building within the changing landscape of Madrid, the museum directors and their superiors at the Fomento proposed turning it into another gated area. As early as August 1875, Agustín Felipe Peró, a municipal architect, warned the City that urban sprawl would make the museum a "ridiculous view" amidst blocks of flats, and proposed that the City establish a protected zone free of construction around Villanueva's structure, destroy the San Jerónimo, build a straight staircase leading to the northern façade, and plant gardens on the two esplanades north of and behind the museum.[67] In June of 1877, *El Globo* published an etching that may have captured the building's appearance shortly before extensive landscaping began. It shows both the northern façade and the esplanade

156

Exterior del Museo del Prado.

FIG. 23 "The Exterior of the Prado Museum," *El Globo* 3 (segunda época), no. 603 (June 5, 1877): 1.

FIG. 24 Hauser y Menet, *The Plaza de Neptuno and the Prado Museum*, c. 1910. Postcard. Author's collection.

untouched, while in front of the western façade stretches a garden with bushes, finely cut trees, and flowers with no wall or gate, enclosed only by a low fence (fig. 23).

In the following years, this view would change drastically. Masses of land would be moved, slopes and hills would be leveled, new streets would be laid north and east of the museum, and the building's architecture would be altered. By June 1879, the whole hill reducing the building's northern façade was gone, and Francisco Jareño, the architect working for the Fomento, had submitted a proposal to build a double-sided, six-flight staircase (fig. 24).[68] When the excavation extended farther north towards the former Tívoli, the archway and a gate that had been regulating access to the San Jerónimo and the Retiro had to go as well.[69] This put the Prado Museum in the center of the emerging urban node that connected several routes leading from the old, Habsburg Madrid to the new recreation centers in the park and east of the Salón del Prado, described above. The numbers of people gathering and passing by made the directors wonder how they could mark the museum's territory as special and distinguished in ways that idle crowds could not destroy. When the Academia San Fernando demanded that the new staircase be in harmony with the building, and the architect proposed a three-part bas-relief representing allegories of Painting, Sculpture, and Architecture, Federico de Madrazo insisted on redirecting the funds to commission sculptures in marble and put them high up on the northern pediment, out of passersby's destructive reach.[70]

Despite these efforts, however, the building remained an ungated structure attracting both the working-class fairground regulars and the bourgeois patrons of the fair in the park. Such a borderline position continued bringing rural and provincial visitors to the museum. Madrid newspapers, which since the late 1860s had been mocking the way that these visitors snapped up discount rail tickets to come to the San Isidro, now coined the word *Isidro* to describe these travelers ready to consume whatever entertainment they could find in the capital. This also included the National Museum. Journalists looked with scorn at the middle-class "out-of-towners" who brought their families to the festivals and the museum, only to run into their own neighbors from home and waste the day discussing food and accommodations instead of looking at paintings.[71] In 1897, commenting on the visit to Madrid of the prince of Siam, one reporter stated that His Majesty acted in exactly the same way as an *Isidro*: "employ half an hour to visit the Prado [Museum], buy souvenirs, and leave."[72] Such visitors were routinely portrayed in the press as keen museum-goers with no clue about art. In 1896, *Militares y paisanos*, the illustrated supplement to *La Correspondencia Militar*, joked that the minister of Fomento had declared visits to the Museum of Paintings during the San Isidro "free of charge and mandatory."[73]

Despite the City's efforts to commercialize the pastimes on the Prado Promenade and the directors' attempts to keep the *Isidros* in the minority and prevent their attitudes from becoming standard, the activities with merry-go-rounds, swings, and open-air dances continued around the museum. In 1884, the assortment of visual attractions added one more spectacle: the *guiñol*, or puppet theater.[74] The word *verbena* now referred not only to nightly gatherings but also to their locations on this urban fairground, which for a while grew wider and remained on the Paseo for longer stretches of time despite all campaigns waged by the museum administration. Eventually, however, this began to change. In 1889, the directors convinced the City not to authorize vending pavilions for the Fall Fair, and by 1902 even managed to push through a ban on installing kiosks in front of Villanueva's building.

The attempts at modernizing pastimes on the Prado Promenade were generating an increasingly more sophisticated visual culture building on the cycle of patron-saint celebrations and old festival attractions yet catering to the bourgeoisie's growing nationalism and unrelenting desire for entertainment.[75] These new attractions occasionally intertwined with museum culture to produce interesting hybrids that were popular while also pretending to be highbrow. In 1880, this mix was depicted in *Madrid Cómico*'s humorous report about a presumed historical panorama—a "cosmography exhibit" soon to be installed in front of the museum. At that time, works were actually underway on the Plaza de la Lealtad to build a real "Grand Panorama" (map 6:8). The installation, which opened in 1881 and ran through 1883, represented the battle of Tetuán, an episode of Spain's last successful colonial war and the subject of a large-scale painting by Mariano Fortuny. The original had been commissioned in the 1860s by the City of Barcelona and remained there, but now the panorama artists sharpened, enlarged, and extended it to simulate complete immersion.[76] The project, executed by a Belgian company, was supposed to satisfy the metropolitan bourgeoisie's fascination with national history. The coverage, however, suggested that in Spain the intended audiences were still woefully lacking in knowledge. The journal's informant, whom the author introduced as a "public official," reportedly confused the scene of his nation's triumph with fairground "representations of popular customs," which turned out to be none other than "The Battle of Salado in Málaga": "the public official claims that the scene features a fellow . . . nicknamed *El Salado* fighting with a *navaja* in his hands against ten or twelve individuals of the same kind, leaving the battlefield covered with corpses."[77] It would be hard to find a more popular version of national history.

Several new establishments in the museum's surroundings now carried the name of "exhibition" and outdid the museum not only in their admission prices but also in popularity. They displayed work that high cultural forms were still officially rejecting. Since the late 1870s, the Platería Martínez across from the Paseo (the former site of the diorama) had housed a commercial "permanent exhibition of fine arts" featuring paintings on popular religious or historical topics that could not find a place at any serious art museum—for example, *Saint Francis of Assisi Receiving an Embrace from Christ Crucified*, supposedly an original by Murillo (map 6:9).[78] Farther west, the Museum of Anatomy and Pathology exhibited over a hundred wax figures, which had

been a part of the Spanish section at the 1878 world's fair in Paris, illustrating different skin infections (map 6:10).[79] By the end of the century, the fusion between high
art, the commercial forms of visual entertainment, and the production of knowledge
also reached the Prado Museum, whose director included in the 1899 events commemorating Velázquez's tercentennial "luminous projections" of the artist's paintings
over the museum's façade. The innovation drew ironic remarks from the *Gedeon*—a
bourgeois erotic magazine—whose editors, unhappy with the show's likeness to mass
entertainment, asked why the planning committee could not simply call the attraction
by its "real" name—the "magic lantern."[80]

Thus, though the last quarter of the nineteenth century really saw the birth of
Spain's modern "exhibitionary complex," unlike the state-controlled disciplinary institutions described by Bennett, on the Prado these displays were marked by a high
degree of influence from popular culture. Yet rather than offer a lasting picture of
social peace, the Promenade remained inclusive only as long as the street was not politicized and the commercial sphere failed to attract the attention of social reformers.
The continuous construction in the area made it unsafe for passersby, and it frequently
figured in the newspapers' incident reports as a place where one could trick or be
tricked, hide or find contraband, and bury or unearth corpses. Because it was situated
in the middle of Madrid's underregulated and unpoliced melting pot, the museum
also became a habitual marker in reports of robberies, suicides, or deaths caused by
malnutrition or gunfire.[81]

Although these accounts did not directly refer to continuing camping at night
and prostitution at all hours around the museum, the reality can be inferred from the
municipal authorities' petitions to the owners of water kiosks on the Prado to assist
them with ending "certain abuses" committed "late at night in their establishments."[82]
The curious comments about the confusion between art and life also reflected the reputation that prostitution was giving to the museum's surroundings: enthralled by the
nudes, male visitors carried their excitement outdoors, facing the risk of being severely
misunderstood. In 1883, a comical "Nocturne" described an ecstatic visitor deploying
the lingo of art criticism in front of a pretty woman just outside the museum, only to
make her think she was being taken for a harlot:

> —Please allow me
>   To admire you *en-face* ecstatically.
> —Sir, please step away.
>   Keep in mind that, although you see me alone,
>   I am a decent girl.[83]

Several robberies at the museum, failed and successful, were recorded during
these years as more and more people began to realize the commercial value of art. In
the past, vandals and thieves had not thought much about paintings, and hence the

damages registered in the museum were insignificant: during its first fifty years, all that disappeared were pieces of lead and iron rods from the window blinds that one of the guards' sons was caught stealing in the 1850s, and precious stones that Grajera found missing from a mosaic table. But by the late 1870s, the criminal appetite for pictorial art had begun to match its growing popularity with the general public. For the time being, the thieves came from the world of art. In 1876, a musician from the orchestra of the Teatro Real was caught carrying a Flemish landscape under his cape.[84] In 1883, a young man, "blinded by his love of art," tried to steal what the reporter identified as "a copy of a painting by Titian that is hanging in the Grand [Central] Gallery, titled *Love and Painting.*"[85] (Catalogues featured no painting by that name, but it could have been *Allegory* [number 497], identified as a copy of a painting by Titian in Madrazo's 1882 catalogue.) Judging by the fact that he carried with him a chain from a paint box that had been missing from the museum for a few days, as well as several portable customs seals, this may have been an inside job.[86]

The newspapers could not be serious even when a real robbery occurred in April of 1897. When a small painting attributed to Murillo (a study for *Saint Anne Teaching the Virgin Mary*) disappeared from the museum, the reporter from *El Siglo Futuro* opined that if the burglar had had any real understanding of art, he would have stolen the nearby *Mater Dolorosa*, a painting comparable in size but more highly valued.[87] With myriads of poor artists coming to Madrid to make it and failing, the distance between studying paintings and stealing them could be short. In 1890, *La Ilustración Artística* published, under the subtitle "A Realist Novel," a story about an impoverished artist-in-training who stole colors from his fellow copyists working at the Prado in order to finish a copy of *Mary Magdalene* by Ribera that could be exchanged for a pair of boots.[88] In turn-of-the-century Spain, those interested in stealing paintings were still likely to know something about art.

Class warfare on the Prado Promenade took new forms and was rising steadily in the end of the nineteenth century. Providing convenient thoroughfares for marching crowds and spacious places for orators to give their speeches, the area from the Botanical Garden all the way to the Salón del Prado was also the home of May Day political demonstrations, the first of which was held in the Jardines del Buen Retiro in 1890. Later in the month it was followed by artists gathering in the museum's portico to protest the jury decisions at the National Exhibition.[89] Peaceful political rallies on the Prado gave socialist writers a chance to portray cleanly dressed male and female workers acting out bourgeois values.[90] Still, in an area that the City tried to secure as the "leisure zone," protesting masses seemed to point to the limits of the peaceful coexistence of all citizens under the benevolent eye of municipal leaders.

While the Prado Promenade acted as a stage for these new civic activities, high-rise Madrid was being built behind the museum, and it was therefore logical that the authorities' main efforts to keep the peace were concentrated on the districts that hitherto had been the Promenade's backwaters. These housing developments had triggered considerable debate, even among the government's advisory bodies. The initial 1877 agreement between the Ministerio de Hacienda and the City reserved the area east of the museum for an English-style garden—something that would offer an alternative to the rural reputation of the Promenade on the other side. Madrid society during the Restoration years took particular interest in trees. In the public's mind, gardens and landscaping became firmly associated with the progress of civilization.[91] In this context, the museum, which in the 1860s had pioneered the use of gardens for decorating public buildings, appeared a perfect location for showcasing rare and useful plants. In 1878, the City even approved a special project for establishing a bird and flower market inside that planned garden, gaining the applause from the liberal press.[92] Still, the museum and its bosses in the Fomento clashed with the government of Madrid and the Hacienda, which were interested in building streets and apartments to expand the city's tax base. Eventually, a beautification project containing a provision to put a fence around the museum's eastern limits prevailed, but there was no longer talk of a bird or flower market, which had moved to the "leisure zones" more successfully established in Madrid Park and the Jardines del Buen Retiro.

The entire back façade and the pavilions built in the museum's two backyards were to be rearranged, and a railing was to be built to enclose the museum's territory, which would be turned into gardens. This area would also house two new pavilions and water hydrants. The apse had to match the height of the building, and a massive renovation inside the Sala de la Reina Isabel would replace the balustrade with a surface that would separate the room into two floors.[93] The remaking of the museum's exterior therefore became interlaced with its interior reorganization and expansion, and the former apse was transformed into an alternative façade overlooking the new Madrid spreading east from the museum's grounds. Debates about how that side would look continued for over a decade. While that remained undecided, without any new construction to carry out, work on the eastern fence began, and the museum's new gate was approved.

Since the museum's modern façades were under permanent construction, its most visible view continued to be the western wall overlooking the Paseo del Prado. The solemn entrance behind the colonnade was still out of use, and in 1879 the monument commemorating Daoíz and Velarde, the martyrs of the 1808 anti-Napoleonic uprising, was installed in front of that door. Initially a part of the collection of the Museo Real, it had been moved to adorn the Retiro in the 1850s and in 1868 was moved to the artillery park of Monteleón, which the revolutionary city planners hoped to transform into a war memorial.[94] Now, although everyone understood that a failed memorial site was no place for the nation's heroes, even the return of the statue to the museum's territory was perceived as political retribution equal to an "imprisonment," as one writer had it, downplaying the heroes' example by reinserting it into the domain of art.[95]

After 1891, when postrevolutionary liberties were restored, talks began about another transfer of the Daoíz and Velarde monument. This time there was a public debate. Still, a new place for the statue was not found until 1899, and when it was, the location again turned out to be far from ideal. As one commentator remarked, the new monument's address in the recently built neighborhood of Moncloa was placing the heroes of the War of Independence in dangerous proximity to the city jail. On that occasion, however, many thought that the end result did justify the means: the Círculo de Bellas Artes had reached an agreement with the City that, in the place where Daoíz and Velarde's monument had been, the museum's main façade would host a monument to none other than Velázquez.[96]

The monument was inaugurated in 1899 as part of the celebration of the artist's tercentennial. Spirits, Luxenberg writes, were low: Spain had just lost its last colonies to the United States, and no celebration, not even a commemoration of Spain's most universally recognized genius, could change the prevalent mood of self-flagellation.[97] Indeed, the historian Francisco José Portela Sandoval emphasizes that, in comparison with the analogous monument erected in the same year in Seville—Velázquez's birthplace, which was claiming back its artist—the statue by the museum was described as low-key, sad, or decadent. Meant to be approachable and familiar, it was not enclosed by a railing or fence.[98] Writing for the newspaper *Gente Vieja*, the writer Enrique Ramírez de Saavedra confessed his anxiety: "I look in fear at the beautiful statue to Velázquez . . . and cannot feel safe."[99] Apparently, the statue seemed out of place in the neighborhood whose reputation the museum still could not improve.

CLASS, GENDER, AND TASTE

As the City's sporadic attempts at regulating public life were failing to produce another "leisure zone" with gates, admission fees, and sports on the Prado Promenade, museum-going continued to be an activity that could have many reasons behind it. The official statistics revealed a steady rise in visitorship on the days of free public admission. More importantly, however, the numbers demonstrate how well the museum's old-regime reputation of a royal estate accessible only to the happy few who could procure an invitation coexisted with the growing acceptance of an entry fee as was normal in bourgeois recreation (table 1). Thus, between 1874 and 1880, the number of paying visitors tripled, while the number of nonpaying ones grew by only 50 percent. Still, the majority of Spaniards, as disenfranchised from the government as they used to be from the court, simply updated their notion of the royal "reserved space" to account for the new state ownership. Since visitors during the week had to either pay or present special passes, those unfamiliar with gated recreation interpreted this as a form of the old-regime privilege. The number of visitors with a special pass indeed remained high.

TABLE I Museum visitor numbers, 1874–80, reported on March 19, 1881. Archivo del Museo Nacional del Prado.

Year	Paid	Pass	Public entry	Total
1874	3,700	2,000	20,000	29,900
1875	4,800	1,600	21,400	27,800
1876	5,600	2,020	25,700	33,320
1877	11,700	1,000	26,800	39,500
1878	9,900	1,700	25,000	36,600
1879	9,700	3,000	30,000	42,700
1880	11,400	2,600	29,800	43,800
Total	57,000	13,920	178,700	249,620

Mocking this approach, the satirical *Periódico para todos* even ran a story about a mayor of a provincial town and his large family, who refused to visit on a day of free public admission because as carriers of special passes they resisted mixing with the "public." In Madrid's press, the habit of describing the museum as royal heritage persisted until the 1890s. As late as 1891, *La Ilustración Ibérica* joked that, instead of the old-time nobility, the places from the new regime charging entrance fees, such as the "Royal Stables, Natural History [Museum], and the Museum of Paintings," should just admit for free rich men adorned with expensive jewelry. The state was emerging as the heir of the statutory system of privileges, and many saw the museum as a prime example.

Despite these criticisms the museum offered a comfortable setting for a debate concerning cultural modernization, the fragmentation of religious experiences, middle-class identity, and the gendering of the public sphere. The museum's directors were more willing than ever before to accommodate casual visitors. Yet as educated Spaniards redirected their political claims into the sphere of the arts and the less educated ones used the arts as entertainment, the museum's growing appeal was hindered by two contradictions. First, the displays were still laid out in a way that assumed that visitors would have skill in aesthetic comparison, which the majority of them were lacking. And second, despite the museum's popularity with the public and foreign museum-goers, among liberal-minded art connoisseurs it still had the backwards reputation it had inherited from its former crowned owners. So while the statistics showed increasing numbers of visitors, journalists insisted that the museum would remain empty were it not for foreigners crazy about Murillo and Velázquez. Some writers lamented the lack of visitors on Sundays, when admission was free, while others deplored its empty rooms on weekdays, when a ticket was required.[100]

Just as had happened in other countries, the museum's opening to social groups beyond the dilettanti and the artists, whom it had previously privileged, had become unavoidable after the official merger with the former National Museum. Yet although

EN EL MUSEO, *por Ignotus.*

—¡María Santísima! ¿Y esto es lo que se ve en Madrid?... ¡Qué vergüenza!

FIG. 25 "—Holy Virgin Mary! And this is what one comes to Madrid to see? . . . What a shame!" Ignotus, "En el Museo," *La Risa* 1 no. 14 (April 1, 1888): 8.

the new structure even left space for individual and corporate patronage of the arts and art education, the takeover by the state—belated in comparison with Spain's neighbors—significantly reduced the nationalistic message that Spaniards could derive from the Prado.[101] The new owner was already falling behind in meeting the growing demand that "self-governance" and "participation" be used as new ways to describe the nation. Compared to how well the first postrevolutionary officials understood museum education, the lack of a clear policy on public art under the Restoration was also a step backward. This further lowered the government's credibility on matters related to art to a point where, in the 1890s, Rodrigo Soriano came to conclude that Spaniards would never develop aesthetic interests unless the National Fine Art Exhibitions were privatized.[102] He was obviously exaggerating, but the message was clear.

Since people in Spain were only getting acquainted with public art that was not religious, the museum's exhibiting efforts led to widespread confusion about the true purpose of the Prado and the difficulty of differentiating between its educational, nationalistic, leisure, and sacred uses. As the result, three types of gaze were soon established as standard for interpreting the paintings: the piety learned in Spain's churches, the commodifying appreciation of realism and the materiality of the paintings' subject matter, and a playful, slightly indecent, and highly gendered "stare" that moved easily from the works of art to the bodies of the visitors themselves. The last type—the curious gaze reflective of the interests of middle-class metropolitan men—prevailed in the descriptions of the Prado in the Spanish press. Depicting people from the periphery, rural newcomers, women, or former colonial subjects staring in shock at the paintings, the writers were, of course, directing the same type of gaze at the visitors, whose citizenship they called into question by criticizing their taste. These written portraits of the *hoi polloi* at the Prado fulfilled a function similar to the autoethnographic *tableaux vivants* that exhibitors all over Europe were arranging to help their compatriots imagine themselves as a nation.

Given that the state officially supported conflating religious and popular aesthetics, one might have expected to see both legitimated in the museum, but that was not the case. In fact, a public debate about the ideological distinction between looking at paintings in the museum or in churches became a noticeable development of the Restoration years. The bourgeois press took the lead in explaining the difference, mocking the indignant working-class visitors who had come with a set of predispositions borrowed from church and were shocked by what they saw at the Prado. Spain's territorial policies were also drawn into play as journalists from Madrid and Barcelona often caricatured confused village folks from Galicia or Andalusia. And, of course, since women were perceived as the most faithful churchgoers, it was they who often appeared disgusted with the museum in these vignettes and cartoons. Through efforts such as these, the press discredited any cultic or religious attitude toward art as uncivilized or uncivic and, in any event, incompatible with a national museum. "Holy Virgin Mary! And this is what one comes to Madrid to see? . . . What a shame!" read the caption to an 1888 cartoon of a peasant woman shocked by the presence of nude statues at the Prado (fig. 25).[103] "You know what I think? . . . There must have been a convent here and when they threw the priests out, they made it a marionette storage," says a woman with a thick Andalusian accent in another vignette as she looks at plaster statues at the Museum of Artistic Reproductions.[104]

Though these humorous denunciations offered a refreshing response to the comparisons to a temple that Federico de Madrazo continued to favor, they did not mean that the authors of these caricatures or their middle-class audience knew any better how to benefit from museum displays. Still, although there is no direct testimony concerning peasant and working-class experiences, some evidence suggests that visitors indeed continued to confuse the museum and the church. For example, a Russian political exile named Isaak Iakovlev (Pavlovskii) saw a "ragged fellow" crossing himself ecstatically before one of Murillo's *Madonnas*.[105] The anarchist-leaning Russian, of course, took the gesture as proof of the innate artistic taste of the common Spaniard. In reality, though, common visitors could go nowhere to learn about public art, so such pious behavior at the Prado was hardly surprising.

The museum's support for a liminal view of its space as a borderland between the church and civil society continued well into the twentieth century. When Federico de Madrazo died in 1894, his successor started a strange tradition exemplifying this confusion: the refurbishment of the museum's main rotunda into funerary chambers for deceased museum directors (fig. 26).[106] Done for the first time at Federico de Madrazo's funeral (and apparently against his orders and the fire-prevention policies that he had established), it was repeated when Palmaroli himself died two years later and then again in 1901 to pay last respects to Luis Álvarez Catalá. On all three occasions, the rotunda was transformed into a sacred space where art recovered its cultic function. For Madrazo's funeral, Velázquez's *Christ Crucified* was hung between two columns, above the body, while an *Immaculate Conception* by Murillo appeared in an improvised altar behind Madrazo's head. A reporter covering the funeral suggested that the images fulfilled a double function: they "symbolize[d] Catholic spirit and relate[d] the memories of the two great artists to the last honors paid to Madrazo."[107] During Palmaroli's funeral, the similitude between the museum and the church was made even clearer by the religious chants that accompanied the "exhibit," according to the reports.[108] Similarly, the journalists covering the funerary chapel of Álvarez Catalá noted that there was an "altar" with a crucifix arranged at the head of the bed.[109]

While the church thus continued providing the framework through which to see exhibits at the museum—and while the museum was emerging as a secular alternative for housing the rituals of the church—it is also clear that these events reflected a crucial change in the exhibiting standards of public art. At that time, it was left up to the wax-figure shows to display scenes of death and assassination to the urban middle classes, who were already repudiating the fairground freak shows but didn't mind having their senses tickled under the respectable cover of historical education. The "exhibition of corpses," as the museum's funerary chambers were called, went even further to blur the boundaries between public art and fairground thrill.

The adamant demand of the audience at the 1881 National Fine Arts Exhibition that the medal of honor be given to one of the bloodiest paintings in Spanish history, José Casado del Alisal's *The Legend of the Monk King* (1880), suggests that by the 1880s the national imagination was linked with sensationalist realism.[110] On that occasion, the audience's enthusiasm for Casado's canvas forced the state to purchase it for the Prado along with another dark and bloody work, Eduardo Rosales's *Death of Lucretia* (1871). If those were the moods of art-savvy Madrileños, the same sort of taste was present in the gory fairground aesthetic, which was effective in delivering images of the national past to rural populations as well. Hence, although journalists continued making fun of common visitors enthralled by Aparicio's *The Famine in Madrid*, to most other people this propagandistic old-regime painting looked more relevant than ever because of its shocking *avant la lettre* naturalism, now becoming standard for representing national history in a way that was comprehensible to everyone. In 1879,

MADRID.—EXPOSICIÓN DEL CADÁVER DEL EXCMO. SR. D. FEDERICO DE MADRAZO
EN LA ROTONDA DEL MUSEO NACIONAL DE PINTURAS.
(Composición y dibujo de D. A. Ferrant.)

FIG. 26   Alejandro Ferrant Fischermans, "Exposición de cadáver del Excmo. Sr. D. Federico de
Madrazo en la rotonda del Museo Nacional de Pinturas" (Exhibition of the corpse of D. Federico de
Madrazo in the rotunda of the National Museum of Paintings), etching, *La Ilustración Española y
Americana* 38, no. 23 (June 22, 1894): 380.

FIG. 27 "Living pictures" at a benefit event at the Conservatorio. Several costumes are inspired by paintings by Velázquez and Goya in the Prado Museum. *La Ilustración Española y Americana* 44, no. 14 (April 15, 1900): 220–21.

Sans even refused to part with the picture, stating that it could not leave the collection because it was "very well known to the public and especially to people from the villages who only come to the museum to see it."[111] By the 1880s, starvation of a different type, public fasting, would receive the name of "hunger art" and become entertainment—so much so that one such "artist," an Italian named Giovanni Succi, displayed himself as he was fasting at the 1888 world's fair in Barcelona.[112]

As coarser tastes were triumphing in the art world and even receiving recognition, despite the occasional objections of educated patrons and juries, there was still no evidence that either educated or uneducated visitors were aware that viewing art at the museum required a special way of looking. Upper- and middle-class fans of bullfighting—a form of popular entertainment that was quickly becoming an industry and a "sportized" activity—exploited this confusion to their advantage.[113] Since the 1880s, bullfighting aficionados and their press had been demanding recognition of this Spanish tradition as an art form by drawing nationalistically tinged comparisons with the Prado Museum. In 1880, one senator defended his proposition to open bullfighting schools in Madrid and Seville by reminding the audience that creating one such school had not prevented Fernando VII from also founding the Museum of Paintings.[114] Although the proposal was later withdrawn, his juxtaposition of the art exhibit and the arena caught on. "Some would say: 'How can you call artistic a show featuring such barbaric and repugnant things?," wrote one author. His answer was unambiguous: "Extremely delicate people who cannot read [Émile] Zola, finding him far too realistic, . . . who understand Murillo and Raphael, . . . who have learned our classics by heart and know every inch of our Museum of Paintings . . . don't miss a bullfight and enjoy watching them and would not trade an afternoon at the ring for anything in the world."[115] Apparently, *goce* (enjoyment), hitherto a word associated only with religious or aesthetic sensibility, was now used to legitimize the emotion one had watching the bulls.

The nationalistic conflations of painting and bullfighting went both ways, as the emotions caused by art were also compared with the affect people would experience in the arena. In this context, bullfighting was cited as a popular show among many others that succeeded where the museum was failing: in attracting the masses. For art spectatorship to become popular as well, it was suggested, its display and propaganda had to elicit similar strong emotions. In 1894, one of the sharpest criticisms of the government's policy on public art (or lack thereof) came from the pages of *La Lidia*, a bullfighting magazine, which formulated a program for private involvement in art at a time when "only foreigners go to the Museum of Painting." Dark-humored and sarcastic, the author—Rodrigo Soriano, mentioned earlier—argued that art exhibitors should learn from those who exhibited commercial goods and directed scandalous performances. "The public is a good person that goes where it is told to go as steel goes to a magnet," he claimed before suggesting a range of activities catering to the baser instincts which could draw Spaniards to museums: "just as impresarios use . . . convoluted displays, art also needs to exhibit its hatreds, its passions, its scandals, to keep the public spirit alive."[116]

Theater was also commonly cited, alongside bullfights, as a source of the museum gaze that Spaniards were learning. The diversification of genres in the second half of the nineteenth century produced a way of looking that could derive differing types of pleasure from different genres, including historical drama, serious or comic opera, and music hall revues (the first music hall, the Alhambra, opened in Madrid in 1894).[117] Just as with bullfighting, the relation between the museum and the theater was mutual: artistic directors would look to the Prado for inspiration for costumes and decorations, while art viewers would look for stories and operatic emotions in paintings (fig. 27). Serious visitors educated in history but not necessarily in art experienced the museum as a collection of prototypes for staging historical opera and drama. Thus, in 1892, Spain's pioneer archaeologist, José Ramón Mélida, argued that researching the history of costume at the Spanish galleries of the Prado would transform theater into a valid tool for educating Spaniards about their history.[118] Three years later, Diego Luque, the set designer of the El Español Theater in Madrid, was reported to have sent his decorators to the Prado to copy Velázquez's paintings, eventually triggering a "scenographic regeneration" of Spanish theater.[119]

FIG. 28 "—I t'ink this is what they call a 'realist (royalist) school' [escuela realista].'"—Really? Then long live the a'solutely a'solute king!" Cilla, "In the Museum," *Madrid Cómico* 7, no. 266 (June 18, 1887): 8.

In the last decades of the nineteenth century, the popular and commercial entertainments that had trained the playful gaze of the urban bourgeoisie increasingly began to capitalize on the display and consumption of the female body.[120] The interplay between the museum and the theater made the Prado the subject of discussions about social morality that centered upon the nude and revealed a growing interest in the museum on the part of Spanish middle-class men.[121] Humorous stories, poems, and cartoons focusing on the reactions of uneducated visitors to the many paintings and sculptures of nudes began appearing in the Spanish press in the early 1880s. In 1883, for example, *Madrid Cómico* featured two peasants seduced so effectively by a painting that they declare themselves "a'solutely a'solutist" supporters of the "royalist/realist school" of art (fig. 28).[122] A serial novel published in 1888 in *La Risa* depicted a young woman of Madrid guiding her provincial mother-in-law swiftly past paintings of men that were "naked although well-shaped."[123] In the same year, the satirical Madrid weekly *La Risa* published a cartoon by "Ignotus" featuring two soldiers still taking the museum for a private residence of long-gone Spanish emperors: they interpreted Titian's *Venus and Music* (*Venus recreándose en la Música*) as a portrait of a lover of the very devout Felipe II (fig. 29).[124] In all of these vignettes, the National Museum provided a convenient setting for the authors to mock bourgeoisie's class antagonists—the aristocrats and the lower classes—and, in the process, reveal that everyone, including the bourgeois, possessed base characteristics.

—Mira, ésta es Venus, querida que dicen que fué de Felipe II.

FIG. 29 "— Look, this is Venus; they say she was Philip II's concubine." Ignotus, "In the Museum of Paintings," *La Risa* 1, no. 10 (March 4, 1888): 4.

171

Since the government privileged historical and religious art, displaying nude images at the Prado was bound to raise many eyebrows in the first place. Their presence, still inexplicable to lay visitors who had yet to learn about ideal form, gave middle-class writers an occasion to reinterpret the Prado as a tantalizing venue for flirtatious encounters. In 1883, writing for the weekly *La América*, Cuban-Spanish writer Tristán de Jesús Medina compared the Prado on a day of public admission to a "carnival of satyrs abducting virginal nymphs" and claimed that visitors who had come "looking for an Easter of Resurrection" through art would instead do something "contrary to the practices of cult," becoming "by force accomplices of terrible rapes."[125] Such opinions transferred the impression left by the nudes on the writers themselves to the attitudes of museum visitors whom they imagined. But they reflected and also fueled the museum's growing popularity among those who sought more carnal pleasures. Asserting continuity between the exhibits and the visitors' bodies, these depictions confirmed the Spanish middle classes' departure from the model of rational *Bildung*, which, as we have seen, had never been fully established even among the aristocratic patrons of the Museo Real. Now, visiting the former royal collection at the National Museum was being recognized as the embodied, collective, and sensual experience that it had always been. Significantly, though, the new standard also naturalized the view of

—¡Conchita, baja los ojos!
—¡Sí, mamá, ya he visto que debía bajarlos!

FIG. 30 "—Look down, Conchita!"
"—Yes, Mother, I've seen that I
wasn't supposed to look." Cubas,
"In the Museum of Paintings,"
Mundo Cómico 4, no. 138 (June 20,
1875): 3.

the museum as a space of male socialization, where women could only figure as com-moditized objects of admiration or as unwelcome intruders. "Look down, Conchita!" a woman orders in one cartoon. "Yes, Mother, I've seen that I wasn't supposed to look," the daughter replies, ostensibly referring to a nude painting, while the reader's eyes are drawn to the figure of a male visitor closely inspecting another canvas behind her back (fig. 30).[126]

Unlike what happened with caricaturesque depictions of peasant and women visitors' confusion between the museum and the church, we know that in the case of nudity in art the educated male museum-goers did, in fact, experience the same type of fascination that they attributed to the objects of their ridicule. Benito Pérez Galdós's novel *The Disinherited* (1881) suggests that even the most canonical Spanish liberal writer, versed in art, was likely to project his thrill in the presence of nude art onto the female museum visitors that he created in his writing. His protagonist, Isidora, on her visit to the Prado cannot help but imagine herself as scantily dressed as a sculpted ancient goddess or a painted Venetian courtesan.[127] Another liberal writer, Leopoldo Alas (Clarín), made the young male protagonist of his novella *Pipá* (1879) imagine that the female paintings on exhibit were looking "at every century's spectator with a gaze of infinite lust."[128] Javier Portús points at over a dozen sensual or frivolous references to the Prado by important Spanish male writers.[129] These references to the museum in contemporary Spanish fiction and the press can be inter-preted both as moral criticism and as testimonies that document the male authors' recurring excitement at the thought of the National Museum and the paintings in its collection.

Often, female foreigners immersed in the contemplation of art became the objects of not-so-disinterested observation for Spanish men. An example is found in *A Family Flight Through Spain*, an 1883 travelogue by the American writer Susan Hale. On their frequent visits to the Prado, Hale writes, she and her female companions would always run into a Spanish man who stayed in the same room with them wherever they went. Hale calls the man "the Amateur, because he was always in the gallery, to fill up his time, apparently, listlessly looking at the pictures, but with more animation at the visitors."[130] He "raise[s] his hat as they passed," obviously trying to establish contact with Hale's party, but receives no reaction. Yet his impression on the book's publishers must have been strong, as his lithographed portrait, depicting such typified traits of a Latin lover as a thick mustache, long nose, and stylish outfit, appears in the book's illustrated edition.

In Spain or anywhere else, nineteenth-century sources record no proposals to feminize the public sphere or even to expose the museum's male gendering. The first, liberal wave of feminist thinkers opted to occupy the museum space on equal terms with educated men, and in Spain this meant that there would be no claims to reconsider female representations or strategies of social inclusion with respect to the Prado. Thus, Emilia Pardo Bazán, the first Spanish writer to be considered a feminist (and a daughter of a successful woman artist), whom we have met copying paintings at the Prado in 1869, invariably made her male protagonists admire the nudes. For example, in a long monologue praising the triumph of "Flemish flesh" on Rubens's canvases, the protagonist of her novel *La Quimera* mentions both male and female subjects.[131] In her personal letters, Pardo Bazán confessed herself a great admirer of Rubens; yet she did not appreciate him as the artist of human flesh, but merely as a colorist.[132]

Between 1873 and 1881, the authorities at the Prado issued authorizations to copy paintings to 990 men and 90 women (presumably only Spanish, since foreigners were counted separately), suggesting that the male-to-female ratio of 10:1 had not changed since prerevolutionary times.[133] Still, this was a considerable number, given that women were excluded from the official institutions of art education.[134] (For comparison, in 1898, observers reported seeing twenty women in a crowd of three thousand participants in a protest on the Paseo del Prado organized by the Socialist and Republican Parties.)[135] In the French Academie des Beaux-Arts, women received equal access to all classes, even life modeling, in 1897.[136] In Spain, where women artists-in-training had to wait until the twentieth century to become equal to their male counterparts, copying works of art or even their printed reproductions was still the only source of education. Asking in 1892 whether women should "forget all shame and begin studying human figure until they know it with the same precision with which artists belonging to the strong sex do," Augusto Danvila Jaldero (a correspondent of the Academia San

Fernando and the author of the vignette about the "marionette storage" mentioned earlier) did not dare to give a straight answer. Indirectly, though, he suggested that women wishing to become anything more than mere "professional aficionadas" should stop at nothing.[137] Despite his well-intentioned declarations, however, he could name

only a handful of women artists, none of whom were Spanish.

Yet there is evidence that women in Spain were beginning to succeed as art professionals. In Barcelona, exhibitions of women artists were held in private venues beginning in 1896, when the first Women Artists' Exhibition was inaugurated in the Sala Parés. (We will have to wait until 1905 to see a similar exhibit in Madrid.) As copyists, women were also competing with men. In 1890, the director of the Prado received a letter from an uncle of Isabel Martos y Beltrán, a young woman copyist who had recently died, requesting the works she had left behind.[138] A museum employee had been selling for a commission her copies of religious paintings from the collection, and now the uncle wanted to take over. The artist, apparently, had worked full time: she had six works ready and had started the seventh at the time of her unexpected death.

As a hybrid institution that succeeded in recasting itself as a men-only club for its middle-class visitors without, nevertheless, contradicting the religious associations that everyone else apparently still supported, the Prado Museum, oddly enough, was considered a respectable place for a single middle-class woman to appear alone and to be seen. And to be seen copying paintings was doubly respectable, besides allowing a woman to come more often and stay longer. The Spanish press often cited the Louvre for its abundance of female copyists, some of them even copying nudes.[139] In the Prado, Russian-French artist Marie Bashkirtseff noticed with delight the number of people coming to see her working on Velázquez, undeterred by her modest Spanish attire: "dressed quietly in black, with a mantilla, such as all the women here wear; yet a great many persons came to stand behind my chair and look on while I worked— one man in particular."[140] The most striking thing about Bashkirtseff's account is her representation of herself as an exhibit of sorts, looking for its own spectators. The modern public sphere relied on the strategies of objectification and the ways of looking developed at "the museum, the theater, and the boutique," to use Mercer's phrase,[141] and so this type of female behavior did little more than extend to the Prado the attitudes already developed in the commercial sphere. The real novelty, however, was to see a woman immersed in the sexualized economy to the point of legitimizing it as high art. Historians of cafés and department stores remark that the proximity of commercial displays produced a similar attitude among female customers, who also came to these places in search of potential suitors. Surrounded by objects designed and exhibited to seduce a buyer, these women, it is argued, began to think of themselves as attractively packaged commodities.

But the museum was different from a store or a restaurant. Or was it? If in 1868 *Gil Blas* could still distinguish between the museum and a place of consumption in order to reprimand conservative provincial museum-goers, a dozen years later it had become much harder to draw the line. In 1880, commenting on the Madrid café owners' new habit of using art to decorate the walls, liberal journalist Miguel Moya proclaimed that soon there would only remain "one café [in Madrid]—the Museum of Paintings."[142] In the meantime, the popular imagination insisted on confusing the Museum of Paintings with stores and commercial establishments dedicated to cultivating or exhibiting bodies.

> Three things are in Madrid
> that are worthy of admiration:
> the Museum of Paintings,
> the opera in the Real
> and the hair salon
> directed by Tomás,[143]

ran a humorous poem in *Madrid Cómico*. Several years later it would be published as an advertisement for Tomás's business, thus using the museum as bait for clients. It seemed very hard for end-of-the-century writers to separate the Prado from the commercial sphere and the world of entertainment.

EDUCATION REFORM, CIVIL ICONOGRAPHY, AND A NEW FLOOR PLAN

If not all visitors were left to their own devices at the museum, it was only thanks to the educational reform of the 1880s, which introduced arts education in the curricula of Spain's public schools and used the contemplation of Spanish art for developing a secular—cultural—alternative to religious nationalism. The reform was propelled from the *Institución Libre de Enseñanza* and the National Pedagogical Museum, mentioned earlier. The philosophers and social reformers, known as the *Krausistas* (the followers of the German philosopher Karl Christian Friedrich Krause) or *Institucionistas* (the intellectual milieu of the Institución Libre de Enseñanza), who stood behind these initiatives were seeking to ground public instruction in a rationalist "intuitive method" of analysis. Since they approached paintings and sculptures as microcosms that allowed pupils to develop the skill of observation, the reformers advocated that art theory and history be required for all, beginning with elementary school.[144]

The high importance put on aesthetic education in the reform can be credited to one man: Manuel Bartolomé de Cossío, the director of the Pedagogical Museum, the head of the aesthetics section in the Madrid Athenaeum, and one of Spain's earliest art historians.[145] An Anglophile who personally knew some of the most prominent British reformers, Cossío developed a theory of educational excursions for all, which followed directly from two British sources: the recreationist ideologies and Ruskin's ideas on worker education.[146] Museums were a part of this wider program. The first elementary school class (1878–79) of the Institución had forty pupils enrolled, but only select groups of seven to nine pupils visited the Prado. The Institución's secondary school was larger and had a more comprehensive art curriculum. During the academic year of 1878–79, the Prado was the destination for 5 out of 24 visits for elementary schoolchildren and 21 out of 111 visits for students at the secondary school. These visits effectively combined art history with comparative aesthetic analysis: learning about the difference between old and modern masters or between Velázquez and Murillo. Contemporary art, cartoons by Goya, and works receiving awards at the National Art Salons received attention as well.

The programs of these visits all followed the same outline, reduced for the younger and expanded for the older pupils. Each visit started with a general overview and moved chronologically from older to contemporary art, including, where possible, visits to the sculpture collections. The tours for younger pupils would cover such topics as "what is a painting" and such fundamentals of aesthetic analysis as drawing, perspective, coloring, subject matter, materials, and techniques. Having first been exposed to general information about the museum, its galleries, and their arrangement, children would then see the old masters, paying particular attention to Raphael. On their next visit, they would look at contemporary paintings, dedicated mostly to history topics and genre painting.[147] Focused on the art of antiquity, the visits to the sculpture sections explained the uses of different materials.

More advanced programs covered in-depth the main periods and schools of painting as well as some of the museum's masterpieces. Students had to take notes. The focus on "schools" and epochs made these tours legitimate heirs of the art education program that the First Republic had proclaimed but never implemented. This was also the first attempt to use the museum to teach aesthetics and the history of art, which planted the seed of the future museum culture. Soon, other institutions, such as the Instituto Internacional (a private school for women), also introduced guided museum visits. But the fruits of their work would not come until the next century. In the meantime, Cossío did all he could to popularize his ideas among the educated public through a program of lectures that he designed for the Madrid Athenaeum and in his own research, which allowed him to "naturalize" El Greco as a Spanish, rather than Venetian, master. The program of lectures that Cossío designed covered two dozen topics and used seventeen speakers. The topics included all periods in the history of painting, sculpture, architecture, and applied arts as well as the issues of general aesthetics and "the arrangement of the Prado Museum."[148]

While the educational activity of the Institución Libre de Enseñanza expanded the circle of people outside of the museum who held opinions about art and its public importance, newspapers hitherto uninterested in art also started to take interest. *El*

Día, a left-leaning daily, provided a platform for Araujo Sánchez's criticism of the Prado, while *Correspondencia de España*, an emphatically neutral evening news source, published the translation of Louis Viardot's old book on Spanish museums. General-interest periodicals with a special focus on art and museums began to appear. In 1882, *La Ilustración Artística* was created in Barcelona. Its regular reviews of exhibitions and museums contributed to making art criticism popular in Spain. In its pages, Pedro de Madrazo made public the first Spanish account of the "Origins of the Prado Museum of Madrid," and Cossío listed the lacunae in its collection.[149] Charnon-Deutsch reminds us, however, that the cult of beautifully rendered etching adopted by the modern illustrated press in Spain also lent itself to racial and gender stereotyping.[150] Manipulating the direction and the depth of engraved lines to establish continuity between the image and the viewer, these illustrations continued in print the "absorption" of spectators that was taking over the display of public art.[151]

A journalist could now trigger huge changes. In November 1891, Mariano de Cavia published in *El Liberal* a piece of unprecedented importance: "Catastrophe last night. Spain is mourning. Fire at the Museum of Paintings."[152] The article described in detail the building covered in flames and the hopeless volunteers trying to save masterpieces by cutting them out of their frames. The catastrophe, the author explained, had started with a coal stove that was left on for the night in one of the guards' apartments; the wooden museum structure caught fire and burned quickly. Readers everywhere panicked, as newspapers all over Spain reproduced the story. The minister of Fomento requested an immediate response from Federico de Madrazo, who had to explain that the article was merely "humorous" and that the museum's fire-prevention system was as solid as it could be. Madrazo also put an official memorandum on the building's door stating that the museum was safe and sound and denouncing the "frivolous" fake news.[153] But this was not enough. Next day, the minister paid a personal visit to the museum to inspect its fire-security system. Using coal heaters was categorically banned, and the wooden roof was to be replaced immediately with a metal one.

The effect of Cavia's article, published soon after Spain had returned to conducting direct general elections in 1890, showed how tightly the politics of the Spanish press was interwoven with the agenda of social participation in the government. Now that more people could vote, the press was reaching beyond simple pro- and antigovernment positions to work with the government and impose its own agenda. As Cavia himself explained in an article titled "Why I Set the Prado Museum on Fire,"[154] the emotions that he stirred helped the ill-funded Fomento receive the money necessary to address the museum's pressing needs. Federico de Madrazo, his political connections notwithstanding, had only been partially successful in getting the funds to protect the building after a *real* fire at a neighboring Royal Armory in 1884. Now, thanks to Cavia's piece of fiction, he obtained all the support necessary to implement much more thorough fire-prevention measures.

Indeed, if in the early years of the Restoration the press was taking on ample responsibility for explaining the museum, its history, its merits, and its deficiencies, in the 1890s it became a real force behind the state's policy. At a time when the museum's directors did not theorize about floor plans and displays, newspapers and journals provided a platform for developing the knowledge that would enable a future modernization. And when state initiative was lacking, they were successful in pushing the government to approve a number of necessary changes. Araujo Sánchez was the first to outline a plan of action after the Bourbons' return: "If the state keeps the museum, all paintings will belong to it; if the [Administration of Royal] Patrimony lays claims to its properties, the state should cede all those that were moved and that remain, including the paintings from the Academia."[155] Two tasks for museum's directors emerged from Araujo's writings: to incorporate a representation of the state into the display, while at the same time paying due respect to the collection's royal origins. They masterfully accomplished both by balancing a whole range of new initiatives.

The parliamentary monarchy made its mark with the first expansions of the museum. Since the years of the Republic, Sans had been refurbishing the lower level and expanding its exhibition space by installing room separators. The first of these new galleries had opened in 1874, but the work continued, and by February 1875 newspapers began to report that the king, accompanied by the princess of Asturias (then a possible heiress to the throne) was coming to view the new galleries before they were open to the public. The royals expressed their satisfaction with the work being done and even consented for the rooms to be named after them.[156] So it seemed that the museum would return to its prerevolutionary ways. However, these developments also made it clear that the government was only paying lip service to the monarchs, whose ownership of the collection was becoming merely symbolic. In the past, naming the gallery containing the greatest masterpieces after Queen Isabel had signaled the monarchy's preeminent cultural role; now this room was rededicated to the other Isabel—Isabel of Braganza, the museum's founding mother. In comparison, the naming of rooms after monarchs during the Restoration made their names look like mere epithets, without any real ideas or meaning behind them. The Prado still exhibited a portrait of the king in a visible place. When remodeling or expansion projects were under way, the royal family could visit the museum and oversee the projects, but public inaugurations were presided over by government officials.

The museum administration's stated goals were to bring natural light to the lower northern galleries through the excavation of the slope outside, which was obstructing the sunlight; build additional stairs; and renovate the upper floor (the still-unfinished location of José de Madrazo's Historical Gallery) to be used as exhibition space. But the first plan was soon abandoned, and the galleries on the lower level did not benefit from the changes brought about by the new plan. As for the upper level, it became the site of the Iconoteca Nacional, a new exhibit featuring civic iconography of the

Spanish state. Created by royal decree on November 26, 1876, the Museo Iconográfico de Españoles Ilustres (Iconographic Museum of Famous Spaniards) was to replace the collection portraying the kings and queens of Spain that José de Madrazo had installed in the 1840s. But this was a much more ambitious enterprise. While Madrazo's gallery had only featured kings and queens, the Iconoteca reflected the new concept of the nation as personified not only by its monarchs but also by its "wise men, philosophers, poets, saints, statesmen, warriors, [and] artists." It was proposed that "all those whose virtue, value, genius, and inspiration have made our motherland shine" would find "their own and logical place in this important collection of national glories."[157] The project was rooted in a rather novel notion of what constituted the nation and what types of activities were most representative of its glory.

179

A special commission, the Junta Iconográfica, incorporating members of the three Academias, was created to identify and acquire suitable paintings. Each commissioner was asked to draft a list of names from the different domains of Spanish history. Though people like Pedro de Madrazo came up with predictable lists of bishops and saints, others gave suggestions that signaled a radically different approach to nationhood. Such was the case with the composer and musicologist Francisco Asenjo Barbieri, whose list contained a section with "hispanicized foreigners" that included, for example, the renowned castrato Farinelli.[158] Barbieri also collected the names of actors and opera singers, hitherto excluded from the canon. Some were women,[159] who would now occupy a venerable place next to Saint Teresa, the two Isabels, and a medieval queen (Doña Urraca). Furthermore, Barbieri added a selection of bullfighters from the eighteenth century onwards, although the large question mark heading his notes on the subject suggests that he doubted his own choices. Still, the fact that such candidacies were even conceivable for the Iconoteca suggested that the new national idea would recognize not just women but even professional entertainers alongside monarchs, clerics, warriors, and writers.

The Iconoteca, furthermore, was taking on some of the more ambitious tasks that Spain's postrevolutionary thinkers had initially devised for the Prado. It was pursuing the line of public opinion that believed the museum could be useful for understanding manifestations of Spain's creative spirit beyond the art of painting. The commission worked to reproduce this idea in the Iconoteca Nacional, although on a very limited scale, arguing that the future collection would provide "to writers and artists and to all Spaniards the means to awaken the grand spirit that moved the hearts of our fathers."[160] The extensive list of artifacts that the Junta Iconográfica was planning to gather included "busts, statues, reliefs, portraits painted or engraved, medals, descriptive, literary, or epigraphic data."[161] It promised to be a comprehensive project that would draw from all visual and discursive sources about famous Spaniards.

In the end, however, the Iconoteca did not succeed in implementing a diverse and inclusive national idea. Of the sixty-eight artifacts acquired by the commission in 1877, all were paintings and only three depicted women (the two queens and Saint Teresa). All of the other subjects were politicians, writers, artists, war heroes, and clergymen. In August of 1877, Sans reported that the Museo Iconográfico would be installed in three months, and in October *La Iberia* covered an official visit to the galleries under construction.[162] Unfortunately, that was the last time that the nineteenth-century public heard about the Iconoteca. The rooms in the attic would soon be open to visitors, but the guidebooks referred to them as "a portrait collection" devoid of any nation-building importance. The Iconoteca was a failed project, the last vestige of the revolutionary view of Spain as a nation represented by its citizens. It was also the last nineteenth-century endeavor that claimed to give the old royal collection the appearance of a national chronology. It did reveal, however, that not only the museum administrators, but also the state and civil society, were changing their attitudes to authority and to the national canon in Spain in ways that could bring the Prado close to the civic iconographies that other European museums were putting on display in the form of portrait galleries.

When we remember that by the end of the 1870s the Senate had begun to claim the right to lead in exhibiting the history of Spain's nationhood, the eclipse of the Iconoteca becomes understandable. The government was crafting its own narrative using, not portraiture, but rather historical paintings that told dramatic, moralizing tales full of tragic losses and providential redemptions. In late nineteenth-century visual culture, these canvases were clearly preferable to static portraits of famous men or women, which left no impression on the new emotional, nationalist gaze. With this last patriotic project failure at the Prado, what story was left it to convey? When Sans died in 1881 and Federico de Madrazo returned as director, he simply refused to engage with the new roles attributed to the museum, choosing instead to fulfill his prerevolutionary concept of it. In November of 1884, he was already reporting to the Fomento that the Prado had a final and definitive floor plan: "all paintings had been classified . . . and occupy definitively the place which corresponds to them in its galleries."[163] The only new task was to bring to fruition one of his initiatives from the 1860s: a classification and a new floor plan for the museum's collection of sculpture.[164] When this was achieved, the administration wanted only to "perfect" the display by improving the way in which works were labeled. This happened in early 1888, when Madrazo asked the director of public instruction to put new, "clear and permanent" plates and numbers with every painting.[165]

This is how Federico de Madrazo planned the museum and how he expected it to stay: mainly concentrated on the main level, it would be distributed into several national "schools," which would sometimes share a room. Thus, only three rooms, to the right and left of the main entrance, and the southern rotunda on the main level were dedicated to one tradition exclusively. Most other salons featured at least two "schools": the central gallery was dedicated to the Spanish (in the first section) and Italian (in the second section) schools, while the galleries to the left and right featured the so-called Germanic school, which Pedro de Madrazo's catalogues did not separate into German, Flemish, and Dutch paintings. The Sala de la Reina Isabel was refurbished in 1892 and remained in place until 1899. Likewise, the collection of royal portraits stayed in the former rest chambers. At the time, the upper level still housed Goya's cartoons for the Royal Tapestry Factory. In 1883, Emilia Pardo Bazán reported that this section had been closed to ordinary visitors and would only be opened following a bribe or a complaint.[166] On the lower level, rooms were named after King Alfonso XII. Araujo Sánchez had no kind words for them in his 1877 columns, arguing that the exhibits were all old paintings on wood, mostly by Spanish and Flemish artists, and that displaying paintings by material rather than historical period was a type of classification that would only make sense in a museum reporting to the forestry services. Works by nineteenth-century artists, including *The Famine in Madrid*, which had been sent into exile and then to the Senate, were back by the small entrance to the central gallery, where they had been hanging since 1819.

As long as eclecticism was the prevailing style in the Western world, it would be hard to find a more eclectic arrangement for a floor plan at the Prado that had all the makings of becoming permanent. But even before the end of Madrazo's tenure, changes had to be made. True, the most notable projects implemented under Madrazo did not touch on classifying the art, and there was no longer talk about reorganizing it on a progressive time line. But in 1892, as work on the apse continued outside, a major reform did away with the most noticeable feature of Villanueva's building. The remodeling of the Sala de Reina Isabel abolished the balustrade that overlooked the lower-level rotunda. The two floors were separated, and the Sala de la Reina Isabel received its own floor and a higher ceiling with natural light coming in. Seven years later, the gallery would close again and undergo another refurbishment. By that time, Madrazo was gone and a new generation of directors was intent on finding new ways to transform the museum into an official place for building up the nation's public memory. When the apse reopened in 1899, newly wallpapered, there was no longer a Sala de la Reina Isabel. The former altar-like niche became the Sala Velázquez.

The seeds of plans for a new exhibit privileging Spain's outstanding master had been planted a few years earlier when special Goya rooms were opened on the lower level. Those galleries were built to house the collection of "dark" paintings that the Prado had received in 1881 from the son of the former owner, Baron d'Erlanger. In 1897, one of the donor's sons decided to visit the collection and, having seen none of those paintings, filed an official protest demanding that the series, which had been sent away to decorate the presidency of the Consejo de Ministros in 1890, be displayed. One is left to wonder what Cánovas had in mind when he decided to decorate the presidency with works such as *Saturn Devouring His Children* and *Two Laughing Women*.[167] Yet when the collection returned to the Prado, it was so successful that the museum administration decided that this was the way to go: forget all their worries about the "Spanish school," consider the collection established and complete, and dedicate new facilities to Spain's most popular artists. The Sala Velázquez confirmed the strategy—naming rooms after most important artists in the collection, rather than royal patrons—that would guide the museum's floor plans in the early 1900s. The Sala Velázquez became the center of celebratory events dedicated to the artist's tercentennial, which in turn gave occasion for many pictures to be taken of Spain's public officials, donors, and intellectual elite posing with the Prado as a backdrop.[168]

The former Sala de la Reina Isabel, inaugurated in 1853 and legitimizing the aesthetic arrangement, had been designed to showcase the monarchy's role as a source of national prosperity. But now there was no longer a need for such a complex metaphoric installation. By the end of the nineteenth century, the taste for aesthetic displays in other European and American museums would silence those critics who were still demanding history from the Prado. Even Cossío did not propose a new display mode but remained content with a more complete representation of different artistic traditions. The canon of Spanish art had become the guiding force behind the floor plan. The museum was being transformed into a show of the nation's—not the kings'—capacity for artistic patronage in the past and present.[169]

By the beginning of the twentieth century, the Prado seemed to ignore every rule of museum development followed abroad: it did not have a historical gallery or a chronological floor plan or an educational program. Nor did it combine arts and crafts. But under the Restoration, such demands had very limited power—and, as we have seen, the museum appealed to much deeper threads of nationalism than those that any traditional national exhibit could convey at that time: it provided middle-class Spaniards a safe place, competing with the church for the right to offer an experience of the sacred, to debate their political differences, and to look at each other surrounded by their rural, provincial, and female compatriots. Moreover, the Prado had a metal roof, a new entrance with an external stairway, and a new façade overlooking the Retiro, enclosed by a fence. Inside, it exhibited a stable collection of paintings arranged by country. And it delivered what most visitors were coming for: an impressive spread of Spanish masterpieces, each in its own gallery. All this helps explain why, apart from those who wanted to use the Prado for teaching art and history, very few people would criticize the display at the end of the century.

CHAPTER FIVE

The Era of the Masses, 1902–1936

WHEN ALFONSO XIII CAME of age and began to pose as a crowned guarantor of Spain's "regeneration," many writers and politicians realized that the Prado Promenade and the museum could provide models for building a civic community on the principles of class solidarity and common values. The new century, however, belonged to the masses—as the philosopher José Ortega y Gasset famously announced in 1929—and these masses were quickly learning how to exert pressure by occupying public spaces.[1] As street politics took over the Paseo del Prado, it became more and more difficult to know whether those gathering there should be classified as fellow citizens, class antagonists, or, simply and nostalgically, "the people." The museum directors José Villegas Cordero (1901–18), Aureliano Beruete y Moret (1918–22), and Fernando Álvarez de Sotomayor (1922–31) and the deputy director Francisco Javier Sánchez Cantón (1922–60), feeling that they could finally succeed in mobilizing public opinion against the celebrations on the Promenade, launched a comprehensive program of guided tours for workers, the general middle-class audience, and art enthusiasts.[2] Although the resulting fusion between leisure and the museum resembled the British recreationists' uses of art for class cohesion, the new roles of the Prado fit much better with Alfonso's early, quasi-Victorian parliamentary monarchy (1902–23) than with what came next: an Italian-style dictatorship in support of the throne (1923–31).[3] Under dictator Primo de Rivera, the behavior of the masses on the Promenade and in the museum became a barometer of civil liberties. Taking a fresh look at the interclass and intersex mingling during festivals on the Prado, members of the writing and reading public had suddenly each been struck by some form of either "verbenophilia" or "verbenophobia"—the love or loathing of patron-saint celebrations—which translated into a new range of opinions about the museum. Writers striving to stay away from politics compared the Prado Museum to a safe refuge where they always felt at home, while their politically committed friends demanded an exhibiting institution that granted education, rather than fun and relaxation, for all.

Alfonso XIII's rule ended abruptly: in 1931, following Primo de Rivera's resignation and the failure of his successor to create a viable cabinet, the king took a one-way trip to Paris. Under the Second Republic (1931–39), standards of leisure received particularly high attention when the elites educated by the Institución Libre de Enseñanza rose to power. The Republic's government changed quickly—from socialist-led reformists (1931–33) to conservatives (1934–36) to the Popular Front coalition that won the election in February of 1936—fueling an ongoing debate concerning the leisure activities on the Paseo del Prado, which was now considered a political commons. When the age-old pastimes of looking at exhibits in the museum and spending time on the Promenade met mass politics, the distinction between autonomous art and the messy world surrounding it became hard to sustain.

EARLY TWENTIETH-CENTURY MUSEUMS

The dawn of the new century was marked by a departure from the philosophical positivism of the previous decades. All across Europe and the Americas, the educated classes, who had only recently glorified reason and exalted experiments with controlled variables, developed an interest in spiritism and theosophy and began founding esoteric societies. Imagination was called on to merge with science for the renewal of the world, now conceptualized in mystical terms. "Genius cannot shine in ignorance and only rises to the light of immortality when it dwells among letters, in the museums, and in the midst of arts," Spanish mathematician and linguist Eduardo Benot wrote in 1902.[4] Museums, only recently expected to provide linear rational displays, now had to become breeding grounds for imagination. As Sheehan points out, the events of the early 1900s shattered the conventions of what art was, the belief that it was best understood through its history, and the expectation that aesthetic contemplation had moral and civic effects.[5] As traditional institutions, museums were deeply affected by the corrosion of nineteenth-century values, and they continued to lose popularity to more successful private exhibitions, traveling displays, and experimental shows.

Many innovative minds demanded the closure of museums and advocated the return of collections to their owners. Others, following the modernist aesthetic of merging art and life, declared that the separation of museums from the surrounding world was becoming philosophically extinct. "Two intellectual currents haunt the art world," Robert de la Sizeranne, a French art critic, wrote in 1904: "one glorifies the beauty of the museums, the other denounces the ugliness of life outside them . . . ; these ideas often dwell in one and the same soul."[6] Such a mindset made maintaining national museums an enterprise as complicated as it was intriguing. Carl E. Schorske explains how the turn-of-the-century expansion of modernist cities such as Vienna created urban spaces where the museum's many roles could be not only debated and contrasted, but also fruitfully juxtaposed.[7] However, such a happy marriage of art and life was an exception. In Berlin, Museum Island, now complete with the Pergamon building finished in 1901 and the Kaiser-Friedrich Museum in 1904, remained isolated from the spaces of politics, worship, and commerce, and thus failed to fulfill the dream of Karl Schinkel, the area's founding father, to build a temple of arts presiding over the life of the city.[8]

The arrival of the 1900s saw a deepening divide between high and low cultures, with the "higher" arts of painting and sculpture relying on museums' support to secure their appeal. Yet the bourgeois belief in the autonomy of art was fracturing under demands from the new generation of artists, who considered such autonomy little short of a bribe that their predecessors had accepted in exchange for giving up their claims to social influence. These avant-garde artists, although they were eagerly learning from the classical works on display, rarely missed an occasion to compare national museums to cemeteries, and even some curators now called their workplaces the "morgues" of art.[9] "From the right-leaning Marinetti to the socialist Malevich, no solution was found except to burn down the museum," Maleuvre writes, adding that these war cries had little consequence since, in an effort to close the breach between art and life, artists focused on making their own art relevant and not on "militating politically against museums."[10] Since this approach did not break up the exhibiting system, the early twentieth century only brought the reputation of museums to a brief crisis, after which they regained their importance as educational institutions.

While national museums were still flourishing, it was private shows and emerging innovative exhibits combining art and performance that were the focus of attention, and there no longer seemed to be a consensus about what a museum was expected to be or do. The budget assigned by the states to former royal galleries was also shrinking, in proportion to what Robin Lenman termed "large-scale mobilization of private wealth."[11] Since new purchases for national museums mostly relied on donations from individuals or associations—Les Amis du Louvre (1897), the National Art Collections Fund in Britain (1903), the Pushkin Museum Trust in Russia, and others—national museums' exhibits began to follow more the tastes of investors. Landscapes, still lifes, and other traditionally private genres that were now being donated to the national museums by trustees were beginning to modify the canons of national schools. Hence, in the twentieth century, it was no longer acceptable to define a national style working only from the history compositions, religious art, portraits, and allegories that used to dominate monarchical, religious, and aristocratic collections. Old national museums were now making space for works that spoke to—and about—the taste of the nation's oligarchs. Still, from Britain all the way to the Soviet Union, cultural policy-makers found ways to redeem these collections, arguing that they were the products of the common people's labor and therefore bore an imprint of folk culture and popular taste.[12]

National museums and democracy, it seemed, could go together. Some private collectors, however, chose to organize their own shows instead of donating works or money to the nation. The extent and longevity of entire artistic currents and movements depended on the preferences of a handful of famous dealers such as Ambroise Vollard, the patron of the Impressionists and their avant-garde successors, and Bernhard Koehler, the collector of Der Blaue Reiter.[13] Although the former resided in France and the latter in Germany, the dealers' specific location meant very little in this extremely mobile art market where artists traveled, founded international groups, and exhibited in any number of European metropolises. Masters old and new were sold internationally, and national museums also had to send emissaries abroad to purchase works and complete their collections.

In the early twentieth-century exhibition world, however, the most noticeable innovations did not happen in a gallery or a museum—whether public or private— but rather on stage or *en plein air*: in the avant-garde performances and in open-air presentations. Decades of "human zoos" and *tableaux vivants* had already prepared European art-lovers to erase the perceptual distinction between inert art objects and moving creatures, and the conflation was now also fueled by the rising popularity of what would become the "moving pictures" par excellence, cinema. Hiring artists, not only to decorate, but also to stage and direct dramas, operas, ballets, and every synthetic form in between was just another step in the same direction. In Paris, transnational events such as the Russian Seasons brought fine arts to the spectacle-loving bourgeois and gave a boost to artists' mobility. The syncretic experiences that these shows provided epitomized the modern quest to merge music, dance, literature, theater, and art.

Although on the surface international avant-garde aesthetics and regionalism seemed incompatible, the modernist insistence on questioning the separation between art and life also gave new breath to ethnographic or autoethnographic exhibits, in vogue since the nineteenth century. The prototype, the Swedish Skansen, inspired regionalist thinkers, politicians, museum creators, and collectors and connoisseurs of crafts, music, dance, and food all across Europe to innovative revival efforts aimed at preserving, popularizing, and displaying regional cultures, which they considered indispensable for competitive nationhood. Ultimately, this transnational take on regionalism opened museum exhibits even further to other arts. Local and regional exhibitors started using vernacular architectural styles to signal, through their visual setup, the continuity between the collection and the everyday life of its community and made use of new sound- and movement-recording technologies, adding to the displays representations of popular music, dances, and rituals.[14]

The thrilling mix of interior and exterior displays in these museum experiments reflected a deeper change in the twentieth-century attitude to space, which, in Walter Benjamin's famous rendering, was influenced by the modern cult of visibility.[15] Since the early 1900s, the avant-garde bourgeoisie had begun to "domesticate" the places of outdoor socialization, making it acceptable and even fashionable to perform outdoor public activities such as eating, lounging, and disrobing: the same things that they had so vehemently chastised as uncivilized and rustic when they spotted people doing them outdoors during the previous decades of rapid urbanization. Even today, transparent arcades and modern cafés with their mirrors, windows, and terrazzos figure prominently in Western cities, reminding their visitors of the moderns' passionate desire to blur the boundaries between dwelling and socializing.[16]

The enthusiasts of early twentieth-century regionalist museums carried this fad further by suggesting that landscape and the lives of people inhabiting it should be viewed as objects of aesthetic enjoyment. In the mid-1930s, these folk exhibits bolstered the ideologies of all shades. The public representations of the Volk were indispensable for the Nazi and Fascist doctrines of "blood and soil." On the opposite side of the political spectrum, among the supporters of the Popular Front and the Communist International (Comintern), which at the time was shifting away from the idea of class struggle, efforts were also underway to typify a broad alliance of people of goodwill united against fascism.[17] Since the nineteenth century, fairground advertisers had been blurring class differences and bringing to the forefront their publics' cultural commonalities, and now these strategies, replicated in the "museums of the people," acquired new importance for the European Left. The 1936 victory of Popular Front coalitions in France and Spain demonstrated the effectiveness of this approach, which was called on to replace the language of proletarian violence. The French National Museum of Popular Art and Tradition was designed at that time (1937). The government of the Spanish Republic managed to implement a similar, albeit much reduced, project called El Museo del Pueblo Español (the Museum of the Spanish People", 1934).[18]

Working people, of course, were also fond of the arts in their own ways, and art exhibits, seeking attention from a lay audience but still trying to promote high-culture attitudes, were pushed into twentieth-century mass politics. The institutions that embraced the modernist aesthetic of art for art's sake became ivory-tower depositories of elitist beauty. Others, by contrast, offered fruitful engagement with present and future social needs, making themselves useful to society by renovating their educational agendas. The nineteenth-century Ruskinian idea that different audiences should be treated to different displays—"one for the public, one for connoisseurs"—was no longer out of the question, as an increasing number of museum reformers recognized visitors without any knowledge of art as legitimate and believed that their tastes should be satisfied.[19] The National Gallery in London was among the first to reorganize itself, even though earlier it had rejected the idea of museum education. This was an intellectual development of the "universalist evolutionary socialism" propagated by the London County Council, whose Progressive Party leadership had dispatched teachers to assess the gallery's didactic potential in the expectation that they would instruct their pupils, who in turn would bring their friends to the museum. Educational public lectures were a later development at the National Gallery, where they started in 1914, three years after the British Museum had implemented a similar program.[20]

Newer nations were the most vehement supporters of common museum-goers, with the U.S. government even commissioning an extensive study about the social role of museums in Europe. The report echoed the mid-nineteenth-century belief that the countries capable of using museums for improving the education of the workers would win the wars and the world's economic competition. Equipping himself with the ideas of British social reformers, American philanthropist Albert Barnes designed a program of regular tours for workers and art workshops aimed at making museums educationally sound. The Barnes Foundation established standards for children's visits to the museum that added an element of play to the teachers' explanations. These practices were quickly copied by European museums under the name of the "museum hour." An even more radical program of bringing people into museums came from the Soviet Union, where citizens were promised collective ownership of the national cultural heritage. The issue of whether or not this was true in reality did not diminish the undisputable impact that such an idea had on Euro-American museum thought.[21] The image of the red flag hovering over the royal palace of the Hermitage, which had been transformed into a museum, spread all around the world, leaving many administrators of culture fascinated by the proletarian government showing so much respect toward the monarchical art collection. In Spain, Andrés Ovejero, who taught art theory at the Universidad Central in Madrid and its worker education extension, declared that Soviet Russia was offering a new paradigm: a "social museum" where everyone would feel at home.[22]

Whether opting to become social or remain "artistic," museums could not exist in isolation from the exhibiting practices of the time that world's fairs and temporary loan exhibitions continued to develop, ushering in the subject matter that old-school royal and aristocratic collectors had ignored. The 1900 International Exhibition in Paris featured the first comprehensive display of drawings, making this hitherto semi-private genre and other works on paper instantly popular. World's fairs had always included contemporary paintings, but the twentieth century further expanded the scope of traveling artifacts to include old masters. As they circulated in the international arena, art collections were also becoming potential victims of international politics. The first attempt to draft a policy for the protection of artistic heritage dated back to the Franco-Prussian War of 1870–71, but it was the shock of seeing expanded war zones completely devastated by air bombers during World War I that made the conservation of artistic treasures a matter of international concern.[23]

The museum world had traditionally defied political borders, yet museum professionals only organized themselves transnationally in 1926, with the creation of L'Office International des Musées (OIM) under the auspices of the Society of Nations. OIM's regular meetings set the foundations of a cross-border cooperation and *Mouseion*, OIM's bulletin, established in 1927, provided an outstanding channel for exchanging information about collections, exhibiting techniques, and policies. The museum world now had its own international framework to rely on. Very soon, however, this fragile consensus about art as a universal value would be shattered. In 1936, a military coup against the Spanish Republic developed into a civil war, in which world powers such as Germany, Italy, and the Soviet Union rehearsed their combat techniques in a preview of World War II. In the early months of the Civil War, Hitler's artillery strikes reached the Prado Promenade, threatening the conservation of the museum building and collection. The art world waited breathlessly to see what would happen.

CORONATION, REGENERATION, AND DICTATORSHIP

Back in early twentieth-century Spain, hardly anyone watching the sportsman heir to the throne take an oath to the constitution and become King Alfonso XIII could have predicted a civil war. On May 17, 1902, the sixteen-year-long regency was completed and the dynastic continuity was restored, along with the hope that the young king would support the full-fledged parliamentary democracy necessary to revive the nation from the colonial debacle of 1898. "Regeneration" was the word of the day. The writer and politician Joaquín Costa had launched it into circulation in the last quarter of the previous century, announcing that a new Spain would emerge from its rural areas. As Madrid was preparing for the coronation, the elites used all channels at their disposal to conjure an image of a Crown working together with the politicians, the army, and the intellectuals for the common good. Museums, fairs, temporary exhibitions, and illustrated magazines competed in tying "regeneration" to their display of progress and prosperity. The Prado boasted the first collection of the works by El Greco, on exhibit in the rotunda, while an enormous exhibition of portraits of famous Spaniards, with works retrieved from the country's national museums, private collections, and royal monasteries, was put together at the Palace of Fine Arts and Industry on the Castellana Promenade, north of the Prado and the Recoletos. Never before had the state, the court, and the elite collaborated on a museum project, and the scope of this one was unprecedented.[24] The Junta Iconográfica, whose work had been abandoned since the 1880s, was reconstituted: it was now charged with collecting and commissioning portraits of famous Spaniards to be exhibited at the Ministerio de Fomento.[25]

The king's birthdays had already been reframed as a part of the San Isidro festival, but in 1902 the organizers rose to the occasion to make this a unique urban celebration.

Combining elements of high and low culture, the festivities of May 1902 showed how popular and civil traditions could be mobilized in unison to display social harmony. At that time, authorities and commercial stakeholders all around Spain were taking interest in reviving centuries-old *verbenas* and pilgrimages for the modern purposes of promoting trade, class interaction, and tourism while also crafting attractive regional identities. Early twentieth-century lithographed announcements of festivals showed old-fashioned and technologically enhanced pastimes complementing each other: horseracing next to motor racing, cinematographs next to bullfights, flower offerings next to firemen's parades. In Madrid, the center of this revival was the gated area of Festival Park around the Campo Grande in the Retiro Park (at the time still called the Parque de Madrid). It was here that the coronation festivities were held in 1902 and where, in the following years, all modern varieties of entertainment were offered during the Spring and Fall Fairs: vending kiosks, riding competitions, parades of flower-decorated cars, and municipal band pageants.

This emerging culture used the cult of patron saints but also competed with it, producing a new scenography and choreography. With their long experience in celebrating coronations, armistices, and anniversaries, the city authorities and civic associations were now acting together with commercial stakeholders and the church. In the epoch thus inaugurated, the questions of modernization and tradition hovered over every events program, leaving a lasting effect on what Spaniards would do on the Prado. When the civil society groups joined forces to transform the festivals into something more palatable, it seemed as if the noisy, smelly, and chaotic days of the patron-saint festivals were over, to be replaced by functions much more organized, "civilized," and modern.

Present-day spectators, however, would be shocked by some of the items on the program of the coronation festivities and would assume that modernization was still only relative. A week after Alfonso XIII's oath-taking, the synergy of all social classes "united in their shared love of national glories" was celebrated in Madrid in a festival that would now be considered morbid, organized by the Writers' and Artists' Association: the recovery, exhibition, and reburial of the bodies of three nineteenth-century liberals—writer Mariano José de Larra, poet José de Espronceda, and artist Eduardo Rosales.[26] Patriotic exhumations had been a common practice since the reburial, in 1820, of Daoíz and Velarde, the heroes of the anti-Napoleonic uprising, and became particularly popular in 1869, when dozens of cherished bodies were taken into the newly built Pantheon. Exactly as had happened on those previous occasions, coverage of the exhumations revealed attitudes oscillating between macabre and scientific. Espronceda's bones were piled up and wrapped in random pieces of decomposed fabric and leather, but his skull was intact and still showed perfect cheek lines. Larra's skull, on the contrary, was half-reduced to dust because the poet had shot himself in the head, while Rosales's funeral attire remained in perfect condition (the artist had only died in 1873).[27] This time, the bodies were taken to the Prado Museum to be exhibited to the public.

The event merged the tradition of liberal civic exhumations and the museum's own practice of arranging funerary chapels for museum directors. This was an unprecedented ritual in which the lower rotunda of the Prado, featuring marble statues, acted as a temple that was both secular and patriotic and that reminded the audience of the democracies of ancient Greece. When the bodies arrived at the Prado, the effect of a temporal stasis encapsulating the nation's past, present, and future was complete when an old woman dressed in black stepped out of the crowd, knelt down, and started praying: she was Larra's daughter. The next morning, Madrid students and schoolteachers, pupils of art academies, members of theater and actors' associations, members of arts and learned societies from the provinces, and "workers related to arts and letters" were invited to carry the bodies to the Pantheon in procession.[28] It would be hard to find a more daring attempt to stage a rebirth of previous-century liberal ideas at the Prado Museum.[29] With the revival of Spain's monarchy, high hopes were bestowed on this institution as a depository of the nation's past, worthy of exhibiting, as material tokens of future revival, not only the works of Spain's geniuses, but also their bodies.

Recycling popular cultural forms, the message of regeneration was crafted to satisfy all tastes. Anticipating the influx of people who would want to pay homage to the new king, the conservative *La Correspondencia Militar* predicted sarcastically that since foreign guests already knew all the museums and public buildings of Madrid better than the locals, they would be much more interested in "things really popular": "the mummy of Saint Isidro" and the "killing of the bulls."[30] Contemplating this officially supported pseudo-folkloric buzz, the socialist *El País* asked its readers, "Is *this* regeneration? Is *this* how the revolution . . . is supposed to look?"[31] For liberal writers, the very form given to the festivities revealed the shaky ground inhabited by a monarchy that styled itself as popular without recognizing the working classes.

Indeed, it did not take long after the coronation for the debate about the political meaning of "regeneration" to emerge. In Joaquín Costa's wording, regeneration would only be possible if Spaniards straightened up two key areas: "school and granary," that is, education and the revival of rural areas. But if Costa was intellectually close to *Krausista* quasi-socialism, in the twentieth century regenerationism took on forms ranging from parliamentary monarchy to republicanism to military dictatorship. Until 1923, the system of a "peaceful rotation" between the liberals and the conservatives established in the 1870s continued despite the growing discontent. Given the king's privilege to hand-pick the president, who would form the government, royal power, in the words of historian José Varela Ortega, was perceived as the "only guaranty of the country's governability."[32] However, it was the Liberal Party that, lacking support from the church, the army, and the industrialists, would seek royal backing each time it was its turn to govern. This made the king's influence particularly relevant for progressive policies aimed at modernization. In order to secure the bond, wishful images of Alfonso XIII as a liberal monarch were used to enlist the Crown in causes as different as the promotion of soccer and the support of fine arts.[33] In 1917, speaking on the behalf of "the lovers and protectors of the artists' work," the academician Pedro Poggio went as far as invite the king to declare himself "the first artist of Spain."[34]

As for the king himself, he was far more sympathetic to the cause of conservative politicians like Prime Minister Antonio Maura, who, ironically, did not support his intrusion into politics. It was a political triangle that did not promise a happy resolution, and the monarch's reputation among all political circles steadily declined. Alfonso XIII had never traveled abroad until he assumed power. He grew to be a king with an anachronistic faith in the monarchy's providential role. In 1905, just three years into Alfonso's rule, an editorial of *El País* already demanded that, if the monarchy could not do any better, the king should at least know "when to abdicate."[35] With time, however, such polite advice would cede place to political actions leading to government crises (in 1906, 1909, 1917, and 1921) that invariably ended with the king seeking support from the church and the military.[36] This did not fail to cause cracks in Spain's parliamentary monarchy, which was only beginning to shed its army-driven politics.

In 1923, following the example of the king of Italy, Victor Emmanuel III, Alfonso XIII legitimized a dictator in an effort to buttress his weakening power. Unlike nineteenth-century coups-d'état, which merely aimed at changing the ruling party, General Miguel Primo de Rivera's Military Directory (1923–30) was a government in itself.[37] The dictator's image was shaped after Benito Mussolini's, but the general did not share the Italian dictator's love of art. Primo de Rivera's regime was styled as modern and industry-friendly and did not rely on the arts for image making, favoring instead, as photo occasions, dedications of highways and dams. His government, however, also sought to make Spain's tourism business effective. This is why the Prado, one of Spain's oldest travel destinations, was slated for reorganization, even though Primo de Rivera himself stayed away from the museum. In 1928, the building of the Prado even appeared on Spain's fifty-peseta banknotes next to a portrait of Velázquez and a reproduction of his *The Surrender of Breda* on the other side.

That was the last currency issued during Alfonso's rule. In January of 1930, Primo de Rivera lost support during the debates about Spain's new constitution and had to resign. Alfonso XIII appointed General Dámaso Berenguer head of the government, with the mandate of reinstating the parliamentary model of 1876. On the occasion of the general's appointment, the illustrated weekly *Nuevo Mundo* ran an interview with Berenguer's daughter, who said that she had a habit of visiting the Prado Museum every Sunday in the company of her father. And with that, the taste for museum-going suddenly appeared a fashionable political marker for a democracy-friendly dictatorship. But in February of 1931, Berenguer resigned, and in April the pro-monarchical parties were defeated in the municipal elections in the major cities. The day after the election—April 14, 1931—several cities across Spain proclaimed the Republic, and an independent Catalan state was declared in Barcelona, while in Madrid the Revolutionary Committee, which had been created a few months earlier, sent to the king and his family an ultimatum to abdicate. Alfonso's answer was to flee to France without abdicating the throne, leaving Spaniards again "a kingless people," as Lord Byron described their nineteenth-century ancestors during the time of the First Republic.

The Revolutionary Committee became the provisional government, which in June 1931 held the general elections bringing to power a coalition of Republican and Socialist parties. In early December, a new constitution was approved, in which, by a very narrow margin, women received full voting rights. In the meantime, a special commission was created to design a comprehensive agrarian reform. Frustrated by the slow pace and the limited scope of the proposed changes, peasants all around Spain, politicized by the anarchist parties, staged violent protests. Facing an urgent need to communicate with the rural population, the central authorities made use of the *Institucionista* belief in cultural citizenship, in which they themselves had been educated. In a surprising move, while the government was reinforcing the civil guards all over Spain, the Ministerio de Instrucción Pública y Bellas Artes (Ministry of Public Instruction and Fine Arts) financed the work of young middle-class men and women from the cities who volunteered to go to the villages, bringing libraries, film projections, theater, and puppet shows and organizing lectures and workshops. Their activities were coordinated through the Patronato de Misiones Pedagógicas (Board of Trustees of the Pedagogical Missions), designed to promote general education and foster civic feeling in rural areas, and was presided over by none other than the art critic Manuel Bartolomé de Cossío.

A NEW PASEO DEL PRADO

The Spanish middle classes now had at their disposal an exhibiting culture that was overtaking the lingering popular traditions and replacing them with new ones; they also had enough support from municipal authorities interested in disavowing uncontrolled uses of the streets—which at that time already meant "political" uses. Commercial brokers wishing to lure people into their indoor or gated domains were also in favor. Around the Prado, the results would soon become very visible. In 1905, the largest wave of redevelopment after Carlos III had begun to transform central Madrid into a twentieth-century capital. Small streets around the Calle Alcalá were cleared to make space for the Gran Via; the Jardines del Buen Retiro were removed to erect a grandiose Palace of Communications—the headquarters of Spain's postal

FIG. 31   Aerial view of the Prado Museum and Promenade from the east, with the museum's new, gated, eastern façade, the modern neighborhood between the Prado and the current Retiro Park, and the Ritz Hotel north of the museum fully visible. *Nuevo Mundo* 36, no. 1839 (April 19, 1929), n.p.

administration (currently housing the government of Madrid); and the Salón del Prado was transformed into a palm grove. In the same year, it was decided that the area of the former Tívoli facing the Prado museum would become the site of a new world-class hotel: the Ritz, finished by 1911 (fig. 31). Meanwhile, the Prado Promenade became less a place for strolling and more an urban artery connecting the new city centers to each other and to the redesigned Paseo de Recoletos while also giving access to the burgeoning development of the Paseo de la Castellana. Different means of public transport, from shared automobile lines to omnibus cars to trams, were now running along the alleys. The streets had to be asphalted, electric poles installed, and rails laid, and larger buildings such as the landmark Platería de Martínez and the Andalusian-style Xifre Palace that were obstructing the passage of cars had to go. There was so much traffic, in fact, that newspapers of the time reported deaths of Madrileños and visitors on foot.

In the meantime, an unannounced war was being waged in the center of the Paseo to conquer it for the upper classes. Complaints had long been filed about the bad state of the fountains closest to the Botanical Garden, which had served as a substitute for a bathroom for the Paseo's homeless dwellers since they were built in the eighteenth century. In 1904, the municipal authorities received well-studied proposals for how to sanitize them, surround them with a railing, and move to the center of the Paseo. When the upcoming construction of the Ritz was announced in 1905, museum directors also redoubled their efforts to stop nighttime camping on the Promenade, and writers followed suit. In 1906, a "Comical Guide to Madrid" penned by humorists calling themselves Nineht and Guripa advised tourists to avoid the museum environs at night unless they wished to see "something very ugly" or to "lose all their feathers" (presumably meaning cash). A vignette published the same year in a comic weekly depicted the statue of Velázquez as a frightened guard "looking in panic at the stone benches even when no one is using them."[38] Now that a debate about the museum's surroundings had emerged and had the authorities' ears, José Villegas Cordero, the director of the Prado from 1901 to 1918, asked the City to dispatch a guard who would prevent paupers from sitting on the stairs during the museum's hours of operation. Perhaps strategically making things sound worse than they were, the director also described the museum as the site of a nightly gathering of "women leading bad lives" (*mujeres de mala vida*), who were blamed for stealing the employees' property, defying the police, and causing disorder.[39]

Policing was one way of stopping unauthorized uses of the museum vicinities, but apparently it was slow to take effect. In 1906 and 1907, the directors insisted on the issues of urban hygiene and public safety. Villegas was in favor of installing electric streetlights in the museum's area while the rest of the Promenade was still lit by gas. One of the subsequent directors, Álvarez Sotomayor, asked the City to pay attention to the fences around the Botanical Garden, where individuals or couples had gone for privacy at night since the eighteenth century.[40] Not only the expensive hotels, but also the rapid growth of luxurious blocks of flats, whose residents found the view from their windows shocking, made it important to minimize the noticeable presence of the working classes on the Paseo. In an attempt to further assist the City in making the area more respectable, it was even reported that the concierges of these buildings would spread petroleum jelly on the benches of the Promenade in order to discourage people from becoming too comfortable.[41]

The battle for the Prado was accompanied by a public discrediting of fairground celebrations, now described as "more and more degenerate and less and less artistic."[42] Instead of offering quality leisure and social cohesion, an author from Barcelona guessed, festivals served the needs of old-school politicking, with deputies attending the fairs to give out free museum tickets to provincials in exchange for their votes.[43] For almost a hundred years, the directors of the Prado had been protesting the fireworks, vending kiosks, horseracing, and late-night drinking on the Promenade during the spring and summer festivals. But now the authorities started listening. First they interfered with the placement and appearance of the vending pavilions and banned the consumption of alcohol on the museum's grounds. Then the decree of April 11, 1905, prohibited the *verbenas* of San Isidro on the Salón del Prado and in the museum's immediate vicinity (the two other, shorter festivals, San Juan and San Pedro, were allowed to remain).[44] Still, a year later, the museum director found it necessary to repeat his complaints to the City, citing the unaesthetic appearance of the vending kiosks, their blockage of museum entrances, and the risk of fire from the sparks from the fireworks. Finally, in 1913, after many years of mostly ignoring such protests, the Madrid council paid attention and, going against the Association of Fairground Vendors, relocated the *verbenas* and kiosks from the Prado closer to the Atocha station. At first, only a small change was enforced, one that didn't help the museum much: vendors and kiosks were confined to the walkways in front of Villanueva's building and the Botanical Garden, "leaving clear all the parts of the Paseo del Prado and the areas adjacent to grand hotels."[45] In an effort to improve the aesthetics of the vending stalls and to bring their design closer to what upper-class travelers would expect from the museum's vicinity, the municipal authorities even requested that vendors have the appearance of their kiosks approved prior to the fair "so that these *verbenas* could offer a more pleasant sight than they currently [do]."[46]

The decisions to move the kiosks, first even closer to the museum and then not far enough from it, of course upset the directors of the Prado, who continued protesting. Assistance, however, came from an unexpected source. In 1915, Pablo Iglesias, the founder of the Socialist Workers' Party (PSOE) and the General Workers' Union (UGT), who at the time was also a representative in the Madrid city government and the Cortes, criticized the mayor's complicity with commerce in allowing "the business-owners to occupy gardens, promenades, and sidewalks."[47] Painting a class-conscious picture of Madrid's public spaces, Iglesias also claimed that "the *verbena* is only good for making the worker drink and get drunk," and requested that the festivals be moved to the outskirts of the city and far away from the Prado Museum.[48] This was, as far as can be determined, the first attempt to ban leisure activities from public spaces in Madrid, and in 1916 all celebrations on the Paseo del Prado were prohibited or transferred to the Pacífico area. In 1922, in an attempt to civilize the Prado even further, the City designated the former fairground of the Paseo del Prado for the "cultured" activity of bookselling. Still, the celebrations on the Paseo had not entirely ended. The very same year, the museum protested again about the crowds making bonfires to celebrate another saint, San Juan.[49]

The political overtones that were starting to permeate working-class festivities were also bringing to extinction the museum's most identifiable mass visitors, the so-called *Isidros*. To a writer for Madrid's *El Liberal*, for example, modernization in the nation's provinces was making the *Isidros* a vanishing species, and those who were left were no longer interested in museum-going anyway. "My *Isidro*," as the writer called the guest he portrayed, only superficially followed the stereotype of a bearded villager with a cane who was not as impressed with the museum as he was with the music halls and the trams. In 1915, a journalist writing for *Nuevo Mundo* under the quasi-traditional pen name of Juan Palomo was already depicting the *Isidros* as nostalgic reminiscences. Collected under the category of "from my archive," Palomo's stories reminded the

Madrileños of the times when these picturesque characters were still a source of easy laughs. The stories included, of course, an inevitable scene in front of the nudes at the Prado, featuring a scandalized *Isidro* explaining, with a thick Aragón accent, that women in Madrid, out of sheer vanity, commissioned portraits of themselves when they couldn't even afford any clothes.[50] With the vanishing of the *Isidros*, the Madrid journalists—themselves mostly provincials who had "made it big" (or not so big) in Madrid—were losing a precious tool for showing the culture of the capital through the eyes of village folks.

Parallel to the unfolding of leisure politics, continuing class struggle presented the authorities with a new question concerning mass leisure: could the *verbenas* bring more harmony to society by providing an alternative to the more dangerous worker-led protests? Or were the *verbenas* themselves merely another manifestation of class warfare? In 1915, commenting on Iglesias's fight against apolitical mass celebrations, mentioned earlier, and on the ensuing displacement of *verbenas* from the Prado, the conservative writer Pedro Mata supported the former, socially optimistic and national-ist view, exalting the *verbenas* as "the only free, picturesque, classic, and clearly popular celebration" available in Madrid.[51] Verbenophilia and verbenophobia cut across all party lines. Among those who disliked them, we find not only Iglesias (and, later on, another important socialist intellectual, Andrés Ovejero) and the conservative-leaning museum authorities, but also the controversial politician Antonio Maura, who pro-moted a "revolution from above" but opposed Primo de Rivera's dictatorship. In the other camp, among those who believed in the *verbenas* were the pro-republican writer Ramón Gómez de la Serna and his pro-fascist friend Ernesto Giménez Caballero. The former, who called himself "the spontaneous son of the Prado," published a richly illus-trated history of the Promenade in 1919, which included photographs of boys doing gymnastics, booksellers' stalls, and other "civilized" and "sportized" leisure activities (figs. 32 and 33).[52]

Political changes under Primo de Rivera would soon add new overtones to the debates about the masses on the Paseo. The majority of journalists opposed the regime, whose strict censorship policies made them channel their political opinions into safer topics, making mass leisure extremely popular. Still, interpretations of the *verbenas* did not always correlate as one might expect with the politics of the writer. The socialist *La Libertad*, for example, supported the booksellers' fight to make the area more respectable and denounced the authorities' leniency toward "horrible instal-lations, merry-go-rounds, raffles, shooting ranges, and filthy tents."[53] Meanwhile, Alberto Insúa, a frequent contributor to the same newspaper, authored an apologetic novel, *A Señorita and a Worker, or A "Flirt" at the Verbena of San Antonio* (1926), sug-gesting that the temporal forgetting of class structure at the *verbenas* was producing the social "miracle of love and democracy."[54] For the moment, the most vocal fans of the Madrid *verbenas* were the avant-garde poets, writers, and artists seeking to give

FIG. 32   Old-books kiosk on the Paseo del Prado. From Ramón Gómez de la Serna, *El Paseo del Prado* (Madrid: G. Hernandez y Galo Sáez, 1919), 34.

FIG. 33   Boys doing gymnastics on the railing on the Paseo del Prado. From Gómez de la Serna, *El Paseo del Prado*, 56.

twentieth-century expression to the traditional forms of folk life, who were gradually making their way into museums (yet not into the Prado).[55] In 1928, the recasting of fairground fun as a subject of determinedly modern paintings inspired by the art deco style propelled the young artist Maruja Mallo (whose real name was Ana María Gómez González) to the forefront of the male-dominated exhibition world. Ortega y Gasset, the godfather and major theoretician of the Spanish avant-garde, gave the highest praise to Mallo's 1927 series of four paintings, *Verbenas*, and immediately organized a solo exhibition for Mallo in the offices of the journal *Revista de Occidente*. Evoking and reworking the Carnival reversal of power, Mallo's compositions depicted the *verbenas* as tacky yet liberating occasions when one might cross the border between races, genders, and classes and weigh the reality of being human against the fantastical presence of deities, animals, automatons, and fairground giants (fig. 34). In her private life, as Shirley Mangini has found, the artist herself and her "modern" female friends used the *verbenas* as an occasion to meet men in public.[56]

FIG. 34   Maruja Mallo, *La verbena I*, oil on canvas, 119 × 165 cm, 1927. Museo Nacional Centro de Arte Reina Sofía.

In 1930, when Alfonso XIII began to dismantle Primo de Rivera's order and the *verbenas* were authorized to take place on the Paseo del Prado again, Gómez de la Serna celebrated the decision as "the best symptom of a new epoch, one with a parliament and a democratic spirit," and as a mark of the times "when one savors again the freedom that Madrid had long not enjoyed."[57] In the same year, Gómez de la Serna and Giménez Caballero presented in the Madrid Cine-Club a film whose title—*La esencia de la verbena* (The essence of verbena) —recovered in the popular celebrations their centuries-old connection to the plant and traced new links to the perfume, which was now mass manufactured. The avant-garde taste for merging tradition and modernity was equally present in the film's innovative language of cross-cutting and double exposure, which restyled Madrid's fairgrounds as a harmonious and inclusive microcosm where "nobody laughs at nobody."[58] Yet until such a utopia became a reality, the directors of the Prado resumed their protests, citing the need to create an environment that would not scare away foreign art-lovers and the occupants of the nearby luxurious hotels. The Círculo de Bellas Artes and the Academia San Fernando stood with the museum, while commercial stakeholders courted the press to publicize the peace and good order reigning at the vending stalls. In the history of the Madrid fairgrounds, the end of the dictatorship in 1930 stands out as the season when everyone seemed to have an opinion.

When the prime minister resigned, Alfonso XIII disappeared, and the Second Republic was proclaimed, the provisional government called on the Constituent Cortes to announce the elections, to be held on June 28—at the time of the San Juan, San Pedro, and San Pablo festivals. Many people in Madrid were curious about, or concerned with, the prospects of the "republican *verbenas*."[59] However, while rumors about possible disruptions to the festivals in other cities (San Sebastian, for example) were spreading, there was no visible change in the capital, whose mayor, Pedro Rico, continued the policy of his predecessor and allowed the fairground on the Paseo. Only in retrospect can one distinguish marks of novelty. Many fundraising *verbenas* were now collecting funds for unemployed workers. Some beauty pageants distributed the title of "Miss Republic," and a small kiosk appeared on the Paseo del Prado selling tickets to a soccer match.[60] Newspapers reporting about the century-old problem of theft during the *verbenas* now adopted a tone somewhere between sarcasm and acceptance: "the bad thing is that people of very different social conditions come to popular celebrations, and into a group of decent people a 'rat' can unfortunately sneak in."[61]

The press saw the *verbenas* as a testing ground for class harmony under the new political circumstances. Yet while the governments were debating the project of land reform or the statutes of Catalonia, the relations between classes were not peaceful. Meetings of over twenty participants were not allowed, and security organizations were keeping an eye on fairground stalls, suspicious that people might be using them for unauthorized political gatherings.[62] During one festival, a group of communists was arrested at a drink kiosk on the Prado and charged with attempting to form a secret cell. Tensions were so high that in 1932 the traders at the Madrid Stock Exchange panicked upon hearing explosions, grabbed their belongings, and ran out of the building—only to see with relief that the noise was coming from the fireworks of the nearby *verbena*.[63] In the same year, the comic pro-monarchical journal *Gracia y Justicia* published a caricature of people running away from the kiosks that sold fried pastry (*churros*), whose smoke and odor reminded them of peasants burning their villages to protest agrarian reform or the lack thereof. And while the tension about the displays of both class struggle and popular celebration hovered above and around the *verbenas* on the Paseo del Prado,[64] newspapers such as *El Heraldo de Madrid* continued their humorous exploration of fairground solidarity. One note reporting a stolen wallet asked that the perpetrators forgive the owner (a journalist) for carrying so little money and begged the thieves to return the documents.[65]

If the *verbenas* were indeed becoming a social laboratory, then it was once again time for reform. This is when the Republic brought its most visible change to the urban festivals: the modern forms of "sportization" reaching beyond the upper- and middle-class horse, bicycle, and car racing. Mass competitions, initially, were registered in areas other than the Promenade. In August 1931, the festival program of La Virgen de la Paloma included boxing matches. In 1932, the San Pedro *verbena* in the Retiro, organized by the Círculo de Bellas Artes, included a swimming competition. During the San Juan festivities of 1933, sport came to the museum's environs in the form of an amateur footrace. In the same year, the Association *Los Hijos de Madrid* (Sons of Madrid), which had been managing the gated fairgrounds of the Retiro, began to explore a new activity in a new location: a nautical *verbena* on the beach of the Manzanares River. Soccer matches first appeared on the program of a festival in Vallecas in July of 1935, but symbolically this sport had already been a part of the experience on the Prado Promenade, which had featured a soccer-themed merry-go-round since 1932.

The *Institucionista* upbringing of many of those now coming to power, and their friendship with Cossío, the educator and art critic, explain the unprecedented importance that the Republic's first government gave to monitored leisure. Just like their nineteenth-century liberal teachers, these politicians believed in the continuity between high and low cultural forms: festival attractions, team sports, and museum-going. Hence, the Republican reformists of the time took a "soft" approach to regulating mass leisure, which would be continued by the 1934–35 conservative-led cabinet. Rather than banning celebrations on the Prado, they gradually developed a list of "civilized" alternatives while also encouraging the development of new venues away from the city center. Meanwhile, the *verbenas* on the Prado were rebranded as a modern neighborhood festival of the Congress district and even included beauty pageants for the title of "Miss Congress."

In every other aspect, the verbenas featured the traditional repertoire of amusements, ranging from serpent tamers and *horchata* kiosks to dancing girls and pleasure rides offering a simulated trip to Shanghai.[66] Despite all of this, in a 1932 guidebook to Madrid, the deputy director of the Prado Museum, Francisco Javier Sánchez Cantón, described the area of the Paseo as merely a site that the museum building shared with "two large modern hotels" and as far less picturesque than it was in the past, when the Prado was still "the fashionable promenade . . . , the scene of love affairs and quarrels, of 'Mars and of exchange in Venus's currency.'"[67] At that time, the City finalized the moving of the Book Fair to the Paseo and even assigned additional funds for building "hygienic and artistic kiosks."[68] This would be, one might think, the end of the *verbenas*. But it was not.

For Socialist and Republican politicians of the Second Republic, fairground celebrations no longer seemed déclassé, commercial, or degrading for the workers. Instead, they were becoming a place to capture the attention of the masses and do politics. In 1933, Indalecio Prieto, then the minister of public works, announced a "subterranean" *verbena* in the recently completed section of a railway tunnel under the Paseo de la Castellana. The event apparently did not take place, but the press took the occasion to joke about a new *tubo de risa* (funhouse; literally "laughing tube" or "tunnel of laughter").[69] In 1935, Manuel Azaña, the leader of the Republican Left, decided to take a walk on the *verbena* on the Prado and was greeted by crowds so large that he was forced to make a hasty retreat by catching a nearby cab.[70] In its next issue, *Gracia y Justicia* advertised "Manolo" (Manuel Azaña) as a new freak show attraction at the *verbena*, ranking somewhere between a fish-woman and a man with five mouths.[71] Concomitant with the populist restyling of his political persona after his release from prison in 1934, however, Azaña's walk foreshadowed one important change that would have to happen: if these celebrations were indeed the place to find the masses, rather than any specific class, the political attitudes of the Left toward these masses needed a revision.

It was, again, the Promenade facing the Prado Museum that provided the arena for most of the numerous political rallies and demonstrations in the months leading to the general election in February 1936, which the Popular Front won in Madrid in a landslide. Azaña, soon to become prime minister, even described the crowd gathering at the Puerta del Sol on the night of the election as another *verbena*.[72] This was not a flattering comparison: the image of the mass festival once again became the embodiment of the winners' fear of uncontrolled gatherings. Could the Popular Front succeed in restraining the popular spirit? After all, its ideology proclaimed interclass solidarity, and the *verbenas* could have been a perfect metaphor for the movement. The antigovernment coup of July 18 and the subsequent war erased this question and the issue of popular leisure in general.

A MODEL OF SELF-GOVERNANCE

Even before the pastimes on the Promenade moved into the center of political debate, the Prado Museum had become a matter of discussions at the Congress and the Senate. Reflecting the museum's growing social prominence, Spain's elected officials drafted proposals ranging from the return of the paintings loaned to the former colonial government of Puerto Rico to the installation of glass screens in the museum's colonnade.[73] (In 1921, the Senate even held a vote on which paintings to put on exhibit in its own gallery and which to keep in the museum—a matter that forty years earlier would have been decided by a verbal agreement or royal decree.) Soriano, the art critic who a decade before had denounced the mismanagement of the Prado in his articles, could now criticize it from his congressional bench as a socialist representative.[74] The press was quick to support this emerging alliance of power, while also suggesting that both the museum and Spain's democracy were victims of a deeper problem: a lack of public interest and participation. One humorous article portrayed a local guide asking a group of provincials on a visit to the nation's capital:

—What impressed you most at the Museum of Paintings?

—The bloody cold.

—Now let's go to see the Congress.

—Won't it be too crowded now that it is in session?

—Not at all! There will be hardly anyone there [now that it is in session], and you get the best seats.[75]

The museum's fate, it seemed, was intertwined with the nation's representative institutions: both were treated like unpopular theater companies.

Still, it was this growing association with the state that paved the way for the museum's most crucial triumph: at the end of 1901, following two years of congressional debates, the Prado took possession of five popular paintings—Goya's two *Majas* and three paintings by Murillo—from the Academia San Fernando, thus crowning the Prado the winner in a century-old competition for social importance.[76] Until recently, the Academia had succeeded in catering to the tastes and aspirations of the educated liberals. But now, as the proposal to centralize Spanish art at the Prado reached the parliament and the press, a columnist of *El Globo* denounced the Academia as a "body of a dubious utility and meager authority, calling itself responsible for Fine Arts while it fails even to include the majority of artists who are making all of us . . . famous all over the world."[77] The Prado became Spain's most relevant exhibiting institution.

Since the previous century, the directors of the Prado had been recruited from outside the Academia San Fernando. In October of 1901, Luis Álvarez Catalá fell victim to the influenza epidemic, and the Ministry of Fomento nominated José Villegas y Cordero, a successful artist who lived in Rome in his specially designed Moorish-style villa.[78] When, soon after the new appointment, he was accepted into the Academia, his inauguration speech was dedicated to the modern subject of the interconnectedness of the arts.[79] Villegas himself set a good example of such interconnectedness by designing Spain's new banknotes and immortalizing Alfonso XIII in a painting for the new building of the National Treasury (Banco de España).[80] The director's success at court was good for the Prado and even allowed early glimpses of the science of the museum display, which was developing abroad and would be brought to Spain. No doubt at Villegas's request, for the first time in history, the state decided to pay for the expense of sending the museum director to see the competitor museums: to study the displays of Spanish art in Germany, Austria, and the Netherlands (1903),[81] and, later on, to oversee the reorganizations in the museums of Italy, Germany, Holland, and France (1911).[82] Once it succeeded in modernizing its image, the Prado's administration could also revisit some of its old projects and plans, one of which was to become a treasury of Spain's painting and sculpture by adding to its holdings works from private and other national collections.

While expanding the display, the new administration also did all it could to modernize the existing exhibition spaces and add new ones in order to keep up with the improvements in other European capitals. A new fire alarm system, safe heaters, electric streetlights, and more respectable surroundings were concerns that had to be addressed in conjunction with a deeper transformation inside and outside the building. In 1911,[83] Villegas made a strong enough case for adding facilities to spur the most decisive museum expansion of the twentieth century, designed by architect Fernando Arbós. Still, the politicians' meddling in the affairs and operations of the Prado did not seem to be ending, causing the Ministry of Development to realize that time had come for allowing the public's direct participation in the museum's governance. Following the example of other nations that gave their museums full autonomy, in June 1912 the ministry issued a decree creating a collective governing body, El Patronato del Museo del Prado (the Board of Trustees of the Prado Museum). Although the budget still depended on the state, the Prado was now getting closer than ever to the ideal of participatory museum that had inspired the first postrevolutionary thinkers.

For the first time since the First Republic, collecting and exhibiting paintings and sculptures became a matter of legislation. The idea, however, was now to take this responsibility away from the state and involve society through the conduit of the experts and the elites. The board included different constituencies—the inspector of fine arts, the museum's director, critics, collectors, and academics—uniting them in a common task. The preamble of the foundational document referred specifically to the need to mitigate the lack of "loving and caring social action" in the matter of developing national art collections.[84] The duke de Alba, the president of the Academia, was elected to preside over the board.

The issues that had dominated the debates about the Prado since its nationalization in 1868–70 were again on the table: steering this "organically constituted" gallery into an exhibit representative of the major "schools" of art and the Spanish school in particular, with a system, a rational time line, and a new catalogue.[85] Although for a museum in the twentieth century this sounded like a return to an unaccomplished yet already dated agenda, the trustees developed an innovative program to address these needs, combining "transformations of, and additions to, the building," cooperating with the grand European museums as well as minor museums of Spain, organizing exhibitions and conferences to advance knowledge of the fine arts, revising old inventories, and verifying the lists of paintings sent as deposits to other institutions.[86] Most importantly, the board signified a major step toward replacing state patronage by private investment. The foundational decree specified that the creation of the new governing body was aimed at securing "honorable and fruitful" public involvement that would "complete and improve official action and add to it the technical expertise that is impossible to obtain otherwise, without running into great expense."[87] Yet if the board was to channel the public's interests, the social base of this "public" was limited to the elites, who, under the pretext of their love of art, were encouraged to employ their wealth to fill the gaps in state funding in exchange for having a say in the museum's future.[88] The board, it was suggested, would dispense to the museum its "daily, solicitous, and effusive attention" and its "warmness and desire," unbound by any "service contract or wage agreement among public servants and the state": a fruit of "the intimate and fervent cult of Art and its glories."[89]

With the creation of the board of trustees, the government therefore sought to attract collectors, who had hitherto remained disenfranchised "due to the notorious lack of synergy between citizens and state centers," to regulate the museum staff, and to make visits to the museum "pleasant to tourists and the lovers of fine art."[90] In the 1870s, the anarchist-leaning Tubino had fantasized about Spaniards of all walks of life being involved in the development of the museum without the government's mediation. This fantasy now seemed to be turning into a partial and somewhat ironic reality. There was only one middle-class trustee, Cossío, and even he stepped down two months after the appointment, making it hard for other board members to support the kind of displays that would educate the masses. Senator Eliseo Tormo, a famous art critic and a professor at the Universidad Central who came to replace Cossío, professed no Ruskinian sympathies, even though he did not hail from the nobility or haut-bourgeoisie. Twenty years later, during the Second Republic, another supporter of worker education, Andrés Ovejero, would also resign after just a few sessions, perhaps finding it hard to work with the board.

Firmly and unquestionably, the board protected the museum's autonomy at all costs, even when this ran counter to the trustees' personal involvement in the debates concerning the state, the church, and the fine arts. This mutual understanding about not taking sides among the trustees allowed the board to move forward with a coherent, albeit limited, agenda focused on collection development, new rules and regulations, admission policies, and the museum's participation in international exhibitions and other artistic exchanges. The trustees supported the hiring of the young historian Francisco Javier Sánchez Cantón as the museum's deputy director, with the special task of producing a new catalogue. Sánchez Cantón's personal archive at the Prado documents several years, during which he painstakingly took notes from a long list of books and articles on museum visitorship, classifications, and the meaning of Spanish art. He spent considerable time thoroughly annotating the contributions of German scholars to these topics. Another young historian, Pedro Beroqui, was hired at the same time to work in the archives and update the registries. Beroqui wrote the first official history of the Prado (published 1931–33).

The ultimate success of the new administration relied, however, on the availability of exhibiting space, and the museum finally began to grow beyond its original limits. Bringing to completion a series of unrealized projects drafted by a succession of architects since 1849, the early twentieth-century expansion put the exhibition space on par with several other European museums that were adding daylit rooms.[91] The construction, fully approved in 1914, was supposed to take seven and a half years, but it took longer due to the architect's death in 1916—which was so sudden that his successor, Amós Salvador, could not even find the original construction plans. This, combined with a wave of builders' strikes in 1921, forced him to step down as the project architect in 1922, without completing the work. A young architect, Pedro Muguruza, came to replace Salvador. According to the architectural historian Moleón Gavilanes, the remodeling, finished in 1923 under Muguruza's leadership but still carrying the name of its first designer, Fernando Arbós, did away with the most salient characteristic of Villanueva's original interior: the three spaces shaped as cul-de-sacs on each floor, connected through the central rotundas.[92] Instead of these unidirectional pathways, the museum could now offer its visitors a free *marche* in any direction. New entrances and exits became necessary, so in 1925 Muguruza finished two staircases connecting what now were the museum's three floors, one of which would soon be equipped with an elevator.

The need for exhibition space, however, could not be fully satisfied by simply expanding the building. The museum's opening to civil society meant that, after a long period of stagnation, the collection had begun to grow thanks to gifts from private donors. In 1904, a donation from Ramón de Errazu set the precedent for the rededication of a section of the exhibit to a private collector rather than a monarch or an artist. Errazu's will named the museum as the heir of several works by classical and best-selling contemporary artists (among them Fortuny and Federico de Madrazo), which in 1905 were all put on display in a specially arranged Sala Errazu.[93] When the board of trustees was created, more donors asked to have galleries named after themselves.[94] In his will, one of the trustees, Pablo Bosch, advised his former colleagues to select for the museum any number of paintings from his three-hundred-item collection, under the condition that these works would be displayed in several contingent rooms bearing Bosch's name and dedicated to the legacy of Count de Romanones, the liberal prime minister who had spurred the creation of the board and who was Bosch's stepfather. Insisting that he was not requesting this "because of some immature vanity, but rather to stimulate others by personal example," Bosch even donated funds to redecorate these galleries "with luxury and good taste, to which foreign museums have us accustomed."[95]

No longer showcasing the tastes of old-regime monarchs, the museum was becoming a monument to the elites sustaining the nation's effort to protect and exhibit its art. The ninety first-rate paintings that the trustees chose upon Bosch's death filled many gaps in the collection of Flemish, French, and Spanish art. These impressive additions, however, came precisely at a time when covering entire walls with pictures was no longer considered acceptable. And so, in 1928, a whole story, with its own staircase, had to be added to the recently completed long gallery in order to house the Bosch collection. By 1930, another large donation, from Xavier Laffitte y Charlesteguy, produced a need for yet another "personal" gallery. On this occasion, it was decided to simply reuse the rooms formerly named after Alfonso XII.

FIG. 35   Detail of the decoration
of the Sala Goya, *Luz*, August 5,
1932, 3.

207

As the display was giving more representation to the nation's collectors, other social groups were beginning to appreciate the museum as a home of their own. In 1906, following the earlier example set in Velázquez's galleries (upholstered in red silk for the 1899 tercentennial), Trinidad de Iturbe (née Scholz), the marquise de Contaminas, decided to fund a luxurious redecoration of Murillo's galleries in red velvet, unveiled in 1910. Early century photographs show that the walls were following the standards and décor of bourgeois residences more and more: the Goya rooms were decorated according to eighteenth-century taste and furbished with neoclassical couches; Titian exhibits hung against luscious silk wallpaper. In 1920, when the collection of El Greco grew large enough to occupy a whole room, that gallery was compared to "a portrait room in a wealthy Castilian mansion, painted in white, with slight and pleasant yellowish tones."[96] The question of the walls became so prominent that in 1927, when the Goya collection was reorganized, the deputy director had to justify its lack of wallpaper, which apparently had become traditional in the museum, on art-historical grounds: "the walls are painted gray, which favors and harmonizes well with the majority of Spanish paintings, which, by a chronic mistake, are usually placed on red."[97] As for the Goya rooms, in 1932 Ramón Gómez de la Serna paid tribute to their upper-class domestic setting by comparing them to "a living and inhabited part of the palace; the dwellings reserved for its last tenant," and praising the ways in which its new lighting interacted with its "contemporary stonework" (fig. 35).[98] Never before had the museum facilities seemed so approachable, and it probably helped that the museum itself could now offer its visitors a toilet and more comfortable staircases, and, in time, better lighting and heating systems.

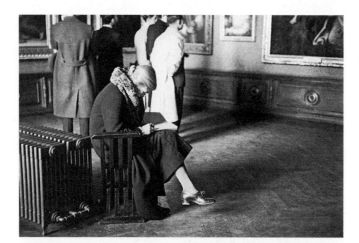

FIG. 36–38 Estudio
Fotográfico "Alfonso"
(Alfonso Sánchez Portela),
The Prado Museum, c.
1935. Archivo General de la
Administración.

A series of photographs taken in the museum and united by the common theme of "dwelling," commissioned just before the end of 1935, captured this new perception well.[99] An old woman draws close to the heater in the Titian gallery to read a book (fig. 36). Another old woman looks disapprovingly at a group of laughing *señoritos* crowding onto the benches (fig. 37). A young couple has a date on another bench (fig. 38). This is also how journalist Antonio Otero Seco would later remember the museum on the days of free public admission, when "some would drift through the waxed beaches of cracking wood toward the red couches that Ramón [Gómez de la Serna] called 'the museum's velvet isles,' seeking the warm caress of nearby radiators, tired of resisting the cold poking their faces outside. Others would look without seeing, their gaze lost in the fake depths of the landscapes, waiting for girlfriends who would always come late, stepping carefully like little birds."[100] If the museum was a home, it was, apparently, one with a view.

A WOMAN-FRIENDLY ENTRYWAY TO THE PUBLIC ARENA

Male writers were the first to imagine the museum as their home, but this particular bourgeois fantasy needed a woman to complete the picture. In 1907, the liberal *La Época* ran a telling humorous dialogue suggesting that "ladies" had to be called in to domesticate the museum and improve the atmosphere. A male interlocutor took pride in not having seen the new Velázquez galleries because "a self-respecting Madrileño never visits the museum. It's a thing for foreigners and people from the provinces."[101] When the speaker's art-loving friend disapprovingly agreed ("That's how good we are with art and proper taste"), the proud Madrileño suggested that, in order to help the situation, "artists, art lovers, and all those who deplore our artistic backwardness should ask the marquise of *** to organize a day *à la mode* to visit the museum. This way, ladies will certainly go." The future of the nation's taste was half-seriously and half-jokingly placed in the hands of its upper-class women, who could make the museum more inviting. Yet as the story continued, it became clear that the nation's political participation could also use some help from the "ladies":

—Not a bad idea . . .
—With tea served by Ideal Room [a catering service] and a sextet playing music.
  And in the spare moments between flirting, a quick look at the paintings.
—With ladies' influence so important, shall we also ask for their support for the
  elections, in view of the current anemia reigning among the electorate?[102]

The comparison of the museum to a home, therefore, did not always indicate a "private refuge." Rather, for this liberal writer the home was a convenient image that allowed

209

him to recognize a woman's role in politics without breaking with the precepts of female domesticity.

The continuing confusion between the public and the private allowed the male fascination with the museum nudes to evolve into a commercially viable visual culture. Claiming that the same gaze was needed to look at all (yet still mostly female) bodies sculpted, painted, or captured in a magazine or on a pornographic postcard, authors and publishers from Madrid and Barcelona coined a special aesthetic category called *sicalipsis* (naughtiness) that overrode the distinction between the naked and the nude across printed media.[103] Reworking old-regime libertinism for the expanding bourgeois audience, sycaliptic imagery was described as "halfway between what is artistically moral and what constitutes the artlessly frivolous: without being completely the former yet without falling into the latter."[104] Such an approach opened new markets for the reproductions of museum paintings, while also making acceptable the public display of nudes outside of the museum. Or at least it now seemed acceptable to cosmopolitan males. In 1904, when the city demanded that a bookstore remove from its window a copy of *The Three Graces*, Peter Paul Rubens's painting from the Prado, because it featured nude women, Mariano de Cavia (the same famous author who had earlier written the sensationalist article about the presumed fire at the Prado) called it the "stigma of our time" that the authorities were no longer able to distinguish a museum masterpiece from pornography.[105] This evolving discussion seemed to suggest that museum masterpieces could become something completely different (and baser, though more exciting) when mechanically reproduced. Starting around 1902, it had become customary for a mixture of etchings and prints of nudes from the Prado's collection with erotic photographs to appear in a range of Spanish illustrated media, from expensive journals such as *Gedeón* and *El Sicalíptico* to medical literature to cheap postcards and paperback novelettes.

Sometimes gathered in separate books or picture sets and referred to as picture galleries of "daring" women (*mujeres galantes*), these images offered a peculiar addition to the analogous series that contributed portraits of "celebrity" women from the Prado and other museums to the national iconography, described at the beginning of this chapter. Taking the issue even further, in 1904, *El Sicalíptico* advertised collections of postcards reproducing Titian's *Danaë* and *Venus and Music* alongside erotic pictures, advising "all artists and lovers of fine arts" to purchase them in order to "have a real museum" of their own.[106] In Maite Zubiaurre's relevant wording, sycalipsis became a "merchandising philosophy" that freed pornography from its identification with lonely pleasures and launched it into wide circulation to support the capitalist gendering of technology and nationalism in Spain.[107] As these discussions unfolded, two apparently unrelated ideologies—feminism and aesthetic "decadentism"—came to the forefront of the public debate, with both questioning the roles reserved to gender in Spanish modernity.[108] It is easy to see, however, how this insertion of the erotic into the bourgeois mainstream was unwittingly facilitated by the blurring of borderlines at the Prado between the space of public interaction and the private homes of the bourgeoisie.

At a time when the civic status of Spanish women was causing a widespread debate, presenting the museum as a space between the public and the private was the same as inviting women to act out their social aspirations in a safe environment. As Judith Keene has shown, among the varying components of the early century preoccupation christened as "the women's question," female suffrage in particular was torn between three approaches: the "feminist" view, which contemplated women's rights as a continuation of the quest for civil liberties; the "new state" model, which looked at suffrage for women as an essential component for creating a reformed modern state apparatus; and the "Latin" way of delaying women's suffrage on the grounds of women's strong link with the conservative wing of the Catholic Church.[109] As the result of these varying influences, only a few feminist opinion-makers supported unrestricted women's suffrage. Both promoters and opponents, however, agreed that Spanish women had not yet achieved emancipation from the church or found a way for themselves into the public sphere. In this context, the Prado Museum, with its traditional public function, its conventional quasi-religious aura, and its newly acquired domestic overtones, became a particularly useful tool for female socialization.

Although dating back to the nineteenth century, such quasi-religious readings of the museum were now recycled to support a new practice among Spaniards: its church-friendly publicness became a perfect arena for women to step out into. Carmen de Burgos, journalist, novelist, and Spain's first suffragist, explicitly told women to visit the Prado if they wanted to achieve emancipation. Significantly, she called the museum "a cathedral": "Seeing how the galleries of the Prado Museum, this cathedral of pictorial art where its most precious treasures are kept, are full of foreign ladies falling ecstatically in front of the genius of our great artists, it occurs to me to advise our women that instead of spending all their time in frivolities they study art and travel in order to achieve superior culture and supreme spiritual enjoyment."[110] In Burgos's opinion, the obstacle in women's path to the museum did not result from a lack of civil liberties, but rather came from within women's own cultures, lifestyles, and traditions. In her own activity, Burgos combined press campaigns that called for the drafting and passing of legislation for the betterment of women (for example, legislation concerning female suffrage, divorce, and so-called crimes of passion) with lectures aimed at making women responsible for their own emancipation "at home, in arts, at work." To become an example for them, she spoke on the subject of Spanish art in women's clubs all over the country.[111]

As she championed museums as a woman's entryway to other public spaces, Burgos was faced with the question of how a woman would feel in this male-gendered space. It was not an easy issue to address at a time when not only male, but also

FIG. 39   José Loygorri, cover of Carmen de Burgos, *The Woman Who Tried to Become Maja* (Madrid: "Novela pasional," 1924).

female artists were defending the right to paint and exhibit nudes as if Spain's cultural modernization depended on it, and Burgos's answer was far from straightforward. To address the topic, she decided to write an erotic novella, *The Woman Who Tried to Become Maja* (c. 1924), which was published as part of a series called the Passionate Novel (*La Novela Pasional*). With illustrations much more daring than the plot, the series was sold in newspaper and magazine kiosks and targeted men as well as women. So, while the pictures by José Loygorri tempted the readers of both sexes with images of women in every stage of disrobing, coded as either "real" (and therefore naked) or copied from Goya and therefore ideal and nude, Burgos told the story of Carola, an upper-middle-class woman wrestling with the desire to be immortalized in a painting as a version of Goya's *Maja*.[112] The underlying message of the story seemed to be that a true modern woman should be able to work with men to determine the best strategy for representing herself and others of her kind. Finding an artist for Carola's portrait, however, turned out to be a passion-ridden adventure that challenged so many of the protagonist's assumptions about nudity and nakedness that the *Maja* that was eventually produced, captured on the novel's front cover, came alarmingly close to the sycaliptic promotion of the female body (fig. 39). Still, this did not cancel the merit of giving women—at least those belonging to the upper and middle classes—agency in using art for redrawing gender roles in the modern public sphere.[113]

A similar interest in the liberating potential of debates about art guided the work of Margarita Nelken, the first woman to lecture at the Prado and one of the three female deputies elected to the Second Republic's Constituent Cortes.[114] A Marxist in her political speeches and writings, Nelken stood firmly on the ground of class analysis, famously claiming that "if all women in Spain were rich, we would most certainly have no feminism."[115] Just as with Burgos, however, Nelken's message was considerably toned down every time she touched the topic of art. In 1932, just weeks after Spanish women received the right to vote, one newspaper even described her as a "socialist 'Mmle. Docteure'"—an ideological fake who "spent her whole life lecturing at the Prado" yet was arrested for instigating a rebellion and spying on the gendarmes.[116] Still, how could she be such an activist yet not question the gender conventions of the aesthetic gaze?

Nelken's views on the situation of Spanish women explained the paradox.[117] Firmly relating the success of the feminist cause to women's learning with and from men, Nelken argued that in Spain this was only happening in the working class. In her quest for models of cross-gender intersubjectivity for the upper classes, she turned to art and museums, where she found both a safe conduit to counter women's deep implication in church matters and an alternative model for relations between the sexes. Since, in her view, these relations had to be based on shared work, she focused on the links between artists and their female models. This was an old topic, yet in her early essays as an art critic Nelken had already distinguished in it a question of female agency. For example, in a piece on Julio Romero de Torres—a contemporary artist who owed his huge commercial success to female portraits—she asserted that his paintings did not represent real women but rather a succession of different heads added to the same body, which existed only in the artist's imagination.[118] Nelken's reading of "Las musas del Museo del Prado" (the Muses of the Prado Museum), as she called her series of lectures, reframed the artist-sitter connection as a form of intersex partnership. Nelken gave her first lecture on this subject in 1930, shortly before she became a member of the Socialist Workers' Party. Though akin to Burgos in her theme and her choice of a venue that resonated with both male and female audiences, Nelken targeted the educated, museum-going public, which did not necessarily read Burgos's less elitist novels.

The subject of Nelken's other lectures—the iconography of the Virgin Mary—derived from her interest in alternative, socialized models of maternity. This was not just a theoretical matter: in the 1910s, she organized free art lessons in Madrid for the children of working-class families. In 1918, she founded an orphanage for the illegitimate children of working mothers.[119] It was, as Paul Preston asserts, the first orphanage in Spain independent of the church, and it caused an outcry from the religious authorities and a subsequent debate in the Senate. Forced to close her establishment in 1920, Nelken dedicated herself to theoretical inquiry, which resulted in her 1926 book *The Science of Mothering and Puericulture*.[120] Later, Nelken's 1929 book on the typology of portraying the Virgin Mary, which replicated some of her lectures at the Prado in the 1930s, applied the same questions about mothering to a subject matter familiar to the museum-going and art-loving audience that an openly feminist publication would not have reached.[121]

During the Second Republic, the Prado was frequently featured in a variety of publications that sought to contest the separation between church and state codified in the new constitution. For example, in 1932–33, when anticlerical groups within the Republic's government and in some areas of Spain began to gain strength, the liberal newspaper *El Imparcial* launched a defense of cultural Catholicism in a series of articles illustrating religious holidays with paintings from the Prado. In this context, Nelken's approach became as effective as it was timely, at least as far as protests from male readers indicate. In 1933, art critic José Francés published a long article in the *Nuevo Mundo* defending the Virgin Mary as "La suprema ejemplaridad humana de la maternidad divina" (the supreme human example of divine motherhood) and an eternal model of femininity against the antireligious propaganda carried out by the Republic's women teachers.[122] Still, it would be hard to deny that at the Prado Nelken's feminist message was coming through in a much more attenuated version than it did at political rallies, thus unwittingly providing support to the bourgeois view of an art museum as a space of social peace.

As feminist opinion-makers were slowly reconsidering public art as a woman-friendly civic arena, male authors who had hitherto only focused their attention on "painted" women (to use Martín Redondo's 1881 joke) began to notice real ones among the museum visitors. In 1930, a joke in the comic (and erotic) magazine *Muchas Gracias* suggested that a young woman's education about "the differences between males and females" was one legitimate outcome of a museum visit. The difference? "A fig leaf!" a female speaker explained to her male friend.[123] Two years later, following the proclamation of the Republic and the granting of the vote to women, the journalist Luis González de Linares told a story portraying women taking full advantage of the museum's gendered structure. It was in the early 1920s (before the Wall Street crash), and the protagonists were American millionaires—a mother and a daughter. Catching a friend of Linares's eyeing female museum visitors, the millionaires decided to try to hire him as an escort. His English rather poor and his masculinity shattering into pieces, the friend thought he was being proposed marriage.[124]

Beyond these gender-bending fantasies about wealthy foreign women acting out the stereotypes of masculine behavior, real Spanish, middle-class female visitors also questioned the museum's privileging of men. For example, the Prado served as a setting for a key scene in Rosa Chacel's semiautobiographical novel *The Maravillas District*. In the story, one of Chacel's twin female protagonists, a nine-year-old girl, has a revelation that her own inability to act is a result of her family putting her "on exhibit" and reducing her to a "vision" (to use Susan Kirkpatrick's term), and attributes this revelation to her viewing a portrait by Carreño de Miranda.[125] Unlike male writers, who always seemed to imagine their women characters identifying themselves with female portraits and nudes, Chacel portrayed her possible alter-ego comparing herself with "moribund" yet "elegant" male sitters: a fitting description for the illness-ridden figure of Carlos II, Spain's last Habsburg king, in Carreño de Miranda's portrait. If the experience described in the novel was actually based on the author's childhood memories, then it is somewhat ironic that male writers still only pictured the Prado of their youth as a place for flirting. Chacel's younger contemporary, Francisco Ayala, for one, remembered that acquiring an "English girlfriend" was considered a customary result of visiting the museum for a young middle-class Spaniard.[126]

Since the museum's potential as a springboard for questioning the conventions of the male gaze remained visible only to women, and since breaking these conventions was something that women calling themselves "modern" would do, female celebrities began to pose as museum-goers if they (or the reporters interviewing them) wished to be seen as avant-garde yet not socially threatening.[127] In 1930, the same year the daughter of the failed dictator Berenguer admitted to going to the Prado every week, a popular photo magazine, *Estampa*, ran an extensive interview with the singer Celia Gámez—at the time the poster child of the emancipation of Spanish women, who often posed wearing pants and holding a cigarette—who confessed some strangely feminine thoughts inspired by El Greco's *Man with a Hand on His Chest*: "I would love this man with all my heart."[128] Gámez was still, of course, declaring her right to choose the object of her affection.

The line between recognizing full female agency and asserting male power was still a fine one. Hence, although in the 1920s and early 1930s women artists, including Maruja Mallo, Remedios Varo, and Ángeles Santos, rose to fame in Spain's avant-garde circles, their success was still measured by their admission into exhibitions together with men.[129] Female copyists also became suddenly visible, even though they had been working in the museum since at least the 1850s. In 1928, José Francés, mentioned earlier but hiding this time under the pen-name "Silvio Lago," even interviewed one such amateur artist, obviously wishing to portray her, again, as unconventional yet unthreatening. The artist, Virginia Palacios Gros, was copying none other than Goya's *Naked Maja* and planned to offer it to the city hall of Zaragoza (the capital of Aragón, which was Goya's and her own native land) (fig. 40).[130]

Indeed, the number of female copyists and visitors was growing quickly. During the seven years between 1873 and early 1881, permission to copy was given to 990 men and 90 women. In 1913 and again in 1914, permission was given to approximately

216

FIG. 40   Artist Virginia Palacios Gros copying Goya's *Naked Maja* (in the background). Photo by Cortés. *Nuevo Mundo* 35, no. 1787 (April 20, 1928), n.p.

35 women and 145 men.[131] This means that the yearly average of women asking for permission to copy at the Prado had grown two- or threefold since the late 1870s and early 1880s, while the number of male copyists remained the same. This was the first time during the eras studied for this book that the ratio of women to men copyists changed. As far as one can infer from the names, about half of the permits given to women copyists were for Spanish women and half for foreigners, but the number of Spanish female artists was growing more quickly. In 1913, approximately sixteen permissions were granted to women with Spanish names; in 1914, the number was twenty-two. The museum was thus becoming a public home of sorts, where women and men felt equally welcome as long as they shared bourgeois values.

AN EXTRAMURAL MUSEUM

A museum as connected to its surroundings as the Prado was bound to be affected by every political change. Yet, as the environs were becoming politicized, part of the museum's audience demanded that this connection become less intimate. Still, although the supporters of autonomous art were eager to retreat from their mundane worries to the Prado, which they loved to compare to a respectable home, their excitement had just as much to do with their feeling of ownership over the museum as it did with their awareness of it as a public space. Spanish anthropologist Julio Caro Baroja remembered going to the Prado as a teenager with his uncle Ricardo, a well-known artist. After each visit his uncle made him stop in the doorway to catch a fresh glimpse of the surroundings outside the museum: "See what there is out here? It has nothing to do with what was in there."[132] The teenager nodded, his thoughts wandering far from his uncle's preaching. (Indeed, there was really no other place around to see a nude!) The middle-class audience had a whole range of reasons for loving the museum, and the detached "aesthetic experience" inside the museum was only one of them.

The bourgeois were keen to see and display paintings and sculpture; however, they no longer needed the state to provide the space. The new player in the field—commercial exhibitions developing on the fringes of the state—enjoyed more popularity than the old museums. Here, for instance, is the story of Ricardo Baroja, the above-mentioned aesthete uncle. In 1925, the official art world declared him anathema after a feisty speech he gave in the Círculo de Bellas Artes against certain influential art critics. Left without a way to exhibit his works, Baroja decided to hang paintings in the entryway of his own house so anyone could stop by, see the artist in his robe and slippers, and purchase his works. The newspaper *El Heraldo de Madrid* publicized the news, and the improvised domestic gallery started receiving commissions from abroad. A year later he was selling his works on display in a prestigious gallery in Paris.[133]

Trading and displaying art was becoming lucrative, and those who did not have a house in which to run their own business could do it in a variety of civic associations. In 1903, the Circulo de Bellas Artes found a new location on the festival grounds of the Retiro Park to display works by women artists (1903) as it also continued to host innovative alternatives to state-run national exhibitions (1908).[134] Reviewers praised the idea of displaying art in a park so the visitors could intermittently find themselves inside and outside, looking at trees painted and real, walking or resting on garden benches, but deplored the charging of an entrance fee and the artists' obsession with the same themes that were already represented in the Prado and the national salons.[135] Modern audiences had high hopes for displays held in the "leisure zone," wishing them to produce something more cheerful than what the royal collections and state-run exhibitions could offer.

Yet it was actually the collection of the Prado Museum that was the source of inspiration for an unexpected move on the part of the leisure-loving public: taking the museum experience outdoors. The change happened just as the San Isidro festival was facing its first crisis. In an effort to "civilize" its offerings, the municipal authorities and corporations had added a series of events that were more appealing to the middle classes: marching bands, free cinematographs, cheap theater performances, and car races. But with tourism (and the government's interest in promoting it) on the rise, some claimed that more had to be done to "attract foreigners and people from provinces where better celebrations are available."[136] This entailed using the unique resources of the capital, among which the Prado was the most prominent. And so, preparing for the Carnival celebration of 1910, one of Madrid's civic associations, Comisión de Espectáculos, organized a special benefit ball whose patrons had to wear Goya-themed costumes.[137] Building on Goya's rising popularity and the continuing fad for reenacting his works, the program included live recreations of the *Burial of the Sardine*—one of Goya's cartoons on exhibit at the Prado.[138] Later in the same year, the Madrid Commission for Industry and Commerce decided to add to the San Isidro *verbena* a parade under the motto "Spiritual Madrid Worshipping the Beauty of Commerce."[139] Local artists and craftsmen were commissioned to decorate dozens of floats, representing everything from agriculture and industry to the army, charity, bullfighting, and stockbreeding. And, perhaps the greatest wonder of all, a portable Prado Museum was part of the parade! The public gathering on the Paseo Rosales on June 8, 1910, could see the museum pass by, identifiable by its façade, with its statue of Velázquez installed on one of the floats and Velázquez's best-known paintings reproduced in oil on the statue's pedestal.[140] Despite the event's elitist tone, newspapers claimed that the spectators were very much impressed by the shapely women acting as live allegories of Sculpture and Painting.[141]

To those who were not content with the exterior impressions of the Prado that they got by merely passing by, the museum authorities eventually began to recommend that they "pass through" the exhibit, thinking of it as a walk, as if the museum was merely part of the Paseo del Prado covered by a roof. Villanueva's building—a product of the century that had ushered in the era of civilized strolling—had been designed for a visitor on the move, but never before had the museum's authorities used its linear structure to encourage visitors to experience the Prado by merely walking through it. The emerging tourism business legitimized this hitherto discouraged "light" approach, and so this was precisely what Sánchez Cantón's guidebook for Madrid suggested to visitors: enter through the northern door and exit by the Botanical Garden to continue the city tour. "After the visit to the Prado Museum, it is difficult to advise an extension of the itinerary, and yet the topography of the city calls for continuation of the route that one has initiated, since this is the only way to obtain a thorough knowledge of Madrid."[142] For more and more people, the museum walls were becoming as transparent as the Crystal Palace in the Retiro.

A similar urge to take the museum "on a walk" was noticeable in the stories about the paintings being taken outside that had proliferated since the turn of the century. Initially, these stories were also linked to the San Isidro festival. In 1905, the humorist Alfonso Pérez Nieva depicted two characters from times gone by meeting outside, both equally horrified by the degradation of the *verbenas* by the museum. One was King Felipe IV from Velázquez's painting; the other was Goya himself. Both nostalgically remembered the fairs of their times, when upper-class women wearing elaborate costumes ennobled the Promenade's crowds.[143] The new literary genre that portrayed the museum as a "home" for characters who left their canvases at night to live normal lives further developed the theme. *Los fantasmas del museo del Prado* (The ghosts of the Prado Museum) by José María Salaverría, which was published in 1921 as a book for young readers and became an instant hit, gave the idea a gothic twist. In later years, such accounts generated a considerable following; even today, the Prado equivalents of Hollywood's *Night at the Museum* occupy an important place in Spanish children's literature.[144]

Next it was the playwrights, especially those working in the genre of musical theater, which a broad cross-section of Spanish society enjoyed, who appropriated, for commercial purposes, the previously aristocratic pastime of *tableaux vivants*. The San Isidro season of 1907, for example, brought to the stage of Madrid's Gran Teatro a successful variety show called *La brocha gorda* (The thick brush; by Jacinto Capella and Joaquín González Pastor), set in the Prado. The cast, who sought to represent the museum as common people would experience or imagine it, included a concierge, a generous supply of museum guards, an *Isidro* from Pamplona, and a *Chula*, a working-class woman from Madrid. The set imitated the central gallery of the Prado but featured an improbable combination of paintings—some made by the stage designers, some projected through a magic lantern onto the stage and the walls—ranging from fifteenth-century religious canvases to contemporary nudes that the Prado, in reality, did not possess.

The plot that framed the songs and dances reflected the museum's reputation as a foreigners' paradise. A certain Míster Eduardo wanted to buy originals from the Prado and tried to bribe the concierge, who replied that Mr. Moneybags would have to content himself with copies, which were then enacted in song and dance, to the audience's great delight. There was, for example, a parody of Patinir's *Temptation of Saint Anthony*, recast as the temptation of General Maura by an altered version of Rubens's *Three Graces*: the Phrase, the Watercolor, and the Sicálipsis, in which they were all completely dressed (fig. 41).[145] Newspapers advertised this and similar variety shows featuring "decorations and costumes replicating the paintings of the Prado" well into the 1920s.[146] Thus, through the conduit of costume, the theater prolonged the connection between the Prado and the fairgrounds, which was otherwise becoming thin.

Around the same time, the Prado also received a different type of thrill: it became a crime scene. On September 20, 1918, the royal collection of vases, chalices, and other objects made of precious and semiprecious stones comprising the so-called Tesoro del Delfín (Dauphin's treasure) was stolen. Since Federico de Madrazo's time, all of these objects, which Spain's first Bourbon, Felipe V, had inherited from his father, who was the son of Louis XIV of France, were exhibited in the Central Gallery in secure and locked glass cabinets, some of which now had parts missing.[147] It was not the first time that things had disappeared from the museum, but never before had the Prado been the victim of a robbery so obviously premeditated and so carefully planned. The museum closed to the public, and for over a month its employees and administration,

FIG. 41   Stage set and a version of *The Three Graces* by Rubens, in *The Thick Brush* at the Gran Teatro in Madrid, 1907. *El Arte del Teatro* 2, no. 30 (June 15, 1907): 6.

its history, and its mores occupied the front pages of all major newspapers, distracting the readers' attention from the news from the battlefields of World War I.

Happy to find new candy for their readers' eyes, newspaper owners were looking for stories that could best use the new format of photo-reportage, and now an inestimable chance arrived. The events, richly illustrated with photographs, had all the characteristics of a good detective plot, in which the hero would be the one who had access to the most up-to-date technology and means of communication. In a matter of hours after the robbery, telegrams were dispatched to all governors and border authorities to warn them about possible attempts to export the treasures. All antique dealers in Madrid and Barcelona were subject to searches,[148] which produced a number of leads and retrieved a few stolen objects. Newspapers were delighted to publish photos of the experts performing dactylographic and anthropometric analyses and studying objects with the help of the new technique of fingerprinting, and of everyone interrogated or detained.[149] The reports read like pulp fiction telling stories of crime and love: "From the Prado Museum. What happened . . . And what could have happened"; "In the evening. — Looking for the lovers."[150] Satirical writers got their fair share of laughs by showing sympathy for the "poor crooks" who didn't know well enough what they were stealing and by chastising the authorities for securing the cabinets after, and not before, their contents disappeared.[151]

The chief investigator received a chance to pose with the members of the board of trustees and became famous overnight (fig. 42).[152] Yet, since he handled the case secretly, the journalists took it as a personal challenge to compete with his agents

FIG. 42   Estudio Fotográfico "Alfonso" (Alfonso Sánchez Portela), *The Board of Trustees and Inspector Luna, September 22, 1918*. Archivo General de la Administración.

in uncovering juicy details, revealing the names of those detained, locating their police records, musing about their fingerprints, and eavesdropping during police interrogations.[153] It became clear later that journalists also collaborated with the police, teasing the public's imagination with exciting leads while in reality they were helping to keep secret the name of the principal suspect,[154] Rafael Fernández Coba, a former museum employee. The press announced with relief that it was now clear that no art authority had been involved and that the criminals were only after money.[155] But now the public demanded more action. The police inspector general declared that the investigation could forever change the organization and custody of Spanish museums, libraries, and archives.[156] Three days after the royal treasures were returned to their cabinets, all the members of the board of trustees announced their resignation. To heighten the suspense even more, while the public was coming to terms with these findings, Coba was still at large. Mass transportation and media facilitated his escape, but they also helped the police to follow his tracks. Weeks later, once he was apprehended and in prison, Coba would admit that he used newspaper reports to find out where his pursuers would be looking for him and avoid those areas.[157] Offering no resistance once captured, he was taken prisoner and delivered to Madrid.[158] "Coba demonstrated that even a child can assault the museum," one newspaper reported.[159]

Thus ended the fascinating story of crime, negligence, and the power of technology in the service of the police and museum administration. Things were not calm at the museum, however. For a month, its internal functioning had been discussed as pieces of a crime puzzle, its galleries as crime scenes, its personnel as real or potential perpetrators, and it seemed that the directors could not live with that image. The deputy director, José Garnelo, presented by journalists as a potential suspect in the early days of the investigation, suffered a nervous breakdown and locked himself up at home. On October 17, director Villegas Cordero stepped down. With the board's resignation a month earlier, the museum administration now seemed to be nonexistent. A week later, the trustees received the news that the king had not accepted their resignations, and they therefore found themselves the museum's only administrators. What they did was truly innovative: for the first time in the history of the Prado, the nominee for director was not an artist, but an art critic, Aureliano Beruete y Moret. On that occasion, Cavia, whose name was still connected to memories of the fake fire announcement, published an article applauding the decision and praising the board for ending a deeply rooted "corruption scheme": "Imagine Raphael de Urbino risen from the dead and nominated to run the Prado Museum. What, do you think, he would do with El Greco, and even with Velázquez and Goya?"[160] Thus bringing to an end the hundred-year-old era of a Prado run by artists for artists, the journalists and press photographers had ushered in a new epoch for the museum, which now had an *Institucionista* art enthusiast for a director and a board of trustees to assist him.

A MOVING DISPLAY

The fact that Coba was one of those lumpen citizens who, in his own words, "thought that it was better to take something from there [the museum], as everyone else did, instead of killing myself toiling," underscored the fact that, for good or bad, the museum had become a fixture in the lives of people from all social strata.[161] Reflecting—and fueling—this growing popularity, in the twentieth century the museum's administration produced highly innovative displays. Some of them addressed the unfinished task of representing a progressive history of fine arts, others followed the new fad of "walk-through museums," and a few went as far as taking the museum itself on the road. Each early century innovation had its own intellectual underpinnings, from late nineteenth-century *Institucionista* thought to the avant-garde merging of art and politics. Giving greater prominence to bourgeois taste while also offering ways to communicate bourgeois values to the working classes, the Prado's twentieth-century floor plans responded to the liberal models of museum-going.

The new generation of aesthetes was particularly interested in the Prado. Known as *novecentistas*—a nickname derived from their claim that the new century needed a modernized system of values—these were well-educated cosmopolitan writers who had more in common with eighteenth-century cultured aficionados than with the nineteenth-century nationalist reformers. Considering the division of the world into broad cultural regions and a Nietzschean theory of eternal repetition more sensible than trying to adjust art history to the changing political map of the world, they valued the exhibits that left their visitors with freedom of interpretation. The Prado, they thought, was a perfect example of such a display. Eugeni d'Ors, one of the better-known *novecentistas*, advised visitors not to "take to the Prado any philosophical, perceptive, or even aesthetic purpose, and . . . not to assign any unique ideal to art."[162] *Three Hours in the Prado Museum*—as D'Ors called his article series, later to become a best-selling book—proposed an itinerary that was structured as a stroll through the collection. D'Ors prescribed visiting the museum on a Sunday morning (still a day of free admission), ideally in the company of a young, intelligent friend who "has instinctively good taste and just a touch of vague and general knowledge about the matters of art."[163] Increasingly indifferent to time lines and classifications aimed at uncovering progress, the visitors of the new generation considered art theory a burden. And so, in the following decades, the museum directors and trustees faced the daunting task of supporting the liberty of interpretation demanded by the moderns and showcasing the progress of national spirit, a task that was *still* unfinished.

Although presentation of the Spanish "school" remained incomplete and controversial, the idea of a twofold exhibit was taking shape. Some rooms were rearranged chronologically, while others (such as the collection of portraits on the lower level) exhibited works from different national schools to facilitate their comparative study.[164] While the needs of visitors seeking education were thus met, the fun-loving, casual spectators enjoyed the expanding arrangement by the celebrity artists Velázquez and Goya. In 1900, the government, to general acclaim, assigned additional funds to expand this reorganization and dedicate special galleries to Murillo, Rubens, and Titian.[165] In 1920, Greco's works were also collected together in one gallery.[166] Hence, by the mid-1920s the Prado featured an eclectic array of exhibits that could satisfy a diverse audience but failed to communicate any cohesive idea—something that the connoisseurs did not fail to criticize. In 1914, the satirical newspaper *El Duende* was still comparing the museum's arrangement to an auction house exhibiting the remainder of its unsold stock or to a "madman's work."[167]

All this, however, had drastically changed by 1927 with the implementation of a new floor plan that architect Fernando Checa called "organic." Indeed, the display that opened to visitors in 1927 epitomized the theory of an "organic" nationhood, as the Krausistas envisioned it: an intertwined unity of diversified and mutually complementing parts.[168] Although the display was not attributed to anyone specific, there is strong evidence to suggest that Sánchez Cantón was behind its design. The new floor plan reflected the idea of complementary difference, termed "diversity," which Sánchez Cantón had already used in 1925 for describing Spanish culture in the tourist guidebook *Spain*. Developing the ideas that Cossío had introduced in the 1880s, the reorganized exhibit at the Prado was an unfolding of the Spanish school as a two-stage movement from uniformity to internal diversification. In this peculiar time line, Spanish art was shown to emerge initially as a unified thread within Italian art and later split into local traditions and individual manners—the diversified yet mutually supporting currents that signaled Spain's maturity as a nation.

In the early twentieth century, the same mindset guided a number of successful modernizing projects, ranging from the tourism industry to the standardization of national food. As a foundation for the redesigned display, it allowed the museum to succeed in what had always seemed unachievable: representing the history of painting as a flow of traditions that had Spain in its center. When the new display was unveiled, Sánchez Cantón published an extensive essay explaining the historical unfolding featured in the itinerary that the museum now offered to its visitors: from "the early Northern schools" and "the fifteenth- and sixteenth-century Italians" at the beginning of the visit, "passing through Veronese, Titian, Tintoretto," and arriving at "El Greco and the central nave at the point when Spanish painting absorbed Venetian teachings."[169] Visually, the new multidirectional space created a way to represent national artistic tradition as a high point of a long historical development and, at the same time, in constant communication with its roots. A new notion of art history was emerging in Sánchez Cantón's interpretation: "a chronological display that did not sacrifice historical rigor"[170] and therefore was unrestrained by a progressive time line. Indeed, three chronologies ran through the new floor plan: the Italian and Northern "prehistories" of Spanish art, the foreign traditions in contact with Spain, and, finally, the history of the Spanish school per se, connected to its origins as well as competitors, and epitomized in its most canonical artists, whose works were collected in the new rooms parallel to the central gallery on the left. The central gallery continued to showcase Spanish art as it used to in the times of Federico de Madrazo, and this meant that the national tradition was still represented by the large-scale religious compositions. Although Sánchez Cantón acknowledged his contemporaries' taste for home-like intimate museum spaces, this was not how the museum construed its most representative collection.[171] The new floor plan, in the author's words, was so "well-ordered and logical" that many learned foreigners could not believe that the building had ever been designed for anything but displaying paintings and sculpture.[172]

Sánchez Cantón stressed that this was an arrangement that would allow a "lay visitor to find out about the historical unfolding" of art.[173] At a time when the middle-class public was no longer demanding a historical display, the authorities turned their attention to educating the working classes. In February 1905 (undoubtedly in the wake of the

FIG. 43   Campúa, "A Group of Workers Entering the Museum of Paintings," *Nuevo Mundo* 15, no. 580 (February 16, 1905): n.p.

LOS OBREROS EN EL MUSEO DE PINTURA

January Revolution in Russia), the illustrated weekly *Nuevo Mundo* ran a photo-rich article dedicated to workers visiting the Prado. The pictures showed around forty tidily dressed males and a few children listening to explanations of the art by Jacinto Octavio Picón, then a member of the University Extension for workers (and later a trustee). The text of the article imparted a message of social peace and harmony, representing the lecturers as apostles and the workers as individuals in need of revelation:

> There is in Madrid a group of intellectuals constituted to exercise with workers a scientific apostolate, articulated in the modern expression of "university extension." They come to workers' societies to give conferences that the latter are solicitously asking for, and take those who wish to sign up to different museums in order to give them artistic or scientific education. . . . While the intellectuals offering their services as teachers give an example of great philanthropy, no less exemplary is the diligence of Madrid workers who show up in huge numbers and with great attention at conferences and visits to the museums of fine arts, archaeology, natural history, etc.[174]

If the photographs (figs. 43 and 44) registered male presence only, the museum's organized tours invited female workers as well, alongside men and children. In 1906, for example, *El País* advertised a Sunday morning visit for "twelve members of the

FIG. 44   Campúa, "Sr. Picón, Member of the University Extension, Explaining to Workers *Jacob's Dream* by Ribera," *Nuevo Mundo* 15, no. 580 (February 16, 1905): n.p.

Universidad Popular (People's University) for children from the orphanage, working women, and working men."[175]

Available statistics do not allow the assessment of the popularity of such events. However, Andrés Ovejero, who taught at the Workers' University in the early years of the twentieth century, remembered whole families coming to the Prado. One day, he later recounted, so many workingmen, women, and children showed up for a visit that the authorities and other museum-goers feared a violent scene. This depiction was probably closer to the truth than the well-intentioned representations of docile workers looking for ways to appease the growing social conflict. Ovejero and his colleagues, however, found a peaceful democratic solution: they asked parents to allow their children to "represent" their families on the tour and promised to organize additional visits for adults later. The description that this prominent socialist thinker gave of the tour, however, suggests that learning democracy through museum education was still steeped in the tradition of British-style bourgeois patronage of the working classes and the habit of guiding the worker audience to the paintings with which they could identify:

> For an hour or two—I am not sure for how long because time ran happily by for me and for them—those children from Madrid were greeting with ingenuous admiration Titian's, Rubens's, Velázquez's, Murillo's, and Goya's children. And

the children from other centuries, other lands, and other skies—Murillo's angels and Ruben's putti, Velázquez's princes and Goya's rascals—seemed to thank the children of the nineteen-hundreds for their greetings, as if yesterday's images and today's children were brothers and sisters, as if they were, as Galdós used to say, "the children of men bringing happiness into life."[176]

The effects of the museum on the parents here also seemed to meet the liberal goals of mellowing morals and preventing class conflict: "with their earlier threatening grimaces changing to grateful smiles," the mothers and fathers waited for their children outside, forming an invincible "guard of the palace of our art."

As he remembered this 1905 incident in his 1934 acceptance speech at the Academia San Fernando, Ovejero portrayed the Prado as a site permeated by class warfare that could nevertheless bring forth social peace: "When I stepped out in order to give the children back to those people, I thought that never had our museum been safer than when it was guarded by workers who had allowed their children be taken in as hostages." That museums could inspire civic values in disenfranchised populations was, indeed, the philosophy behind the innovative program of museum education implemented by the Second Republic. In 1931–34, responding to the peasant violence induced by the limitations of the agrarian reform, the Republic's reformist government undertook an unprecedented campaign aimed at making the museum experience— along with the portable libraries, touring theaters, and cinematographs—available in smaller towns and villages (fig. 45). Cossío, who designed this program, called Misiones Pedagógicas (Pedagogical Missions), and presided over the Patronato de Misiones Pedagógicas until his death in 1935, finally realized his most daring dream: to bring everyone to the Prado (fig. 46).

Two "itinerant museums," "traveling museums," or, officially, the Museo del Pueblo (People's Museums) were sent out from Madrid in October and December of 1932 to deliver life-sized, high-quality copies of certain works from the Prado to provincial and municipal centers to be displayed when people from adjacent towns and villages were gathering there for seasonal fairs. Bundling the museum together with spectacular innovations such as "light projections" (of films and slides, including the slides of paintings) and gramophones that played music inside the exhibition rooms, Cossío revived for the new political era the century-old connection between the museum and the fairground, stating that the "people's museum" would "represent another—free-of-charge—item on the festival program, next to the procession, dances, competitions, sports, and fireworks."[177] Photo coverage of these events gives glimpses of outdoor, improvised museums in places where there was no interior space big enough to house one. A snapshot from the village of Pedraza featured a missionary (future filmmaker José Val del Omar) and a uniformed guard displaying a copy of El Greco's *Resurrection* from the balcony of the city hall to the visitors gathered below (fig. 47).[178]

228

FIG. 45   The Museo del Pueblo in Turégano (Segovia), January 6–9, 1933. Archivo de la Residencia de Estudiantes.

FIG. 46   Unloading the copy by Ramón Gaya of Diego Velázquez's *Portrait of Prince Balthasar Carlos on Horseback*, c. 1932. Archivo de la Residencia de Estudiantes.

Those in the early years of the century who imagined the paintings escaping for a walk could hardly have thought that they could actually be exhibited outdoors. These would become, however, some of the most emblematic testimonies of the role that art played in the Republic's political life. In Jordana Mendelson's incisive analysis, the continuous photographic coverage that the illustrated press was giving to the traveling museums' sojourns in villages around the country transmitted the message of social harmony and modernization by delivering to the cities images of cleanly clad peasants engaging in cultured, quiet contemplation.[179] Importantly, though, this innovative

FIG. 47   Showing a copy of El
Greco's *Resurrection* from the
traveling museum from a balcony
of the City Hall, Pedraza, Segovia,
c. 1932. *Residencia*, February 1933.
Archivo de la Residencia de
Estudiantes.

experience of rural urbanity was a result of Cossío's conscious program of juxtaposing
museums and fairgrounds. Since this was how, after all, Madrileños and visitors to
Madrid had always unofficially experienced the Prado Museum, bringing together
town and country went even further than Cossío might have suspected. Translated
into the language of agrarian reform, these images of rural museum-goers were a sort
of promise that the experience of art could help to overcome not only cultural, but
also political contradictions between town and country by transforming peasants into
citizens, capable of governing themselves. At the time, many hoped that the police and
the army would not have to do anything about the unrest among the peasants as long
as a museum could be brought in.[180]

At the end of 1933, when the Republic's reformist cabinet collapsed and extraordinary elections were called, the winning conservative government cut the funding
for the Misiones Pedagógicas and their traveling museums. Only when the Popular
Front coalition won the election in February 1936 and proclaimed, as its main objective, the defense of culture and the well-being of all citizens did the Prado Museum

regain its prominence as a political force. In the same year, when the general elections in France also brought victory to the Popular Front, something similar to the Spanish traveling museum could be observed on the streets of Paris, where replicas of Goya's *May 3 Rebellion* and Cimabue's *Madonna* appeared next to Delacroix's *Liberty at the Barricades* on placards at a rally celebration during Bastille Day. "We were carrying the museums onto the streets, and it was we who, making colossal reproductions of [Honoré Daumier's *The Massacre of the*] *Rue Transnonain* and [Goya's] *Third of May*, brought to the people the knowledge of these sublime images," artist Boris Taslitzky remembered.[181] Back in Madrid, however, history would soon bring a tragic twist to both metaphors of the museum that the twentieth century had ushered in: the museum as a home and as an extramural exhibit. The Prado was set to indeed become a "museum without walls," to use the phrase that the translators of Andre Malraux's 1947 *Le musée imaginaire* (Imaginary museum) would later coin.[182]

In 1927, journalist Manuel Herrera y Ges rhetorically asked in the pages of the Catholic *El Siglo Futuro* why the Prado did not receive more donations. The answer, in his view, had to do with the people's continuing mistrust of the state.[183] However, that did not mean, he continued, that the Prado or other museums in Madrid or Barcelona were unpopular with the people. To illustrate his argument (and emphasize its centralist message at a time when antimonarchical nationalism was gaining strength in Catalonia), the author described a scene that he had witnessed at the museum: a visitor who appeared to be a mason or a builder professed vocal admiration of the Prado in the Velázquez room, saying, "This is unique and unprecedented. Only Spain has it!"[184] While Spaniards' relationship with the state was in reality becoming more complicated, the Prado Museum, which had been appropriated by the middle class during the first decades of the century, was now seeking to establish a bond with working-class visitors.

Epilogue

"MORE IMPORTANT FOR SPAIN THAN THE REPUBLIC AND THE MONARCHY COMBINED"

QUESTIONING THE CONVENTION THAT "museum culture" ought to portray the nation from a privileged spot in its capital's center, the People's Museum program of the Second Republic created an innovative setting for art, where the gaze of the peasant and provincial population could be recognized and empowered. These traveling museums added a new dimension to the debate between the center and the periphery that the display of the "Spanish school" had not succeeded in neutralizing for over hundred years. But also, more importantly for this book's argument, by substituting copies for the originals, taking them outside Madrid, and inserting them strategically into the world of festivals and fairgrounds, Cossío and his supporters closed the cycle of mutual hostility and attraction underpinning the parallel histories of leisure and the arts on the Prado Promenade. Despite the ideological tone of the Pedagogical Missions' reports, which makes it difficult to judge the project's real achievements, conceptually this short-lived experiment proved that the Prado Museum had become a keystone of democracy in the eyes of Spain's social reformers. Never and nowhere before had art museums played such an extraordinary role in promoting a nation's territorial cohesion, bridging between town and country, and harmonizing class relations.

As Spain was moving through modernization, the Prado Museum mediated between the elites and the populace, the provinces and the metropolis, the citizens and the government, and now that this unacknowledged mission was becoming explicit, high art was embracing reproduction and morphing into modern, technologically enhanced, and socially inclusive leisure. Modernized fairgrounds could open up to museum masterpieces detached from the "aura" of authenticity, and religious festivals were given a chance to reinvent themselves as popular celebrations of liberalism and the school of civility.[1] It seemed as if the forces set in motion by modernity were about to arrive at a dialectical synthesis, announcing an era in which "leisure culture" would cease being an oxymoron and become, instead, a reality—a reality that would also fix the contradiction between centralism and localism and the decomposition of the festival world into leisure, cult, and commerce. As one reviewer of the Pedagogical Missions suggested, the police and the army would have nothing to do as long as a museum could be brought in.[2] Reports such as this were adding a tinge of humor to the actual hopes that culture and fairgrounds could merge, enjoyment could become the standard outcome of a museum visit, and, with the assistance of the illustrated press, Spaniards from all regions and walks of life would see each other as neighbors admiring the same paintings.

This would have been the happy end of my story about the Prado—a museum haunted and shaped by the changing forms of leisure overtaking the Promenade— had only the political history of the early twentieth century been less averse to such neat endings. As the fights for, and against, democracy shattered the fragile balance of power in Spain, it became clear that the Republic's cultural reformers, though well aware of the political potential of popular leisure, still did not go far enough in meeting the needs of an agricultural nation. Fearing proletarian mobilization even more than peasant revolt, they idealized folk culture in the hope that an innovative fairground-museum would strengthen the government's positions vis-à-vis organized labor among rural dwellers and counter the perceived degrading effects of urban commercial entertainment on recent urban immigrants. These fears and hopes would ultimately send the museum—and the Republican reformism itself—down quite a different path. In November 1933, having failed to stop peasant violence, the reformist government was voted out and replaced by a conservative cabinet that preferred political repression to their predecessors' course of cultural nation-building. One of its most memorable acts was to deploy the army to shoot striking workers and miners across Spain, especially in Catalonia and Asturias. The resulting bloodshed marked the political rise of General Francisco Franco, Spain's future dictator, who in October 1934 was dispatched to "pacify" the Asturian miners, who had armed themselves. When the delegates to the 1934 meeting of the Office International des Musées gathered in Madrid at the end of that October, the agenda included issues such as packing and climate-control requirements for transporting artifacts, the real and ominous purpose of which—preparedness for war—remained undisclosed until 1936.[3] By late April 1935, an imminent violent conflict in Madrid was perceptible enough for the board of trustees of the Prado Museum to prepare a list of the most important paintings and begin looking for a place where they could be moved in the face of a threat. Having discussed several locations, the trustees agreed that the vaults of the Banco de España (the National Treasury) across the Paseo del Prado would provide the most reliable shelter for the museum's collection.[4]

Ironically, while the duke de Alba, who presided over the board, and other trustees were voicing their concern for the protection of museum artifacts against a revolutionary outbreak, the defense of culture against another enemy, fascism, was becoming an important issue for the European Left. In June 1935, in Paris, the First International Writers' Congress for the Defense of Culture discussed the safeguarding of artistic heritage as a cause shared by all people of goodwill. Alongside the protection of peace, health, and well-being, the preservation of culture was becoming a key component in the Popular Front's calls, supported by the Comintern, to forge broad cross-class solidarity against the threat of fascism. In Spain, when the electoral coalition of the Republican and Socialist Parties was created in January 1936 under the leadership of Manuel Azaña (the president of the Republic's first government), it refrained from following its French counterpart in calling itself "Popular Front." When in February 1936 Azaña's platform, by that time already known as the Popular Front, won the election, it included only one worker party.[5] Only in September of 1936, when the far-right rebellion grew into a full-fledged war with the backing of Fascist Italy and Nazi Germany (and in which the USSR, appearing to hold on to the politics of nonintervention proclaimed by the Comintern, initially only provided unofficial support to the Republic), Communists moved into the government, giving the Comintern a greater, although still largely invisible, role. The events of the Civil War soon put an end to the century of the codevelopment of leisure and culture on the Prado Promenade.

By the end of summer 1936, Spain was a mosaic of Republican and Nationalist territories—the latter being the name adopted by the rebels who would soon accept Franco as leader. Madrid, loyal to the Republic, became the target of the fast-approaching Nationalist troops. The Prado remained open until August 30, after which, fearing an attack on Madrid, the staff began to move the exhibits, starting with Velázquez's *The Surrender of Breda* (one of the largest in the collection) into the lower-level rotunda. The activities also included fortifying door openings and windows, wrapping statues, and isolating several storage rooms with sandbags. Since the proclamation of the Republic in 1931, the Prado had had only a nominal director—writer Ramón Pérez de Ayala, who doubled as the Spanish ambassador to the United Kingdom—and was in actuality run by the deputy director, Sánchez Cantón. On September 19, 1936, a new director was appointed: Pablo Picasso, who resided in Paris and thus could not guide the museum any better than his predecessor.[6] In the absence of a real director, it fell on Sánchez Cantón to determine the museum's wartime policy. According to his postwar testimony, less than a week after the July 1936 coup, two museum workers demanded the dissolution of the board of trustees and denounced some of the staff members as secret supporters of the anti-Republic rebels. The decree of August 4, 1936, abolished the board and placed the museum directly under the Ministry of Public Instruction and Fine Arts. Sánchez Cantón continued on as the museum's acting director, carrying out the emergency plan that the trustees had drafted earlier, until early November 1936, when the government decided to move to Valencia, taking along the most important works from the museum's collection. The move, which revolutionized international norms and agreements as well as the museum's own safety measures, was justified retrospectively by the Nazi bombings of the Prado in mid-November of 1936.

234

Though extreme secrecy surrounded the operation, the photographs taken by the institutions involved come across as eerily similar to the earlier, joyful pictures of the Pedagogical Missions' trucks carrying the copies of masterpieces to the country-side; this time, however, it was the originals, not copies, that trucks carried through woods and fields (fig. 48). Thus began the museum's three-year odyssey—away from home and back again.[7] When the paintings were safely installed in Valencia and the press was allowed to cover the operation, the story fit neatly with the mission of the defense of culture that had consolidated the Popular Front movements since 1935. On the flip side, the evacuation of art was a good way to illustrate the need for military assistance to the Republic from outside Spain, which had so far been ignored or denied. For a while, Spain's representatives at the Comintern in Paris had been demanding military aid, but up until early 1937, the only result that they could obtain was encouragement to organize more "solidarity campaigns."[8] So, back in Spain, the Alliance of Anti-Fascist Intellectuals—the organization that carried out the bulk of the Republic's propaganda—began describing the dangers that the Nationalist air raids were posing to cultural heritage as a coded message evidenc-ing an urgent need for international military support.[9] Numerous pamphlets were published at that time documenting the destruction of the National Library of Spain, the former royal palace, and other historical monuments—making it clear that help was needed immediately.[10] The damage caused by incendiary bombs that fell on Villanueva's building on November 16, 1936, was one of the most striking examples of what was then called the "fascist barbarity"—a barbarity that the Nazi propagandists, on their part, attributed to the Republic's own army, which, according to one Nazi publication, bombed the Prado in order to justify the smuggling of its masterpieces abroad.[11]

Meanwhile, for the Republic's government, concerned with projecting an image of control and order abroad and with countering the anarchist violence at home, the rescue of the Prado acquired additional connotations that continued the reformists' earlier take on the traveling museums as agents of social harmony.[12] Emphasizing the civic maturity of common Spaniards (who, unlike the peasant protagonists of the Pedagogical Missions' narratives, were now bearing arms), artists, poets, and writers as famous as Pablo Picasso, Josep Renau, Antonio Machado, Rafael Alberti, and María Teresa León asserted that the Prado was saved by illiterate militiamen who

FIG. 48   Fernando Gallego Fernández, *A Truck of the Junta del Tesoro Artístico with an Escort and Convoy Turning off the Chiva Highway to Enter Valencia.* Archivo de la Junta Delegada de Incautación y Protección del Tesoro Artístico de Madrid; Madrid, Archivo IPCE.

understood the importance of art without understanding art itself. To support the image of people united for the protection of the nation's art treasures, newspapers ran pictures of young men with guns enjoying an exhibit of salvaged paintings in Valencia (fig. 49). In reality, the paintings at that exhibit, which indeed opened in December of 1936, were rescued from the collection of the duke de Alba, the president of the board of trustees of the Prado, who was in London representing Nationalist Spain while his Madrid palace was converted into the headquarters of the Communist People's Militia. The palace was heavily damaged during the same artillery attack that hit the Prado Museum in mid-November 1936, and so the images of militiamen enjoying the duke's collection, which they had saved, were closer to the truth than the intended message of the coverage: that the Prado collection had been rescued, supposedly by the militiamen, thanks to the Communist leadership.[13] It was, however, that latter story, authored by Rafael Alberti and frequently repeated, that moved to the forefront of the Republic's propaganda, eclipsing other, more accurate narratives.[14] While the documentation that could help us understand why the Republic's government, hastily organizing its own retreat, decided to evacuate the Prado is either lost or never existed, hardly anyone now doubts that, if the paintings survived the ordeal, it was thanks to museum workers, from Sánchez Cantón and Pedro Muguruza all the way down to the restorers Manuel Arpe Retamino and Tomás Pérez Alférez.[15]

Neither Alberti, nor Renau or León, who elaborated and popularized the legendary story about the rescue of the Prado, claimed that the common people understood the artwork that they were saving. Rather, these and other authors reserved an unusual role for the museum's presumed saviors: to safeguard cultural heritage, become its custodians, and hand it over to the nation when the danger passed, without necessarily understanding or even claiming to understand it. Renau, the artist and director general of the fine arts, remembered fondly the "simple civilians or members of people's

FIG. 49 The exhibition of paintings rescued from Madrid at the Colegio del Patriarca in Valencia, 1936 (Exposición Alba). Fototeca del Patrimonio Cultural de España, Fondo Vaamonde; Madrid, Archivo IPCE.

militia, mostly illiterate, undertaking long and difficult journeys only to bring to the Delegación General de Bellas Artes simple etchings and canvases of minimal value, convinced that these were works of art."[16] Likewise, León, who led the initial evacuation on behalf of the Alliance of Anti-Fascist Intellectuals, portrayed her assistants as "men entrusted to rescue what they did not understand, of which they had been deprived in the partition of common goods."[17]

Unusually for a propaganda message, the people's role in the museum was therefore reduced to a transcendental, albeit merely physical, activity. The texts and images produced in the course of the operation—some published and others preserved in the archives—supported this story by portraying common people moving, loading, wrapping, unwrapping, hanging, guarding, and otherwise interacting with works of art as merely material objects (fig. 50). This plot ran parallel to narratives about the rescue of other cultural objects—religious statuary or books, among others—which insisted that the intervention of common people was decisive for their survival, even though the saviors did not realize the importance of their own work. Cuban writer Juan Marinello, delegate to the Second Congress of Antifascist Writers, held in Valencia in 1937, put this idea on the lips of a militiaman: "Many of these things we do not know for sure what they represent or cost. Books written in Latin or the Castilian of old times, we do not understand them, but our superiors have told us that it was important to conserve them all, so that, come victory, Spanish culture would have suffered the least damage possible."[18] The story of the rescue of the museum was thus becoming an open-ended narrative, in which the common people of Spain received the new function of safeguarding cultural heritage physically, with a teleological effect that would be only revealed after the war ended.

The early months of the Civil War were marked by many burnings of churches and their religious paintings, which organizations such as the Alliance of Anti-Fascist Intellectuals and its affiliates were determined to stop. On October 3, 1936, the

FIG. 50   David Seymour, *Madrid, October/November, 1936: Woman Making an Inventory of the Paintings in the Collection of Las Descalzas Reales with Two Republican Soldiers.* Negative from the "Mexican Suitcase."

anarchist-leaning newspaper *La Libertad* ran verses by Luis de Tapia containing "Questions" (the title of the poem) such as these:

> Why wouldn't the Iberian people
> Become a little bit of an art dealer? . . .
> Why do they not exchange their Titians
> For some bombs for airplane missions?[19]

The fact that these might not have been just rhetorical questions, but rather a real reflection of the popular attitude to the cultural heritage of the upper classes, was part of what fueled articles in frontline newspapers and informational leaflets about the rescue of the artifacts. Meanwhile, internationally the publications about art-loving militiamen helped to refute the bad press portraying Spain as a frightening "red" peninsula. The Pavilion of the Spanish Republic at the 1937 International Exhibition in Paris featured a wall-sized collage by Renau illustrating the evacuation of the Prado Museum to Valencia, while Pablo Picasso exalted the actions of the militiamen in order to explain his own absence from the museum: "I have not being able to take charge. . . . At this time, artists cannot be the real museum curators: the real curators are aviators, tank crews, and the soldiers of the People's Army."[20]

The murky waters of late 1930s international politics have not allowed contemporaries—or historians who have studied the operation—to agree on the reasons why the Prado was evacuated.[21] From London, the duke de Alba speculated in early 1937 that the Spanish government had plans to sell the Prado's collection abroad. Republican officials, for their part, took great pains to explain the evacuation of the Prado, producing abundant proof that the original safety plans prepared by the museum staff were unviable or insufficient. Between March and July 1937, Prime Minister Juan Negrín negotiated with the French authorities to put together an exhibition at the Louvre that would place the paintings in a neutral land, awaiting a time when they could return to a liberated Spain.[22] The documents preserved in the archive of the embassy of the Spanish Republic in Paris make it clear that the preparations were aborted on August 14, 1937, but do not explain the reasons for this sudden change. In 1936 and 1937, the governments of Basque Country and Catalonia, more successful in their rescue efforts, organized similar exhibits in Paris, and even as late as August 1938 there were talks of sending a selection of paintings from the Prado to the upcoming International Exhibition in New York.[23]

By that time, however, the progress of the Nationalist troops and the firm resistance of the French to taking sides chased the Republic's besieged government to Barcelona (October 1937) and then to the Franco-Catalan border, carrying Goya's and Velázquez's paintings along with them. It no longer mattered whether the Republic had any plans besides ensuring that these works did not perish. If the earlier mobilization of the Prado had already given it heavy ideological clout, the subsequent changes in the location of the government—and the paintings—carried the meaning of the museum further away from the world of art and into the realm of politics. The collection received an uncertain shelter wherever President Manuel Azaña and Prime Minister Juan Negrín resided—be it a castle in Figueras or in the village of La Vajol on the Franco-Catalan border. Meanwhile, from Rome, the artist José María Sert managed to mobilize international museum professionals, who began negotiating with the leaders of the Republic the extradition of the evacuated collection to the Palace of the League of Nations in Geneva. Correctly predicting that the League of Nations would cede the paintings to Franco's rebels if they were victorious rather than guard the masterpieces in expectation of the next armed conflict that would wipe fascism off the face of the earth, the Republic's representatives were reluctant to accept the offer, insisting that the collection not be given back to anyone besides the Spanish people and their legitimate representatives.

In his memoirs, Azaña would later confess that his heart sank every time he heard an air bomber, fearing the destruction of Velázquez's *Las Meninas* more than he feared the loss of his own life. The Nationalists, meanwhile, claimed that the Republic's government made it known that the president and the paintings traveled together in order to turn the masterpieces into his own sacred shields. In early February 1939, the government of the Republic agreed to entrust the collection to the League of Nations. Timoteo Pérez Rubio, president of the Republic's Junta Central del Tesoro Artístico, remembered that the final protocols were written in the light of car headlights because

Franco's air raid had destroyed the power plant the previous night.[24] The Prado was "more important than the Republic and the monarchy combined," Azaña remembered telling Negrín a few months before.[25] Still, he knew only too well that the works would eventually be repatriated to the country ruled by Franco, a man whose authority he would never recognize as legitimate.

The story of the evacuation and restitution of the Prado Museum had enough drama, mystery, and suspense to inspire an unending chain of memoirs, historiographical findings, novels, fictional films, and mockumentaries.[26] Yet what makes it the culminating point of *this* book is not its highly debatable chain of events, but rather how these events redefined the relationship between the Prado and Spain. Considering that, during the first hundred and twenty years of the museum's existence, Spain's most educated and democratically minded individuals expressed serious doubts about the collection's significance beyond its identification with the Crown, the church, or an imperfect system of state institutions, while its directors continued to put the interests of monarchs, artists, and foreigners before those of common domestic visitors, the Republic's custody of the collection during the fire of war was extraordinary in its acknowledgment that the Prado had to be conserved no matter which side prevailed. As Peter Aronsson and Gabriella Elgenius argue, only truly successful national museums survive through periods of such radical political change, gaining the reputation of "a cultural asset and force unto themselves that are to be regarded and rearranged but seldom destroyed by new socio-political groups and visions."[27] This suggests that the actions and even the eventual defeat of the Republic's government brought about a breakthrough in the museum's history. Ceasing to be the playground of the elites and a mirror for the princes and heads of state, at least for a visionary leader such as Azaña the Prado was in the process of becoming the nation's most cherished treasure in a way that made the stories about the Spaniards protecting cultural heritage sound prophetic: it was, indeed, the physical support of people who were considered common custodians that, in the final account, preserved the museum as the ultimate custodian of these very people's cultural identity, beyond the military defeats and imminent repression to come.

This new mindset differed from the idea that the real spirit of the people should go into exile to be freed from the limitations of statehood, famously voiced in the 1940s verse by the Communist emigrant poet León Felipe, which cast doubt over the future of Spain once the poets headed across the border, taking along all of Spain's songs.[28] While diaspora intellectuals have insisted that their nation's "songs" could incubate in transnational enclaves in the hope that political change would one day allow them back, this ending of the Prado's saga suggests the opposite: that the nation's cultural foundations could also be preserved inland, under any regime. Since the end of the Civil War, the Loyalists and anti-Francoists in exile and in internal opposition had considered the Prado Museum a cornerstone of the culture of resistance and a highly visible place of deeply hidden Republican memory. Art historians Enrique Lafuente Ferrari and Juan Antonio Gaya Nuño, marginalized due to their former links to the Republic, dedicated to the Prado some of their most inspired texts, while the playwright Antonio Buero Vallejo, a member of the clandestine Communist party, authored works exploring how the playful baroque optic of Velázquez's art could show to all Spaniards an escape from Franco's oppressive control.[29]

Though opposition intellectuals' view of the Prado as an island of freedom seemed to offer hope and promise, it also pushed the museum even deeper into the modern ideological war zone, thereby limiting the Republic's earlier hopes that Spaniards of all sexes, regions, and income levels would experience the museum as their own realm of enjoyment. For its part, Franco's New State sought to bring the meaning of "national" in the museum's name closer to the ideology of its self-defined Nationalist cause: strong centralization, official Catholicism, and traditional family values and gender roles. Just like Mussolini and Hitler, Franco was an amateur artist—the author of rather dull landscapes. Though Franco's visits to the Prado were few and far between, during the early postwar months he used the museum as a symbol of reconstruction and peace at home and abroad. The return of the paintings to, and the reinauguration of, the Prado in 1939 became highly publicized events, even as the most important pieces of the collection still remained on exhibit in Geneva. The profascist magazine *Vértice* ran a series of articles with photographs of paintings transported and unwrapped, this time by uniformed guards and museum professionals. A few years later, Franco used the arrival of the Vichy government in France to negotiate the return from the Louvre of the so-called *Soult Madonna*—the *Immaculate Virgin Mary* by Murillo, which had avoided post-Napoleonic restitution—and the *Dama de Elche*—an archaeological find of startling beauty and uncertain origin discovered and exported by a French archaeological team in the early 1900s. Each of these "returns" provided an occasion for Franco's government to pose as the good shepherd of national artistic treasures.

The signs of care for cultural heritage—welcomed and energetically applauded by the Prado's restituted board of trustees and by Sánchez Cantón, who, following the purging process, was reappointed and received word of praise for his acts "under the red rule"—firmly recemented the identification between the museum and the state that had seemed to be gone at the end of the Civil War.[30] Franco's peculiar dictatorship, halfway between military and religious, was no friend of mass celebrations on the Prado Promenade. Coupled with an aversion to uncontrolled mass gatherings—in fact, with a ban on gatherings of more than two people, the violation of which led to arrest—the government's ideological approach put an end to the indoor-outdoor, leisure-culture dynamic that had marked the museum's existence since its inception. In the mid-1940s, Sánchez Cantón retrieved all the petitions intending to isolate the territory of the Prado from its surroundings that his predecessors had unsuccessfully filed over the course of the past hundred and twenty years, insisting that the time to bring them to fruition had finally arrived.[31] It was probably only the regime's lack of funds or lack of real interest on the part of the government that made the project fail again. Just as it had been for the past century, a merely symbolic chain around the patches of grass and trees in front of the main façade remained the museum's only sign of distinction from its surroundings.

If the Prado Promenade ceased to serve a gathering spot, becoming instead a car and bus route, a modern nonplace, was there really any reason to demand a fence? With all the alleys except the central one asphalted and turned into roads for traffic, and only the tidy secondhand book vendors' stalls left as a reminder of the fairground that used to sprawl across the former Atocha (now Paseo de Claudio Moyano), the directors of the Prado had little to fear. The gymnastic facilities, merry-go-rounds, music, and water kiosks that used to surround the museum would never be back. And although visitors coming inside—and the onlookers outside—surely continued to have fun, this was a different "culture and leisure" story, without disorderly *verbenas*, without the challenge of a world of objects on sale around the temple of arts, and without the uncertain borderline between town and country that the Prado Promenade was now ceasing to be in order to become a heavily asphalted thoroughfare. The dark shadow of official culture would stretch far, and as late as the 1970s, the anti-Francoist writer Juan Goytisolo would state that the only artist he was interested in at the Prado (as well as the Louvre, Metropolitan, the British Museum, and so on) was one named "Uscita, Salida, Exit, Sortie, or Ausgang."[32]

In 1955, Gaya Nuño denounced the rare combination of extreme centralization, total control, and "total contempt for the visitor's curiosity" reigning over Franco's museum policy.[33] While the catalogues and publications authored by Sánchez Cantón and other art historians working in the Prado maintained the highest intellectual standards, as an exhibit and a public space the Prado was firmly inscribed into the system of state-controlled cultural institutions. The collective imagination pictured it as a respectable visiting spot for school and tourist groups, and, in a curious reversal of roles, the only stories told about the Prado suggesting anything playful or unlawful now involved foreigners, not Spaniards. Such was, for example, the 1959 Italo-French-Spanish film *Toto in Madrid*, starring the famous comic Louis de Funés, with a complicated plot revolving around an Italian impostor's scheme to prove the existence of—and gainfully sell—Goya's third Maja, *Maja in Lingerie*.[34]

By the early 1960s, when a new cabinet envisioned that an influx of mass tourism would rescue the country from economic stagnation and political isolation, the Prado Museum must have offered such a hopelessly gloomy view that Manuel Fraga Iribarne, the new Minister of Information and Tourism and the main designer of the regime's tourism-induced economic recovery, demanded that the museum be spiced up. As a boy, Fraga had seen or heard about an improvised museum that the Republic's government had dispatched to Galicia,[35] and now, as a high government official, he imagined his own traveling museum with a Catholic twist: take the masterpieces from the Prado to the streets "for the locals and guests to enjoy" as part of a modernized rite of Holy Week.[36] Although this particular vision was never realized, the minister used other means for bringing his dreams to life. One of them was the improvised museum of Spanish art at the 1964 World's Fair in New York, featuring works from the Prado alongside paintings by modern artists such as Salvador Dalí, who had returned to Spain in the 1950s, and Pablo Picasso, who continued to see the regime as illegitimate.[37]

The 1960s plan to bring Spain out into the global leisure market is now considered the first page in the history of its "pre-post-Francoist" revival.[38] Hence, although the story of the political developments at the Prado Museum after Franco's death in 1975 has been well told in Spanish and even in English—in Selma Holo's highly informative *Beyond the Prado*[39]—historians have yet to trace the connection between the museum's current image, the 1960s engagements with neoliberalism, and their nineteenth-century liberal, *Institucionista* underpinnings, which Fraga's politics had borrowed from the Republican reformism, adjusting them to fit his own need to give dictatorship a facelift. I have taken here the first steps toward such a new genealogy of present-day museum politics by bringing back into one volume the history of the liberal debates about and around the Prado. As we have seen, early thinkers saw the separation between leisure, culture, and cult at the Prado as wishful thinking rather than a *fait accompli*. Yet the museum and the leisure grounds surrounding it evolved together, and by the 1870s the continuity between the museum and the modernized fairgrounds, both of which the bourgeois began to like, stopped being a problem. At the beginning of the twentieth century, inspired by the British example of parliamentary monarchy and German religious modernism, a new generation of liberals welcomed a museum that could be experienced outdoors as well as inside and propagated a new meaning of museum enjoyment, conflating aesthetic pleasure and leisure.

Considering the well-articulated line of liberal thought about the Prado Museum and its role in Spanish society that I have described in this book, it is hardly surprising that the most recent and drastic changes in the Prado and its vicinity have followed so closely the nineteenth-century projects recounted here. The new extension designed by Rafael Moneo incorporated the cloisters of the San Jerónimo monastery that the two generations of Madrazo directors wanted to annex. Likewise, the new façade with the beautiful door by Cristina Iglesias, the terraced garden, and the newly visible Villanueva's apse facing Calle Ruiz de Alarcón have finally fulfilled the City and the museum's joint intention since the nationalization of the Museo Real after 1868 to provide the Prado with an attractive back entrance and surround it with a garden. Preparing to celebrate the inauguration of these improvements, the museum's administration and the City of Madrid established extended hours of free admission, just as had happened in the past during the patron-saint festivals, and in 2008, on a patriotic anniversary of the anti-Napoleonic uprising of May 2, 1808, visitors were greeted by actors dressed as characters from Goya's paintings. Special studies carried out by the museum administration together with the Instituto de Estudios Turísticos—the government body responsible for analyzing Spain's tourism market—provide evidence that, in the absence of a beach, the Prado constitutes the prime component of the brand named "Madrid" and that, unlike many other tourism attractions, it makes Spain's capital equally interesting to foreign and domestic visitors.[40]

Over the course of the nineteenth and early twentieth centuries, Spaniards, as well as those in the Iberian Peninsula who resisted this name, lived through a dozen coups d'état and revolutions, fought in four civil wars, witnessed the breakdown of the old regime, saw two republics proclaimed and undone, and survived two dictatorships. Most of this period's violent events took place in close proximity to the museum, yet no matter how severe the conflict, whenever the collection was threatened, the governments and the citizens have managed to put their differences aside long enough to protect it—if only, in some cases, to reappropriate it for their own political needs. At times it was the only thing about which the fighting factions could not afford to disagree, fearing to pay too high a political price if the art was damaged or lost. How could people develop such an attachment to the museum even though their education provided them with no tools for understanding its exhibits? This story of the Prado as a museum without walls connected to the Promenade, a "contact zone" between town and country, and a familiar touchstone for a modernizing nation begins to answer this question.

Notes

Newspaper and magazine articles are cited according to Hemeroteca Digital, Biblioteca Nacional de España, Madrid.

ABBREVIATIONS

AGA: Archivo General de la Administración, Alcalá de Henares, Spain
AGP: Archivo General del Palacio, Madrid
Archivo MNP: Archivo del Museo Nacional del Prado
Archivo RABASF: Archivo de la Real Academia de Bellas Artes San Fernando
Archivo RAH: Archivo de la Real Academia de la Historia

INTRODUCTION

1. Libro de visitas 1864 a 1870, fol. 191, Archivo MNP, L-176.

2. Lopezosa Aparicio, "Consideraciones," 216.

3. Lopezosa Aparicio, "Fiesta oficial" and "Devociones populares."

4. Guerra de la Vega, *Juan de Villanueva*, 125.

5. According to Jürgen Habermas's classical model, the "public sphere" encapsulates the way in which social communication is organized in the modern world. In the early system that Habermas identifies as feudal or medieval "representative publicity," this communication was ceremonially structured through the rituals making the sovereign's power present to the participants referred to as "the public." In the sixteenth century, the fast transmission of the print media opened new possibilities for kings' indirect communication with their vassals. Concomitantly, absolutist royal power produced an extended network of institutions, referred to as the "sphere of public authority" or simply "the state," whose connections with the persona of the monarch became less and less direct. Habermas envisions the "public sphere" as a set of institutions, activities, and discourses of public opinion mediating between the state and the private lives of its subjects. In seventeenth-century France, "the public" already referred not only to the readers

of the press, writers, and journalists, but also to the attendees of theater performances and the consumers of art practicing their taste in museums. In other parts of Europe, the notion of "the public" developed in stages that were uneven although comparable (Habermas, *Structural Transformation of the Public Sphere*).

6. Rumeu de Armas, *Origen*.

7. Moleón Gavilanes, *Proyectos y obras*, 41–43.

8. Chueca Goitia, *El Museo del Prado*, 22, cit. Moleón Gavilanes, *Proyectos y obras*, 33. See also Moleón Gavilanes, *Proyectos y obras*, 36–37, and *Juan de Villanueva*, 141, 152, 159.

9. Moleón Gavilanes, *Proyectos y obras*, 53, 152.

10. Mesonero Romanos, *Manual de Madrid*, 286.

11. Madoz, *Madrid*, 403.

12. Carlos Sambricio, "Ideal historicista," qtd. Moleón Gavilanes, *Proyectos y obras*, 36.

13. Mesonero Romanos, *Memorias*, 1:107.

14. As reported in "Francia," *Revista Española* 109 (October 25, 1833): 1.

15. Reproduced in Moleón Gavilanes, *Proyectos y obras*, 101.

16. "Tragedia que si no ha sucedido puede suceder, escrita casi en verso y *ad libitum* por Serapio Papamoscas," *El Papamoscas y su tío*, July 28, 1848, 129–32; "Predicar en desierto," *El Clamor Público*, June 15, 1853, 3. The author was making a pun: *cuadros* in Spanish means both "pictures" and "scenes."

17. The renewed version was published in *Diario de Madrid*, May 30, 1816, 665–66.

18. Deleito y Piñuela, . . . *También se divierte*, 55–62.

19. Castellanos, *Bibliotecario*, 38.

20. Caro Baroja, *Estación de Amor*, 132–34.

21. Mesonero Romanos (El Curioso Parlante), "Costumbres de Madrid. La Exposición de Pinturas," *Semanario Pintoresco Español* 131 (September 30, 1838): 720–22.

22. Burke, "Viewpoint."

23. Letter, February 23, 1843. AGP, Sección Administrativa, Legajo 460–3, Carpeta "Museo de pinturas fechos en 1844," Exp. 20 de junio de 1840, José de Madrazo a Intendente Gral. de la Rl. Casa y Patrimonio.

24. Luis Bermejo, "Las ferias de Madrid," *Blanco y Negro*, October 2, 1897, 3–4. Bermejo refers to the mid-nineteenth century.

246

25. Anon., "Las verbenas," *El Globo*, June 21, 1913, 3.

26. Géal, "Admirar y recordar."

27. Rancière, *Spectator*, 69.

28. Bruford, *German Tradition*.

29. Sherman and Rogoff, introduction, ix–xix. Hooper-Greenhill offers a relevant discussion concerning the origins and evolution of "museum culture" in *Shaping of Knowledge*.

30. Huizinga, *Homo Ludens*; Bataille, *Part maudite*; Caillois, *Jeux*; Bakhtín, *Франсуа Рабле*.

31. In Bourdieu's terminology, as explained in *Distinction* and in the essays collected by Randall Johnson in *Pierre Bourdieu*. Bourdieu coined this soccer-inspired term to account for the processes of legitimation of power through the false distinction between economic, social, and cultural forms of capital.

32. I am following the theories of embodiment that examine art as a prosthetic medium connecting the artists and the viewers thought the conduit of affect. This interpretation draws but also departs from the analysis of the haptic elements in pictorial art that Fried has developed in a number of books, from *Absorption* to *Menzel's Realism*.

33. Hooper-Greenhill, *Museums and Their Visitors*, 2.

34. Foley and McPherson, "Museums as Leisure"; Lorente, *Museums of Contemporary Art*; and Horner and Swarbrooke, *Leisure Management*, 343–45. A useful summary of the visitors' responses to such a refurbishing of art museums as leisure can be found in Hanquinet and Savage, "'Educative Leisure."

35. Ivanovic, *Cultural Tourism*. The place of art museums in leisure economy is explained in French and Runyard, *Marketing*, 44–46.

36. Falk, *Museum Experience*, 11–24; Prentice, "Experiential"; Weil, "From Being"; Silverman, "Visitor Meaning-Making"; Konlaan, "Visiting."

37. Ruiz Mantilla, "'Los museos.'"

38. Prior ("Museums," 41) cites Nochlin's definition of museums as suffering "schizophrenia from the start" ("Museums and Radicals," 646).

39. Prior, "Museums," 27–28.

40. Bairoch and Goertz, "Factors of Urbanization," 288.

41. Bahamonde Magro and Toro Mérida, *Burguesía*.

42. Mikkelsen, "Working-Class Formation."

43. Salmi, *Europe*, 89.

44. The model, often referred to as "disciplinary museum" and building on Michel Foucault's *Discipline and Punish*, was first formulated by Hooper-Greenhill in *Museums and the Shaping of Knowledge*, 189. Developed further in Bennett's *The Birth of the Museum*, it has laid the foundation for a

whole line of research in museum studies. See, for example, Hill, *Culture and Class*; Hooper-Greenhill, *Museums and Education*; Prior, "Museums" and *Museums and Modernity*, 13–65; Woodson-Boulton, *Transformative Beauty*, 12–15. Trodd offers a relevant discussion of this theory in "The Discipline of Pleasure."

45. Cunningham, *Leisure*, 76–109; Judd, "'Oddest Combination'"; Philips, *Fairground Attractions*.

46. Abrams, *Workers' Culture*, 9.

47. Mumford, *Culture of Cities*, 265.

48. Ibid., 263–64.

49. Prior, "Museums," 32.

50. Foucault, "Of Other Spaces."

51. Gadamer, *Truth and Method*, 86–87.

52. Belting, *Germans and Their Art*, 44–48; Whitehead, "Cartography."

53. Pearce, *Museums, Objects, and Collections*, 206. Relevant sources about the museum's narrative structures include ibid., 196–207; Hall, *On Display*, 25–29; Ravelli, *Museum Texts*, 119–48; Bal, "Telling, Showing, Showing Off."

54. Bennett, *Birth*; Duncan, *Civilizing Rituals*. A relevant discussion on the museums' changing roles can be found in Mandler, "Art in a Cool Climate."

55. Duncan, *Civilizing Rituals*, 11–32; Perry, *History's Beauties*.

56. Sheehan, *Museums in the German Art World*; Whitehead, *Public Art Museum*; Hoock, "Reforming Culture"; Prior, *Museums and Modernity*; McClellan, *Inventing the Louvre*.

57. Qtd. Trodd, "Paths," 40.

58. Duncan, paraphrasing Samuel Beckett.

59. Adorno, "Valéry Proust Museum," 175; Bazin, *Museum Age*, 264–65.

60. Duncan, "Museums and Department Stores."

61. Koven, "Whitechapel Picture Exhibitions," 23.

62. Abrams, *Workers' Culture*, 34–63.

63. Lefebvre, "La signification de la Commune"; [Debord et al.], "L'historien Lefebvre" and "*Aux poubelles de l'Histoire!*"

64. Billinge, "Time and Place."

65. Clarke and Critcher, *Devil Makes Work*, 134.

66. Elias, introduction and "Essay on Sport and Violence."

67. Elias, *Civilizing Process*.

68. Foucault, *Foucault Effect*; Best, *Leisure Studies*.

69. Garland-Thompson, *Staring*; Gerber, "The Careers."

70. Burke, "Viewpoint."

71. Afinoguénova, "Entre pitos y flautas."

72. The author wishes to thank Jesús Cruz for this reference. See also Cruz, "Símbolos de la modernidad."

73. Bailey, "Adventures in Space," 3.
74. Ibid.
75. Ibid.
76. Osterhammel, *Transformation of the World*, 761.
77. Sarlo coined the term "peripheral modernity" to account for the specificities of cultural production in countries such as Argentina, where "tools of modernity have arrived but where the mental habits and perspectives of traditional culture still persist" (*Modernidad periférica*, 28).
78. Sandberg, *Living Pictures*.
79. Labanyi, "Horror."
80. Hansen, *Babel and Babylon*, 65.
81. Pratt, "Contact Zone" and *Imperial Eyes*, 7.
82. Foucault, "Of Other Spaces," 26.
83. Portús, *Museo del Prado*, 16.
84. Moleón Gavilanes, *Biografía*. I owe the term "biography" to Geraldine Norman's *Hermitage*.
85. Beroqui, "Apuntes para la historia del Museo del Prado" and *Museo del Prado*; Mariano de Madrazo, *Historia*; Gaya Nuño, *Historia*; Pérez Sánchez, *Museo del Prado* and *Pasado, presente, futuro*; Alcolea Blanch, *Museo del Prado*; Calvo Serraller, *Breve historia*; and Javier Portús, *Museo del Prado*.
86. Bal, "Telling"; Duncan, *Civilizing Rituals* and "Putting the 'Nation'"; Hall, *On Display*; Macdonald and Silverstone, "Rewriting"; Pearce, *Museums, Objects, and Collections*; Whitehead, *Public Art Museum*.
87. Bolaños, *Historia*; Géal, *Naissance*; Holo, *Beyond the Prado*; Lanzarote Guiral, "National Museums."
88. Luxenberg, *Galerie Espagnole*.
89. Vázquez, *Inventing*.
90. *El Grafoscopio*, 22 de junio–26 de septiembre, 2004, curated by José Manuel Matilla y Javier Portús.
91. *Arte protegido: Memoria de la Junta del Tesoro Artístico durante la Guerra Civil*, 26 de junio–14 de septiembre, 2003, curated by Isabel Argerich and Judith Ara Lázaro.
92. *El Museo de la Trinidad en El Prado*, 13 de julio–19 de septiembre, 1994, curated by José Álvarez Lopera.
93. *Sala Reservada y el desnudo en el Museo del Prado*, 28 de junio–29 de septiembre, 2002; *El Palacio del Rey Planeta*, 6 de julio–27 de noviembre, 2005, both curated by Javier Portús.
94. *El siglo XIX en el Prado*, 31 de octubre, 2007–20 de abril, 2008, curated by José Luis Díez.
95. Fundación Amigos del Museo del Prado, *Enciclopedia del Museo del Prado*.
96. Álvarez Lopera, *Política de bienes culturales* and "La Junta del Tesoro"; Colorado Castellary, *Museo del Prado* and the revised 2nd ed., *Éxodo y exilio del arte*.

97. Colorado Castellary, "Arte salvado," 6–19.
98. *Arte Salvado. 70 aniversario del salvamento del patrimonio artístico español y de la intervención internacional*, 25 de enero–21 de marzo, 2010, El Paseo del Prado, Madrid, curated by Arturo Colorado Castellary. Following the route of the evacuation of the Prado in 1936-1939, this traveling exhibition made stops in Valencia (Universitat de Valencia, Claustro de La Nau, March 30–May 30, 2010), Sitges (Racó de la Fragata, June 5–August 1, 2010, Figueres (Castell de Sant Ferrán, August 5–October 19, 2010), Teruel (Plaza de San Juan, November 9, 2010–January 9, 2011), Genève (Promenade Saint-Antoine, April 8–June 29, 2011), A Coruña (Museo de Belas Artes, June 10–October 16, 2011), and L'Alfàs del Pi Alicante (Fundación Frax, October 23, 2011–February 26, 2012).
99. Baker, *Materiales para escribir Madrid*; Cruz, *Rise of Middle-Class Culture*; Frost, *Cultivating Madrid*; Uría González, *Sociedad, ocio y cultura*; Valis, *Culture of "Cursilería."*
100. Blanco, *Cultura y conciencia imperial*; Charnon-Deutsch, *Hold That Pose*; Susan Martín Márquez, *Disorientations*; Mercer, *Urbanism and Urbanity*; Zubiaurre, *Cultures of the Erotic*; Charnon-Deutsch and Labanyi, *Culture and Gender*.
101. Ginger, *Cultural Modernity*; Larson, *Constructing and Resisting Modernity*; Parsons, *Cultural History of Madrid*; Salaün and Serrano, *1900 en España*; Ortega, *Ojos que ven* (especially the chapters by Simón Palmer, "La publicidad y la imagen en Madrid [1840–1874]," Riego, "Visibilidades diferenciadas," and Mornat, "Espectáculos de vistas a Madrid [1840–1875]"); Larson and Woods, *Visualizing*.
102. Ferrer, *Visión Castiza*; Lopezosa Aparicio, *Paseo del Prado*; Mariblanca Caneyro, *Retiro*; Simón Palmer, *Jardines*.
103. Botti, *Cielo y dinero*; Flitter, *Spanish Romanticism*; Sánchez-Llama, *Galería*; Urigüen González, *Orígenes*.
104. Pommier, *Musées en Europe*; Bergvelt and Meijers, *Napoleon's Legacy*; and, more recently, Knell et al., *National Museums*; Paul, *First Modern Museums*; Meyer and Savoy, *Museum Is Open*.
105. Juan Sin Tierra, "Madrid," *Nuevo Mundo*, May 31, 1899, 91.

CHAPTER 1

1. Moleón Gavilanes, *Proyectos y obras*, 53.
2. Sommelier du corps was a high position at the court, at the time undergoing a change. The 1817 and 1822 dictionaries of the Spanish Royal Academy defined "Sumiller de Corps" as "a very distinguished person in the palace in charge of assisting the king

247

248

at his toilet, with getting dressed and undressed, and with everything related to royal bed." The 1832 dictionary, however, employed the past tense, describing the sommelier as "a very distinguished person in the palace who used to be in charge of assisting the king in his room" (*Nuevo Tesoro Lexicográfico*)

3. AGP, Reinados, Fernando VII, Caja 401, Exp. 40.

4. Marqués de Santa Cruz, November 25, 1819. AGP, Reinados, Fernando VII, Caja 401, Exp. 40.

5. Gaya Nuño, *Historia*, 9.

6. Mérimée, *Lettres d'Espagne*, 125.

7. "Noticias Extrangeras," *El Restaurador* 150 (December 16, 1823): 1301.

8. "Crónica de diciembre de 1829, Baviera," *El Mercurio de España*, December 1929, 425.

9. Sheehan, *Museums*, 15.

10. Mandler, "Cool Climate," 102.

11. Sheehan, *Museums*, 62–70.

12. Sheehan, "Art and Its Publics," 9.

13. Hoock, *The King's Artists*, qtd. Mandler, "Cool Climate," 105.

14. Bertini, "Parma and Piacenza," 73–89.

15. A useful overview is Paul's preface to *The First Modern Museums of Art*, x–xix. Paul identifies Rome's Capitoline Museum, founded in 1733, as the earliest example of an "institutional" museum—in this case, channeling the municipal, rather than national, power (Paul, "Capitoline Museum, Rome").

16. Conlin, *Nation's Mantelpiece*, 48.

17. Sheehan, *Museums*, 72.

18. Roger de Piles's *Balance des Peintres* rated Renaissance and Baroque painters according to a system based on four academic classifications: "Composition," "Dessein," "Coloris," and "Expression." In Spain, the doctrine was known firsthand, but also from Céan Bermúdez's 1827 translation of Francesco Milizia's *The Art of Seeing*, which defined only three "parts": argument, exactness of form, and variety of lines (*Arte de ver en las bellas artes del diseño*, 110–11). Cross-national traditions of comparative viewing are described in Paul, introduction to *First Modern Museums of Art*, 7–8.

19. Pearce, *Museums, Objects, and Collections*, 98–109; Meijers, "Classification comme principe."

20. Belting, *Germans*, 37–38.

21. Whitehead, "National Art Museum," 105–22.

22. De Certeau notes a structural connection between early history and a gallery: images and effigies connect people and events no longer present with the time of the visitors' own itinerary. Historiography, in de Certeau's words, fulfills the same function: "it represents the dead along a narrative itinerary" (*Writing of History*, 100). A

philosopher influenced by poststructuralist thought, de Certeau reveals that the main function of connecting the "dead" to the present, be that through a gallery or a historical narrative, consists in covering up, and filling, the hiatus between the collective or personal past and the individual present. In his scheme, the approach to history through writing, however, differs from a mere demonstration since writing does not only connect the past to the present, but also fulfills the functions of burial and symbolization: it assures us that the past is past and finds for it a place in the present that is symbolic rather than factual.

23. McClellan, *Inventing the Louvre*, 107–16; Whitehead, "Manifesto," 48–60.

24. Wezel, "Denon's Louvre," 158.

25. Sheehan, *Museums*, 80.

26. Qtd. Géal, *Naissance*, 126. Géal cites Menéndez Rexach, "Separación," 97.

27. Manuel Godoy (1767–1851) was Spain's prime minister under Carlos IV, the father of Fernando VII, and the favorite of Queen María Luisa, Fernando's mother. Supporter and signatory of the failed Fontainebleau Treaty with Napoleon, which opened Spain to the French invasion, he was first imprisoned and then exiled to France and Italy. In 1808, Carlos IV confiscated his properties to appease the participants in the Mutiny of Aranjuez. Godoy was one of the most prominent art collectors of his time, and his dismantled private gallery included, among others, Velázquez's *Venus at Her Mirror* and both of Goya's *Majas* (Rose–de Viejo, "Colección"). A detailed summary of the debates around the Buenavista Palace can be found in Beroqui, *Museo*, 1:76–81; Valentín de Sambricio, "Museo Fernandino"; Navarrete Martínez, *Academia*, 330–37; and Géal, *Naissance*, 123–26.

28. López Aguado, "Descripción," qtd. Moleón Gavilanes, *Proyectos y obras*, 45.

29. For an 1804 inventory of the collection of paintings of the Academia, see Bédat, *Real Academia*, 310–24.

30. Géal, *Naissance*, 128.

31. Approved June 9, 1816. AGP Reinados, Fernando VII, Caja 401, Exp. 65.

32. Géal, *Naissance*, 136. García-Monsalve Escriña convincingly attributes the discord to Fernando's restoration of the Mayordomía Mayor, which made the state's authority uncertain and the fiscal situation uninspiring ("Historia jurídica," 80, 174–75).

33. Ford, *Handbook*, 681.

34. Beroqui, "Apuntes," 190; Mariano de Madrazo, *Historia*, 89–90; Moleón Gavilanes, *Proyectos y obras*, 51–52.

35. Moleón Gavilanes, *Proyectos y obras*, 161.

36. Qtd. Gaya Nuño, *Historia*, 65.

37. Beroqui, *Museo del Prado*, 1:54–56; Antiguedad, "Primera colección." For a discussion in English, see Schulz, "Museo Nacional del Prado," 240–41.

38. Qtd. Beroqui, "Apuntes," 151.

39. See Géal's detailed account in *Naissance*, 117–23, esp. 118. Géal cites Rose–de Viejo, *Manuel Godoy*, 1:505.

40. Calvo Serraller, *Breve historia*, 12.

41. Qtd. Beroqui, "Apuntes," 160–61.

42. The royal decree concerning reorganization of Roya Postal service was adopted November 29, 1817 (*Mercurio de España*, June 1819, 137–39).

43. Bernardo López Piquer, *María Isabel de Braganza, Queen of Spain, as the Foundress of the Prado Museum*, 1829, oil on canvas, 258 ´ 174 cm, P00863. For more about the painting, see Sánchez Cantón, *España, itinerarios*, 81. For a detailed examination of this legend, refuted already by Pedro de Madrazo in 1882, see Beroqui, "Apuntes," 102–6.

44. Beroqui, "Apuntes," 106–7, quotes the description of Montenegro by Fernando's contemporary Michael J. Quin (*Memorias históricas*, vol. 1, 287). Montenegro's position in Spanish sounded like "Gentihombre de la cámara con entrada" (Beroqui, *Museo*, 94).

45. Ford, *Handbook*, 744.

46. Moleón Gavilanes, *Proyectos y obras*, 153. The sculptures were completed and delivered to Madrid in 1826. AGP, Reinados, Fernando VII, Caja 351, Exp. 22.

47. Comellas, "Españoles," 6, 11–12.

48. Caro Baroja, *Estación de Amor*.

49. Carlos Sambricio, "Fiestas," 165–66.

50. See also "Fígaro" (Mariano José de Larra). "La vida de Madrid," *El Observador* 151 (December 12, 1834): 3-4; "La sociedad," "Jardines públicos," "Don Timoteo o El literato."

51. [Mackenzie], *Year in Spain*, 149.

52. Anon., "Promenade on the Prado at Madrid," 529.

53. Fischer, *Picture of Madrid*, 52.

54. [Mackenzie], *Year in Spain*, 146.

55. Anon., "Promenade on the Prado at Madrid," 530.

56. Fischer, *Picture of Madrid*, 53–54.

57. [Mackenzie], *Year in Spain*, 239.

58. Mesonero Romanos, *Guía de Madrid*, 310–11.

59. Eusebi, *Noticia*, 1828, Advertencia, n.p.

60. "El que no sabe," *Correspondencia* (Madrid), September 12, 1828, 3.

61. Varey, *Cartelera*. I owe the reference to Rebecca Haidt.

62. "Ventas," *Diario de Avisos de Madrid*, June 4, 1826, 619–20; Thomas, *Romanticism*.

63. Alongside the views of Seville and farther-removed places such as Saint Petersburg and Mexico City, the vista of the Promenade was a stable part of the Cosmorama exhibited continuously in 1828–29. A great number of these mechanized views are on display at the Musée des Arts et Métiers in Paris.

64. 1827, "Sobre un fenomeno," qtd. Varey, *Cartelera*, 355.

65. February 18, 1821, qtd. Varey, *Cartelera*, 313–14.

66. Varey, *Cartelera*, 314; see also Varey, "'Bleeding Nun' and 'Our Lady of Paris.'"

67. Qtd. Varey, *Cartelera*, 349–50.

68. Mesonero Romanos, *Memorias*, 263.

69. Fernández de los Ríos, *Guía de Madrid*, 333, quoting from Madoz, *Madrid*, 406; Perla, "El Hotel Ritz."

70. Lopezosa Aparicio, "Ocio y negocio," 272.

71. Varey, *Cartelera*, 77, 344.

72. Madoz, *Madrid*, 406.

73. [Eusebi], *Catálogo*, 1819, "Bodegones," "Fruteros," y "Floreros," nos. 33, 43, 46, 47, 48, 51, 52, 53, 56, 57, 58, 66, 67, and many others; "La Feria de Madrid en la plazuela de la Cebada: por D. Manuel Cruz," no. 88 (*The Madrid Fair*, 1770–80, oil on canvas, 84 ´ 94 cm, P00693, currently on deposit at the Museo de Historia de Madrid); "Merienda de majos: por Bayeu," no. 45 (probably *The Country Picnic* by Ramón Bayeu, 1784–85, no. P00607, oil on canvas, 37 ´ 56 cm); "Una Merienda en el canal de Madrid: Por Bayeu," no. 91 (probably *Bridge over the Madrid Canal* by Francisco de Bayeu, 1784–85, P00605, oil on canvas, 36 ´ 95 cm).

74. [Eusebi], *Catálogo*, 1819, "Vista de un paseo: por D. Francisco Bayeu," no. 44; "Coches y comitiva entrando en un bosque: Por Velázquez," no. 59 (probably *Calle de la Reina, in Aranjuez* by Juan Bautista Martínez del Mazo, seventeenth century, P01214, oil on canvas, 245 × 202 cm; there are no people eating depicted on that canvas, however), "Felipe IV de caza: por Velázquez," no. 78.

75. [Eusebi], *Catálogo*, 1819.

76. [Eusebi], *Noticia*, Advertencia, s.p.

77. AGP, Reinados, Fernando VII, Caja 352, Exp. 30.

78. Ibid.

79. Afinoguénova, "Painted in Spanish"; Portús, *Concepto*.

80. [Eusebi], *Catálogo*, 1824, 25, same wording in [Eusebi], *Noticia*, Advertencia, n.p.

81. [Eusebi], *Catálogo*, 1824, 27; [Eusebi], *Noticia*, Advertencia, n.p.; Eusebi 1824, 27, Eusebi 1828, 81.

82. Vega, *Litografía*.

83. Ceán Bermúdez, *Diccionario histórico*.

84. Qtd. Mariano de Madrazo, *Historia*, 148.

85. Espinosa Martín, "Luis Eusebi"; Pardo Canalís, "Noticias y escritos."

86. Eusebi, "Llave."

87. Ibid., 111–12.

88. Ceán Bermúdez, "Historia." Eusebi does not quote this work, but he does quote Ceán's *Dictionary* extensively.

89. In Ceán's view, these masters had neglected all other elements of the art and therefore "no longer knew essential beauty of art and nature, which is the result of all those things that they ignored" ("Historia," 6:130–31). In a later section, dedicated to the Andalusian school, Ceán paid due tribute to Romantic ways of thinking by emphasizing Velázquez's mastery of art against the backdrop of the general decadence (ibid., 7:237).

90. Ibid., 7:308.

91. Eusebi, *Ensayo*, xv–xvi.

92. Viardot, "Musée," also in *Étude*, 389.

93. Calvo Serraller, *Breve historia*, 20–21.

94. *Mercurio de España* (April 1821): 333. In the budget for 1823 approved by the Cortes in 1822, one finds 72,000 reales, the equivalent of three monthly contributions from the king, assigned to the museum from the "Gobierno político y económico del reino," which may signal that the government was posing as the museum's guarantor (Cortes, *Colección*, 9:511).

95. AGP, Reinados, Fernando VII, Caja 401, Exp. 3, 1819.

96. Alcolea Blanch, "Marqués de Santa Cruz," in *Enciclopedia del Museo del Prado* online; Portús, *Sala Reservada*.

97. Beroqui, *Museo*, 105.

98. Alcolea Blanch, *Prado*, 34–36.

99. Beroqui, *Museo*, 111; Gaya Nuño, *Historia*, 71, Alcolea Blanch, *Prado*, 34–35.

100. November 14, 1826. AGP, Reinados, Fernando VII, Caja 401, Exp. 77.

101. [Eusebi], *Catalogo*, 1821; *Noticia*, 1824.

102. AGP, Reinados, Fernando VII, Caja 401, Exp. 20.

103. Ibid., Exp. 71, October 2, 1818; February 11, 1819.

104. November 18, 1828; August 20, 1830. AGP, Reinados, Fernando VII, Caja 401, Exp. 94.

105. Mariano de Madrazo, *Historia*, 113; Seseña, "Retrete"; Pérez Sánchez, "Autor de la decoración."

106. AGP, Reinados, Fernando VII, Caja 399, Exp. 38: "Solicitud del duque de Hijar que se expongan en la rotonda del museo las estatuas de los Reyes Padres" (1826); Caja 12, Exp. 31; Caja 401, Exp. 81.

107. [Eusebi], *Catálogo* 1819, 4 (no. 29); Schulz, "Museo Nacional del Prado," 252.

108. Qtd. Mariano de Madrazo, 105; Moleón Gavilanes, *Proyectos y obras*, 153.

109. Mariano de Madrazo, *Historia*, 106.

110. Ibid., 114 and 118; [Eusebi], *Catálogo*, 1828, 73. Schulz ("Museo Nacional del Prado," 252) adds to the list *Disembarkation of Fernando VII in Puerto de Santa María* by José Aparicio, but while newspapers of the time indeed reveal an intention to exhibit this canvas in the Museo Real, there is no evidence that it had ever been implemented. For more on this painting, see Pardo Canalís, "'El desembarco.'"

111. [Eusebi], *Noticia*, 1824, 26; [Eusebi], *Catálogo*, 1828, 76.

112. Pedro de Madrazo, *Catalogo*, 1843, 121.

113. "Museo Real de Nápoles: Noticias y Variedades," *Crónica Artística y Literaria*, January 26, 1819, 3; "Artes: Descripción de la Tribuna en Florencia," *Crónica Científica y Literaria* 282 (December 10, 1819): 1–3.

114. "Bellas Artes: Museo de la Cámara de Pares de Francia," *Mercurio de España*, August 1818, 329–54; October 1818, 171–72.

115. *Crónica Artística*, March 23, 1820, qtd. Ariza, "Los proyectos de museos," 425; Bolaños, *Historia*, 182; Alcolea Blanch, *Prado*, 33. See also José María Halcón, "Continuación de la carta inserta en el número anterior," *Miscelánea de Comercio, Arte y Literatura*, February 16, 1820, 3–4.

116. *Miscelánea de Comercio, Arte y Literatura*, May 7, 1820, 3.

117. El testigo de vista, "Bellas Artes," *El Espectador*, July 1, 1821, 311; "Libros," *Diario de Madrid* 249 (September 7, 1822): 6; "Anuncios," *Nuevo Diario de Madrid* 288 (October 16, 1822): 1264.

118. *El Restaurador* 112 (November 1, 1823): 1000; *El Restaurador* 115 (November 5, 1823): 1027.

119. "Correspondencia," *Correo Literario y Mercantil* 27 (September 12, 1828): 3.

120. "España," *Mercurio de España* (September 1828): 184.

121. Géal, *Naissance*, 320. See also Bolaños, *Historia* (1st ed.), 169–74.

122. Qtd. Beroqui, *Museo del Prado*, 160–61.

123. January 3, 1826. AGP, Reinados, Fernando VII, Caja 400, Exp. 24, cuentas, carta de Vicente López.

124. Viardot, *Étude*, 432, 434. See also Luxenberg, *Galerie Espagnole*, 104.

125. AGP, Reinados, Fernando VII, Caja 351, Exp. 24.

126. Viardot, *Étude*, 388.

127. Through the beginning of the nineteenth century, the academicians insisted that art education follow the neoclassical standards of learning from the ancient masters, or, as Bédat has it, put "the statues of antiquity as a necessary intermediate between nature and a projected painting or sculpture" (*Real academia*, 231). Hinging on Mengs's teachings, this

principle persisted through the end of the studied period. Navarrete quotes José de Madrazo's 1819 proposal for the program of study of the color techniques, heavily reminiscent of Mengs's own views, and the versions authored by Jovellanos that Bédat quotes (*Academia*, 216–19).

128. Weichlein, "Cosmopolitanism," 84.
129. Viardot, *Étude*, 389.
130. Mérimée, *Lettres d'Espagne*, 126.
131. AGP, Reinados, Fernando VII, Caja 351, Exp. 24.
132. Ibid.
133. *Real Orden*, March 12, 1827.
134. July 13, 1827. AGP, Reinados, Fernando VII, Caja 351, Exp. 81.
135. August 11, 1831. AGP, Reinados, Fernando VII, Caja 351, Exp. 31.
136. *Cartas Españolas*, March 1832, 141.

CHAPTER 2

1. Beroqui, *Museo*, 145–49.
2. "Edgardo," "Revista de nobles artes," *La España*, February 1, 1855, 1.
3. Duncan and Wallach, "Universal Survey Museum."
4. Blanning, *Nineteenth-Century Europe*, 6–9; Osterhammel, *Transformation*, 58–62.
5. Bennett, "Exhibitionary Complex."
6. Barlow, "'Fire, Flatulence, and Fog.'"
7. Nora, *Les lieux*, vol. 2, pt. 3, 96.
8. Babelon, "Louvre."
9. Kerckhof, Bussers, and Bücken, *Peintre*, 195–200; Streidt and Feierabend, *Prussia*, 392.
10. Qtd. Tomlinson, "State Galleries," 25–26.
11. Whitehead, "Cartography."
12. Conlin, *Nation's Mantelpiece*, 87.
13. Paul, *First*, ix.
14. Smith, *Victorian Nude*, 68–75; Pointon, *Naked Authority*, 11–16. On the definition of "bourgeoisie," see Osterhammel, *Transformation*, 761. My use of an opposition between the naked and the nude is based on Clark's oft-cited *The Nude*. The term "distinction" belongs to Pierre Bourdieu.
15. Duncan, *Civilizing Rituals*, 72–100.
16. Smith, *Victorian Nude*, 4, 121; Afinoguénova, "Nation Disrobed."
17. Charnon-Deutsch, *Fictions of the Feminine*, 127–73.
18. Holt, *Triumph of Art*; *Art of All Nations*; and *Emerging Role*.
19. Koven, "Whitechapel."
20. Lorente, *Museums*, 39–65.
21. Haskell, *Ephemeral Museum*.
22. Qtd. Lockhurst, *Story of Exhibitions*, 112.

23. Lockhurst, *Story*, 116; Holt, *Expanding World*, 11–13; Drachkovitch, *The Revolutionary Internationals*, 5. Some of these authors state that the meeting was held at the 1855 Paris exhibition. I could not find a confirmation for this earlier date.
24. "Cinematograph," 1905, qtd. Sazatornil Ruiz and Lasheras Peña, *París y la española*.
25. Holt, *Triumph of Art*, 416.
26. S. Rejano, "Exposición de pinturas," *El Popular*, October 11, 1849, n.p.
27. Larra [Fígaro], "*Cuasi*."
28. Glendinning and Macartney, *Spanish Art*.
29. Luxenberg, *Galerie Espagnole*, 79.
30. There were legal grounds for the decision: the so-called Pragmatic Law, dating back to medieval Castilian tradition and adopted under Fernando's father Carlos IV in 1789 but never ratified.
31. White, "Liberty, Honor, Order."
32. Reyero, "Ideología e imagen," 131.
33. Pérez Sánchez, *Pasado, presente y futuro*, 23–24.
34. Gaya Nuño, *Historia*, 83; Alcolea Blanch, *Prado*, 47.
35. May 26, 1857. AGP, Sección Administrativa, Legajo 461, Carpeta 1 "Real Museo de Pintura y Escultura, 1850 a 1859," Real Orden.
36. See Madrazo's rebuttal, *El Clamor Público*, September 30, 1845, n.p.
37. Duncan, "'Putting the 'Nation,'" 101–11.
38. Afinoguénova, "'Painted in Spanish.'"
39. "Exposición de bellas artes en la Academia San Fernando" II, *El Heraldo*, October 19, 1848, 1.
40. Federico de Madrazo, "Recuerdos de mi vida," 66.
41. Mesonero Romanos, "Costumbres de Madrid."
42. José de Madrazo, *Epistolario*, 321 (March 23, 1839).
43. J. Honibato García de Quevedo, "Esposicion de la Academia de San Fernando," *El Clamor Público*, October 9, 1845, 4; "Esposición de la Real Academia de San Fernando," *La España*, September 6, 1850, 4; José Galofre, "Nobles Artes: La Real Academia de San Fernando," *El Heraldo*, December 13, 1853, 3; see also *La Época*, November 24, 1855, 3.
44. Cueva Merino and López Villaverde, *Clericalismo y asociacionismo*, 30.
45. Callahan, "Church and State," 59–60.
46. Pageard, Fontanella, and Cabra Loredo, *SEM*; Burdiel, *SEM*.
47. *La Cruz: Periódico de Religión, de Literatura y de Política*, qtd. Urigüen González, *Orígenes*, 164; "the Madrazo boys" in Pérez Galdós, *Mendizábal*.
48. González López and Martí Ayxelà, *El mundo*, 319.

49. P. de M. (Pedro de Madrazo), "Vínculo social," *El Áncora*, Barcelona, January 20, 1850, 1–3; see also Afinoguénova, "Providencialismo."

50. *La Iberia*, August 6, 1854, 3.

51. Qtd. Beroqui, *Museo*, 148.

52. Pedro de Madrazo, *Poesías dedicadas á S.M. la Reina*.

53. Simón Segura, "Desamortización"; Fernández García, "Evolución social," 17.

54. Only the Plazas Tirso de Molina and Vázquez Mella were built on former convent lands. A few other plots of confiscated land were used to widen the streets.

55. In 1804 the estimated population of Madrid was 176,374. The ensuing censuses registered the following growth: 1825, 207,334; 1836, 224,312; 1857, 281,170; 1860, 298,426; 1869, 304,489 (Ringrose, *Madrid*). Only the numbers corresponding to 1857 are taken from the census; the rest are widely accepted projections. See, for example, Bahamonde Magro and Toro Mérida, *Burguesía*, 171.

56. Fernández de la Ríos, *Guía de Madrid*, 604.

57. Cruz, *Middle-Class Culture*, 5–6.

58. Carballo Barra, "Orígenes"; Ayuntamiento de Madrid, *Plan Castro*, 5.

59. Ariza Muñoz, *Jardines*, 228–34, Frost, *Cultivating Madrid*; Cruz, "Símbolos."

60. Bahamonde Magro and Toro Mérida, "Mendicidad."

61. Cuevas, "Aproximación," 168.

62. Anon., *Madrid in 1835*, 1:76–77.

63. Billinge, "A Time and Place"; Bailey, *Leisure and Class*.

64. "La recreación es grata a la conservación de la vida," *El Diario de Avisos de Madrid*, April 21, 1834, 5.

65. "Junta Superior de Sanidad," *Eco del Comercio* 68 (July 7, 1834): 2.

66. "Viena," *El Instructor, ó Repertorio de historia, bellas letras y artes* 4, no. 40 (1837): 98; "Paseos Públicos," *El Instructor, ó Repertorio de historia, bellas letras y artes* 5, no. 49 (1838): 28–29.

67. "Modas: Madrid," *Correo de las Damas* 1, no. 22 (November 27, 1833): 174.

68. "Noticias de Madrid," *Correo de las Damas* 3, no. 4 (January 28, 1835): 200.

69. "El Prado," *Correo de las Damas* 3, no. 15 (April 21, 1835): 113.

70. "Noticias de Madrid."

71. Mercer, *Urbanism and Urbanity*, 67.

72. Nemesio Fernández Cuesta, for example, left detailed and very sarcastic portrait of water-selling women and "their amiable, serviceable, and accommodating character" ("Revista de la semana," *El Museo Universal* 8, no. 26 [June 26, 1864]: 201–2).

73. Antonio López de Guzmán, "¡Qué tiempos tan felices! Novela de costumbres políticas y sociales. tomo 2º, parte primera, cap 1, 'Una vuelta por el Prado,'" *Eco del Comercio* 1484 (August 3, 1847): 1.

74. *La Revista Española* 212 (May 12, 1834): 464.

75. *Eco del Comercio* 173 (October 20, 1834); "Pillos que venden candela," *La Revista Española* 231 (June 3, 1834): 538.

76. M.-P.S., "La verbena de S. Pedro," *El Jorobado* 106 (July 5, 1836): 2.

77. "M.L.," "La verbena de San Juan," *Fr. Gerundio* 8º trimestre (June 25, 1839): 418.

78. "El circo 'Fama del Prado,'" *Diario de Madrid*, July 16, 1837, 4.

79. *El Observador*, June 24, 1851.

80. "Costumbres: Las verbenas en Madrid," *La Época*, June 27, 1853, 2.

81. *Diario de Avisos de Madrid*, June 23, 1837, 1.

82. *Diario de Madrid*, September 16, 1838, 4.

83. February 23, 1843. AGP, Sección Administrativa, Legajo 460–3, Carpeta "Museo de pinturas fechos en 1844," Exp. 20 de junio de 1840.

84. "Higiene," *La España*, March 18, 1853, 4.

85. Ibid.

86. "Conservación de un edificio," *El Clamor Público*, March 18, 1853, 4.

87. AGP, Sección Administrativa, Administración General, Legajo 460–4, Carpeta "Real Museo fechos en 1852."

88. April 12, 1853. AGP, Sección Administrativa, Administración General, Legajo 460–4, Carpeta "Real Museo fechos en 1852."

89. September 1, 1856. AGP, Sección Administrativa, Administración General, Legajo 460–4, Carpeta "Real Museo de Pintura y Escultura fechos en 1856."

90. Barcelona, not Madrid, became the first railroad hub in Spain with the inauguration of the Barcelona–Mataró line in 1848. The Madrid-Aranjuez railroad was inaugurated in 1851, but it was reserved for the royal family.

91. [Mesonero Romanos], "Los paletos en Madrid."

92. "Variedades, Crónica de la capital: Oscuridad," *El Clamor Público*, October 6, 1859, 4.

93. "Apuntes de un Castellano Viejo," *Gil Blas*, May 21, 1868, 2.

94. "Advertencia," *Correo de las Damas* 3 no. 30 (August 14, 1835): 239.

95. Mariano de Madrazo, *Historia*, 211.

96. *La Correspondencia*, June 16, 1870, 3.

97. Frost, *Cultivating Madrid*.

98. *La Época*, May 29, 1868, 3.

99. Moleón Gavilanes, *Proyectos y obras*, 69.

100. There were plans for transferring there the gate that separated the northern façade from the Tivoli: "Buen Retiro," *La España*, July 16, 1851, 4; *La Iberia*, October 31, 1861, 3; "A tiempo estamos," *El*

Clamor Público, April 2, 1864, 3; *La Época*, March 3, 1866, 4. The gate was eventually moved to the entrance to the Retiro park in 1880 (*La Iberia*, August 11, 1880, 3).

101. Published in *La Época*, November 30, 1849, 1–2.

102. "Proyecto," *El Clamor Público*, February 3, 1847, 3.

103. *La Correspondencia*, April 20, 1860, 2.

104. "Anales de la Catedral de Madrid," *La Época*, December 7, 1864, 2.

105. *El Observador*, April 2, 1849; *El Clamor Público*, April 3, 1849, 3; *La España*, April 8, 1849, 4.

106. Moleón Gavilanes, *Proyectos y obras*, 163.

107. *La Época*, May 7, 1864, 3.

108. Vinuesa, "La restauración."

109. July 31, 1844. AGP, Sección Administrativa, Legajo 460–3, Carpeta "Museo de pinturas fechos en 1844," Exp. "Prejuicio que puede ocasionar al Real Museo la pólvora depositada en San Gerónimo."

110. July 12, 1847. Archivo MNP, Caja 1339, Registros de salida, 1839–69.

111. "Tragedia que si no ha sucedido puede suceder, escrita casi en verso y *ad libitum* por Serapio Papamoscas," *El Papamoscas y su tío*, July 28, 1848, 129–32.

112. AGP, Sección Administrativa, Administración General, Legajo 460–4, Carpeta "Museo 1838–56, Expedientes de Contaduría de varios años," Exp. 8133.

113. February 10, 1842. AGP, Sección Administrativa, Legajo 460–3, Carpeta "Museo de pinturas fechos en 1844."

114. *La Esperanza*, November 4, 1851, 4.

115. Flitter, *Spanish Romanticism*.

116. José de Madrazo, *Epistolario*, October 5, 1838.

117. December 1, 1847. AGP, Sección Administrativa, Museo de Pintura y Escultura, Legajo 460, Carpeta 1, Exp. "Relacionado a la Galería Histórica, 1847 y 1848."

118. Ibid., December 4, 1847.

119. AGP, Sección Administrativa, Museo de Pintura y Escultura, Legajo 460–3, Caja "Museo fechos en 1847."

120. *El Popular*, Madrid, January 26, 1848, 4; "Museo Historico Nacional," *El Popular* (January 28, 1848), 4. See also Gilarranz, "Estado-nación."

121. December 1, 1847. AGP, Sección Administrativa, Real Museo de Pintura y Escultura, Legajo 460, Carpeta 1, Exp. "Relacionado a la Galería Histórica, 1847 y 1848."

122. Having assumed the functions of the museum's director when José de Madrazo stepped down, Juan Antonio de Ribera found that only the portraits of the kings and queens of Aragon, the Habsburgs, and the Bourbons were displayed in chronological order. In Ribera's own words,

he proceeded to rearrange the Historical Gallery "so that every portrait could find its corresponding place" (January 24, 1859. AGP, Sección Administrativa, Museo de Pintura y Escultura, Legajo 460–3, Carpeta "Museos, 1857, 58 y 59"). This work was interrupted by Ribera's sudden death in 1860.

123. Newspapers reported that he was painting the portrait for the museum on December 30, 1846.

124. Federico de Madrazo, "Recuerdos de mi vida," 66.

125. José Muñoz Gaviria, *Semanario Pintoresco español*, 33 (1856): 259.

126. "Una pregunta," *El Clamor Público*, March 5, 1850, 3.

127. M.L., "El teatro Nacional," *El Clamor Público*, May 24, 1864, 3. In the 1840s, Lafuente, under the name of "Fray Gerundio," published a compendium on theater, *Teatro social*.

128. "Descuido," *El Clamor Público*, December 30, 1853, 3; concerning women, see *El Heraldo de Madrid*, November 17, 1853, 3.

129. The name featured in Pedro de Madrazo's 1854 catalogue.

130. *La Época*, January 20, 1854, n.p.

131. Pedro de Madrazo, *Catálogo*, 1843, v.

132. José de Madrazo, *Catálogo*, 6.

133. Federico de Madrazo, *Epistolario*, 147.

134. To be sure, the Madrazos never fully resolved the issue of heterogeneity and continued citing Ceán Bermúdez and recognizing, at times, at least two "schools" in Spain, the Castilian and the Andalusian one.

135. Qtd. Pedro de Madrazo, *Catálogo descriptivo e histórico*, xxiv–xxv.

136. Ibid., xxxii.

137. *La Esperanza*, September 12, 1868, 4.

138. "Variedades," *El Arte en España* 3 (1865): 39.

139. Vázquez, *Inventing the Art Collection*, 8–10.

140. "Esposición de la Real Academia de San Fernando," *La Época*, November 24, 1955, 3. Writers and artists agreed that, to meet the standards set at the Paris salons, the exhibitions at the San Fernando and the Fall Fair had to be split.

141. Fontanella, *Historia de la fotografía*; Carabias Álvaro, "Diorama," 974.

142. "Diorama," *Diario de Madrid* 2662, July 10, 1842, 4

143. *Semanario Pintoresco Español* 119 (1838): 627–28; *Diario de Avisos*, July 8, 1838, n.p.

144. Luxenberg, *Galerie Espagnole*, 75.

145. Martínez, *Lectura*, 193.

146. *La Moda Elegante Ilustrada*, July 6, 1868, 202.

147. Flint, *Victorians*.

148. Vega, "Del espectáculo."

149. "El pantógrafo," *Semanario Pintoresco español* 2 (1837): 71–72.

253

254

150. Castellote, "España," 31.

151. Wood, *Shock of the Real.*

152. "La Nobleza," *El Jorobado* 21 (March 24, 1836): 2. *Diario de Madrid*, November 17, 1838, qtd. Geal, *Naissance*, 318–19. Starting in 1838, the galleries dedicated to paintings were open on Sundays, while the sculpture galleries were open only Mondays and Wednesdays.

153. Qtd. Mariano de Madrazo, *Historia*, 179n.

154. Pedro de Madrazo, *Catálogo*, 1843, xi–xii.

155. "P. de M.," "Pintura," *El Artista* 2 (1835): 14–16, 14 (italics in original).

156. Federico de Madrazo, "Recuerdos de mi vida," 74 (italics in original).

157. Valis, *Culture*, 34.

158. Antonio Flores, "Una semana en Madrid: Artículo séptimo y último," *El Laberinto*, May 1, 1844, 172.

159. Géal, *Naissance*, 326–36.

160. April 12, 1856. AGP, Sección Administrativa, Legajo 461, Carpeta 1, Exp. "Real Museo de Pintura y Escultura, 1850 a 1859."

161. Real Museo de Pintura y escultura de S.M., REGLAS *que para el buen orden y decoro de este Real Establecimiento deben observar los individuos que concursan a sus salas y galerías en los días que no son de exposición pública*, Archivo MNP, Caja 359, Madrid, January 31, 1863.

162. Géal, *Naissance*, 334.

163. *Libros-registro de los nombres de las personas que visitan las salas del Real Museo de Pintura y Escultura de S.M.*, several vols., 1854–65. Archivo MNP.

164. *La Época*, November 24, 1855, 3; "Esposición de la Real Academia de San Fernando."

165. "Delación risible," *La Linterna Mágica* 4 (1849): 100.

166. "P. de M.," "Pintura," 15 (italics in original). My reading of class at the Museo Real hinges on Pierre Bourdieu's *Love of Art.*

167. "P. de M.," "Dibujante—Colorista—Bello-Ideal," *El Artista* 1 (1834): 290.

168. Eladio Lezama, "El panecillo del cuadro del hambre," *El Arte: Periódico semanal de literatura y bellas artes* 1, no. 8 (1866): 2.

169. "Museo de las clases pasivas," *El Clamor Público*, October 13, 1848, 4 (italics in original).

170. "Diario de las Cortes," *El Español*, April 18, 1847, 1.

171. "Revista de teatros," *El Imparcial*, February 19, 1865, 1.

172. Benito Vicens y Gil de Tejada, "Una restauración muy completa de un fragmento de estatua muy escaso," *El Arte en España* 3 (1865): 92–3.

173. *El Popular*, May 11, 1849, 4.

174. Ramón de Navarrete, "Revista de Madrid," *La Ilustracion, Periódico Universal* 9 (March 2, 1850): 67.

175. *La Discusión*, September 5, 1865, 3.

176. "Predicar en desierto," *El Clamor Público*, June 15, 1853, 3.

177. "Noticias extranjeras," *El Clamor Público*, March 6, 1847, 4; "Observaciones," *La Iberia*, April 24, 1861.

178. "Retazos," *La Posdata: Periódico Joco-Serio* 775 (August 20, 1844), 4.

179. Pedro de Madrazo, *Catálogo de los cuadros*, 1850, iii–x.

180. Mariano de Madrazo, *Historia*, 180–81.

181. Afinoguénova, "Art Education."

182. April 17, 1856, AGP, Sección Administrativa, Legajo 461, Carpeta 1, Real Museo de Pintura y Escultura, 1850 to 1859.

183. Viardot, *Musées d'Espagne*, 5, 7–10.

184. Francisco Pi y Margall, "Real Museo de Pintura y Escultura" I and II, *El Museo Universal*, January 30, 1858, 39–40; February 15, 1858, 47–48; this quote II, 47–48.

185. Eugenio de Ochoa, "El gobierno y las bellas artes," *La América*, March 13, 1867, 4.

186. Ibid.

187. "Cuadros de Goya," *El Clamor Público*, November 24, 1854.

188. José Fernández Giménez, "Las bellas artes en España: Con motivo de la Exposición en Madrid de 1866," *Revista Hispano-Americana*, February 28, 1867, 118.

189. Gregorio Cruzada Villaamil, "Juicio crítico de las exposiciones de bellas artes," *El Arte en España* 5 (1867): 113.

CHAPTER 3

1. November 4, 1868. Archivo MNP, Caja 14294.

2. *Libro-registro de los nombres de las personas que visitan las salas del Real Museo de Pintura y Escultura de S.M. Madrid, 1864-1870.* Archivo MNP, Caja L-74, fols. 209–10.

3. Pearce, *Museums, Objects, and Collections*, 100.

4. Fernández de los Ríos, "Estudios en la emigración: El Futuro Madrid; Paseos mentales por la capital de España, tal cual es y tal cual debe dejarla transformada la Revolución," *La Época*, October 29, 1868, 1.

5. Granger, *L'empereur et les arts.*

6. Meijers, "Dutch Method"; Bodenstein, "National Museums in the Netherlands."

7. Troilo, "National Museums in Italy," 468.

8. Aronsson and Bentz, "National Museums in Germany," 402.

9. *La Esperanza*, January 26, 1869, 1.

10. Perry, *History's Beauties.*

11. Fernando Cos-Gayón, *Revista de España*, July–August 1872, 137.

12. Hill, *Culture and Class*, 5.

13. Koehler, "American Preface."

14. Bennett, *Birth of the Museum* and *Museums and Citizenship*, 5–6.

15. Bennett notes that museums, panoramas, world's fairs, and other mid-nineteenth-century exhibition venues contributed to disciplining British society by "simultaneously ordering objects for public inspection and ordering the public that inspected" ("Exhibitionary Complex," 74).

16. Strobel, *Spanish Revolution*, 32–33.

17. Ibid., 69.

18. February 17, 1870, AGA Grupo de fondos 5, fondo 1.7, Caja 31 6783.

19. Alcolea Blanch, *Prado*, 59.

20. AGA Grupo de fondos 5, fondo 1.7, Caja 31 6783.

21. October 8, 1870, "Al Director General de Instrucción Pública," AGA Grupo de fondos 5, fondo 1.7, Caja 31 6783.

22. Letter from Antonio Gisbert to the Minister of Fomento, April 19, 1870, AGA Grupo de fondos 5, fondo 1.7, Caja 31 6783.

23. Ibid.

24. As referenced by "Eguren" in Madoz, *Diccionario*, 859, qtd. Alcolea Blanch, *Prado*, 61.

25. Decree of November 25, 1870. Full text in English in Alcolea Blanch, *Prado*, 62–63.

26. December 2, 1870. AGA Grupo de fondos 5, fondo 1.7, Caja 31 6783. Al Excmo. Sr. Ministro de Fomento, Excmo. Sr., D. Pedro de Madrazo, 9.

27. In his 1870 proposal for merging the two museums, quoted above.

28. The fire is cited in the preamble of the royal decree of March 22; reported in *El Café*, March 18, 1872, 44.

29. Decree of March 23, 1872.

30. *El Imparcial*, July 23, 1872, 3; *La Esperanza*, July 29, 1872, 4.

31. Perez Sánchez, *Pasado, presente y futuro*, 30–32.

32. February 27, 1886. AGA Grupo de fondos 5, fondo 7.1, Caja 31 6797, "1886, Asuntos Generales."

33. The most recent *Enciclopedia del Museo del Prado* online states that it fell again under the jurisdiction of the Ministry of Hacienda, although my sources suggest that it remained subordinated to the Fomento.

34. July 16, 1873. Archivo MNP, Caja 1378 Legajo 11 282, Exp. 2.

35. *Enciclopedia del Museo del Prado* online.

36. Decree of November 14, 1873.

37. June 15, 1874. AGP, Sección Administrativa, Museo de Pintura y Escultura, Legajo 460.

38. *La América*, 12, no. 20 (October 28, 1868): 5–7.

39. "Las reformas del Retiro," *La Época*, April 28, 1874, 1.

40. AGA Grupo de fondos 5, fondo 1.7, Caja 31 6783, "Acta de entrega 6 de Mayo."

41. *Gil Blas*, October 15, 1868, 4.

42. Ibid.; Hugo, *Notre-Dame de Paris*.

43. Victorino López Fabra's letter to *La Época*, quoted above, specifically mentioned the need to avoid the museum ending up "sunk under the hill" covered with new blocks of flats.

44. *La Gaceta de Madrid*, June 27, 1871, 4; *La Época*, June 26, 1871, 3.

45. *La Época*, August 16, 1869, 3; *La Esperanza*, August 15, 1870, 3.

46. *La Iberia*, March 23, 1869, 1.

47. *La Época*, March 23, 1869, 3.

48. Nicolás Díaz Benjumea, "Revista de la semana," *El Museo Universal*, February 14, 1869, 2.

49. June 26, 1869. AGP, Sección Administrativa, Legajo 460–2, Exp. "D. Antonio Pérez solicita permiso para colocar sillas de hierro en el Jardín del Museo de Pintura."

50. September 12, 1873. Archivo MNP, Caja 1429.

51. De Amicis, *Spain*, 122.

52. Boyd, "Un lugar de memoria olvidado."

53. José Picón, "Diálogo entre D. Ventura Rodríguez y D. Juan de Villanueva," *La América* 13, no. 12 (1869): 8.

54. *La Iberia*, April 4, 1869.

55. "Ley de aranceles," 1869.

56. "En un Museo de pinturas," *Periódico para todos*, January 31, 1874, 15.

57. Valis, *The Culture of "Cursilería."*

58. Salez Mayo, *Condesita*; see also Rodríguez de Rivera, "Placer solitario."

59. Fernando Martín Redondo, "Manufacturas poéticas," *La Ilustración Española y Americana* 18, no. 31 (August 22, 1874): 6.

60. Archivo MNP, Registro de Copiantes, 1864–73.

61. María del Pilar Sinués de Marco, "Los Mártires del siglo XIX," *La Moda Elegante*, August 14, 1869, 239; for an in-depth analysis of Sinués de Marco's four-volume *Gallery of Famous Women* [*Galería de mujeres célebres*], see Sánchez Llama, *Galería*, 347–65.

62. *La guirnalda*, November 16, 1873.

63. Charnon-Deutsch, *Fictions of the Feminine*, 97–101.

64. Salvador Maria de Fábregues, "La cruz de Santiago," *La Moda Elegante* 29, no. 27 (July 22, 1870): 222; no. 28 (July 30, 1870): 227–29.

255

65. "La semana del hambre," *Gil Blas*, July 8, 1869, 2; "Cabos sueltos," *Gil Blas*, October 11, 1871, 4; "Cabos sueltos," *Gil Blas*, October 26, 1871, 4.

66. Ponzano, "En el museo de pinturas," *El Mundo Cómico*, June 1, 1873, 3.

67. *La Iberia*, April 4, 1869, 2.

68. *El Combate*, March 5, 1872, 4.

69. "Allí están mejor," *La Iberia*, February 17, 1870, 3; *La Esperanza*, April 1, 1872, 4.

70. Géal, "Salón de la Reina Isabel," 168. For an in-depth overview of the reception of Goya, see Glendinning, *Goya*; Smith, "Recepción."

71. *El Imparcial*, March 24, 1871, 3; *La Época*, March 24, 1871, 4.

72. April 22, 1871. Archivo MNP, Caja 359; June 10, 1874. AGA Grupo de fondos 5, fondo 1.7, Caja 31 6784.

73. June 10, 1874. AGA, Grupo de fondos 5, fondo 1.7, Caja 31 6784.

74. Giner de los Ríos, *Manual de Estética*, viii; López-Ocón Cabrera, "El papel de Juan Facundo Riaño," 86.

75. Published in *La Esperanza*, February 20, 1869, 2.

76. *La Correspondencia de España*, December 5, 1868, 4.

77. Bolaños, *Historia de los museos en España*, 226–31.

78. *La Esperanza*, May 19, 1870, 2; *La Esperanza*, August 24, 1870, 1.

79. April 10, 1872. AGA, Grupo de fondos 5, fondo 1.7, Caja 31 6783.

80. Poleró, *Breves observaciones*, 6.

81. Poleró, "Museos de Madrid," 1871, 4.

82. Ibid.

83. *El Arte en España* 6 (1868): 268–78; Hernando Carrasco, *Bellas artes*.

84. Cruzada Villaamil, "Lo que ha hecho," 268, 269.

85. Ibid., 269.

86. Tubino dedicated to the topic two extensive articles published in the liberal magazine *Revista de España*: "El Museo del Prado, la Academia de Bellas Artes y el Catálogo del Señor Madrazo," *Revista de España* 119 (November–December 1872): 506–30, and "La reforma artística," *Revista de España*, March 1873, 170–85.

87. Tubino, "El Museo del Prado," 507

88. Ibid.

89. Ibid., 511.

90. Ibid., 512–13.

91. Ibid., 508; Tubino, "La reforma artística," 175.

92. Tubino, "Museo del Prado," 517.

93. Tubino, "Reforma artística," 171.

94. Ibid.

95. Ibid., 176.

96. Ceferino Araujo Sánchez, "El Museo de Madrid, la Academia de San Fernando y el Nuevo Catálogo del Señor Don Pedro de Madrazo," *Revista de España*, March 1873, 477.

97. Araujo Sánchez, "Museo de Madrid," 480.

98. Initially published as Ceferino Araujo Sánchez, "Los Museos de España" I, *Revista Europea* 71 (July 4, 1875): 18–19.

99. Ibid., 19.

100. The initial draft (October 30, 1870. AGA, Grupo de fondos 5, fondo 7.1, Caja 31 6784) was prepared by an official working for the Dirección General de Instrucción Pública. The Ministerio de Fomento issued the decree on November 25, 1870 (*Decreto nombrando una Comisión encargada de proponer las bases para refundir en uno los Museos de Pintura y Escultura del Prado y de la Trinidad*, published in the *Gaceta de Madrid*, November 27, 1870). See also Antigüedad and Alzaga Ruiz, *Colecciones*, 116–18.

101. AGA, Grupo de fondos 5, fondo 1.7, Caja 31 6707, "Temas propuestos para el concurso conforme el Capítulo 3 del reglamento de 5 de julio de 1871, Sección de Museos."

102. *La Discusión*, November 28, 1868, 4.

103. *La Época*, November 24, 1873, 1–2.

104. October 16, 1868. AGP, Sección Administrativa, Museo de Pintura y Escultura, Legajo 460–3, Carpeta "Fechos en 1851."

105. For a summary of Federico de Madrazo's proposal, see October 30, 1868. AGP, Sección Administrativa, Museo de Pintura y Escultura, Legajo 460–3, Carpeta "Fechos en 1851," Exp. s/n.

106. November 23, 1868. AGP, Sección Administrativa, Museo de Pintura y Escultura, Legajo 460–2, Carpeta "Museo en 1868," Exp. 15.

107. December 10, 1868. AGP, Sección Administrativa, Museo de Pintura y Escultura, Legajo 460–2, Carpeta "Museo en 1868," Exp. s/n.

108. October 30, 1870. AGA, Grupo de fondos 5, fondo 1.7, Caja 31 6784.

109. August 20, 1874. AGA, Grupo de fondos 5, fondo 1.7, Caja 31 6793.

110. Sans's memorandum of October 7, 1874, contained a detailed explanation of his plans for the future of the museum's expansion. AGA, Grupo de fondos 5, fondo 1.7, Caja 31 6793.

111. *La Época*, March 24, 1871, 4.

112. November 18, 1872. AGA, Grupo de fondos 5, fondo 1.7, Caja 31 6784.

113. See, for example, Sans's proposals to Bellas Artes concerning the exchange of holdings with other museums starting June 15, 1874. AGA, Grupo de fondos 5, fondo 1.7, Caja 31 6784.

114. Ibid.

115. Petitions of December 10, 1873, and February 10, 1874. AGA, Grupo de fondos 5, fondo 1.7, Caja 31 6784.

116. "4° trimestre de 1873–74." AGA, Grupo de fondos 5, fondo 1.7, Caja 31 6793.

117. January 22, 1875. AGA, Grupo de fondos 5, fondo 1.7, Caja 31 6793.

CHAPTER 4

1. "Dinero para la Guerra," *El País*, July 2, 1898, 1. The most radical position in support of selling the paintings belonged to José Nakens, republican anticlerical writer and the founder of *El Motín*, a satirical weekly, where he ran a series of articles against maintaining the museum: "Palos y pedradas," August 23, 1885, 3; "El dedo en la llaga," November 22, 1885, 3; "Al general de moda," June 5, 1887, 1.

2. Rodrigo Soriano, "500.000.000," *El Imparcial*, October 24, 1898, 3–4.

3. Alcolea Blanch cites Soriano's 1923 article "Arte, millones . . ." in *La Libertad*, testifying that the assessment of the collection was no joke, at least in the framework of postwar reparations (*Prado*, 72). Gaya Nuño quotes Alice B. Saarinen's testimony concerning Henry Havemeyer's wish that the United States indeed request the Prado in exchange for the Philippines (Saarinen, *Proud Possessors*, 163, qtd. Gaya Nuño, *Historia*, 132). Back in Spain, the consensus among Spaniards that the museum could not be sold may have been stronger than it seems: in 1901 Nakens's *El Motín* praised a collection of articles by Soriano that included an eloquent defense of the museum, "Lo que vale un museo" ("Las flores rojas," *El Motín*, June 8, 1901, 3).

4. Facos and Hirsch, *Art, Culture*.

5. Storm, *Culture of Regionalism*.

6. Widén, "National Museums in Sweden," 1056–57.

7. Silverman, *Art Nouveau*, 153.

8. Koselleck, "On the Anthropological."

9. Weiner, *Architecture*, 19–26.

10. Dowling, *Vulgarization*, 43. Nietzsche, in "What Do Ascetic Ideals Mean?," famously criticized the Kantian ideal of "disinterested" contemplation, using the example of the nude female statue. Relevant texts against the moralizing function of art include Joris-Karl Huysmans's *À rebours* (1884) and Oscar Wilde's *The Picture of Dorian Gray* (1891).

11. As exemplified by Whistler's philippics against Ruskin, analyzed in Dowling, *Vulgarization of Art*, 46–49. See also Bailey, *Leisure and Class*, 116–32, and Maleuvre, *Museum Memories*.

12. Conlin, *Nation's Mantelpiece*, 237.

13. Ibid., 235–39.

14. Carrier, *Museum Skepticism*.

15. Koven, "Whitechapel."

16. That film required a special—collective—spectatorship was argued in Benjamin's 1936 "The Work of Art." Sandberg's *Living Pictures* has been the most influential text for tracing continuities between end-of-the-century art and cinema spectatorship.

17. Faulkner, Sánchez-Biosca, and Smith, "Cinema"; López Serrano, *Madrid*.

18. Maleuvre, *Museum Memories*, 3.

19. Bailey, "Adventures in Space."

20. Switzer, "Hungarian Self-Representation"; Hirsh, "Swiss Art."

21. Qureshi, *Peoples on Parade*; on "autoethnography," see Buzard, *Disorienting Fiction*.

22. Qtd. Widén, "National Museums in Sweden."

23. Silverman, *Art Nouveau*.

24. Holt, *Expanding World*, vol. 2, 138–46.

25. Zola, *L'assommoir*, 441–46.

26. Harris, "Museums."

27. Duncan, "Museums and Department Stores"; Bastida de la Calle, "Imagen de la mujer pintora."

28. Brown and Dodd, "Society of Female Artists"; D'Souza and McDonough, *Invisible Flâneuse?*

29. Brown and Dodd, "Society of Female Artists," 87.

30. Ceferino Araujo Sánchez, "Deficiencias del arte oficial," *El Día*, January 1, 1887, 1.

31. "Discurso de 25 de febrero de 1877," *El Globo*, February 28, 1877, 3.

32. Direct universal suffrage was established on June 26, 1890. The article was published in *La Monarquía*, May 27, 1890, 3.

33. November 22, 1890. Archivo MNP, Caja 1304; AGA, Caja 31 6797.

34. *El Día*, March 29, 1887, 1.

35. Bolaños, "Bellezas prestadas."

36. *El Día*, March 29, 1887, 1.

37. Bolaños, *Historia*, 249–301.

38. González López and Martí Ayxelà, *Los Madrazo*.

39. González Cuevas, "El rey," 191.

40. "El Palacio del Senado: Memoria del Sr. Maques de Barzanallana. Continuación," *Diario Oficial de Avisos de Madrid*, July 31, 1882, 4.

41. The Anthropological Museum and colonial exhibitions were more politicized than the Prado, as shown in Bolaños, *Historia*, 268–78, and Martín Márquez, *Disorientations*, 64–100.

42. Emilio Castelar, "14 Julio 1895," in *Crónica internacional 1890–1898*, http://www.biblioteca.org.ar/libros/70821.pdf.

43. Gaya Nuño, *Historia*, 123–25; Alcolea Blanch, *Prado*, 70–71.

44. *La Gaceta de Instrucción Pública*, January 30, 1896, 6.

45. S., "Pradilla," *El Imparcial*, February 3, 1896, 1–2. The author was playing on the allegory of The

Conquest of Granada, one of Pradilla's paintings. *Gaceta de Instrucción pública*, January 31, 1896, 6.

46. M. de C. [Mariano de Cavia?], "Españolería andante," *Correspondencia de España*, February 12, 1897, 1; *La Iberia*, January 26, 1897, 3; "Pradilla," *Diario Oficial de Avisos de Madrid*, February 12, 1897, 2.

47. *Correspondencia de España*, November 1, 1896, 4. For the donations that the museum received under Pradilla, as well as lost opportunities to expand the collection, see Alcolea Blanch, *Prado*, 71.

48. *La Discusión*, February 11, 3.

49. Half of the ushers (four out of eight) were appointed after 1868, but only one of the four doormen had been appointed after 1868. The museum's oldest employee, José Sieres, had been working since 1838.

50. July 26, 1884. AGA, Grupo de fondos 5, fondo 1.7, Caja 32 6797.

51. December 6, 1887. AGA, Grupo de fondos 5, fondo 1.7, Caja 31 6797. There are eleven signatures under the petition.

52. Araujo Sánchez, "Deficiencias del arte oficial," *El Día*, January 1, 1887, 1.

53. "Ecos de Madrid," *La Época*, July 1, 1875, 4.

54. Mariblanca Caneyro, *Retiro*, 201.

55. José Fernández Bremón, "Crónica general," *La Ilustración Española y Americana* 21, no. 46 (December 15, 1877): 370.

56. *La Iberia*, November 25, 1877, 3; *La Iberia*, December 26, 1877, 3; *La Época*, January 9, 1878, 4.

57. See also the overview by Fernandez Bremón, quoted above (*La Ilustración Española y Americana* 21, no. 46 [December 15, 1877]: 370).

58. *La Iberia*, January 1, 1878, 3.

59. *El Globo*, December 11, 1877, 3.

60. Fernández Bremón, "Crónica General," *La Ilustración española y Americana* 23, no. 19 (May 22, 1879): 330.

61. Blanco, *Cultura y conciencia*, 49–78; Sánchez Gómez, *Un imperio en la vitrina*, 71.

62. Sánchez Gómez, *Un imperio en la vitrina*, 47, 69–70.

63. Blanco, *Cultura y conciencia*, 63.

64. Versteeg, *Jornaleros*.

65. "Sección de noticias," *El Imparcial*, May 13, 1878, 1.

66. "Bazar de Postizos," *El Globo*, September 7, 1878, 4.

67. Qtd. Moleón Gavilanes, *Proyectos y obras*, 191.

68. Ibid., 76, 200–207.

69. Ibid., 207, 214.

70. November 3, 1881. AGA, Grupo de fondos 5, fondo 7.1, Caja 31 6797.

71. "Gente de fuera," *El Imparcial*, June 16, 1890, 6–7.

72. Leopoldo López de Saa, "Notas de la semana," *Nuevo Mundo*, October 27, 1897, 4.

73. "Tiroteos," *Militares y paisanos*, Suplemento semanal ilustrado a *La Correspondencia Militar*, May 17, 1896, 7.

74. *El Liberal*, May 14, 1884, 4. Facing the museum, the puppet theater was installed next to the building of the former Platería Martínez, by that time a private art show. The date suggests that the puppet theater was a part of the San Isidro Fair.

75. Afinoguenova, "Entre pitos y flautas."

76. López Serrano, *Madrid*, 24.

77. Ricardo de la Vega, "De todo un poco," *Madrid Cómico* 1, no. 38 (September 19, 1880): 1-2.

78. *La Correspondencia de España*, April 5, 1877, 3.

79. "Museo patológico anatómico," *La Iberia*, December 27, 1882, 3. For European prototypes and colonial sources, see García González, *Cuerpo abierto*, 305.

80. "Las fiestas de Velázquez," *Gedeón*, June 7, 1899, 3.

81. *El Globo*, March 15, 1877, 3; *La Correspondencia de España*, March 15, 1877, 3; "Varios sucesos," *La Época*, November 14, 1897, 3; *Diario Oficial de Avisos*, May 13, 1877, 2; *El Siglo Futuro*, May 22, 1885, 4; *El Imparcial*, June 24, 1891, 3.

82. "Noticias: Madrid," *El País*, July 14, 1887, 2.

83. José López Silva, "Nocturnos," *Madrid Cómico* 3, no. 29 (September 9, 1883): 7.

84. February 9, 1876. AGA, Grupo de fondos 5, fondo 7.1, Caja 31 6784.

85. *El Globo*, February 16, 1883, 3.

86. *El Imparcial*, February 16, 1883, 2.

87. *El Siglo Futuro*, April 6, 1897, 2.

88. Rafael de Nieva, "Las botas de mi amigo Ricardo (novela realista)," *La Ilustración Artística* 9, no. 426 (February 24, 1890): 498–51.

89. *El Imparcial*, May 26, 1890, 1–2.

90. This was particularly noticeable when covering the rally of the *cigarreras*, women workers at the Madrid tobacco factory, held in June 1896. *El País*, June 27, 1896, 1.

91. Frost, *Cultivating Madrid*.

92. *La Iberia*, December 20, 1878, 2.

93. Moleón Gavilanes, *Proyectos y obras*, 221.

94. Hernando Carrasco, *Bellas artes*, 87–89; Géal, "Admirar y recordar"; *La Iberia*, January 21, 1879, 2; "Impresiones políticas," *La Unión*, January 22, 1879, 1; *La Iberia*, January 22, 1879, 2.

95. "Estatuas de Velarde y Daoíz," *El Globo*, May 2, 1898, 2.

96. Luxenberg, "Regenerating Velázquez." As Luxenberg notes, the location in front of the museum, now seemingly logical, was actually not the first on the list. Just like the monument to Murillo, the statue to Velázquez was a civil undertaking carried out by individuals and corporations with some government support.

97. Ibid.

98. Portela Sandoval, "La ciudad," 75.

99. Ramírez de Saavedra Rivas, *De literatura y arte*, 218.

100. Carlos Ossorio y Gallardo, "Las papeletas," *El Álbum Ibero Americano* 7, no. 35 (September 22, 1899): 416; Kasabal, "Madrid," *La Ilustración Ibérica*, Barcelona 8, no. 383 (May 3, 1890): 274. These claims may not have been unwarranted given the museum's increasing popularity among foreign artists such as John Singer Sargent and Mary Cassatt (Boone, *Vistas*).

101. Bolaños, *Historia*, 249–78.

102. Rodrigo Soriano, "La exposición del Círculo de Bellas Artes" II, *La Lidia: Revista Semanal Ilustrada* 12, no. 13 (June 10, 1894): 140.

103. Ignotus, "En el Museo," *La Risa* 1, no. 14 (April 1, 1888): 8.

104. A. Danvila Jaldero, "Diálogos Matritenses," *La Ilustración Artística*, Barcelona 13, no. 651 (June 18, 1894): 388.

105. Iakovlev, Очерки, 198.

106. Afinoguénova, "El neocatolicismo."

107. *La Época*, June 12, 1894, 3.

108. José Fernández Bremón, "Crónica general," *La Ilustración española y americana* 40, no. 4 (January 30, 1896): 58.

109. *La Correspondencia de España*, October 5, 1901, 1; "Entierro de D. Luis Álvarez," *La Época*, October 5, 1901, 3.

110. Labanyi, "Horror."

111. February 6, 1879. AGA, Grupo de fondos 5, fondo 1.7, Caja 31 6785.

112. Nieto-Galán, "Marvels." I am grateful to José María Lanzarote Guiral for drawing my attention to the subject of "hunger art."

113. Shubert, *Death and Money*, 14-16 and throughout.

114. *Boletín de Loterías y de Toros*, March 8, 1880, 3–4.

115. "El arte y los toros," *La Lidia: Revista Taurina* 6, no. 17 (July 25, 1887): 1.

116. Soriano, "La exposición del Círculo de Bellas Artes" II, *La Lidia: Revista Semanal Ilustrada* 12, no. 13 (June 10, 1894): 140.

117. Salaün, "Apogeo," 138.

118. José Ramón Mélida, "La arqueología en el teatro," *La España Moderna* 29 (March 15, 1892): 161.

119. "Augusto Ferri," *La Gran Vía* 13, no. 127 (December 14, 1895): 4.

120. Gies, *Theatre*, 1-39.

121. Smith, *Victorian Nude*, 68–75.

122. Cilla, "En el museo," *Madrid Cómico* 7, no. 266 (June 18, 1887): 8.

123. Carlos Frontaura, "La viuda de Zaragata" II, *La Risa* 1, no. 33 (August 12, 1888): 10.

124. Ignotus, "En el Museo de Pinturas," *La Risa* 1, no. 10 (March 4, 1888): 4.

125. Tristán de Jesús Medina, "Visita a los muertos," *La América* 24, no. 22 (November 28, 1883): 11.

126. Cubas, "En el Museo de Pinturas," *El Mundo Cómico* 4, no. 138 (June 20, 1875): 3.

127. Pérez Galdós, *La desheredada*, 64.

128. Alas (Clarín), *Pipá*, 139.

129. Portús, *Sala Reservada*, 277–83.

130. Hale, *Family Flight*, 289.

131. Pardo Bazán, *Quimera*, 76–77.

132. Qtd. González Herrán, "Pardo Bazán."

133. March 19, 1881. Archivo MNP, Caja 1429. The document states that authorizations were also given to 161 foreigners, but it is not clear whether this was in addition to the ones given above. At any rate, clearly many more Spaniards than foreigners were working at the museum at the end of the 1870s.

134. Diego, *La mujer y la pintura*.

135. "La manifestación de ayer," *El Imparcial*, April 4, 1898, 1.

136. Sauer, *L'entrée des femmes*.

137. Augusto Danvila Jaldero, "Las aficionadas a la pintura," *La Ilustración Artística*, Barcelona, 11 no. 538 (April 18, 1892): 250.

138. Archivo MNP, Caja 1429.

139. Ramón Balsa de la Vega, "Crónica del arte," *La Ilustración Artística*, Barcelona, 11, no. 539 (April 25, 1892): 258.

140. Bashkirtseff, *Journal*, 257. Bashkirtseff visited the Prado in 1881.

141. Mercer, *Urbanism*, 67.

142. Miguel Moya, "El Café," *La América*, 21, no. 11 (June 8, 1880): 14.

143. *El Madrid Cómico*, July 25, 1891, 8.

144. Giner de los Ríos, *Manual*, ix.

145. Portús and Vega, *Descubrimiento*.

146. Otero Urtaza, "Expediciones"; Afinoguénova, "Leisure."

147. "El combate naval de Trafalgar.—La muerte de Virginia.—Carlos V en Yuste.—La educación del príncipe don Juan.—Don Fernando el Emplazado, Juana la Loca.—El perro y el trozo de carne, de Pablo de Voss" ("Excursiones Instructivas," *Boletín de la Institución Libre de Enseñanza* 3 [1879]: 55).

148. Archivo RAH 61-1167, c. 1883–85; Cossío, "La pintura española: Ideas generales," *Boletín de la Institución Libre de Enseñanza* 9 (1885): 375. See also Portús, *Pintura española*; and Afinoguénova, "'Painted.'"

149. Pedro de Madrazo, "Orígenes del Museo del Prado de Madrid," *La Ilustración Artística*, Barcelona, 1, no. 45 (November 5, 1882): 354–58; Manuel Bartolomé de Cossío, "Algunos vacíos del Museo del Prado," *La Ilustración Artística*, Barcelona, 2, no. 86 (August 20, 1883): 271–72.

150. Charnon-Deutsch, *Hold That Pose*, 9–44.

151. Ibid., 65–67; on "absorption," see Fried, *Absorption*.

259

152. Mariano de Cavia, "La catástrofe de anoche: España está de luto; Incendio del Museo de Pinturas," *El Liberal*, November 26, 1891, 2. For a detailed account and reproduction, see Gaya Nuño, *Historia*, 114–21.

153. Mariano de Cavia, "Por qué he incendiado el Museo del Prado," *El Liberal*, November 26, 1891, 1.

154. Ibid.

155. Araujo Sánchez, *Museos de España*, 10–11.

156. March 30, 1875. AGA, Grupo de fondos 5, fondo 1.7, Caja 31 6784.

157. AGA, Grupo de fondos 5, fondo 1.7, Caja 31 6784.

158. Casares, *Barbieri*.

159. Maria Ladvenant, La Caramba, La Tirana, Lorenza Correa, Rita Luna, Isabel Colbrán (Rossini's wife), Antera Baus, Manuela Oreiro y Lema. AGA Grupo de fondos 5, fondo 1.7, Caja 31 6784.

160. AGA, Grupo de fondos 5, fondo 1.7, Caja 31 6784.

161. Ibid.

162. August 28, 1877. AGA, Grupo de fondos 5, fondo 1.7, Caja 31 6784; *La Iberia*, October 24, 1876, 2.

163. November 27, 1884. AGA, Grupo de fondos 5, fondo 1.7, Caja 31 679.

164. November 25, 1884. AGA, Grupo de fondos 5, fondo 1.7, Caja 31 6797.

165. January 11, 1888. AGA, Grupo de fondos 5, fondo 1.7, Caja 31 6797.

166. "Exposiciones," 1883, in *Nuevo Teatro Critico* (Madrid: Administración, 1892), 33.

167. Gaya Nuño, *Historia*, 111.

168. Luxenberg, "Regenerating Velázquez."

169. Meanwhile, the sculpture collection was also reorganized. Its floor plan testifies to a certain tendency toward a chronological arrangement, although inconsistently followed. The art of ancient Greece was located in the apse, underneath the Gallery of Reina Isabel and later of Velázquez. Roman art would occupy the central rotunda leading into this gallery and the room to the right. All following galleries exhibited European works from the sixteenth to the eighteenth centuries in the final rotunda.

CHAPTER 5

1. José Ortega y Gasset's *La rebelión de las masas* first appeared in chapters in *El Sol* between October and November 1929 and was later issued as a book.

2. The period ended with the directorship of the writer Ramón Pérez de Ayala during the Second Republic (1931–36). His was, however, an honorary position: on the very day when the trustees elected him the director of the Prado, Pérez de Ayala was also appointed ambassador for the Republic to the United Kingdom and soon left for London. The bulk of responsibilities was carried out by the deputy director, Francisco Javier Sánchez Cantón, who would become the director of the Prado in 1960.

3. Dowling, *Vulgarization of Art*, 43; Bennett, *Birth* and *Museums and Citizenship*, 5–6.

4. Eduardo Benot, "La loca de la casa," *La Ilustración Artística*, Barcelona, 21, no. 1044 (January 1, 1902), 16.

5. Sheehan, *Museums*, 139.

6. Sizeranne, *Les questions*, 291, qtd. Ovejero, *Concepto*.

7. Schorske, *Fin-de-siècle Vienna*, 100–110.

8. Scheehan, *Museums*, 170.

9. Bazin, *Museum Age*, 265. For a useful summary of museum-bashing moods among modern artists, see Hughes, *Shock*.

10. Maleuvre, *Museum Memories*, 50.

11. Lenman, *Artists and Society in Germany*, 164.

12. Groys, "Struggle."

13. Rabinow, *Cézanne to Picasso*, 176–84.

14. Jenkins, *Provincial Modernity*; Poulot, "Identity as Self-Discovery," 68–69.

15. Benjamin, *Arcades*.

16. Schwarz, *Spectacular Realities*.

17. Eley, *Forging Democracy*, 261–77; Wolikow, *L'internationale Communiste*; Dell, *Image*.

18. Barañano and Cátedra, "Representación"; Schammah Gesser, "Museos."

19. Bazin, *Museum Age*, 363; Hoffmann, "German Art Museum," 13.

20. Conlin, *Nation's Mantelpiece*, 343.

21. Norman, *Hermitage*.

22. Ovejero, *Concepto actual*.

23. Lambourne, *War Damage*, 12–41; Bruquetas Galán, "Protección"; Visscher, "Protection," 266–69. The initial legal framework for the protection of heritage during wartime was established during the Brussels Conference (1874); it was later taken on at the next Brussels Conference (1907) and at the Hague Convention (1907). Unless the monuments were used for military purposes, the protection to monuments and works of art was declared a responsibility of the attacking army. In 1923, in another meeting in The Hague, a packet of measures was discussed for protecting monuments and works of art against air attacks; these included establishing, around those monuments, neutral zones with oversight from international experts. These measures were collected in article 26 of the Protocol of Rules of Air Warfare, which was never ratified, although it had support from the major human rights experts of the time.

24. There were 1,675 paintings exhibited.

25. While the Junta was slowly negotiating the details—which were never agreed on—publishers swiftly produced three beautiful books with the portraits of famous Spanish men and women from the Prado: *Retratos de mujeres por Goya*, *Retratos de hombres célebres del Museo del Prado*, and *Retratos de Mujeres célebres del Museo del Prado*, all part of the the series Los grandes maestros de la pintura en España (Madrid: Fernando Fe, 1909).

26. "El panteón de hombres ilustres," *La Época*, May 19, 1902, 2.

27. "La exhumación de Larra, Espronceda y Rosales," *El Liberal*, May 25, 1902, 1.

28. "El panteón de hombres ilustres"; "El panteón de hombres ilustres," *El Liberal*, May 24, 1902, 2.

29. Boyd, "Lugar de memoria."

30. R. Mesa de la Peña, "Bocetos: Los extranjeros," *La Correspondencia Militar*, April 1, 1902, 1.

31. "Los toros y la monarquía," *El País*, May 23, 1902, 1.

32. Qtd. La Parra López, "Alfonso XIII," 433.

33. Quiroga, *Football*.

34. "El primer congreso español de bellas artes," *La Ilustración Española y Americana* 62, no. 19 (May 22, 1918): 292.

35. "Sin gobiernos," *El País*, July 1, 1905, 1.

36. Moreno Luzón, *Alfonso XIII*, 15.

37. Quiroga, *Making Spaniards*, 6.

38. *Monos*, June 23, 1906, 8.

39. Archivo MNP, Caja 369.

40. Archivo MNP, Fondo Álvarez Sotomayor, 1923.

41. "Nuestro activo Consejo: Las influencias poderosas de los porteros de casa rica," *La Voz*, December 23, 1924, 8.

42. Julio Esquivel, "Rosquillas y Pitos," *Iris*, May 12, 1900, 11.

43. This was, however, hardly true because the museum was usually free during these days.

44. Archivo MNP, 1905: "quedan prohibidas las verbenas en las inmediaciones del Museo de Pintura." June 1909, identical decree.

45. "Las verbenas," *El Globo*, June 21, 1913, 3.

46. Ibid.

47. "Ayuntamiento.—La Sesión de ayer," *El Imparcial*, July 24, 1915, 5.

48. Pedro Mata, "El odio a la Verbena," *ABC* (Madrid), May 14, 1916, 14.

49. *La Época*, July 1, 1930, 4.

50. Juan Palomo, "De mi archivo: Cien dibujos," *Nuevo Mundo* 22, no. 1116 (May 29, 1915): 35.

51. Pedro Mata, "El odio a la Verbena."

52. Gómez de la Serna, *Paseo*, 1.

53. Antonio Zozaya, "Divulgadores humildes," *La Libertad*, November 2, 1924, 1–2.

54. Insúa, *Señorita*, 60.

55. Bonet, "De la verbena a Vallecas"; Mangini, *Maruja Mallo*, 66–80. See also Pérez Rojas, *Ciudad placentera*.

56. Mangini, "Madrid es un cabaret."

57. Ramón Gómez de la Serna, "Una verbena bien situada," *El Sol*, July 6, 1930, 3.

58. Ernesto Giménez Caballero, dir., *La esencia de la verbena* (1930), 12 min.; the quotation occurs at 7:30.

59. "La primera verbena republicana," *El Heraldo de Madrid*, May 2, 1931, 1.

60. "A favor de los obreros sin trabajo," *El Heraldo de Madrid*, June 20, 1931, 2; "La tradicional verbena de Montepío de actores españoles," *La Libertad*, July 14, 1931, n.p.; "'Futball. La final del XXII Campeonato de España . . . y la del II Campeonato Amateur," *El Heraldo de Madrid*, June 20, 1931, 10.

61. "Noches verbeneras," *La Voz*, June 20, 1931, 6.

62. "Trece comunistas detenidos," *La Libertad*, August 13, 1931, 8.

63. "Comentarios," *El Imparcial*, June 24, 1932, 6.

64. Juliá, *Madrid 1931–1934*.

65. "Aviso a los señores carteristas," *El Heraldo de Madrid*, June 20, 1933, 4.

66. "La verbena de San Juan—Programa de festejos," *El Sol*, June 25, 1933, 3; "Las bellas durmientes del salón del Prado, o un paseo por la verbena en la octava de San Juan," *La Voz*, June 27, 1934, 3; "La típica verbena de San Pedro," *El Madrid Ilustrado* 2, no. 8 (June 1935): 2.

67. Sánchez Cantón, *Walks Through Madrid*, 15–16 (adapted from the original English translation—E.A.).

68. "Vida municipal," *La Época*, January 23, 1934, 4.

69. "Una verbena en el tubo de la risa," *El Siglo Futuro*, July 20, 1933, 1; "El tubo de la risa," *La Voz*, July 20, 1933, 1.

70. "El Sr. Azaña fue objeto de una manifestación de entusiasmo cuando paseaba por la verbena," *El Heraldo de Madrid*, July 8, 1835, 1.

71. "Como temíamos, Manolo acaba exhibiéndose en una verbena," *Gracia y Justicia* 4, no. 186 (July 13, 1935): 8.

72. "Some [political] novices were very impressed, but I remembered the night of April 14, 1931, and also the one in May that preceded the burning of convents, and to me all that seemed like a verbena" (Azaña, *Obras completas*, 4:569).

73. "En el senado," *La Correspondencia de España*, December 6, 1910, 5 (El Sr. Pulido), and "Retablo parlamentario: Los abuelos de la patria y la batalla de Bailén," *La Voz*, June 3, 1921, 4.

74. December 27, 1901.

75. "Viendo Madrid," *La Correspondencia de España*, February 4, 1902, 2.

76. Portús, *Concepto*, 147.

77. "Particularismos," *El Globo*, December 11, 1901, 1.

78. "Panorama universal," *Hojas Selectas: Revista para todos*, Barcelona, 1 (1902): 77.

79. "Recepción," *La Dinastía*, March 2, 1903, 1.

80. *El Siglo Futuro*, March 3, 1903.

81. AGA, Grupo de fondos 5, fondo 1.7, Caja 31 6798.

82. "Noticias," *Revista General de Enseñanza y Bellas Artes* 35 (June 1, 1911): 12.

83. *El Imparcial*, February 23, 1911, 3.

84. "Real Decreto creando un Patronato del Museo Nacional de Pintura y Escultura, encargado de recoger y emplear los recursos destinado á la adquisición de cuadros á objetos que por su valor artístico deban figurar en dicho Museo Nacional," *Gaceta de Madrid*, June 9, 1912, 569–71.

85. Ibid., 569–70.

86. Ibid.

87. Ibid., 570.

88. Gaya Nuño, *Historia*, 139.

89. "Real Decreto creando un Patronato," 570.

90. Ibid.

91. Moleón Gavilanes, *Proyectos y obras*, 86-87.

92. Ibid., 88.

93. Barón, *Errazu*.

94. Gaya Nuño, *Historia*, 141–42.

95. *Enciclopedia del Museo Nacional del Prado* online, http://www.museodelprado. es/ enciclopedia/enciclopedia-on-line/voz/ bosch-y-barrau-pablo/.

96. "La vida en Madrid," *La Correspondencia de España*, October 14, 1920, 1.

97. Sánchez Cantón, "Reorganización," 292.

98. Ramón Gómez de la Serna, "Angulos de Madrid: El Reloj de Goya," *Luz*, August 5, 1932, 3.

99. Currently at the AGA, together with the rest of materials from Alfonso Sánchez Portela's studio. In the archive, the series is dated "November 1936." By that date, however, the museum was closed and its paintings transported to Valencia. In fact, these photographs are from 1935. They accompanied the article by Felipe Morales ("El Museo del Prado, de doce a una. Los niños, los soldados, los enamorados y los campesinos frente a Goya y Murillo"), published in *Informaciones* on 21 November, 1935 (Archivo MNP).

100. Antonio de la Serena [Antonio Otero Seco], "Lo que se ha llevado la guerra. Jueves: Visita a los copistas del Museo," *Mundo Gráfico* 27 (June 30, 1937): n.p.

101. M., "La vida madrileña," *La Época*, Madrid, March 8, 1907, 1.

102. Ibid.

103. Zubiaurre, *Cultures of the Erotic*.

104. Félix Limendoux, *Las mujeres galantes*, vol. 1 (Madrid: Ramón Sopena, 1902), back cover.

105. Mariano de Cavia, "Un estigma de los tiempos," *Las Dominicales: Semanario Librepensador* 4, no. 152 (1904): 3.

106. "El desnudo en el arte," *Sicalíptico: Revista semanal ilustrada*, Barcelona, 1, no. 43 (October 29, 1904): 13.

107. Zubiaurre, *Cultures of the Erotic*, 213.

108. Johnson, *Gender and Nation*; Tsuchiya, *Marginal Subjects*.

109. Keene, "Clear Air"; Offen, "Aventura del sufragio" and "Feminists Campaign in 'Public Space.'"

110. "Turistas," *El Heraldo de Madrid* (September 18, 1906), 1.

111. *El Pueblo*, May 29, 1907, qtd. Núñez Rey, "Carmen de Burgos"; see also Louis, *Women and Law* and "Carmen de Burgos"; Rotjer Rødtjer, "Ancestral Line," chap. 8.

112. Burgos (Colombine), *La que quiso ser Maja*. I am grateful to Rocio Rødtjer for drawing my attention to the importance of this novel.

113. Such a gender-inclusive version of modernism constituted, in Johnson's argument, Burgos's major contribution to an otherwise male-centered discussion of Spain's social modernization ("Carmen de Burgos and Spanish Modernism").

114. Cabañas Bravo, "Nelken," 464. During the Second Republic, Nelken was a trustee of the Museo de Arte Moderno (Museum of Modern Art) in Madrid. Her first collection of essays about art, *Glosario*, was published in 1917. In 1930, Nelken's guidebook for the Prado Museum, called in Spanish *Meditaciones sobre el Prado* (Madrid: CIAP) and in French *Guide spirituel du Prado* (Paris: Van Oest) was listed as "in press" on the promotional pages at the end of her *Las escritoras españolas* (Madrid: Labor, 1930), 236. Neither Cabanillas ("Las mujeres y la crítica") nor I has been able to find this text in either French or Spanish, suggesting that it may not have been published.

115. Nelken, *Condición*, 14–15. On Nelken's political persona and specifically on the social responses to the aforementioned book, see Preston, *Doves of War*, 307–9.

116. *El Crisol*, January 6, 1932, 9.

117. Capel Martínez, *Sufragio*, 162–92.

118. Nelken, *Glosario*.

119. Preston, *Doves of War*, 307.

120. Nelken, *Maternología*. According to Cabañas Bravo ("Margarita Nelken," 465), Nelken received an honorary recognition from the Consejo Superior de Protección a la Infancia.

121. Nelken, *Tres tipos de Vírgen*.

122. José Francés, "La suprema ejemplaridad humana de la maternidad divina," *Nuevo Mundo*, December 22, 1933, n.p.

123. José S. Santonja, "Una pequeña diferencia," *Muchas Gracias* 7, no. 347 (October 4, 1930): 7.

124. Luis González de Linares, "Ya no es negocio copiar cuadros en el museo del Prado . . . porque los millonarios norteamericanos han perdido mucho dinero en Wall Street," *Estampa* 5, no. 209 (January 9, 1932): 8.

125. Kirkpatrick, *Mujer*, 67; Chacel, *Maravillas*, 33. If Isabel was indeed, as the critics agree, the autobiographical alter ego of Chacel (who was born in 1898), then the scene at the Prado is set around 1908, the year of Chacel's arrival in Madrid.

126. Qtd. Hiriart, *Conversaciones*.

127. Mangini, *Modernas*.

128. Vicente Sánchez-Ocaña, "Celia Gámez, a la puerta del convento," *Estampa* 3, no. 137 (August 26, 1930): n.p.

129. Mangini, *Maruja Mallo*; Diego, *Mujer*; Muñoz López, "Mujeres," 83–85.

130. Silvio Lago [José Francés], "Las copias de Goya que se envían al extranjero," Fotos por Cortés, *Nuevo Mundo* 35, no. 1787 (April 20, 1928), n.p.

131. Archivo MNP, Caja 1377 (my calculation—E.A.).

132. Caro Baroja, *Los Baroja*, 422, qtd. Portús, *Memoria escrita*, 297.

133. "Conversaciones: Ricardo Baroja va a representar una exposición de pinturas en París, dice que los fotógrafos lo hacen mejor que los pintores," *El Heraldo de Madrid*, December 23, 1927, 16.

134. The Catholic *La Lectura Dominical* dismissively called the event "exposición de pintores hembras" and stated that "women do not feel color except when they put it on their faces" (June 28, 1903).

135. "La exposición en broma: Telas y Barro," *Blanco y Negro*, May 9, 1908, 17.

136. "Los festejos de Mayo," *El País*, May 5, 1910, 1.

137. "Las fiestas de Carnaval," *El País*, January 13, 1910, 2.

138. Ibid.

139. "La Cabalgata del Comercio," *La Correspondencia de España*, June 2, 1910, 4.

140. Ibid., 5.

141. "Festejos: La Cabalgata de ayer," *Informaciones de Madrid*, June 9, 1910, 4.

142. Sánchez Cantón, *Walks Through Madrid*, 35. The book was a translation of Sánchez Cantón's 1930 *Paseos por Madrid y excursiones a Toledo, Alcalá, El Escorial y Aranjuez*.

143. In 1904 one journalist reported that "many special visits" were paid to the museum in the wake of a masquerade ball in the house of the marquises of Monteagudo (S.-A., "Crónicas Masdrileñas," *El Heraldo de Madrid*, February 8, 1904), 1).

144. Hidalgo, *La infanta baila*; Cansino, *Misterio*, among many others.

145. Enrique Sá del Rey, "*La brocha gorda*: Revista en un acto, en prosa y verso, dividido en tres cuadros y un prólogo, original de los Sres. Capella y González Pastor, música de los maestros Torregrosa y Calleja, estrenada en el Gran Teatro," *El Arte del Teatro: Revista Quincenal Ilustrada* 2, no. 30 (June 15, 1907): 6–8.

146. "Estampa de navidad: Gazetillas," *La Voz*, December 23, 1924, 7.

147. La enciclopedia del Prado online; "Robo insólito en el Museo de Pinturas," *La Acción*, September 20, 1918, 6; Gaya Nuño, *Historia*, 143–54.

148. "Robo escandaloso en el Museo del Prado," *El Heraldo de Madrid*, September 22, 1918, 1.

149. "El robo del Tesoro de Delfín," *La Nación*, September 27, 1918, 4; "Robo en el Museo de Pinturas," *El Globo*, September 27, 1918, 3; *La Nación*, September 26, 1918, 1; "Varias notas gráficas del robo en el Museo del Prado," *El Día*, September 27, 1918, 8.

150. "Del Museo del Prado: Lo que ha ocurrido . . . y lo que puede haber ocurrido," *El Liberal*, September 26, 1918, 1; "Por la tarde.—Nuevas declaraciones.—Villa, incomunicado.––Su amante.—En busca de los amantes," *La Nación*, September 27, 1918, 4.

151. "Retablillo," *El Día*, September 26, 1918, 1; *El Día*, September 27, 1918, 1.

152. Silvio Lago (Jose Francés), "El robo en el Museo del Prado.— La culpable negligencia," *Nuevo Mundo* 25, no. 1290 (September 27, 1918): n.p.; "El robo del Tesoro del Delfín," *La Ilustración Española y Americana* 36 (September 30, 1918): 549.

153. "El robo en el Museo del Prado: Todo está descubierto," *El Heraldo de Madrid*, September 29, 1918, 2.

154. "Robo en el Museo de Pinturas," *El Globo*, September 27, 1918, 3.

155. "El robo del Museo de Pinturas," *El Heraldo de Madrid*, September 29, 1918, 2.

156. "Se comprueba la intervención de un celador del Museo," *El Sol*, September 28, 1918, 3.

157. "El robo del Museo del Prado," *El Liberal*, October 23, 1918, 2.

158. "El robo en el Museo de Pinturas," *La Nación*, October 14, 1918, 5.

159. *El Sol*, October 23, 1918, 2.

160. Mariano de Cavia, "La Dirección del Museo del Prado," *El Sol*, December 4, 1918, 2.

161. *La Libertad*, October 23, 1918, 2.

162. D'Ors, *Tres horas*, 8.

163. Ibid., 7.

164. "Los cuadros religiosos de Velázquez," *El Imparcial*, May 20, 1921, 1; "En el Museo del Prado. Se abren seis nuevas salas," *La Época*, May 17, 1922, 2; "SSMM Los reyes de Portugal," *La Correspondencia de España*, March 14, 1906, 2.

165. "En el Parlamento: Senado; Sesión del 3 de diciembre de 1900," *El Globo*, December 3, 1900, 3.

166. Juan de la Encina (Ricardo Gutiérrez Abascal), "La nueva sala del Greco," *La Voz*, September 21, 1920, 3.

167. "Unas cuantas observaciones al actual director del Museo del Prado," *El Duende*, March 8, 1914, 10–11, 11.

168. Afinoguénova, "Organic Nation."

169. Sánchez Cantón, "La reorganización del Museo del Prado," 291.

170. Ibid., 292.

171. Ibid., 291–92.

172. Ibid., 291.

173. Ibid.

174. "Los obreros en el Museo de Pintura," *Nuevo Mundo* 15, no. 580 (February 16, 1905): n.p.

175. "Madrid: Universidad Popular," *El País*, March 24, 1906, 3.

176. Ovejero, *Concepto*, 84–85.

177. *Memoria del Patronato de Misiones Pedagógicas*, 51–52, 106–7, 109; see also Afinoguénova, "Leisure and Agrarian Reform."

178. Published in L.S. [Luis Santullano], "Patronato de Misiones Pedagógicas," *Residencia*, February 1933, 1–21.

179. Mendelson, *Documenting Spain*, 39–124.

180. Jose Montero Alonso, "La siembra que no será estéril: El Museo Circulante," *Nuevo Mundo* 30, no. 2042 (May 5, 1933): 23–24.

181. Taslitzky, "Le Front Populaire et les intellectuelles. Temoignage 1," 13; see also Held, "Political Effects," 35.

182. In 1967, Stuart Gilbert and Francis Price, the translators of André Malraux's 1947 *Le musée imaginaire*, coined this popular term—"museum without walls"—to represent the museum as a cultural ideal.

183. Manuel Herrera y Ges, "Caso insólito," *El Siglo Futuro*, April 2, 1927, 1.

184. Ibid.

EPILOGUE

1. Benjamin, "Work of Art."

2. Jose Montero Alonso, "La siembra que no será estéril: El Museo Circulante," *Nuevo Mundo* 30, no. 2042 (May 5, 1933): 23–24..

3. Oulebsir, *Usages*, 194; Foundoukidis, "L'Office international," 187; Afinoguénova, "Arte de élites," 342.

4. *Libro de Actas del Patronato del Museo Nacional del Prado*, 1930–42. Acta 344, 55bis. Madrid, Archivo MNP, Caja 1350.

5. Calero Delso, *Gobierno de la anarquía*, 16–21.

6. On the details of Picasso's appointment, see Renau, *Arte en peligro*, 19.

7. Colorado Castellary, *Éxodo y exilio*.

8. Kowalsky, *Soviet Union*, 167; Schauff, *Victoria frustrada*, 123–40.

9. Álvarez Lopera, *Política*, 1:32–35, 115–16.

10. See Junta Central del Tesoro Artístico, *El fascismo al desnudo* and *Propaganda cultural*; Antonio Machado, "El Museo del Prado y la Biblioteca nacional han sido bombardeados sin otro motivo bélico que la fatal necesidad de destruir que siente el fascismo," *La Libertad*, November 29, 1936, 5.

11. "La heroica aviación fascista y su misión histórica de destrucción y barbarie," *El Mundo Obrero*, November 19, 1936, 1; *El fascismo intenta destruir el museo del Prado*; Argerich and Ara Lázaro, *Arte Protegido*. For the Nazi and Nationalist propaganda, see "Wie die Roten Madrid verheerten: Zerstörte Museen und Bibliotheken—Bisher 25000 Erschiessungen," *Berliner Tageblatt*, January 23, 1937, 1, 5; P. de La Mora, "La destrucción del tesoro nacional por la revolución marxista," *Orientación española*, Buenos Aires, May 15, 1938, 32–33, qtd. Alted, *Política*, 91.

12. Afinoguenova, "Arte de élites."

13. "Reportaje Gráfico: Capilla de uno de los palacios incautados protegida por los milicianos. Foto Díaz Casariego," *ABC*, July 28, 1936, 4; "¿Quiénes son los verdaderos amigos del arte y de la Cultura? El Partido Comunista de Madrid, que se ha incautado del antiguo Palacio de Liria mantiene y conserva en el mayor orden sus obras de arte. Así lo acredita la Junta del patrimonio Artístico," *El Mundo Obrero* (August 6, 1936), 2; "Notas de Arte. El Nuevo Tesoro Artístico Nacional y su custodia por los milicianos," *ABC*, July 31, 1936, 8; see also the compilation by Álvarez Casado, "Noticias."

14. Alberti, "Mi última visita al Museo del Prado," *El Mono Azul*, *La Voz*, May 3, 1937, 3; later developed into the play *Noche de guerra en el Museo del Prado* (1956).

15. Álvarez Lopera, *Política*, 1:158; Alonso Alonso, "Taller de Restauración."

16. Renau, "Défense," 58.

17. León, *La historia*, 65.

18. Marinello, *Cultura*, 7–8.

19. Luis de Tapia, "Preguntas," *La Libertad*, October 3, 1936, 1.

20. Pablo Picasso, "'Los verdaderos conservadores de él son ahora los aviadores, los tanquistas y los soldados del Ejército del pueblo que luchan a las puertas de Madrid,'" *El Mundo Obrero*, September 14, 1937, 3.

21. Álvarez Lopera, *Política*, 1:158–60.

22. Colorado Castellary, *Museo*, 53–59; Granger, "Évacuation," 345–46.

23. Muñoz Fernández, "Guerra, Arte," 93–95; AGA (10)96 Caja 54/11254, Exp. 6246; AGA (10)96 Caja 54/11209, Exp. 7382.

24. Qtd. Colorado Castellary, *Patrimonio*, 19.

25. Azaña, letter to Angel Ossorio, June 28, 1939, in *Diarios completos*, 1271.

26. Arce, *Los colores de guerra*; Antonio Mercero, dir., *La hora de los valientes* (1998); Alberto Porlán, dir., *Las cajas españolas* (2004); Alfonso Arteseros, dir., *Salvemos el Prado: El frente del arte en la Guerra Civil española* (2004).

27. In Aronsson and Elgenius, *Building National Museums*, 6.

28. León Felipe, "Hay dos Españas."

29. Portús and Vega, *Descubrimiento*; Antonio Buero Vallejo, *Las Meninas: Fantasía velazqueña en dos partes*, Teatro Español, Madrid, December 9, 1960; *Primer Acto* 19 (January 1961); *El tragaluz: Experimento en dos partes*, Teatro de Bellas Artes, Madrid, October 7, 1967; *Primer Acto* 90 (November 1967).

30. *Libro de Actas del Patronato*, Acta 364, May 16, 1939, 86bis. For more information concerning the postwar debates about cultural heritage, see Llorente Hernández, *Arte e ideología*, 51, 235.

31. Archivo MNP, Caja 1429.

32. Goytisolo, "El museo Dillinger," 183.

33. Gaya Nuño, *Historia y guía*, 13; Bolaños, *Historia*, 370–411. Gaya Nuño did, however, remark that the catalogues of the Prado were an exception.

34. Steno, dir., *Toto in Madrid* (*La culpa fue de Eva*) (Italy–France–Spain, 1959).

35. I owe this information to Rafael Rodríguez Tranche.

36. Fraga Iribarne, *Pregón*, 51–52.

37. Bolaños, "Modern Art Museums," 141–42.

38. Using the narrator's expression from Eduardo Mendoza's novel *El misterio de la cripta embrujada* (1979).

39. Holo, *Beyond the Prado*.

40. Instituto de Estudios Turísticos, *Encuesta a los visitantes*.

Bibliography

ARCHIVES

Archivo de la Real Academia de Bellas Artes San
    Fernando
Archivo de la Real Academia de la Historia
Archivo de la Villa de Madrid
Archivo del Museo Nacional del Prado
Archivo General de la Administración, Alcalá de
    Henares, Spain
Archivo General del Palacio, Madrid
Archivo Histórico Nacional
Archivo Manuel Bartolomé de Cossío, Residencia
    de estudiantes, Madrid

SECONDARY SOURCES

Abrams, Lynn. *Workers' Culture in Imperial
    Germany: Leisure and Recreation in the
    Rhineland and Westphalia*. London:
    Routledge, 1992.
Adorno, Theodor W. "Valéry Proust Museum." 1953.
    In *Prisms*, translated by Samuel Weber
    and Shierry Weber, 173–85. Boston: MIT
    Press, 1981.
Afinoguénova, Eugenia. "Arte de élites, política de
    masas: Los 'milicianos de la Humanidad' y
    la defensa de la cultura en el relato sobre el
    rescate del Museo del Prado." In *La España
    del Frente Popular: Política, sociedad, cultura
    y conflicto en la España de 1936*, edited
    by Rocío Navarro Comás and Eduardo
    González Calleja, 339–53. Granada:
    Comares Historia, 2011.
———. "Art Education, Class, and Gender in a
    Foreign Art Gallery: Nineteenth-Century
    Cultural Travelers and the Prado Museum
    in Madrid." *Nineteenth-Century Contexts*
    32, no. 1 (2010): 47–63.
———. "Entre pitos y flautas: La modernización
    de la romería de San Isidro en Madrid."
    In *Sociabilidades en la historia: VIII
    congreso de historia social*, edited by

Santiago Castillo. Madrid: Universidad
    Complutense, 2015.
———. "Leisure and Agrarian Reform: Liberal
    Governance in the Traveling Museums of
    Spanish Misiones Pedagógicas (1931–
    1933)." *Hispanic Review* 79, no. 2 (2011):
    261–90.
———. "El neocatolicismo, la exhibición de
    figuras humanas y las capillas ardientes
    en el Museo del Prado." In *Las Artes y la
    Arquitectura del Poder*, edited by Víctor
    Mínguez, 2631–52. Castellón: Universidad
    Jaume I, 2013.
———. "'Painted in Spanish': The Prado Museum
    and the Naturalization of the 'Spanish
    School' in the Nineteenth Century."
    Journal of Spanish Cultural Studies 10, no. 3
    (2009): 319–40.
———. "El providencialismo histórico y la misión
    del arte en la obra de Pedro de Madrazo."
    Boletín de la Biblioteca de Menéndez Pelayo
    74 (2008): 209–40.
Alas, Leopoldo (Clarín). *Pipá*. In *Pipá*, 3rd ed., 1–74.
    Madrid: Librería de Fernando Fe, 1886.
Alberti, Rafael. *Noche de guerra en el Museo del
    Prado (aguaferte, en un prólogo y un acto)*.
    Buenos Aires: Ediciones Losange, 1956.
Alcolea Blanch, Santiago. *Museo del Prado*. Madrid:
    Poligrafía, 1991.
———. *The Prado*. Translated by Richard-Lewis
    Rees and Angela Patricia Hall. New York:
    Harry N. Abrams, 1991.
Alonso Alonso, Rafael. "La actuación del Taller
    de Restauración del Museo Nacional del
    Prado durante la Guerra Civil." In Ara
    Lázaro and Argerich Fernández, *Arte
    protegido*, 165–86.
Alted Vigil, Alicia. *Política del nuevo Estado sobre el
    patrimonio cultural y la educación durante
    la guerra civil española*. Madrid: Ministerio
    de Cultura, 1984.
Álvarez Junco, José, and Adrian Shubert, eds.
    Spanish History Since 1808. London:
    Arnold, 2000.

Álvarez Lopera, José. "La Junta del Tesoro Artístico de Madrid y la protección del patrimonio en la Guerra Civil." In Ara Lázaro and Argerich Fernández, *Arte Protegido*, 27–62.

———. *El Museo de la Trinidad en El Prado: Catálogo de la exposición, 13 de julio–19 de septiembre 1994.* Madrid: Museo Nacional del Prado, 2004.

———. *La política de bienes culturales del gobierno republicano durante la guerra civil española.* 2 vols. Madrid: Ministerio de Cultura, 1982.

Anon. *Madrid in 1835; or, Sketches of the metropolis of Spain, by a Resident Officer.* 2 vols. London: Saunders and Otley, 1836.

———. "A Promenade on the Prado at Madrid." *London Magazine* 2 (November 1820): 528–30.

Antiguedad, María Dolores. "La primera colección pública en España: El Museo Josefino." *Fragmentos* 11 (1987): 67–85.

Antigüedad, María Dolores, and Amaya Alzaga Ruiz, eds. *Colecciones, expolio, museos y mercado artístico en España en los siglos XVIII y XIX.* Madrid: Editorial Universitaria Ramón Areces, 2011.

Araujo Sánchez, Ceferino. *Los museos de España.* Madrid: Medina y Navarro, 1875.

Arce, Juan Carlos. *Los colores de guerra.* Barcelona: Planeta, 2002.

Argerich Fernández, Isabel, and Judith Ara Lázaro, eds. *Arte protegido: Memoria de la Junta del Tesoro Artístico durante la Guerra Civil, 26 de junio–14 de septiembre, 2003.* Madrid: Instituto de Patrimonio Cultural de España, Museo Nacional del Prado, 2003.

Ariza, Rosa María. "Los proyectos de museos que conserva la Real Academia de San Fernando." *Boletín de la Real Academia de Bellas Artes de San Fernando* 83 (1996): 415–57.

Ariza Muñoz, Carmen. *Jardines de Madrid: paseos arbolados, plazas y parques.* Madrid: Lunwerg, 2001.

Aronsson, Peter, and Emma Bentz. "National Museums in Germany: Anchoring Competing Communities." In Aronsson and Elgenius, *Building National Museums*, 327–62.

Aronsson, Peter, and Gabriella Elgenius, eds. *Building National Museums in Europe, 1750–2010.* Conference Proceedings from EuNaMus, European National Museums: Identity Politics, the Uses of the Past and the European Citizen, Bologna, April 28–30, 2011. Linköping: Linköping University Electronic Press, 2012.

Ayguals de Izco, Wenceslao. *María, la hija de un jornalero.* Illustrated ed. 2 vols. Madrid: Wenceslao Ayguals de Izco, 1847.

Ayuntamiento de Madrid. *Plan Castro 150 años.* Madrid: Ayuntamiento de Madrid, 2010, ebook.

Azaña, Manuel. *Carta a Angel Ossorio 28 de junio de 1939.* In *Diarios completos: Monarquía, República, Guerra Civil,* edited by Santos Julia, 1258–75. Barcelona: Crítica, 2000.

———. *Obras completas.* Vol. 4. Mexico City: Oasis, 1968.

Babelon, Jean-Pierre. "The Louvre: Royal Residence and the Temple to the Arts." In *Les lieux de Memoire III,* translated by Mary Seidman Trouille, 253–89. Chicago: University of Chicago Press, 2001.

Bahamonde Magro, Angel, and Julián Toro Mérida. *Burguesía, especulación y cuestión social en el Madrid del siglo XIX.* Madrid: Siglo XXI, 1998.

———. "Mendicidad y paro en el Madrid de la Restauración." *Estudios de Historia Social* 7 (1978): 353–60.

Bailey, Peter. "Adventures in Space: Victorian Railway Erotics, or Taking Alienation for a Ride." *Journal of Victorian Culture* 9, no. 1 (2004): 1–21.

———. *Leisure and Class in Victorian England: Rational Recreation and the Contest for Control, 1830–1885.* London: Methuen, 1987.

Bairoch, Paul, and Gary Goertz. "Factors of Urbanisation in the Nineteenth Century Developed Countries: A Descriptive and Econometric Analysis." *Urban Studies* 23, no. 4 (1986): 285–305.

Baker, Edward. *Materiales para escribir Madrid: Literatura y espacio urbano de Moratín a Galdós.* Madrid: Siglo Veintiuno Editores, 1991.

Bakhtin, Mikhaíl. *Творчество Франсуа Рабле у народная культура Средневековья и Ренессанса.* Moscow: Nauka, 1965.

Bal, Mieke. "Telling, Showing, Showing Off." *Critical Inquiry* 18, no. 3 (1992): 556–94.

Barañano, Ascensión, and María Cátedra. "La representación del poder y el poder de la representación: La política cultural en los Museos de Antropología y la creación del Museo del Traje." *Política y Sociedad* 42, no. 3 (2005): 227–50.

Barlow, Paul. "'Fire, Flatulence, and Fog': The Decoration of Westminster Palace and the Aesthetics of Prudence." In Barlow and Trodd, *Governing Cultures*, 69–82.

Barlow, Paul, and Colin Trodd, eds. *Governing Cultures: Art Institutions in Victorian London*. Aldershot: Ashgate, 2000.

Bashkirtseff, Marie. *The Journal of a Young Artist, 1860–1884*. Translated by Maria Serrano. New York: Cassell, 1889.

Bataille, Georges. *La part maudite: Essai d'économie générale*. Paris: Minuit, 1949.

Bazin, Germain. *The Museum Age*. Translated by Jane van Nuis Cahill. New York: Universe Books, 1967.

Bédat, Claude. *La Real Academia de Bellas Artes de San Fernando (1744–1808)*. Madrid: Fundación Universitaria Española, 1989.

Belting, Hans. *The Germans and Their Art: A Troublesome Relationship*. Translated by Scott Kleager. New Haven: Yale University Press, 1998.

Benjamin, Walter. *The Arcades Project*. Translated by Howard Eiland and Kevin McLaughlin. Edited by Rolf Tiederman. Cambridge, Mass.: Harvard University Press, 1999.

———. "The Work of Art in the Age of Mechanical Reproduction." In *Illuminations*, edited by Hannah Arendt, translated by Harry Zorn, 217–52. New York: Schocken Books, 1968.

Bennett, Tony. *The Birth of the Museum: History, Theory, Politics*. London: Routledge, 1995.

———. "The Exhibitionary Complex." *new formations* 4 (1988): 73–102.

———, ed. *Museums and Citizenship: A Resource Book*. Brisbane: Queensland Museum, 1996.

Bergvelt, Ellinoor, Debora J. Meijers, Lieske Tibbe, and Elsa van Wezel, eds. *Napoleon's Legacy: The Rise of National Museums*. Berliner Schriften zur Museumsforschung 27. Berlin: G+H Verlag, 2009.

Beroqui, Pedro. "Apuntes para la historia del Museo del Prado." *Boletín de la Sociedad Española de Excursiones* 39 (1931) and 40 (1932).

———. *El Museo del Prado: Notas para su historia*. Vol. 1, *El Museo Real 1819–1933*. Madrid: Gráficas Marinas, 1933.

Bertini, Giuseppe. "Art Works from the Duchy of Parma and Piacenza Transported to Paris During the Napoleonic Time and Their Restitution." In Bergvelt et al., *Napoleon's Legacy*, 73–89.

Best, Shaun. *Leisure Studies: Themes and Perspectives*. London: Sage, 2010.

Billinge, Mark. "A Time and Place for Everything: An Essay on Recreation, Re-Creation, and the Victorians." *Journal of Historical Geography* 22, no. 4 (1996): 817–44.

Blanco, Alda. *Cultura y conciencia imperial en la España del siglo XIX*. Valencia: Universitat de Valencia, 2012.

Blanning, Tim, ed. *The Nineteenth Century: Europe, 1789–1914*. New York: Oxford University Press, 2000.

Blanning, Tim, and Hagen Schulze, eds. *Unity and Diversity in European Culture, c. 1800*. Proceedings of the British Academy 134. Oxford: Oxford University Press, 2006.

Bodenstein, Felicity. "National Museums in the Netherlands." In Aronsson and Elgenius, *Building National Museums*, 709–40.

Bolaños, María. "Bellezas prestadas: La colección nacional de reproducciones artísticas." *Culture and History Culture & History Digital Journal* 2 (2013): e025. doi: http://dx.doi.org/10.3989/chdj.2013.025.

———. *Historia de los museos en España: Memoria, cultura, sociedad*. Gijón: Trea, 1997.

———. "Modern Art Museums Under Franco: Routines, Isolation, and Some Exceptions." In *Spain Is (Still) Different: Tourism and Discourse in Spanish Identity*, edited by Eugenia Afinoguénova and Jaume Martí-Olivella, 129–50. Lanham, Md.: Lexington Books, 2008.

Bonet, Juan Manuel. "De la verbena a Vallecas: Divagaciones en torno a la primera Maruja Mallo." *Arte y Parte* 82 (August–September 2009): 30–39.

Boone, Mary Elizabeth. *Vistas de España: American Views of Art and Life in Spain, 1860–1914*. New Haven: Yale University Press, 2007.

Botti, Alfonso. *Cielo y dinero: El nacional catolicismo en España (1881–1975)*. Madrid: Alianza, 1992.

Bourdieu, Pierre. *Distinction: A Social Critique of the Judgment of Taste*. Translated by Richard Nice. Cambridge, Mass.: Harvard University Press, 1984.

Bourdieu, Pierre, with Dominique Schnapper. *The Love of Art: European Art Museums and Their Public*. Translated by Caroline Beattie and Nick Merriman. Stanford: Stanford University Press, 1990.

Bourdieu, Pierre, and Randall Johnson. *The Field of Cultural Production: Essays on Art and Literature*. New York: Columbia University Press, 1993.

Boyd, Carolyn. "Un lugar de memoria olvidado: El Panteón de Hombres Ilustres en Madrid." *Historia y Política* 12 (2004): 15–40.

Brown, Stephanie, and Sara Dodd. "The Society of Female Artists and the Song of the

Sisterhood." In Barlow and Trodd, *Governing Cultures*, 85–97.

Bruford, Walter Horace. *The German Tradition of Self-Cultivation: "Bildung" from Humboldt to Thomas Mann*. London: Cambridge University Press, 1975.

Bruquetas Galán, Rocío. "La protección de monumentos y obras de arte en tiempos de guerra: La acción de la Junta del Tesoro Artístico y su repercusión internacional." In Ara Lázaro and Argerich Fernández, *Arte protegido*, 201–20.

Burdiel, Isabel, ed. *SEM: Los Borbones en Pelota*. Zaragoza: IFC, 2012.

Burgos, Carmen de (Colombine). *La que quiso ser Maja*. Novela pasional 23 (1924). Seville: Renacimiento, 2000.

Burke, Peter. "Viewpoint: The Invention of Leisure in Early Modern Europe." *Past and Present* 146, no. 1 (1995): 136–50.

Buzard, James. *Disorienting Fiction: The Autoethnographic Work of Nineteenth-Century British Novels*. Princeton: Princeton University Press, 2005.

Cabanillas Casafranca, África. "Las mujeres y la crítica de arte en España (1875–1936)." *Espacio, Tiempo y Forma*, 7th ser., 20–21 (2007–8): 363–89.

Cabañas Bravo, Manuel. "Margarita Nelken: Una mujer ante el arte." In *La mujer en el Arte Español: VIII Jornadas de Arte*, 463–84. Madrid: Alpuerto, 1997.

Caillois, Roger. *Les jeux et les hommes: Le masque et le vertige*. Paris: Gallimard, 1967.

Calero Delso, Juan Pablo. *El gobierno de la anarquía*. Barcelona: Síntesis, 2011.

Callahan, William J. "Church and State, 1808–1874." In Alvarez Junco and Shubert, *Spanish History Since 1808*, 49–63.

Calle, Maria Dolores Bastida de la. *La Comisión de Reformas Sociales 1883–1903: Política social y conflicto de intereses*. Madrid: Ministerio de Trabajo y Seguridad Social, 1989.

———. "La imagen de la mujer pintora en la ilustración popular del siglo XIX." *Espacio, Tiempo y Forma* 7 (1994): 265–73.

Calvo Serraller, Francisco. *Breve historia del Museo del Prado*. Madrid: Alianza Editorial, 1994.

Cansino, Eliacer. *El misterio Velázquez*. Madrid: Bruño, 1998.

Capel Martínez, Rosa. *El sufragio femenino en la Segunda República española*. Madrid: Horas y Horas, 1992.

Carabias Álvaro, Mónica. "El diorama de la Fábrica-Platería Martínez: La representación del Monasterio del Escorial." In *Literatura e imagen en El Escorial*, 969–82. El Escorial: R.C.U. Escorial––Ma. Cristina Servicio de Publicaciones, 1996.

Carballo Barra, Borja. "Los orígenes del Moderno Madrid: El Ensanche Este (1860–1878)." Trabajo fin de Máster [equivalent to M.A. thesis], Universidad Complutense de Madrid, 2007.

Caro Baroja, Julio. *La estación de Amor (Fiestas populares de Mayo a San Juan)*. Madrid: Taurus, 1979.

———. *Los Baroja: memorias familiares*. Madrid: Taurus, 1972.

Carrier, David. *Museum Skepticism: A History of the Display of Art in Public Galleries*. Durham: Duke University Press, 2006.

Casares, Emilio. *Francisco Asenjo Barbieri: El hombre y el creador*. Madrid: Universidad Complutense de Madrid, 1994.

Castelar, Emilio. *Discursos políticos de Emilio Castelar: Dentro y fuera del parlamento en los años de 1871 a 1873*. Madrid: A. Lopez, 1873.

Castellanos, Basilio Sebastián. *El bibliotecario y el trovador español: Colección de documentos interesantes sobre nuestra historia nacional, y de poesías inéditas de nuestros poetas antiguos y modernos, y de artículos de costumbres antiguas españolas*. Madrid: I. Sancha, 1841.

Castellote, Alejandro. "España: Fragmentos propios y ajenos de nuestro imaginario visual." In *España a través de la fotografía, 1839–2010*, edited by Pablo Jiménez Burillo, 27–93. Madrid: Santillana, 2013.

Ceán Bermúdez, Juan Agustín. *Diccionario histórico de los profesores ilustres de las Bellas artes en España*. Madrid: Academia San Fernando, 1800.

———. "Historia del arte de pintura." 11 vols. Unpublished manuscript. Madrid, RABASF.

Chacel, Rosa. *El Barrio de Maravillas*. Barcelona: Seix Barral, 1976.

Charnon-Deutsch, Lou. *Fictions of the Feminine in the Nineteenth-Century Spanish Press*. University Park: Penn State University Press, 2010.

———. *Hold That Pose: Visual Culture in the Late Nineteenth-Century Spanish Periodical*. University Park: Penn State University Press, 2008.

Charnon-Deutsch, Lou, and Jo Labanyi, eds. *Culture and Gender in Nineteenth-Century Spain*. Oxford: Clarendon Press, 1995.

Chueca Goitia, Fernando. *El Museo del Prado: Guiones de arquitectura*. Madrid: Misiones de Arte, 1952.

Clark, Kenneth. *The Nude: A Study in Ideal Form*. New York: Pantheon Books, 1956.

Clarke, John N., and Charles Critcher. *The Devil Makes Work: Leisure in Capitalist Britain*. Urbana: University of Illinois Press, 1985.

Colorado Castellary, Arturo. "Arte salvado: Los antecedentes de una deuda histórica." In *Arte Salvado: 70 aniversario del salvamento del patrimonio artístico español y de la intervención internacional*, 6–19. Madrid: Gobierno de España, Ministerio de Cultura, Sociedad Estatal de Conmemoraciones Culturales, 2010.

———. *Éxodo y exilio del arte: La odisea del Museo del Prado durante la Guerra Civil*. Madrid: Cátedra, 2008.

———. *El Museo del Prado y la Guerra Civil: Figueras-Ginebra, 1939*. Madrid: Museo Nacional del Prado, 1991.

———, ed. *Patrimonio, Guerra Civil y posguerra*. Madrid: Universidad Complutense de Madrid, 2010.

Comellas, José Luis. "Los españoles del primer tercio del siglo XIX." In *Del antiguo al nuevo régimen: Hasta la muerte de Fernando VII*, edited by José Luis Comellas. Historia general de España y América 12. Madrid: Rialp, 1981.

Conlin, Jonathan. *The Nation's Mantelpiece: A History of the National Gallery*. London: Pallas Athene, 2006.

Cos-Gayón, Fernando. *Historia jurídica del Patrimonio Real*. Madrid: E. de la Riva, 1881.

Cruz, Jesús. "The Moderate Ascendancy, 1843–1868." In Álvarez Junco and Shubert, *Spanish History Since 1808*, 33–47.

———. *The Rise of Middle-Class Culture in Nineteenth-Century Spain*. Baton Rouge: Louisiana State University Press, 2011.

———. "Símbolos de modernidad: La historia olvidada de los jardines de recreo en la España del siglo XIX." In Pilar Folguera, Juan Carlos Pereira Castañares, Carmen García García et al., eds., *Pensar con la historia desde el siglo XXI: Actas del XII Congreso de la Asociación de Historia Contemporánea*, 5245–73. Madrid: Universidad Complutense de Madrid, 2015.

Cueva Merino, Julio de la, and Ángel Luis López Villaverde, eds. *Clericalismo y asociacionismo católico en España: De la Restauración a la Transición*. Cuenca: Ediciones de la Universidad de Castilla–La Mancha, 2005.

Cuevas, Matilde. "Aproximación a la consideración social de la prostitución madrileña." In *Madrid en la sociedad del siglo XIX*, edited by Luis E. Otero Carvajal and Angel Bahamonde Magro, vol. 2, *Capas populares y conflictividad social: Población, abastecimientos y crisis de subsistencias*, 163–73. Madrid: Comunidad de Madrid, 1986.

Cunningham, Hugh. *Leisure in the Industrial Revolution, c. 1780–c. 1880*. London: Croom Helm, 1980.

De Amicis, Edmondo. *Spain and the Spaniards*, translated by Wilhelmina W. Cady. New York: Putnam's Sons, 1880.

[Debord, Guy, et al.] "Aux poubelles de l'Histoire!" *Internationale Situationniste* 12 (September 1969): 108–11.

———. "L'historien Lefebvre." *Internationale Situationniste* 10 (March 1966): 73–75.

de Certeau, Michel. *The Writing of History*. Translated by Tom Conley. New York: Columbia University Press, 1988.

de Diego, Estrella. *La mujer y la pintura en la España del Siglo XIX: Mujeres pintoras en Madrid, 1868–1910*. Madrid: Universidad Complutense de Madrid, 1987.

de la Sizeranne, Robert. *Les questions esthétiques contemporaines*. Paris: Hachette, 1904.

Deleito y Piñuela, José. . . . *También se divierte el pueblo (Recuerdos de hace tres siglos)*. 2nd ed. Madrid: Espasa-Calpe, 1954.

Dell, Simon. *The Image of the Popular Front: The Masses and the Media in Interwar France*. Basingstoke: Palgrave Macmillan, 2006.

de Sales Mayo, Francisco. *La condesita: (memorias de una doncella): estudio fisiológico no ménos interesante al facultativo que al hombre de mundo*. Madrid: Oficina Tipográfica del Hospicio, 1869.

Díez, José Luis, ed. *La pintura de historia del siglo XIX en España*. Madrid: Museo Nacional del Prado, 1992.

Díez, José Luis, and Javier Barón, eds. *The Nineteenth Century in the Prado*. Madrid: Museo Nacional del Prado, 2008.

d'Ors, Eugeni. *Tres horas en el Museo del Prado: Itinerario estético, seguido de los Avisos al visitante de las exposiciones de pinturas*. Madrid: Aguilar, 1963.

Dowling, Linda C. *The Vulgarization of Art: The Victorians and Aesthetic Democracy*.

271

Charlottesville: University Press of Virginia, 1996.

Drachkovitch, Milorad M. *The Revolutionary Internationals, 1864–1943*. Stanford: Stanford University Press, 1966.

D'Souza, Aruna, and Tom McDonough, eds. *The Invisible Flâneuse? Gender, Public Space, and Visual Culture in Nineteenth-Century Paris*. Manchester: Manchester University Press, 2006.

Duncan, Carol. *Civilizing Rituals: Inside Public Art Museums*. London: Routledge, 1995.

———. "Museums and Department Stores: Close Encounters." In *High-Pop: Making Culture into Popular Entertainment*, edited by Jim Collins, 129–55. Oxford: Wiley-Blackwell, 2002.

———. "Putting the 'Nation' in London's National Gallery." In *The Formation of National Collections of Art and Archaelogy*, edited by Gwendolyn Wright, 100–11. Hanover: University Press of New England, 1996.

Duncan, Carol, and Alan Wallach. "The Universal Survey Museum." *Art History* 3, no. 4 (1980): 448–69.

Eley, Geoff. *Forging Democracy: The History of the Left in Europe, 1850–2000*. Oxford: Oxford University Press, 2002.

Elias, Norbert. *The Civilizing Process: The History of Manners*. Translated by Edmund Jephcott. Oxford: Blackwell, 1991.

———. "An Essay on Sport and Violence." In *Quest for Excitement: Sport and Leisure in the Civilizing Process*, edited by Norbert Elias and Eric Dunning. Oxford: Blackwell, 1986, 150–74.

———. Introduction to Elias and Dunning, *Quest for Excitement*, 19–62.

Enders, Victoria Lorée, and Pamela Beth Radcliff, eds. *Constructing Spanish Womanhood: Female Identity in Modern Spain*. Albany: SUNY Press, 1999.

Espinosa Martín, Carmen. "Luis Eusebi (1773–1829): Pintor miniaturista y primer conserje del Museo del Prado." *Goya* 285 (November–December 2001): 332–38.

[Eusebi, Luis.] *Catálogo de los cuadros de la Escuela Española que existen en el Real Museo del Prado*. Madrid: Imprenta Real, 1819.

———. *Catálogo de los cuadros que existen colocados en el Real Museo del Prado*. Madrid: Imprenta nacional, 1821.

———. *Catálogo de los cuadros que existen colocados en el Real Museo de Pinturas del Prado*. Madrid: Oficina de Francisco Martínez Dávila, 1824.

———. *Ensayo sobre las diferentes Escuelas de Pintura*. Madrid, 1822.

———. "Llave para la introducción al conocimiento; de los Cuadros que posee el Rey N.S. de las Escuelas Flamenca, Olandesa, y Alemana para ilustración de los mismos, indagar el Autor de cada una de ellos, clasificarlos para su colocación, y para la formación del Catálogo del Real Museo de Pinturas, o, Historia de los Pintores Flamencos, Olandeses, y Alemanes. Año de sus nacimientos, sus nombres y sus apodos, sus respectivos Maestros, época de su muerte, y carácter distintivo de su estilo y manera, para reconocerlos en sus obras. Desde el origen de la pintura al olio, y el restablecimiento de las Artes, hasta el Siglo XVIII." Archivo y Biblioteca de la Fundación Lázaro Galdiano, Madrid.

———. *Noticia de los cuadros que se hallan colocados en la galería del Museo del Rey Nuestro Señor, sito en El Prado de esta Corte*. Madrid: La Hija del Francisco Martínez Dávila, impresor de Cámara de S.M., 1828.

Facos, Michelle, and Sharon L. Hirsch, eds. *Art, Culture, and National Identity in Fin-de-Siècle Europe*. Cambridge: Cambridge University Press, 2003.

Falk, John H. *The Museum Experience*. Washington, D.C.: Howells House, 1992.

El fascismo intenta destruir el museo del Prado. Madrid: Publicaciones del 5º Regimiento, 1936.

Faulkner, Sally, Vicente Sánchez-Biosca, and Paul Julian Smith. "Cinema, Popular Entertainment, Literature, and Television." In *A Companion to Spanish Cinema*, edited by Jo Labanyi and Tatjana Pavlović, 5th ed., 489–520. London: Blackwell, 2013.

Fernández de los Ríos, Ángel. *Guía de Madrid*. Madrid: Oficinas de la Ilustración Española y Americana, 1876.

Fernández García, Antonio. "La evolución social de Madrid en la época liberal (1834–1900)." In *Arquitectura y espacio urbano de Madrid en el siglo XIX*, 10–29. Madrid: COAM, 2008.

Ferrer, José María. *Visión castiza de Madrid*. Madrid: Viajes Ilustrados, 1997.

Fischer, Christian Augustus. *A Picture of Madrid: Taken on the Spot*. London: J. Mawman, 1808.

Flint, Kate. *The Victorians and the Visual Imagination*. Cambridge: Cambridge University Press, 2000.

Flitter, Derek. *Spanish Romanticism and the Uses of History: Ideology and the Historical Imagination*. London: Legenda, 2006.

Foley, Malcolm, and Gayle McPherson. "Museums as Leisure." *International Journal of Heritage Studies* 6, no. 2 (2000): 161–74.

Fontanella, Lee. *La historia de la fotografía en España, desde sus orígenes hasta 1900*. Madrid: El Viso, 1981.

Ford, Richard. *A Handbook for Travellers in Spain*. 3rd ed. Part II. London: Murray and Sons, 1855.

Foucault, Michel. *Discipline and Punish: The Birth of the Prison*. Translated by Alan Sheridan. New York: Vintage Books, 1995.

———. *The Foucault Effect: Studies in Governmentality; With Two Lectures by and an Interview with Michel Foucault*. Edited by Graham Burchell, Colin Gordon, and Peter Miller. Chicago: University of Chicago Press, 1991.

———. "Of Other Spaces." Translated by Jay Miskowiec. *Diacritics* 16, no. 1 (1986): 22–27.

Foundoukidis, Euripide. "L'office international des Musées et la protection des monuments et oeuvres d'art en temps de guerre." *Mouseion* 35–36 (1936): 187–200.

Fraga Iribarne, Manuel. "Pregón de la Semana Santa madrileña." 1963. In *Cinco loas*, 51–52. Madrid: Editora Nacional, 1965.

French, Ylva, and Sue Runyard. *Marketing and Public Relations for Museums, Galleries, Cultural and Heritage Attractions*. London: Routledge, 2012.

Fried, Michael. *Absorption and Theatricality: Painting and Beholder in the Age of Diderot*. Berkeley: University of California Press, 1980.

———. *Menzel's Realism: Art and Embodiment in Nineteenth-Century Berlin*. New Haven: Yale University Press, 2002.

Frost, Daniel. *Cultivating Madrid: Public Space and Middle-Class Culture in the Spanish Capital, 1833–1890*. Lewisburg: Bucknell University Press, 2008.

Fundación Amigos del Museo del Prado. *Enciclopedia del Museo del Prado*. 6 vols. Madrid: Fundación Amigos del Museo del Prado, 2007. Online module: http://www.museodelprado.es/enciclopedia/.

Gadamer, Hans Georg. *Truth and Method*. 2nd rev. ed.. Translation revised by Joel Weinsheimer and Donald G. Marshall. London: Continuum, 2004.

García González, Armando. *Cuerpo abierto: Ciencia, enseñanza y coleccionismo andaluces en Cuba en el siglo xix*. Madrid: CSIC, 2010.

García-Monsalve Escriña, Antonio. "Historia jurídica del Museo del Prado." Ph.D. diss., Universidad Complutense de Madrid, 2002.

Garland-Thomson, Rosemarie, ed. *Freakery: Cultural Spectacles of the Extraordinary Body*. New York: NYU Press, 1996.

———. *Staring: How We Look*. Oxford: Oxford University Press, 2009.

Gaya Nuño, Juan Antonio. *Historia del Museo del Prado, 1890–1969*. León: Everest, 1969.

———. *Historia y guía de los museos de España*. Madrid: Espasa-Calpe, 1955.

Géal, Pierre. "Admirar y recordar: Las apropiaciones conflictivas del monumento a Daoíz y Velarde de Antonio Solá." In *Arte y memoria: Grupo de investigación Arte y memoria 2*, edited by José Prieto Martín and Vega Ruiz Capellán, 135–54. N.p.: Tervalis, 2014.

———. *La naissance des musées d'art en Espagne (XVIIIe–XIXe siècle)*. Madrid: Casa de Velázquez, 2005.

———. "El Salón de la Reina Isabel en el Museo del Prado (1853–1899)." *Boletín del Museo del Prado* 19, no. 37 (2001): 143–72.

Gerber, David. "The Careers of People Exhibited in Freak Shows: The Problem of Volition and Valorization." In Garland-Thomson, *Freakery*, 38–54.

Gies, David T. *The Theatre in Nineteenth-Century Spain*. Cambridge: Cambridge University Press, 1994.

Gilarranz, Ainhoa. "El estado-nación español y su implicación en el desarrollo artístico del xix: Imaginarios, representaciones, colecciones y museos." Ph.D. diss., Universidad Autónoma de Madrid, forthcoming.

Giner de los Ríos, Hermenegildo. *Manual de Estética y Teoría del Arte e Historia abreviada de las artes principales hasta el cristianismo*. Nueva edición con 168 grabados intercalados en el texto. Madrid: Saénz de Jubera Hnos., 1895.

Ginger, Andrew. *Painting and the Turn to Cultural Modernity in Spain: The Time of Eugenio Lucas Velázquez*. Selinsgrove: Susquehanna University Press, 2007.

Glendinning, Nigel. *Goya and His Critics*. New Haven: Yale University Press, 1977.

Glendinning, Nigel, and Hilary Macartney, eds. *Spanish Art in Britain and Ireland, 1750–1920: Studies in Reception in Memory*

273

274

of *Enriqueta Harris Frankfort*. Woodbridge: Tamesis, 2010.

Gómez de la Serna, Ramón. *El Paseo del Prado*. Madrid: G. Hernández y Galo Sáez, 1919.

González Cuevas, Pedro Carlos. "El rey y la corte." In Luzón, *Alfonso XIII*, 187–212.

González Herrán, José Manuel. "Emilia Pardo Bazán en el epistolario de Marcelino Menéndez Pelayo." *Cuadernos de Estudios Gallegos* 36, no. 101 (1986): 325–42. Digital copy, Alicante, Biblioteca Virtual Miguel de Cervantes, 2003.

González López, Carlos, and Montserrat Martí Ayxelà, eds. *El mundo de los Madrazo*. Madrid: Comunidad de Madrid, 2007.

Goytisolo, Juan. "El museo Dillinger." In *Contracorrientes*, 181–91. Barcelona: Montesinos, 1985.

Granger, Catherine. *L'empereur et les arts: La liste civile de Napoléon III*. Paris: Écoles des Chartres, 2005.

———. "L'évacuation des collections des musées espagnols et françaises." In Colorado Castellary, *Patrimonio*, 339–56.

Groys, Boris. "The Struggle Against the Museum, or: The Display of Art in Totalitarian Space." In Sherman and Rogoff, *Museum Culture*, 144–62.

Guerra de la Vega, Ramón. *Juan de Villanueva*. Vol. 2, *Museo del Prado y Jardín Botánico*. Madrid: Edición del autor, 1987.

Habermas, Jürgen. *The Structural Transformation of the Public Sphere: An Inquiry into a Category of Bourgeois Society*. Translated by Thomas Burger. Cambridge, Mass.: MIT Press, 1991.

Hale, Susan. *A Family Flight Through Spain*. Boston: D. Lothrop, 1883.

Hall, Margaret. *On Display: A Design Grammar for Museum Exhibitions*. London: Lund Humphries, 1986.

Hanquinet, Laurie, and Mike Savage, "'Educative Leisure' and the Art Museum." *museum and society* 10, no. 1 (2012): 42–59.

Hansen, Miriam. *Babel and Babylon: Spectatorship in American Silent Film*. Cambridge, Mass.: Harvard University Press, 1994.

Harris, Neil. "Museums, Merchandizing, and Popular Taste: The Struggle for Influence." In *Material Culture and the Study of American Life*, edited by Ian M. G. Quimby, 140–74. New York: W. W. Norton, 1978.

Haskell, Francis. *The Ephemeral Museum: Old Master Paintings and the Rise of the Art Exhibition*. New Haven: Yale University Press, 2000.

Held, Jutta. "How Do the Political Effects of Pictures Come About? The Case of Picasso's *Guernica*." *Oxford Art Journal* 11, no. 1 (1988): 33–39.

Hernando Carrasco, Javier. *Las bellas artes y la revolución de 1868*. Oviedo: Universidad de Oviedo, 1987.

Hidalgo, Manuel. *La infanta baila*, Barcelona: Plaza & Janés, 1997.

Hill, Kate. *Culture and Class in English Public Museums, 1850–1914*. Aldershot: Ashgate, 2005.

Hiriart, Rosario. *Conversaciones con Francisco de Ayala*. Madrid: Espasa-Calpe, 1982.

Hirsh, Sharon L. "Swiss Art and National Identity at the Turn of the Twentieth Century." In Facos and Hirsch, *Art, Culture, and National Identity*, 250–85.

Hobsbawm, Eric J. *Nations and Nationalism Since 1780: Programme, Myth, Reality*. Cambridge: Cambridge University Press, 1990.

Hoffmann, Detlef. "The German Art Museum and the History of the Nation." In Sherman and Rogoff, *Museum Culture*, 3–21.

Holo, Selma. *Beyond the Prado*. Washington, D.C.: Smithsonian Institution, 1999.

Holt, Elizabeth Gilmore, ed. *The Art of All Nations, 1850–73: The Emerging Role of Exhibitions and Critics*. Princeton: Princeton University Press, 1981.

———, ed. *The Expanding World of Art, 1874–1902*. 2 vols. New Haven: Yale University Press, 1988.

———, ed. *The Triumph of Art for the Public: The Emerging Role of Exhibitions and Critics*. Washington, D.C.: Decatur House Press, 1980.

Hoock, Holger. *The King's Artists: The Royal Academy of Arts as a National Institution, c. 1768–1820*. Oxford: Clarendon Press, 2003.

———. "Reforming Culture: National Art Institutions in the Age of Reform." In *Rethinking the Age of Reform: Britain, 1780–1850*, edited by Arthur Burns and Joanna Innes, 254–70. Cambridge: Cambridge University Press, 2003.

Hooper-Greenhill, Eilean. *Museums and Education: Purpose, Pedagogy, Performance*. London: Routledge, 2007.

———. *Museums and Their Visitors*. 2nd ed. London: Routledge, 2013.

———. *Museums and the Shaping of Knowledge*. London: Routledge, 1992.

Horner, Susan, and John Swarbrooke. *Leisure Management: A Global Perspective.* London: Elsevier, 2005.

Hughes, Robert. *The Shock of the New.* New York: Knopf, 1981.

Hugo, Victor. *Notre-Dame de Paris.* Paris: Furne, 1844.

Huizinga, Johan. *Homo Ludens: A Study of the Play-Element in Culture.* London: Routledge and Kegan Paul, 1949.

Huysmans, Joris-Karl. *À rebours.* Paris: Presses Universitaires de France, 1987.

Iakovlev (Pavlovskii), Isaak. *Очерки современной Испании (1884–1885).* Saint Petersburg: A. S. Suvorin, 1889.

Inglis, Henry David. *Spain in 1830.* Vol. 1. London: Whittaker, Treacher, 1831.

Instituto de Estudios Turísticos. *Encuesta a los visitantes del Museo del Prado, Año 2011: Caracterización de los visitantes.* Madrid: Ministerio de Industria, Energía y Turismo, Instituto de Turismo de España, Instituto de Estudios Turísticos, 2012.

Insúa, Alberto. *La señorita y el obrero, o un "flirt" en la verbena de San Antonio.* Madrid: La Novela Mundial vol. 33, 1926.

Ivanovic, Milena. *Cultural Tourism.* Claremont, South Africa: Juta, 2009.

Jenkins, Jennifer. *Provincial Modernity: Local Culture and Liberal Politics in Fin-de-siècle Hamburg.* Ithaca: Cornell University Press, 2003.

Johnson, Roberta. "Carmen de Burgos and Spanish Modernism." In "Spain Modern and Postmodern at the Millennium," edited by Janet Pérez, special issue, *South-Central Review* 18, nos. 1/2 (2001): 66–77.

———. *Gender and Nation in the Spanish Modernist Novel.* Nashville: Vanderbilt University Press, 2003.

Jordan, David P. Introduction to *Rethinking France / Les lieux de Memoire,* vol. 1, translated by Mary Seidman Trouille. Chicago: University of Chicago Press, 2001.

Judd, Mark. "'The Oddest Combination of Town and Country': Popular Culture and the London Fairs, 1800–60." In *Leisure in Britain, 1780–1939,* edited by John K. Walton and James Walvin, 11–30. Manchester: Manchester University Press, 1988.

Juliá Díaz, Santos. *Madrid 1931–1934: De la fiesta popular a la lucha de clases.* Madrid: Siglo XXI, 1998.

Junta Central del Tesoro Artístico. *El fascismo al desnudo.* Valencia: Junta Central del Tesoro Artístico, 1937.

———. *Propaganda cultural.* Valencia: Junta Central del Tesoro Artístico, 1937.

Keene, Judith. "Into the Clear Air of the Plaza: Spanish Women Achieve the Vote in 1931." In Enders and Radcliff, *Constructing Spanish Womanhood,* 325–47.

Kerckhof, Véronique Van de, Helena Bussers, and Véronique Bücken, eds. *Le peintre et l'arpenteur: Images de Bruxelles et de l'ancien duché de Brabant.* Brussels: Dexia Banque; Tournai: Renaissance du livre, 2000.

Kerr-Lawson, E., ed. *A Catalogue of the Paintings in the Museo del Prado at Madrid.* London: W. Heinemann, 1896.

Kirkpatrick, Susan. *Mujer, modernismo y vanguardia en España: 1898–1931.* Translated by Jacqueline Cruz. Valencia: Universitat de Valencia, 2003.

Knell, Simon, et al., eds. *National Museums: New Studies from Around the World.* London: Routledge, 2011.

Koehler, Sylvester Rosa. "American Preface." In *Modern Art Education: Its Practical and Aesthetic Character Educationally Considered,* by Josef Langl, translated by Sylvester Rosa Koehler, iii–l. Boston: L. Prang, 1875.

Konlaan, Boinkum B. "Visiting the Cinema, Concerts, Museums, or Art Exhibitions as Determinant of Survival: A Swedish Fourteen-Year Cohort Follow-Up." *Scandinavian Journal of Public Health* 28, no. 3 (2000): 174–78.

Koselleck, Reinhart. "On the Anthropological and Semantic Structure of 'Bildung.'" In *The Practice of Conceptual History: Timing History, Spacing Concepts,* translated by Todd Samuel Presner et al., 170–207. Stanford: Stanford University Press, 2002.

Koven, Seth. "The Whitechapel Picture Exhibitions and the Politics of Seeing." In Sherman and Rogoff, *Museum Culture,* 22–48.

Kowalsky, Daniel. *Stalin and the Spanish Civil War.* New York: Columbia University Press, 2004.

Krause, Karl Christian Friedrich. *Ideal de la humanidad para la vida.* 2nd ed. Madrid: F. Martínez García, 1871.

Labanyi, Jo. "Horror, Spectacle, and Nation-Formation: Historical Paintings in Late-Nineteenth-Century Spain." In Larson and Woods, *Visualizing Spanish Modernity,* 64–80.

Lambourne, Nicola. *War Damage in Western Europe: The Destruction of Historic Monuments During the Second World War*. Edinburgh: Edinburgh University Press, 2001.

Lanzarote Guiral, José María. "National Museums in Spain: A History of Crown, Church and People." In Aronsson and Elgenius, *Building National Museums*, 847–80.

La Parra López, Emilio. "Los intentos de renovación del Sistema (1902-1916)". In Paredes Alonso, *Historia Contemporánea*, 429-52.

Larson, Susan. *Constructing and Resisting Modernity: Madrid, 1900–1936*. Madrid: Iberoamericana Vervuert, 2011.

Larson, Susan, and Eva Woods, eds. *Visualizing Spanish Modernity*. Oxford: Berg, 2005.

Lefebvre, Henri. "La signification de la Commune." *Arguments* 27–28 (1962): 11–19.

Lenman, Robin. *Artists and Society in Germany, 1850–1914*. Manchester: Manchester University Press, 1997.

León, María Teresa. *La historia tiene la palabra*. Buenos Aires: Patronato Hispano-Argentino de Cultura, 1943.

León Felipe. "Hay dos Españas." In *Antología rota*, edited by Miguel Galindo, 301. Madrid: Cátedra, 2008.

Llorente Hernández, Ángel. *Arte e ideología en el franquismo: 1936-1951*. Madrid: Visor, 1995.

Lockhurst, Kenneth. *The Story of Exhibitions*. London: The Studio, 1951.

Lorente, Jesús Pedro. *The Museums of Contemporary Art: Notion and Development*. Aldershot: Ashgate, 2011.

López Morillas, Juan. *Krausismo: Estética y literatura*. Barcelona: Lumen, 1973.

López-Ocón Cabrera, Leoncio. "El papel de Juan Facundo Riaño como inductor del proyecto cultural del Catálogo Monumental de España." In *El catálogo monumental de España (1900–1961): Investigación, restauración y difusión*, edited by Amelia López-Yarto Elizalde, 49–74. Madrid: Ministerio de Cultura, 2012.

Lopezosa Aparicio, Concepción. "Consideraciones y síntesis de un proyecto: El Paseo del Prado." *Anales de Historia del Arte* 3 (1991–92): 215–29.

———. "Devociones populares en el Paseo del Prado: San Blas, Santo Ángel de la Guarda y San Fermín." In *El culto a los santos: Cofradías, devoción, fiestas y arte*, edited by F. Javier Campos y Fernández de Sevilla, 151–64. El Escorial: Ediciones Escurialense, 2008.

———. "Fiesta oficial y configuración de la ciudad: El caso del madrileño Paseo del Prado." *Anales de Historia del Arte* 12 (2002): 79–92.

———. "Ocio y negocio: El jardín del Tívoli en el Paseo del Prado de Madrid." *Anales de Historia del Arte* 15 (2005): 269–79.

———. *El Paseo del Prado de Madrid: Arquitectura y desarrollo urbano en los siglos XVII y XVIII*. Madrid: Fundación de Apoyo a la Historia del Arte Hispánico, 2006.

López Serrano, Fernando. *Madrid, figuras y sombras: De los teatros de títeres a los salones de cine*. Madrid: Editorial Complutense de Madrid, 1999.

Louis, Anja. "Carmen de Burgos and the Question of Divorce." *Journal of Iberian and Latin American Studies* 5, no. 1 (1999): 49–63.

———. *Women and the Law: Carmen de Burgos, an Early Feminist*. Woodbridge: Tamesis, 2005.

Luxenberg, Alisa. *The Galerie Espagnole and the Museo Nacional, 1835–1853: Saving Spanish Art, or The Politics of Patrimony*. Aldershot: Ashgate, 2008.

———. "Regenerating Velázquez in Spain and France in the 1890s." *Boletín del Museo del Prado* 35 (1999): 125–51.

Macdonald, Sharon, and Roger Silverstone. "Rewriting the Museums' Fictions: Taxonomies, Stories, and Readers." *Cultural Studies* 4, no. 2 (1990): 176–91.

[Mackenzie, Alexander Slidell]. *A Year in Spain, by a Young American*. Boston: Hilliard, Gray, Little and Wilkins, 1829.

Madoz, Pascual. *Madrid: Audiencia, provincia, intendencia, vicaria, partido y villa*. Madrid, 1848.

Madrazo, Federico de. *Epistolario*. Edited by José Luis Díez. 2 vols. Madrid: Museo Nacional del Prado, 1994.

———. "Recuerdos de mi vida." In *Federico de Madrazo (1815–1894): Museo Romántico (5 de octubre–13 de noviembre de 1994)*, edited by Carlos González López and Monserrat Martí Ayxelá. Madrid: Amigos del Museo Romántico, 1994.

Madrazo, José de. *Catálogo de la galería de cuadros del Exmo: Sr. D. José de Madrazo*. Madrid: Cipriano López, 1856.

———. *Epistolario*. Edited by José Luis Díez. Santander: Fundación Marcelino Botín, 1998.

Madrazo, Mariano de. *Historia del Museo del Prado (1818–1868)*. Madrid: Ministerio de Asuntos Exteriores, 1945.

Madrazo, Pedro de. *Catálogo de los cuadros del Real Museo de Pintura y Escultura de S.M.* Madrid: Oficina de Aguado, 1843.

———. *Catálogo de los cuadros del Real Museo de Pintura y Escultura de S.M.* Madrid: J. M. Alonso, 1854.

———. *Catálogo descriptivo e histórico del Museo del Prado de Madrid: Seguido de una sinopsis de las varias escuelas . . . y de una noticia histórica sobre las colecciones de pinturas de los palacios reales de España y sobre la formación y progreso de este establecimiento.* Madrid: Rivadeneyra, 1872.

———. *Poesías dedicadas á S.M. la Reina Dña. Isabel II al ceder á la Nación la mayor parte de su Rl. Patrimonio.* Madrid: Rivadeneyra, 1865.

Maleuvre, Didier. *Museum Memories: History, Technology, Art.* Stanford: Stanford University Press, 1999.

Malraux, André. *Museum Without Walls.* Translated by Stuart Gilbert and Francis Price. Garden City, N.Y.: Doubleday, 1967.

Mandler, Peter. "Art in a Cool Climate: The Cultural Policy of the British State in European Context, c. 1780 to c. 1850." In Blanning and Schulze, *Unity and Diversity,* 101–20.

Mangini, Shirley. "Madrid es un cabaret y Maruja Mallo la protagonista." Lectures du genre 11. http://www.lecturesdugenre.fr/ Lectures_du_genre_numero_11.

———. *Maruja Mallo and the Spanish Avant-Garde.* Aldershot: Ashgate, 2010.

———. *Las modernas de Madrid.* Barcelona: Península, 2001.

Mariblanca Caneyro, Rosario. *El Retiro: Sus orígenes y todo lo demás . . . (1460–1988).* Madrid: Junta Municipal, 1991.

Marinello, Juan. *Cultura en la España republicana.* New York: Spanish Information Bureau, 1937.

Martínez, Jesús A. *Lectura y lectores en el Madrid del siglo XIX.* Madrid: CSIC, 1991.

Martín Márquez, Susan. *Disorientations: Spanish Colonialism in Africa and the Performance of Identity.* New Haven: Yale University Press, 2008.

Matilla Rodríguez, José Manuel, and Javier Portús, eds. *El Grafoscopio,* June 22–September 26, 2004. Madrid: Museo Nacional del Prado, 2004.

McClellan, Andrew. *Inventing the Louvre: Art, Politics, and the Origins of the Museum in Eighteenth-Century Paris.* Cambridge: Cambridge University Press, 1994.

Meijers, Deborah. "La classification comme principe: La transformation de la Galerie Impériale de Vienne en 'histoire visible de l'art.'" In Pommier *Les Musées en Europe,* 591–613.

———. "The Dutch Method of Developing a National Art Museum: How Crucial Were the French Confiscations of 1795?" In Bergvelt et al., *Napoleon's Legacy,* 41–53.

Memoria del Patronato de Misiones Pedagógicas, Septiembre de 1931–Diciembre de 1933. Madrid: Aguirre, 1934.

Mendelson, Jordana. *Documenting Spain: Artists, Exhibition Culture, and the Modern Nation, 1929–1939.* University Park: Penn State University Press, 2005.

Menéndez Rexach, Antonio. "La separación entre la Casa del Rey y la administración del Estado (1814–1820)." *Revista de estudios políticos* (Nueva época) 55 (1987): 55–121.

Mercer, Leigh. *Urbanism and Urbanity: The Spanish Bourgeois Novel and Contemporary Customs (1845–1925).* Lewisburg: Bucknell University Press, 2012.

Mérimée, Prosper. *Lettres d'Espagne.* Edited by Gérard Chaliand. Paris: Éditions Complexe, 1989.

Mesonero Romanos, Ramón. *Guía de Madrid.* 2nd ed. Madrid: D. M. Burgos, 1833.

———. *Manual de Madrid: Descripción de la corte y de la villa.* Madrid: D. M. Burgos, 1831.

———. *Memorias de un setentón.* Vol. 1, 1808–24. Madrid: Ilustración española e hispano-americana, 1881.

Meyer, Andrea, and Bénédicte Savoy, eds. *The Museum Is Open: Towards a Transnational History of Museum.* Berlin: Walter de Gruyter, 2014.

Mikkelsen, Flemming. "Working-Class Formation in Europe and Forms of Integration: History and Theory." *Labor History* 46, no. 3 (2005): 277–306.

Milizia, Francesco. *Arte de ver en las bellas artes del diseño: Según los principios de Sulzer y de Mengs; Escrito en italiano por Francisco de Milizia y traducido al castellano con notas e ilustraciones por Juan Agustín Ceán-Bermúdez.* Madrid: Imprenta Real, 1827.

Moleón Gavilanes, Pedro. *Juan de Villanueva.* Madrid: AKAL, 1998.

———. *El Museo del Prado. Biografía del edificio.* Madrid: Museo Nacional del Prado, 2012.

———. *Proyectos y obras para el Museo del Prado.* Madrid: Museo Nacional del Prado, 1996.

278

Moreno Luzón, Javier, ed. *Alfonso XIII: Un político en el trono*. Madrid: Marcial Pons, 2003.

Mornat, Isabelle. "Espectáculos de vistas a Madrid (1840–1875): Des fabriques de réalité." In Ortega, *Ojos que ven, ojos que leen*, 75–82.

Mumford, Lewis. *The Culture of Cities*. New York: Harcourt Brace Jovanovich, 1966.

Muñoz Fernández, Francisco Javier. "Guerra, arte y exilio en el País Vasco." In Colorado Castellary, *Patrimonio*, 87–98.

Muñoz López, Pilar. "Mujeres españolas en las artes plásticas." *Arte, Individuo y Sociedad* 21 (2009): 73–88.

Navarrete Martínez, Esperanza. *La academia de Bellas Artes de San Fernando y la pintura en la primera mitad del siglo XIX*. Madrid: Fundación Universitaria Española, 1999.

Nelken, Margarita. *La condición social de la mujer en España: Su estado actual, su posible desarrollo*. Madrid: Minerva, 1919.

———. *Glosario: Obras y artistas*. Madrid: Fernando Fe, 1917.

———, trans. *Historia del arte*, by Élie Faure. 4 vols. Madrid: Renacimiento, 1924–28.

———. *Maternología y Puericultura*. Valencia: Biblioteca Editorial Generación Consciente, 1926.

———. *Tres tipos de Virgen: Angélico, Rafael, Alonso Cano*. Madrid: Ciudad Lineal, 1929.

Nieto-Galan, Agustí. "Scientific 'Marvels' in the Public Sphere: Barcelona and Its 1888 International Exhibition." *Host: Journal of History of Science and Technology* 6 (2012): 7–38.

Nietzsche, Friedrich. "What Do Ascetic Ideals Mean?" In *On the Genealogy of Morality: A Polemic*, translated by Maudemarie Clark and Alan J. Swensen, 67–118. Indianapolis: Hackett, 1998.

Nochlin, Linda. "Museums and Radicals: A History of Emergencies." *Art in America* 59, no. 4 (1971): 26–39.

Nora, Pierre, ed. *Les lieux de mémoire*. Vol. 2, *La nation*, pt. 3. Paris: Gallimard, 1986.

Norman, Geraldine. *The Hermitage: The Biography of a Great Museum*. New York: Fromm, 1997.

Offen, Karen. "La aventura del sufragio femenino en el mundo." In *Historia de una conquista: Clara Campoamor y el voto femenino*, edited by Rosa Capel Martínez, 11–33. Madrid: Ayuntamiento de Madrid, 2007.

———. "Feminists Campaign in 'Public Space': Civil Society, Gender Justice, and the History of European Feminism." In *Civil Society and Gender Justice: Historical and Comparative Perspectives*, edited by Karen Hagemann, Sonya Michel, and Gunilla-Friederike Budde, 97–116. New York: Berghahn Books, 2008.

Ortega, Marie-Linda, ed. *Ojos que ven, ojos que leen: Textos e imágenes en la España Isabelina*. Madrid: Visor Libros and Presses Universitaires de Marne-la-Vallée, 2004.

Ortega y Gasset, José. *La rebelión de las masas*. Madrid: Revista de Occidente, 1930.

Osterhammel, Jürgen. *The Transformation of the World: A Global History of the Nineteenth Century*. Translated by Patrick Camiller. Princeton: Princeton University Press, 2014.

Otero Urtaza, Eugenio. "Las primeras expediciones de maestros de la Junta para Ampliación de Estudios y sus antecedentes: Los viajes de estudio de Cossío entre 1880 y 1889." *Revista de Educación* (2007): 45–66.

Oulebsir, Nabila. *Les usages du patrimoine: Monuments, musées et politique coloniale en Algérie (1830–1930)*. Paris: Éditions de la Maison des sciences de l'homme, 2004.

Ovejero, Andrés. *Concepto actual del museo artístico: Discurso de ingreso; Recepción pública celebrada en día 24 de junio de 1934*. Madrid: Sucesores de Rivadeneyra, 1934.

Pageard, Robert, Lee Fontanella, and María Dolores Cabra Loredo, eds. *Sem: Los Borbones en pelota*. Madrid: Ediciones El Museo Universal, 1991.

Pardo Bazán, Emilia. *La Quimera*. Vol. 29 of *Obras completas*. Madrid: Administración, n.d.

Pardo Canalís, Enrique. "'El desembarco de Fernando VII en el Puerto de Santa Maria,' por Jose Aparicio." *Anales del Instituto de Estudios Madrileños* 22 (1985): 129–57.

———. "Noticias y escritos de Luis Eusebi." *Revista de ideas estéticas* (1968): 179–200.

Paredes Alonso, Francisco Javier, ed. *Historia contemporánea de España: Siglo XX*. Barcelona: Ariel, 2004.

Parsons, Deborah L. *A Cultural History of Madrid*. Oxford: Berg, 2003.

Paul, Carole, ed. *The First Modern Museums of Art: The Birth of an Institution in 18th- and Early 19th-Century Europe*. Los Angeles: Paul J. Getty Museum, 2012.

Pearce, Susan M. *Museums, Objects, and Collections: A Cultural Study*. Washington, D.C.: Smithsonian Institution Press, 1992.

Pérez Galdós, Benito. *La desheredada*. Madrid: Librería de Perlado, 1909.

Pérez Rojas, Francisco Javier, ed. *La ciudad placentera: Noche y día de la vida moderna; Centro cultural El Monte, Sala Villasís mayo–junio 2005*. Valencia: Fundación el Monte, 2005.

Pérez Sánchez, Alfonso. "El autor de la decoración del Retrete de Fernando VII en el Prado." *Boletín del Museo del Prado* 7, no. 19 (1986): 33–38.

———. *El Museo del Prado*. Madrid: Museo del Prado, 1974.

———. *Pasado, presente, futuro del Museo del Prado*. Madrid: Museo del Prado, 1977.

Perla, Antonio. "El Hotel Ritz de Madrid: Apuntes históricos y antecedentes; El Tívoli y el Real Establecimiento Tipográfico." *Espacio, Tiempo y Forma, Serie VII, Historia del Arte* 22–23 (2009–10): 235–73.

Perry, Lara. *History's Beauties: Women in the National Portrait Gallery, 1856–1900*. Aldershot: Ashgate, 2006.

Philips, Deborah. *Fairground Attractions: A Genealogy of the Pleasure Ground*. London: Bloomsbury Academic, 2012.

Pieper, Josef. *Leisure: The Basis of Culture*. New York: Pantheon, 1952.

Pointon, Marcia. *Naked Authority: The Body in Western Painting, 1830–1908*. Cambridge: Cambridge University Press, 1990.

Poleró y Toledo, Vicente. *Breves observaciones sobre la utilidad y conveniencia de reunir en uno solo los dos museos de pintura de Madrid, y sobre el verdadero estado de conservación de los cuadros de constituyen el Museo del Prado*. Madrid: Eduardo Cuesta, 1868.

Pommier, Edouard, ed. *Les musées en Europe à la veille de l'ouverture du Louvre*. Paris: Klincksieck–Musée du Louvre, 1995.

Portela Sandoval, Francisco José. "La ciudad y el monumento público en España." In *La dimensión artística y social de la ciudad*, edited by Juan Antonio Sánchez García-Saúco, 51–82. Madrid: Ministerio de Educación, 2002.

Portús Pérez, Javier. *El concepto de pintura española: Historia de un problema*. Madrid: Verbum, 2012.

———. *Museo del Prado, Memoria escrita, 1849–1994*. Madrid: Museo Nacional del Prado, 1994.

———. *El Palacio del Rey Planeta, July 6–November 27, 2005*. Madrid: Museo Nacional del Prado, 2005.

———. *Sala Reservada y el desnudo en el Museo del Prado, June 28–September 29, 2002*. Madrid: Museo Nacional del Prado, 2002.

Portús Pérez, Javier, and Jesusa Vega. *El descubrimiento del arte español: Cossío, Lafuente, Gaya Nuño*. Madrid: Nivola Libros y Ediciones, 2004.

Poulot, Dominique. "Identity as Self-Discovery: The Ecomuseum in France." In Sherman and Rogoff, *Museum Culture*, 66–84.

Pratt, Mary-Louise. "Arts of the Contact Zone." *Profession* 91 (1991): 33–40.

———. *Imperial Eyes: Travel Writing and Transculturation*. London: Routledge, 1992.

Prentice, Richard. "Experiential Cultural Tourism: Museums and the Marketing of the New Romanticism of Evoked Authenticity." *Museum Management and Curatorship* 19, no. 1 (2001): 5–26.

Preston, Paul. *Doves of War: Four Women of Spain*. London: HarperCollins, 2002.

Prior, Nick. *Museums and Modernity: Art Galleries and the Making of Modern Culture*. Oxford: Berg, 2003.

———. "Museums: Leisure Between State and Distinction." In *Histories of Leisure*, edited by Rudy Koshar, 27–44. Oxford: Berg, 2002.

Quin, Michael J. *Memoirs of Ferdinand VII, King of the Spains. By don ***** Advocate of the Spanish Tribunals. Translated from the Original Spanish Manuscript*. London: Hurst, Robinson, 1824.

———. *Memorias históricas sobre Fernando VII, rey de España*. Valencia: Imprenta de Gimeno, 1840.

Quiroga, Alejandro. *Football and National Identities in Spain*. New York: Palgrave Macmillan, 2013.

———. *Making Spaniards: Primo de Rivera and the Nationalization of the Masses, 1923–1930*. New York: Palgrave Macmillan, 2007.

Qureshi, Sadiah. *Peoples on Parade: Exhibitions, Empire, and Anthropology in Nineteenth-Century Britain*. Chicago: University of Chicago Press, 2011.

Rabinow, Rebecca A. *Cézanne to Picasso: Ambroise Vollard, Patron of the Avant-Garde*. New York: Metropolitan Museum of Art, 2006.

Ramírez de Saavedra Rivas, Enrique. *De literatura y arte: Discursos, cartas y otros escritos*. Madrid: Tello, 1903.

Rancière, Jacques. *The Emancipated Spectator*. Translated by Gregory Elliot. London: Verso, 2010.

Ravelli, Louise. *Museum Texts: Communication Frameworks*. London: Routledge, 2006.

Renau, Josep. "L'organisation de la défense du patrimoine artistique et historique espagnol

280

pendant la guerre civile." *Mouseion* 11, nos. 39–40 (1937): 7–64.

Reyero, Carlos. "Ideología e imagen del artista español del siglo XIX entre París y Roma." In *El arte español entre Roma y París*, edited by Luis Sazatornil Ruiz and Frédéric Jiménо, 129-44. Madrid, Casa de Velázquez, 2014.

Riego, Bernardo. "Visibilidades diferenciadas: Usos sociales de las imágenes en la España Isabelina." In Ortega, *Ojos que ven, ojos que leen*, 55–74.

Ringrose, David. *Madrid y la economía española, 1560–1850: Ciudad, Corte y país en el Antiguo Régimen*. Madrid: Alianza, 1985.

Rodríguez de Rivera, Itziar. "Placer solitario y homoerotismo femenino en *La Condesita. (Memorias de una doncella)* (1869) de Francisco de Sales Mayo: Otro peligroso suplemento." *Revista de Estudios Hispánicos* 48, no. 1 (2014): 25–48.

Rødtjer, Rocío. "Whose Ancestral Line Is It Anyway? Women, Legitimacy, and the Nineteenth Century Genealogical Imagination." Ph.D. diss., King's College London, 2015.

Rose–de Viejo, Isadora. "Colección de Manuel Godoy." *Enciclopedia del Prado* online.

———. *Manuel Godoy, patrón de artes y coleccionista*. Vol. 1. Madrid: Universidad Complutense, 1983.

Ruiz Mantilla, José. "'Los museos están a medio camino entre Disneylandia y la Iglesia': Entrevista con Mikhail Piotrovsky." *El País*, February 27, 2011. http://elpais.com/diario/2011/02/27/eps/1298791613_850215.html.

Rumeu de Armas, Antonio. *Origen y fundación del Museo del Prado*. Madrid: Instituto de España, 1980.

Saarinen, Alice B. *The Proud Possessors: The Lives, Times, and Tastes of Some Adventurous American Art Collectors*. New York: Random House, 1958.

Salaün, Serge. "Apogeo y decadencia de la sicálipsis." In *Discurso erótico y discurso transgresor en la cultura peninsular: Siglos XI al XX*, edited by Myriam Díaz-Diocaretz and Iris M. Zavala, 129–53. Madrid: Ediciones Tuero, 1992.

Salaün, Serge, and Carlos Serrano, eds. *1900 en España*. Madrid: Espasa-Calpe, 1991.

Salaverría, José María. *Los fantasmas del museo*. Barcelona: Guinart y Pujolar, 1920.

Salmi, Hannu. *Nineteenth Century Europe: A Cultural History*. Oxford: Wiley, 2013.

Sambricio, Carlos. "Fiestas, celebraciones y espacios públicos en el Madrid josefino." In *La guerra de Napoleón en España*, edited by Emilio La Parra López, 149–76. Alicando: Universidad de Alicante, 2010.

———. "El ideal historicista en la obra de Juan de Villanueva." In *La arquitectura española de la Ilustración*, 233–60. Madrid: CSCAE-IEAL, 1986.

Sambricio, Valentín de. "El Museo Fernandino, su creación y causas de su fracaso." *Archivo español de arte* 15 (1942): 132–46, 262–83, 320–35.

Sánchez Cantón, Francisco Javier. *España, itinerarios de arte*. Madrid: CSIC, 1974.

———. "La reorganización del Museo del Prado," *Arte español* 1927, 290-93.

———. *Spain*. Madrid: PNT, 1921.

———. *Walks Through Madrid and Excursions to Its Environs*. Madrid: PNT, 1932.

Sánchez Gómez, Luis Ángel. *Un imperio en la vitrina: El colonialismo español en el Pacífico y la exposición de Filipinas de 1887*. Madrid: CSIC, 2003.

Sánchez-Llama, Íñigo. *Galería de escritoras isabelinas: La prensa periódica entre 1833 y 1895*. Madrid: Cátedra, 2000.

Sancho, José Luis. *Las vistas de los Sitios Reales de Brambilla: La Granja de San Ildefonso*. Madrid: Doce Calles, Patrimonio Nacional, 2000.

Sandberg, Mark B. *Living Pictures, Missing Persons: Mannequins, Museums, and Modernity*. Princeton: Princeton University Press, 2002.

Sarlo, Beatriz. *Una modernidad periférica: Buenos Aires, 1920 y 1930*. Buenos Aires: Nueva Visión, 1988.

Sauer, Marina. *L'entrée des femmes à l'Ecole des Beaux-Arts, 1880–1923*. Paris: Ecole Nationale Supérieure des Beaux-Arts, 1990.

Sazatornil Ruiz, Luis, and Frédéric Jiménо, eds. *El arte español entre Roma y París (siglos XVIII y XIX): Intercambios artísticos y circulación de modelos*. Madrid: Casa de Velázquez, 2014.

Sazatornil Ruiz, Luis, and Ana Belén Lasheras Peña. "*París y la españolada*: Casticismo y estereotipos nacionales en las exposiciones universales (1855–1900)." *Mélanges de la Casa Velázquez* 35, no. 2 (2005).

Schammah Gesser, Silvina. "Museos, Etnología y Folklor(ismo) en el Madrid franquista: Sobre precariedad, rupturas y continuidades de un proyecto inacabado." In *Imaginarios y representaciones de España durante el franquismo*, edited by Stéphane Michonneau and Xosé-M. Núñez-Seixas, 221–30. Madrid: Casa de Velázquez, 2014.

Schauff, Frank. *La victoria frustrada: La Unión Soviética, la Internacional Comunista y la Guerra Civil Española*. Barcelona: Debate, 2008.

Schorske, Carl E. *Fin-de-siècle Vienna: Politics and Culture*. New York: Knopf, 1980.

Schulz, Andrew. "Museo Nacional del Prado, Madrid: Absolutism and Nationalism in Early 19th-Century Madrid." In Paul, *First Modern Museums of Art*, 237–59.

Schwarz, Vanessa R. *Spectacular Realities: Early Mass Culture in Fin-de-siècle Paris*. Berkeley: University of California Press, 1999.

Seseña, Natasha. "Retrete de Fernando VII." In *Museo del Prado, Enciclopedia del Prado* online.

Sheehan, James J. "Art and Its Publics, c. 1800." In Blanning and Schulze, *Unity and Diversity*, 5–18.

———. *Museums in the German Art World: From the End of the Old Regime to the Rise of Modernism*. Oxford: Oxford University Press, 2000.

Sherman, Daniel J., and Irit Rogoff. Introduction to Sherman and Rogoff, *Museum Culture*, iii–xix.

———. *Museum Culture: Histories, Discourses, Spectacles*. Minneapolis, University of Minnesota Press, 1994.

Shubert, Adrian. *Death and Money in the Afternoon: A History of the Spanish Bullfight*. Oxford: Oxford University Press, 1999.

Silverman, Debora L. *Art Nouveau in Fin-de-siècle France: Politics, Psychology, and Style*. Berkeley: University of California Press, 1989.

Silverman, Lois H. "Visitor Meaning-Making in Museums for a New Age." *Curator: The Museum Journal* 38, no. 3 (1995): 161–70.

Simón Palmer, María del Carmen. *Los jardines del Buen Retiro*. 2nd ed. Madrid: La Librería, 2001.

———. "La publicidad y la imagen en Madrid (1840–1874)." In Ortega, *Ojos que ven, ojos que leen*, 11–36.

Smith, Alan E. "La recepción de la primera edición de *Los desastres de la Guerra* de Goya (marzo, 1863) en el Madrid del joven Galdós." *Bulletin of Spanish Studies*, 86 (2009): 459–74.

Smith, Alison. *The Victorian Nude: Sexuality, Morality, and Art*. Manchester: Manchester University Press, 1996.

Storm, Eric. *The Culture of Regionalism: Art, Architecture, and International Exhibitions in France, Germany, and Spain, 1890–1939*. Manchester: Manchester University Press, 2011.

Streidt, Gert, and Peter Feierabend, eds. *Prussia: Art and Architecture*. Cologne: Könemann, 1999.

Strobel, Edward Henry. *The Spanish Revolution, 1868–1875*. Boston: Small, Maynard, 1898.

Switzer, Terri. "Hungarian Self-Representation in an International Context: The Magyar Exhibited at International Expositions and World Fairs." In Facos and Hirsch, *Art, Culture, and National Identity*, 160–85.

Taslitzky, Boris. "Le Front Populaire et les intellectuelles: *Témoignage 1.*" *La Nouvelle Critique* 7, no. 70 (1955): 11–16.

Thomas, Sophie. *Romanticism and Visuality: Fragments, History, Spectacle*. London: Routledge, 2008.

Thompson, Edward Palmer. *The Making of the English Working Class*. New York: Pantheon Books, 1964.

Tomlinson, Janis A. "State Galleries and the Formation of National Artistic Identity in Spain, England and France, 1814–1851." In Facos and Hirsch, *Art, Culture, and National Identity*, 16–38.

Trodd, Colin. "The Discipline of Pleasure; or, How Art History Looks at the Art Museum." *museum and society* 1, no. 1 (2003): 17–29.

———. "The Paths to the National Gallery." In Barlow and Trodd, *Governing Culture*, 29–43.

Troilo, Simona. "National Museums in Italy: A Matter of Multifaceted Identity." In Aronsson and Elgenius, *Building National Museums*, 461–95.

Tsuchiya, Akiko. *Marginal Subjects: : Gender and Deviance in Fin-de-siècle Spain*. Toronto: University of Toronto Press, 2011.

Úbeda de los Cobos, Andrés. *Paintings for the Planet King: Philip IV and the Buen Retiro Palace*. Madrid: Museo Nacional del Prado, 2005.

Uría González, Jorge. *Sociedad, ocio y cultura en Asturias (1898–1914)*. Oviedo: Universidad de Oviedo, 1991.

Urigüen González, Maria Begoña. *Orígenes y evolución de la derecha española: El neocatolicismo*. Madrid: CSIC, 1986.

Valis, Noël. *The Culture of "Cursilería": Bad Taste, Kitsch, and Class in Modern Spain*. Durham: Duke University Press, 2002.

Varey, John E. "'The Bleeding Nun' and 'Our Lady of Paris.'" In *Spain and Its Literature: Essays in Memory of E. Allison Peers*. Edited by Ann L. Mackenzie, 283–301. Liverpool: Liverpool University Press, 1997.

———. *La cartelera de títeres y otras diversiones populares de Madrid, 1758–1840: Estudio y documentos*. Madrid: Tamesis, 1995.

Vázquez, Oscar E. *Inventing the Art Collection: Patrons, Markets, and the State in Nineteenth-Century Spain*. University Park: Penn State University Press, 2001.

Vega, Jesusa. "Del espectáculo de la ciencia a la práctica artística cortesana: Apuntes sobre la fortuna de la fotografía en España." *Revista de dialectología y tradiciones populares* 63, no. 2 (2013): 359–83.

———. *Origen de la litografía en España: El Real Establecimiento Litográfico*. Madrid: Casa de la Moneda, 1990.

Versteeg, Margot. *Jornaleros de la pluma: La (re) definición del papel del escritor-periodista en la revista "Madrid Cómico."* Madrid: Iberoamericana, 2001.

Viardot, Louis. *Etude sur l'histoire des institutions: De la littérature, du théâtre et des beaux-arts en Espagne*. Paris: Paulin, 1835.

———. "Le musée de Madrid." *Revue Républicaine* (December 1834).

Vilches, Jorge. *Progreso y Libertad: El Partido Progresista en la Revolución Liberal Española*. Madrid: Alianza Editorial, 2001.

Vinuesa, Celia. "La restauración del Claustro de los Jerónimos en las obras de ampliación del Museo del Prado (I)." http://art-edemadrid.wordpress.com/2009/03/22. Accessed November 25, 2010.

Visscher, Charles de. "La protection internationale del objets d'art et de monuments historiques." *Revue de droit international et de législation comparée* (1935): 32–75, 246–88.

Weddigen, Tristan. "The Picture Galleries of Dresden, Düsseldorf, and Kassel: Princely Collections in Eighteenth-Century Germany." In Paul, *First Modern Museums of Art*, 145–66.

Weichlein, Siegfried. "Cosmopolitanism, Patriotism, Nationalism." In Blanning and Schulze, *Unity and Diversity*, 77–100.

Weil, Stephen E. "From Being About Something to Being for Somebody: The Ongoing Transformation of the American Museum." *Daedalus* 128, no. 3 (1999): 229–58.

Weiner, Deborah E. B. *Architecture and Social Reform in Late-Victorian London*. Manchester: Manchester University Press, 1994.

Wezel, Elsa van. "Denon's Louvre and Schinkel's Alte Museum: War Trophy Museum Versus Monument to Peace." In Bergvelt et al., *Napoleon's Legacy*, 157–72.

White, Sarah L. "Liberty, Honor, Order: Gender and Political Discourse in Nineteenth-Century Spain." In Enders and Radcliff, *Constructing Spanish Womanhood*, 233–58.

Whitehead, Christopher. "Establishing the Manifesto: Art Histories in the Nineteenth-Century Museum." In *Museum Revolutions*, edited by Simon J. Knell, Susan MacLeod, and Sheila Watson, 48–60. London: Routledge, 2007.

———. "National Art Museum Practice as Political Cartography in Nineteenth-Century Britain." In Knell et al., *National Museums*, 105–22.

———. *The Public Art Museum in Nineteenth-Century Britain*. Aldershot: Ashgate, 2005.

Widén, Per. "National Museums in Sweden: A History of Denied Empire and a Neutral State." In Aronsson and Elgenius, *Building National Museums*, 1039–66.

Wolikow, Serge. *L'Internationale Communiste, 1919–1943: Le Komintern ou le rêve déchu du parti mondial de la révolution*. Ivry-sur-Seine: Les Éditions de l'Atelier / Editions Ouvrières, 2010.

Wood, Gillen D'Arcy. *The Shock of the Real: Romanticism and Visual Culture, 1760–1860*. New York: Palgrave Macmillan, 2001.

Woodson-Boulton, Amy. *Transformative Beauty: Art Museums in Industrial Britain*. Stanford: Stanford University Press, 2012.

Yonan, Michael. "Kunsthistorisches Museum / Belvedere, Vienna: Dynasticism and the Function of Art." In Paul, *First Modern Museums of Art*, 167–90.

Zola, Émile. *L'assommoir: Les Rougon-Macquart II*. Paris: Gallimard, 1961.

Zubiaurre, Maite. *Cultures of the Erotic in Spain, 1898–1930*. Nashville: Vanderbilt University Press, 2010.

Index

284